Pa S0-AFS-341

Statistical Process Control

OTHER STATISTICS TEXTS FROM
CHAPMAN AND HALL

Practical Statistics for Medical Research
Douglas Altman
The Analysis of Time Series
C. Chatfield
Problem Solving: A Statistician's Guide
C. Chatfield
Statistics for Technology
C. Chatfield
Introduction to Multivariate Analysis
C. Chatfield and A. J. Collins
Applied Statistics
D. R. Cox and E. J. Snell
An Introduction to Statistical Modelling
A. J. Dobson
Introduction to Optimization Methods and their Application in Statistics
B. S. Everitt
Multivariate Statistics – A Practical Approach
B. Flury and H. Riedwyl
Readings in Decision Analysis
S. French
Multivariate Analysis of Variance and Repeated Measures
D. J. Hand and C. C. Taylor
Multivariate Statistical Methods – A Primer
Bryan F. Manley
Statistical Methods in Agriculture and Experimental Biology
R. Mead and R. N. Curnow
Elements of Simulation
B. J. T. Morgan
Probability: Methods and Measurement
A. O'Hagan
Essential Statistics
D. G. Rees
Foundations of Statistics
D. G. Rees
Decision Analysis: A Bayesian Approach
J. Q. Smith
Applied Statistics: A Handbook of BMDP Analyses
E. J. Snell
Elementary Applications of Probability Theory
H. C. Tuckwell
Intermediate Statistical Methods
G. B. Wetherill

Further information of the complete range of Chapman and Hall *statistics books is available from the publishers.*

Statistical Process Control

Theory and practice

G. Barrie Wetherill

Director, Industrial Statistics Research Unit,
University of Newcastle upon Tyne

Don W. Brown

Consultant in Mathematics and Statistics
ICI Chemicals and Polymers Ltd

CHAPMAN AND HALL

LONDON • NEW YORK • TOKYO • MELBOURNE • MADRAS

UK   Chapman and Hall, 2–6 Boundary Row, London SE1 8HN

USA   Chapman and Hall, 29 West 35th Street, New York NY10001

JAPAN   Chapman and Hall Japan, Thomson Publishing Japan,
            Hirakawacho Nemoto Building, 7F, 1-7-11 Hirakawa-cho,
            Chiyoda-ku, Tokyo 102

AUSTRALIA   Chapman and Hall Australia, Thomas Nelson Australia,
            102 Dodds Street, South Melbourne, Victoria 3205

INDIA   Chapman and Hall India, R. Seshadri, 32 Second Main Road,
            CIT East, Madras 600 035

First edition 1991

© 1991 G. Barrie Wetherill and Don W. Brown

Typeset in 10/12 Times by
KEYTEC, Bridport, Dorset
Printed in Great Britain by
T. J. Press (Padstow) Ltd, Padstow, Cornwall

ISBN 0 412 35700 3

British Library Cataloguing in Publication Data
Wetherhill, G. Barrie (George Barrie), 1932-
Statistical process control.
1. Industries. Quality control. Statistical methods
I. Title II. Brown, Don W.
658.562015195

ISBN 0-412-35700-3

Library of Congress Cataloguing in Publication Data
Wetherhill, G. Barrie.
    Statistical process control: theory and practice / G. Barrie
Wetherhill, Don W. Brown — 1st ed.
    p. cm.
    Includes bibliographical references and index.
    ISBN 0-412-35700-3
    1. Process control — Statistical methods. I. Brown, Don W.
II. Title.
TS156.8.W455 1990
670.42 — dc20   90-2560
                                                          CIP

Contents

Method summaries

x Method summaries

Acknowledgements

We gratefully acknowledge permission to reproduce material from the following:

Biometrika Trustees for permission to reproduce tables of normal and related distributions;

The British Standards Institution for permissin to reproduce extracts from Standards. Complete copies of the Standards can be obtained from BSI Sales, Linford Wood, Milton Keynes, MK14 6LE, UK, or from Natinal Standards Offices;

Professors C. W. Champ and W. H. Woodall, and the American Statistical Association for permission to quote results given in Chapter 8;

Controller of HMSO for permission to reproduce figures contained in Chapter 12;

Professor B. Kumar Ghosh for permission to reproduce Tables 5.10, 8.9 and 8.10 from K. Tuprah and Ncube (1987) A Comparison of Dispersion Control Charts. *Sequential Analysis* (ed. B. K. Ghosh), Marcel Dekker, USA, **6**, 155–64;

Professor A. M. Goel for permission to reproduce the nomogram in Chapter 7;

Dr R. J. Rowlands for permission to reproduce ARL data contained in Chapters 7 and 8;

Professor Dr P.-Th. Wilrich for permission to use nomograms in Chapters 9 and 12.

Preface

Statistical process control (SPC) is now recognized as having a very important role to play in modern industry. Our aim in this book has been to present SPC techniques in a simple and clear way, and also to present some of the underlying theory and properties of the techniques.

This volume arises partly out of a revision of Wetherill (1977), and partly out of experience in teaching and implementing SPC at industrial sites, especially with ICI. It would have been impossible to come to our present understanding of this field without the joint efforts of industry and university.

A number of features of this book are new:

(1) The special emphasis on process industry problems, including one-at-a-time data.
(2) The discussion of between and within-group variation, and the effects of this on charting and on process capability analysis.
(3) The derivation of the properties of the techniques has not been gathered together before.
(4) The presentation of sampling by variables contains many new features.

The techniques themselves are presented in a very simple way by using 'method summaries', and these could be a basis for training when SPC is implemented.

We hope that this volume will be used in courses in universities and polytechnics. Some of the more mathematical sections and chapters are marked with an asterisk, and these can be omitted at first reading. It is important to get a good intuitive grasp of the subject before delving into the theory. Two sets of exercises are provided at the ends of chapters. Those labelled 'A' explore the techniques themselves whereas those under 'B' are more mathematical or theoretical. A separate and parallel volume is being produced, *Statistical Process Control – a Manual for Practitioners*, which avoids theoretical aspects, and which covers practical issues omitted from this text.

The book divides into two major areas. Chapters 1–10 largely deal with charting, and Chapters 11–14 with sampling inspection.

Modern industry is very complex, particularly the process industries. It is important for some of the SPC staff to have an understanding of the properties of SPC techniques under a variety of assumptions. Surprisingly enough, there are many points which need further research, and some of these are pointed out in the text.

We are indebted to many people in the production of this book. The initiatives of Total Quality of ICI Chemicals and Polymers and ICI Films lead to a 'Teaching Company Scheme' in SPC between ICI and the University of Newcastle upon Tyne. This scheme covered six projects and gave the university staff inside experience of the problems of implementing SPC. Discussions with ICI staff and Teaching Company Associates have helped. Further discussions with ICI staff at SPC courses have deepened our understanding.

Although this volume arises partly out of a revision of Wetherill (1977), and much of the writing has been done by G. B. Wetherill, much has been done in collaboration with ICI, especially D. W. Brown, in writing an SPC manual for the company. The emphasis on problems associated with process industries owes a lot to DWB and contributions from ICI.

Colleagues Marion Gerson and Jim Rowlands in the Industrial Statistics Research Unit at the University of Newcastle upon Tyne have helped enormously. There have been numerous discussions on methodology and approach as we studied the implementation of SPC at various sites.

We are indebted to Mr W. Dobson for producing many of the diagrams and the sampling datasets. We are also grateful to Mr S. King for help with proof-reading.

Appendix C contains a list of National and International Standards relating to quality control. It is the first time that such a list has been available. The authors have made every effort to check the list but cannot vouch for inaccuracies or omissions. Students intending to work in the quality area ought to be familiar with the major Standards. The authors are indebted to David Baillie, with the help of John Mallaby of the British Standards Institution, and Tsuneo Yokoh of the Japanese Standards Association for provision of this list.

This project has taken a lot of time and energy, but it is one which we feel has been very worthwhile. We hope that the book proves to be useful and interesting to others.

G. Barrie Wetherill
Don W. Brown

1

Statistical process control

1.1 DEVELOPMENT OF SPC

Statistical process control and allied techniques of sampling inspection and quality control were developed in the 1920s. In May 1924, Walter A. Shewhart of Bell Telephone Laboratories developed the first sketch of a modern control chart. Work by him, H. F. Dodge, H. G. Romig, W. J. Jennett and others continued apace. In 1931 a crucial paper on the new techniques was presented to the Royal Statistical Society, which stimulated interest in the UK.

SPC was used extensively in World War II both in the UK and in the USA, but lost its importance as industries converted to peacetime production. However people in the West taught it to the Japanese, and W. E. Deming in particular made a big impact in Japan in the 1950s. Japanese industry applied SPC widely and proved that SPC saves money and attracts customers. US and UK industries are now being forced to introduce it in order to compete with the Japanese.

As part of the UK National Quality Campaign, a group representing UK industrial interests went to Hong Kong, Japan and the USA in the summer of 1984. As a result of their visits, all members of the group became alarmed at the competition faced by UK industry, and were especially convinced about the need for a radical reappraisal of our attitude to quality. The Japanese philosophy is that good quality products sell, consistent good quality leads to greater productivity, and that there is *no* conflict between price and quality. One of the Japanese who spoke to the group explained that 'It would take you ten years to get to where we are . . . *and we know you won't do it!*'

The Japanese have applied very successfully the statistical techniques they learned in the West from Deming, Juran and others. The message is clear: these techniques must be applied widely in the West.

1.2 WHAT SPC IS AND IS NOT

Statistical process control is not a magic formula for curing all production ills; it is a very useful tool to be used in promoting and maintaining the health of a commercial or industrial enterprise. Although many of the statistical ideas originated in Britain and America, they have been grossly under-used and misunderstood for many years. It is the Japanese who have seen the important contribution of SPC within industry and combined it with a totally different approach to quality and to management. The result is slowly filtering through to the West chiefly via the USA.

Although we shall not always need to differentiate in this text it is worth noting here that SPC is used:

(1) To improve *quality* (in the Crosby sense of conformance to requirements; for details see the references).

When information about production and control over it leads to the reduction or elimination of non-conforming product this can lead to:
   (a) Reduced manufacturing costs, due to less
   - Scrap
   - Added value to defective product
   - Rescheduling
   - Inspection/re-work
   (b) Increased reputation/customer satisfaction
   (c) Tighter specification limits and hence improved product claims.

(2) To increase *yield* (or maintain yield at reduced cost).

In many chemical and some other process industries it is important to maximize output value relative to inputs. Small differences in yield may have a significant effect on profit, so it is as important to capitalize on positive causes of variation as to detect and eliminate those causes that have a negative effect.

A very important part of this process is the role played by measurement. It is necessary for us to have some data measuring the quality of our output, data on quality costs, data on how a process is performing, etc. This leads directly to the use of statistics. Statistical methods for process control have been taught for about 60 years now, and there are many examples of how important and successful statistical process control can be. Simple statistical methods can be used in order to:

(1) Have evidence of what a process is doing, and what it is likely to do.
(2) Provide an assessment of the quality levels your process is currently capable of meeting.
(3) Tell when to look for trouble and when not to.

(4) Provide clues as to where trouble is likely to occur.
(5) Help towards an understanding of the operation of the system and so help in making improvements to the process or product.

The results of the statistical methods must be interpreted by the operating staff, using their experience, perceptions and common sense. They are not blind tools, but they are extremely helpful in the context of a management system committed to achieving quality and productivity.

1.3 ON-LINE SPC METHODS

SPC methods can be described as *on-line* or *off-line*. We deal first with on-line methods, which again divide into two types, *screening* or *preventative* and these can be seen in Fig. 1.1.

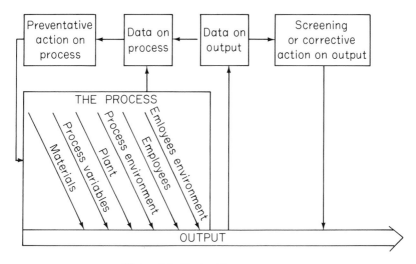

Figure 1.1 Controlling a process.

In *screening*, we inspect the output, and if the quality is not satisfactory, we screen out the substandard items for reworking, for selling at a reduced price or for scrap. This is usually done by a system of sampling inspection, and can be done by methods discussed in Chapters 11–14. Screening for quality is usually very expensive, and not recommended.

In *preventative* SPC methods we inspect the process, and try to use process control to avoid defective items being produced. Typical preventative SPC methods are:

(1) Shewhart control charts for process variables (Chapters 5 and 6).
(2) CuSum control charts for process variables (Chapter 7).
(3) Sampling inspection of input material (Chapters 11–13).
(4) Continuous production inspection of product (Chapter 14).

Some people contrast control charts, as preventative methods, with sampling inspection as a screening procedure. This distinction is not correct. Control charts *can* be used as a screening mechanism, and sampling inspection *can* be used in a preventative manner. But the importance of on-line SPC methods lies in their use as *preventative* procedures.

SPC methods concentrate on trying to control process average level and process spread. In particular, process spread or variability is a special enemy of quality, and needs to be tackled with some vigour. Indeed the vast majority of discussions on quality between manufacturers, their customers and suppliers is centred around the *consistency* of feedstocks and products.

1.4 OFF-LINE PROCESS CONTROL

This is often the next stage on from on-line SPC, although ideally it should be built into designing and setting up a product and its production process from the start.

The aim is to reduce or remove the effect of potential causes of variability by modifying the process, or the product, so making it less sensitive to these causes. This generally requires skill and ingenuity from a team of people with different expertise, one of whom will be a statistician. It is not possible to give general rules or simple guidelines, but in a short introduction the following examples may help illustrate the possibilities. This type of use of experimental design has been pushed by Taguchi (1985, 1986a, 1986b).

Example 1.1

A number of different factors were postulated as possible causes of variability in large ceramic insulators. A properly designed experiment was carried out to determine which of these had significant effects. This identified firing temperature (which could be different in different parts of the kiln, depending on loading etc.) as a major factor. A programme of work was put in hand to find a ceramic mix that would be less sensitive. In addition, one of the lesser sources of variation was found to be the length of time that elapsed between manufacture of an insulator and firing. (A firing batch would be collected over a period of time.)

This was largely eliminated by setting up a small holding store with a suitable atmosphere.

Example 1.2

Gorsky (1987) reported an experiment run at some Ford Motor Company plants. The problem concerned the 3.8L V6 camshaft, and there were two objectives:

(1) To reduce the percent carbide content variation, lobe to lobe, on a given camshaft.
(2) To achieve higher lobe hardness.

A brainstorming session was held in order to identify factors worthy of study in an experiment. Two sorts of factors were identified, tooling factors and process factors.

The tooling factors affect the configuration of the machine. Five factors were selected, each at two levels, and it was decided to perform a fractional factorial experiment of eight runs, in order to find the optimum configuration.

The process factors represent 'noise', which are more difficult or impossible to control. Six such factors were identified, each at two levels, and a fractional factorial experiment of sixteen runs was selected.

Under the system proposed by Taguchi (1986b), each of the tooling factor runs was performed at each combination of noise factors. For full details see the original article, but in all about 1500 camshafts were made.

The objective of the analysis was to find a combination of tooling factors which achieved the objectives consistently across the noise factors. Because the experiments were of the fractional factorial type, confirmatory runs had to be made before implementing the conclusions.

Example 1.2 illustrates the contrast between what Taguchi calls 'control' and 'noise' factors. By carefully designed experiments it is possible to find control factor combinations which perform consistently well across the less well-controlled noise factors. In Example 1.1 a change to the product was necessary to achieve the objectives, whereas in Example 1.2 the change is more to the process.

Example 1.3

Becknell (1987) reported an experiment run on throttle bodies for the Ford Motor Company. The component was die cast, and although quality was satisfactory from most points of view, it was subject to gas porosity voids which affect visual quality. A brainstorming session was held after which seven factors were selected for examination. These were metal cleanliness, shot size, spray pattern, intensification, profile velocity, die temperature and metal temperature. Each of these factors was selected at two levels, but a fractional factorial experiment of only eight runs was used. The optimum combination of factor levels was tested in a confirmatory run. The results achieved a 73% reduction in visual porosity, and an estimated annual saving of over £200 000.

Off-line quality control employs a considerable amount of experimental design work, and some special types of design favoured by Taguchi. There is now a very large literature on this topic: see for example American Supplier Institute (1987).

In some cases the use of off-line quality control may eliminate the need for on-line methods, but in most cases on-line methods are a vital part of the quality initiative. The text to follow concentrates on on-line methods.

1.5 SPC METHODOLOGY

SPC should be seen as an objective statistical analysis of process variation and its causes. Often large gains can be made by using quite simple statistical methods. The difference between decisions made on a basis of facts and data rather than gut-feel and intuition can be enormous.

In some industries of the component manufacturing type, filling lines, etc., the charting methods which form much of the book can be readily applied. It is sometimes obvious what to plot on the chart, such as a dimension, and it may also be reasonably clear what to do when a 'process out of control' signal is given.

In other industries, particularly in the process industries, the situation is very complicated and it is not at all clear what to plot, nor what to do at 'out of control' signals.

In process industries the processes involve recycling, automatic control loops, and many stages of mixing, blending or interaction. Typically, a process industry has:

(1) About 10 variables defining the quality of the product.
(2) About 200–500 process parameters or variables.
(3) About 30 variables defining quality and amounts of input raw material.

There is frequently only vague knowledge of the relationships between many of these variables.

An SPC study into such a process involves much more than charting, and based on our experience we suggest the following stages. Greater discussion will be given in the companion volume *Statistical Process Control – a Manual for Practitioners*.

Stage 1 Process flow

1.1 Draw a schematic diagram of the flow of the process, and note the stages or phases in the process.

1.2 Study the flow of data from the process. Note where and when this data is stored, communication links, etc.

Stage 2 Determine the problem

2.1 Collect peoples' opinions about the problem, including the customer.

2.2 Determine the important product variables, whether or not they are measured.

2.3 Collect and analyse data on these variables using moving averages, CuSums, and process capability studies (Chapters 2–4).

2.4 Calculate the costs of non-conforming product.

2.5 Interpret the data using process log books, and by consultation with process engineers and operators.

Stage 3 Explore the process

3.1 Collect information about the process:
   (a) Known from technical sources and reports
   (b) Relationships or material believed, sometimes strongly
   (c) Conjectures and opinions.

3.2 Break the process down into modules, if possible, and decide on any extra data necessary to achieve this.

3.3 Collect data available from quality control or other routine operations. Decide on extra data required and collect it.

3.4 Analyse and interpret the data using graphs, CuSum plots, multiple regression or multivariate statistical methods.

3.5 Design and carry out experiments on the plant in order to test and establish empirical or theoretical models.

3.6 Choose the types of SPC charts to use and decide where to put them.

3.7 Implement SPC. This stage will often involve training, and some sort of 'public relations' exercise with staff.

A key point with a complex system is to break the process into modules. Multivariate methods such as principal components can be used to trace back variations through the process. Often some time-series analysis will also be required.

The experimental design stage is often essential, for without it there is insufficient knowledge of the process to implement SPC.

This section has mentioned numerous statistical techniques not covered in this book, such as experimental design, multivariate analysis or time-series analysis. For these we refer readers to standard texts. Versions of texts adapted to the quality field do not seem yet to exist.

1.6 OTHER FACTORS AFFECTING THE SUCCESS OF SPC

The technical side of SPC is clearly essential in gathering information about processes, setting up control charts, and showing how quality or yield can be improved and then maintained at a high level. But as the Japanese have shown, and as practitioners of SPC and quality management such as Crosby and Deming have also realized, there is a great deal more to it than technical expertise.

The company has to be prepared to make substantial inputs of training, capital and equipment where these are shown to be beneficial. It is also essential to have a management philosophy and structure which permits and encourages workers at all levels to work for high-quality

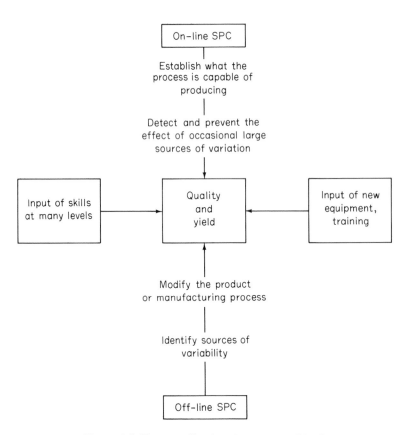

Figure 1.2 Factors affecting the success of SPC.

production. The success of SPC and other quality initiatives in Japan, and its lack of success in Britain and the USA where the techniques originated, is thought to be very largely due to a failure on our part to develop our own industrial philosophy and strategies. In particular, successful management of the work-force, both skilled and unskilled, depends on an understanding of what the company is, and the reasons that people will work well within it.

Many people depend on the continued health and profitability of a large company. Those directly involved include personal investors, both large and small, pension funds etc., but the structure and wealth of society is also affected because of direct taxation of the company, taxation of its employees, and the maintenance of the many service industries catering for employees.

But the people who have the greatest stake in the present and future well-being of the company are the people who work for it at every level. They make substantial inputs of time and effort and require satisfactory returns, not all of which are financial.

Although people will often work longer hours (and sometimes harder) for more money, for the majority of people this is not a motive for a high standard of work. To achieve this latter, a person must be motivated by a sense of achievement and of self-worth. Most of us motivate ourselves quite well over long periods of time and in remarkably difficult conditions. This is especially true if we are in a position to see that the work we are doing is well done or has a value of its own, including the value of providing for ourselves and for our dependents. But we do also need external appreciation of various kinds if we are to continue to think and work to the best of our ability. Awards for quality improvement (as suggested by Crosby) are one part of this, and so is the appreciation shown 'little and often' by superiors or within a peer group. This is one of the important requirements that management cannot afford to overlook in a quality improvement exercise, or they will find that the programme is relatively short-lived in its effectiveness. In particular if the 'appreciation' of management is shown by making workers redundant as a result of improved quality or lower production costs, then sensible people who see colleagues treated in this way will know how to react to subsequent quality drives. Redeployment and retraining cost money, but not as much as is lost by demoralizing the work-force at all levels.

In the final analysis the company is a highly sophisticated tool for shaping our society. Its importance lies only in the effects it has on large numbers of different people. Like many tools the edges are inclined to get blunt and require sharpening, parts wear and need replacing. And the first and most important step in doing this is to perceive the need.

1.7 OUTLINE OF THE BOOK

This book is intended to be accessible to people at a range of levels, including technical management in industry and statistics, engineering and mathematics undergraduates on degree and degree-level courses. Chapters 1–7 and 10 (omitting starred sections) should be accessible to a wide range of readers, provided the material contained in Chapter 2 is studied in detail. Chapters 8, 9 and 11 onwards are at a higher technical level.

Two sets of exercises have been provided at the ends of chapters; those marked 'A' are general data exercises to be done by everyone. Exercises marked 'B' are intended to be more mathematical, and to enable readers to achieve a deeper understanding of the techniques. The exercises should not be skipped.

Most of the techniques used are presented in a very simple step-by-step summary form, called **Method summaries**. These summaries should make the techniques quite clear, and they should be used as a basis of training when SPC is implemented.

EXERCISES 1A

1. Write out a detailed flow chart for a process that you are familiar with. List separately the
   (a) Input variables. Variables connected with the input raw materials.
   (b) Process variables. Variables which describe process conditions.
   (c) Product variables. Variables which describe the quality of the product.

   Discuss the possible points in this process at which SPC charting, sampling inspection, or off-line quality control might be applied.

2
Some basic distributions

2.1 INTRODUCTION

2.1.1 Layout of this chapter

A large part of this book is taken up with the construction of various types of control chart, and with the derivation of some of the properties of these charts. All of these charts are based on an underlying model for the data, and in this chapter we review the main models used. In section 2.1.2 we describe the types of data we meet, and we shall need models to cover these. Also, in section 2.2 and to some extent in section 2.7 a list of basic results is given. In fact, a large part of the book can be understood with a fairly shallow understanding of these ideas.

A revision of the binomial, Poisson, geometric and normal distributions is given in sections 2.3–7. Those familiar with the material on distributions should read sections 2.1 and 2.9, with sections 2.10 and 2.11 as optional.

Scientists interested mainly in the applications need not study the detailed theory but should read the basic definitions in each section.

2.1.2 Types of data

There are three main types of data: attribute, countable and continuous data.

(a) *Attribute data*
In attribute data, each item of data is classified as belonging to one of a number of categories, and the most common case is when there are just two categories. Examples are as follows:

(1) An article on a production line is inspected and classified as either effective or defective.
(2) A sample of a chemical is inspected and analysed for the percentage of a certain impurity. This result is simply recorded as either within or not within specified tolerances.

(3) A sample of 200 invoices is inspected, and each invoice is classified as correct or incorrect.
(4) In inspection at an electronics factory, it is recorded which of five 'setting stations' produced a given item.

(b) *Countable data*

Countable data arises when each data item is the count of the number of faults, accidents etc. for a given length of time or quantity of material. For countable data, observations range over the values 0, 1, 2, . . ., and examples are as follows:

(1) A sample of plastic chips are inspected, and the number of misshapen pieces recorded.
(2) In the production of electronic equipment, final production was subject to strict inspection. The number of defects for each item inspected was noted.
(3) A sample of 200 invoices was inspected and the number of errors in each noted.

(c) *Continuous data*

Many variables are measured on a continuous scale such as the following:

(1) The hardness of a metal, or of a plastic.
(2) The tensile strength of a piece of plastic.
(3) The water content, in parts per million, of a sample of antifreeze.
(4) The weight of a powder packed in a capsule or container.

(d) *Multivariate data*

Most SPC methods to date deal with one variable at a time, whereas in fact most practical situations are multivariate. For example, in the manufacture of film, a set of variables which describes the product might include hardness, profile, luminescence, yellowness. Similarly, a set of variables describing the process might include the shift number, batch number, processing times at various stages, critical temperatures, draw ratios, etc. For the same application, a further collection of variables might describe the quality and amounts of input raw materials. It is often vital to keep a clear distinction between these input, process and product variables.

Multivariate data is especially common in applications in the process industries, but multivariate SPC methods are not yet well developed.

2.2 SOME BASIC DEFINITIONS

We have just described some kinds of data which we shall meet in statistical process control. In order to proceed we shall need some basic ideas and definitions. A full explanation of these can be found in books on elementary statistics, such as Chatfield (1984) or Wetherill (1982).

Suppose we take samples of 1 kg from successive batches of production of an engineering plastic, and examine them for longs (unusual-shaped pieces). The numbers of longs for successive batches might be

$$0, 3, 0, 1, 2, 1, 1, 0, 2, 5, \ldots$$

If we let the successive results be denoted $x_1, x_2, \ldots$, then for the first n we can calculate the *sample mean*

$$\bar{x} = \sum x_i / n$$

and the *sample variance*

$$s^2 = \sum (x_i - \bar{x})^2 / (n - 1)$$

or the *standard deviation* s, which is the square root of the variance.

We regard any data set, such as a collection of 100 successive results, as a *random sample* from a *population*. For the example we are considering the population is summarized by the *relative frequency table* for a very large set of results taken under the same conditions. (In practice, it is not possible to sample under identical conditions due to variations in the process; we shall discuss this later.) Models for populations are *probability distributions*. For countable data, as in our example above, a suitable probability distribution is a set of values $p(r)$, for $r = 0, 1, 2, \ldots$, such that $p(r) \geq 0$ and

$$\sum p(r) = 1$$

For continuous data, a suitable probability distribution is defined by a probability density function $f(x)$ such that $f(x) \geq 0$,

$$\int_{-\infty}^{\infty} f(x) \, dx = 1$$

and the probability of getting a result between L and U is

$$\int_{L}^{U} f(x) \, dx.$$

Examples of these distributions are given in the following sections of this chapter.

The mean of the population, rather than the sample, is called the *expectation*, and is defined by

$$E(r) = \sum rp(r)$$

for countable data, and by

$$E(X) = \int xf(x)\,dx$$

for continuous data. The *variance* of the population is given by

$$V(X) = \int (x - \mu)^2 f(x)\,dx$$

where μ is the expectation. These quantities can be regarded as the sample mean and variance, but calculated for the whole population rather than for a sample.

2.3 ATTRIBUTE DATA – BINOMIAL DISTRIBUTION

The most common distribution which arises for attribute data is the *binomial distribution*. This arises in the following situation:
  Carry out n independent trials, the result of which is either 0 or 1.
  The probability of a '1' result is constant from trial to trial and is denoted p.
  The outcome X of each trial is independent of all others.
  With these assumptions, the probability distribution of the number of '1' results is

$$Pr(X = r) = \binom{n}{r} p^r (1 - p)^{n-r}, \qquad r = 0, 1, \ldots, n \qquad (2.1)$$

and some values are given in Table 2.1.
  For this distribution we find that the expectation and variance are

$$E(X) = np, \qquad V(X) = np(1 - p).$$

The binomial distribution approaches the normal distribution as $n \to \infty$. The normal distribution is discussed in section 2.6, and the normal approximation to the binomial distribution is studied in section 2.10.

Example 2.1 Acceptance inspection
As batches of items come into a production line, a sample of 20 items is selected and the number defective counted. The distribution of the observed number of defects will be binomial, theoretically. We find that

$$Pr(\text{Number of defectives} = r) = \binom{20}{r} p^r (1 - p)^{20-r}$$

Table 2.1 Binomial distribution for a selection of *p*-values with $n = 20$

r \ p	0.05	0.10	0.20	0.40
0	0.3585	0.1216	0.0115	0.0000
1	0.3774	0.2702	0.0576	0.0005
2	0.1887	0.2852	0.1369	0.0031
3	0.0596	0.1901	0.2054	0.0123
4	0.0133	0.0898	0.2182	0.0350
5	0.0022	0.0319	0.1746	0.0746
6	0.0003	0.0089	0.1091	0.1244
7	0	0.0020	0.0545	0.1659
8		0.0004	0.0222	0.1797
9		0.0001	0.0074	0.1597
10		0	0.0020	0.1171
11			0.0005	0.0710
12			0.0001	0.0355
13			0	0.0146
14				0.0049
15				0.0013
16				0.0003
17				0
18				
19				
20	0	0	0	0
Mean	1.00	2.00	4.00	8.00
St.Dev.	0.975	1.342	1.789	2.191

where p is the probability of a defective. This is the basis of acceptance inspection, and will be discussed later.

A 'model' of the binomial distribution can be made as follows. Suppose we have a container with discs in it, a proportion p of which are labelled '1' and the rest '0'. To simulate the binomial distribution with, say $n = 10$, take 10 separate drawings, *replacing* the disc each time. Record the total number of '1' responses. This is precisely the same as drawing 10 items from a batch with replacement, a proportion p of which are defective.

2.4 COUNTABLE DATA – POISSON DISTRIBUTION

Countable data occurs very frequently, and one of the most common distributions which applies is the Poisson distribution. This distribution applies when certain 'events' occur at random in time or space, and the observation recorded is the number of events in a given interval.

Examples of cases where the Poisson distribution applies are the number of incoming telephone calls to an exchange in a five-minute period, and the number of 'specks' per gram of a powder.

In general, let the expected number of 'events' in a unit time interval be μ, so that the probability of an event in the interval $(t, t + \delta t)$ is $\mu \delta t$, independently of events in other time intervals. From these assumptions it can be shown that the probability distribution of the number, X, of events in a given (unit) time interval is

$$\Pr(X = r) = e^{-\mu}\mu^r/r!, \qquad r = 0, 1, 2, \ldots \tag{2.2}$$

For this distribution we find that the expectation and variance are both μ.

The Poisson distribution approximates the Normal distribution for large μ, and the Normal approximation to the Poisson distribution is studied in section 2.11.

A historic data set which fit the Poisson distribution will illustrate the basic idea.

Example 2.2 Radioactive emissions
The emission of α-particles from a radioactive source are events which are independent of each other, and completely randomly distributed in time. Rutherford *et al.* (1920) reported the results of observing the number of emissions from each of 2608 periods of 7.5 seconds, and the results are shown in Table 2.2.

Table 2.2 The number of emissions from a radioactive source

No. of emissions	Frequency	Poisson distribution, Probability	$\mu = 3.870$ $2608 \times$ Prob
0	57	0.0209	54.399
1	203	0.0807	210.523
2	383	0.1562	407.361
3	525	0.2015	525.496
4	532	0.1949	508.418
5	408	0.1509	393.515
6	273	0.0973	253.817
7	139	0.0538	140.325
8	45	0.0260	67.882
9	27	0.0112	29.189
10	10 ⎫		
11	4 ⎬	0.0066	17.075
12	2 ⎭		

The Poission distribution can be worked out theoretically, and it depends on one parameter, μ, which we set equal to the average $\bar{x}$. In column 4 of Table 2.2 we show the fitting Poisson distribution, and there is very good agreement. A formal statistical test can be done to show that the agreement is within what we might expect from random variation.

The point about Example 2.2 is that it is an example where the assumptions of the Poisson distribution do seem to hold. When we go to industrial data we often have reasons to doubt that the assumptions hold.

Example 2.3
Data was collected on the number of accidents in a certain factory each month for four years. Table 2.3 shows a comparison with a Poisson distribution of the same mean (3.354 per month).

Table 2.3 Accidents per month for 48 months

No. of accidents	Frequency	Poisson distribution, Probability	$\mu = 3.354$ $48 \times$ Prob
0	3	0.0349	1.68
1	5	0.1172	5.63
2	7	0.1965	9.43
3	12	0.2197	10.55
4	7	0.1843	8.84
5	9	0.1236	5.93
6	2	0.0691	3.31
7	3	0.0331	1.59
≥ 8	0	0.0216	1.04

Although the agreement with the Poisson distribution is fairly good in Example 2.3, there are reasons to doubt the Poisson fit. For example, winter may be worse than summer for accidents, and the rate is likely to depend on the man-hours worked. The occurrence of an accident may make others more careful so that accidents are not independent of each other. In fact, the Poisson distribution often fits accident data surprisingly well.

If now we consider the distribution of the number of 'specks' in a kilogram of a powder from an industrial process, then for the Poisson distribution to hold we would need to assume that the production conditions hold constant over the period during which the data was collected, and this may well be unlikely. We would be likely to see a greater dispersion in the data than a Poisson distribution would allow. However, the Poisson distribution fits many situations very well. It can also be used as an approximation to the binomial distribution when n is large and p is small, by setting $\mu = np$. In Table 2.4 some Poisson distribution are tabulated, and also one case of a binomial distribution, showing the close approximation to a Poisson distribution.

Table 2.4 The Poisson distribution

r	$\mu = 1$	2	4	8	Binomial $n = 20\ p = 0.4\ np = 8$
0	0.3679	0.1353	0.0183	0.0003	0.0000
1	0.3679	0.2707	0.0733	0.0027	0.0005
2	0.1839	0.2707	0.1463	0.0107	0.0031
3	0.0613	0.1804	0.1954	0.0286	0.0123
4	0.0153	0.0902	0.1954	0.0573	0.0350
5	0.0031	0.0361	0.1563	0.0912	0.0742
6	0.0005	0.0120	0.1042	0.1221	0.1244
7	0.0001	0.0034	0.0595	0.1396	0.1659
8	0	0.0009	0.0298	0.1396	0.1797
9		0.0002	0.0132	0.1241	0.1597
10		0	0.0053	0.0993	0.1171
11			0.0019	0.0722	0.0710
12			0.0006	0.0481	0.0355
13			0.0002	0.0296	0.0146
14			0.0001	0.0169	0.0049
15			0	0.0090	0.0013
16				0.0045	0.0003
17				0.0021	0
18				0.0009	
19				0.0004	
20	0	0	0	0.0002	0
Mean	1	2	4	8	8
St.Dev.	1	1.414	2	2.828	2.191

2.5 GEOMETRIC DISTRIBUTION

The geometric distribution arises in the following situation.

Carry out a series of independent trials, the results of which is either 0 or 1.

The probability of a '1' result is constant from trial to trial and is denoted p.

The outcome X of each trial is independent of all others.

The result is the number of trials up to the first '1'.

With these assumptions, the probability distribution is

$$\Pr(X = r) = (1 - p)^{r-1}p, \qquad r = 1, 2, 3, \ldots \qquad (2.3)$$

and we find that the expectation and variance are

$$E(X) = 1/p \qquad V(X) = (1 - p)/p^2$$

Example 2.4

In a certain factory process inspections are made every half-hour, as a result of which the process is declared to be either 'in control' or 'out of control'. The probability of detecting the 'out of control' state is p. The probability distribution of the number of inspection periods until an 'out of control' state is recorded is geometric, with parameter p. (This assumes that the process remains statistically stable in the period.)

Some values of the geometric distribution are given in Table 2.5.

In SPC work, the geometric distribution usually occurs with a very low value of p, in which case the tail of the distribution is very long.

Table 2.5 The Geometric distribution

r / p	1	2	3	4	5	6	7	8
0.99	0.99	0.0099	0.0001	0	0	0	0	0
0.95	0.95	0.0475	0.0024	0.0001	0	0	0	0
0.9	0.9	0.09	0.009	0.0009	0.0001	0	0	0
0.8	0.8	0.16	0.032	0.0064	0.0013	0.0003	0.0001	0
0.7	0.7	0.21	0.063	0.0189	0.0057	0.0017	0.0005	0.0002
0.6	0.6	0.24	0.096	0.0384	0.0154	0.0061	0.0025	0.0010
0.5	0.5	0.25	0.125	0.0625	0.0312	0.0156	0.0078	0.0039
0.4	0.4	0.24	0.144	0.0864	0.0518	0.0311	0.0187	0.0112

r / p	9	10	11	12	13	14	15	16	17
0.99	0	0	0	0	0	0	0	0	0
0.95	0	0	0	0	0	0	0	0	0
0.9	0	0	0	0	0	0	0	0	0
0.8	0	0	0	0	0	0	0	0	0
0.7	0	0	0	0	0	0	0	0	0
0.6	0.0004	0.0002	0.0001	0	0	0	0	0	0
0.5	0.002	0.001	0.0005	0.0002	0.0001	0.0001	0	0	0
0.4	0.0067	0.0004	0.0024	0.0015	0.0009	0.0005	0.0003	0.0002	0.0001

2.6 THE NORMAL DISTRIBUTION

Many measurements of continuous variables follow the normal distribution, which has the shape shown in Fig. 2.1. The reason for this is a powerful result called the 'central limit theorem'. Basically it states that if we add enough effects together, none predominating, then a normal distribution results. Because of this result, we often find good fits to practical data by the normal distribution.

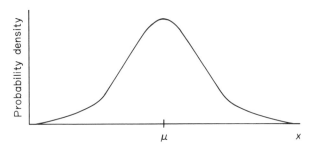

Figure 2.1 The normal distribution.

The distribution is symmetrical and bell-shaped and is determined by its expectation and variance,

$$E(X) = \mu, \qquad V(X) = \sigma^2$$

and has a probability density function

$$\frac{1}{\sqrt{(2\pi)}\sigma} \exp\left\{-\frac{1}{2}\left(\frac{x - \mu}{\sigma}\right)^2\right\}. \tag{2.4}$$

We call this an $N(\mu, \sigma^2)$ distribution. The distribution is such that

$$\Pr(X > \mu + 3.09\sigma) = 0.001$$

$$\Pr(X > \mu + 1.96\sigma) = 0.025.$$

Table 2.6 The normal distribution

$$p = \int_{-\infty}^{z} \exp(-x^2/2)\,dx/\sqrt{(2\pi)}$$

z	0	0.5	1.0	1.5	2.0	2.5	3.0	3.5	4.0
p	0.5	0.6915	0.8413	0.9332	0.9772	0.9938	0.9986	0.99977	0.99997
p	0.5	0.6	0.7	0.8	0.9	0.95	0.975	0.99	0.999
z	0	0.25	0.52	0.84	1.28	1.64	1.96	2.33	3.09

For further values see the Appendix tables.

Other values of probability can be read from Table 2.6. The tables only give results for the *standard normal* distribution in which $\mu = 0$ and $\sigma = 1$; for other cases of μ and σ we use the transformation

$$z = (x - \mu)/\sigma$$

and look up z in the tables. Thus,

$$\Pr(x > 5.94 | \mu = 3, \sigma = 1.5) = \Pr\left(z > \frac{5.94 - 3}{1.5} \,\middle|\, \mu = 0, \sigma = 1\right)$$

$$= \Pr(z > 1.96 | \mu = 0, \sigma = 1)$$

$$= 0.025$$

2.7 DISTRIBUTIONS DERIVED FROM THE NORMAL DISTRIBUTION

2.7.1 Sample mean

The distribution of the mean of n observations drawn from a normal population with expectation μ and variance σ^2 is normal with expectation and variance:

$$E(\bar{X}) = \mu \qquad V(\bar{X}) = \sigma^2/n$$

(see Fig. 2.2).

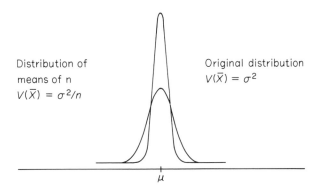

Distribution of
means of n
$V(\bar{X}) = \sigma^2/n$

Original distribution
$V(\bar{X}) = \sigma^2$

μ

Figure 2.2 Sampling from the normal distribution.

This result is used a great deal in the sequel. Because of the 'central limit theorem' the distribution of means are very often normal even if the original distribution is markedly non-normal.

2.7.2 Sample variance

The distribution of s^2, the sample variance drawn independently from a $N(\mu, \sigma^2)$ population is such that $(n - 1)s^2/\sigma^2$ has a χ^2_{n-1} distribution. Tables of the χ^2 distribution are given in Table 2.7, and methods of inference based on this are given in elementary statistics texts.

Table 2.7 The χ^2 distribution

Degrees of freedom	Lower percentage points		Upper percentage points			
	1%	5%	10%	5%	1%	0.1%
3	0.115	0.352	6.25	7.81	11.34	16.27
4	0.297	0.711	7.78	9.49	13.28	18.47
5	0.554	1.15	9.24	11.07	15.09	20.52

For further values see the Appendix tables.

The amount of information on which the sample variance is calculated is called the *degrees of freedom*. For a sample of n observations, there are only $n - 1$ independent differences, and so $n - 1$ degrees of freedom.

2.7.3 The sample range

The distribution of the sample range

$$R = (\max x_i) - (\min x_i)$$

of n independent observations from an $N(\mu, \sigma^2)$ population is not so easy to represent. Tables of the distribution are given in Table 2.8.

Table 2.8 Percentage points of the distribution of the relative range (range/σ)

Sample size	99.0	95.0	5.0	2.5	1.0	0.1
3	0.19	0.43	3.31	3.68	4.12	5.06
4	0.43	0.76	3.63	3.98	4.40	5.31
5	0.66	1.03	3.86	4.20	4.60	5.48

For further values see the Appendix tables.

From this table we see that, for example, in a sample of size 5, 98% of sample ranges will fall in the interval

$$(0.66\sigma, \ 4.60\sigma)$$

Ranges can be used to estimate σ, instead of using the sample standard deviation. The method is simply to get the sample range, and divide by the factor d_n given in Table 2.9. (This is often referred to as d_2 in the literature.)

Table 2.9 Conversion of range to standard deviation

n	d_n	n	d_n	n	d_n	n	d_n
2	1.128	6	2.534	10	3.078	14	3.407
3	1.683	7	2.704	11	3.173	15	3.472
4	2.059	8	2.847	12	3.258	16	3.532
5	2.326	9	2.970	13	3.336	17	3.588

Example 2.5
If our data is

$$2.1 \quad 1.7 \ 2.4 \quad 1.9 \quad 2.6$$

then we have

$$\text{range} = 2.6 - 1.7 = 0.9$$
$$\hat{\sigma} = 0.9 \div 2.326 = 0.387$$

2.8 APPLICATION OF RESULTS – A SIMPLE CONTROL CHART

In a certain production process, titanium buttons were being produced. Samples of four were drawn from the process every 15 minutes, and measurements of hardness (DPN) made on each button. The data for 25 samples are given in Table 2.10, together with the means and ranges of each sample.

Data of this kind are usually part of a process control procedure, and our intention is to distinguish between

(1) those samples such that the variation can be adequately accounted for by random variation, and
(2) those samples which indicate that some special cause of variation is likely to be present.

Table 2.10 Hardness measurements of titanium buttons

Sample number	Hardness	(DPN)			Mean $(\bar{x})$	Range (R)
1	125.8	128.4	129.0	121.0	126.1	8.0
2	125.2	127.0	130.4	124.6	126.8	5.8
3	121.8	126.8	127.2	129.8	126.6	8.0
4	131.0	130.0	127.2	127.0	128.8	4.0
5	128.6	122.8	125.4	126.4	125.8	5.8
6	122.0	123.8	131.2	121.8	124.7	9.4
7	122.9	129.3	126.2	128.8	126.8	6.4
8	120.2	130.0	125.6	144.0	130.0	23.8
9	124.8	123.7	130.2	128.8	126.9	6.5
10	127.0	126.4	122.2	129.0	126.2	6.8
11	131.8	127.6	123.8	123.2	126.6	8.6
12	129.8	125.6	128.2	127.6	127.8	4.2
13	127.6	125.6	128.2	126.8	127.1	2.6
14	124.2	122.8	124.8	124.6	124.1	2.0
15	125.4	129.4	123.6	127.2	126.4	5.8
16	130.8	122.8	125.4	126.2	126.3	8.0
17	127.4	131.0	123.0	122.8	126.1	8.2
18	124.8	122.6	122.8	123.6	123.5	2.2
19	123.8	130.0	128.4	130.0	128.1	6.2
20	128.8	141.2	138.8	136.2	136.3	12.4
21	126.4	123.8	128.8	129.6	127.2	5.8
22	130.8	127.4	126.0	125.2	127.4	5.6
23	129.6	128.4	123.2	125.8	126.8	6.4
24	124.4	127.0	130.0	122.8	126.1	7.2
25	129.2	126.2	128.0	123.2	126.7	6.0
				Totals	3175.0	175.6

When we get samples of type (2), we carry out some investigation of the process in order to control it. Now if we look at Fig. 2.3 and Fig 2.4 we see that samples 8 and 20 seem to show unusual behaviour. However, there are other samples which we might question, and we obviously need some rule to help us to interpret charts such as Figs. 2.3 and 2.4.

We approach this by assuming that for most of the time, sampling the process is just like drawing samples from a single normal population. The results of the previous section enable us to draw boundaries which will contain almost all of the data, under normal conditions.

Clearly, in any practical case we would test the normality assumption

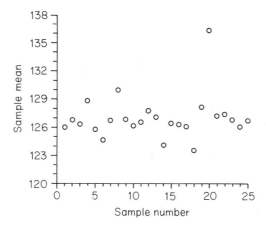

Figure 2.3 Plot of means of titanium hardness data.

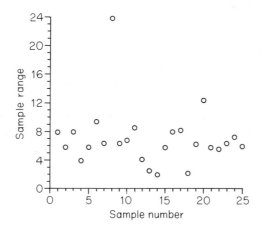

Figure 2.4 Plot of ranges of titanium hardness data.

before proceeding. Furthermore, we shall soon see that the underlying process is often more complex than our simple model allows. For the present we assume a normal population and proceed to estimate μ and σ for the population representing our 'hardness' data.

The best estimate of μ is given by the overall average,

$$\hat{\mu} = 3175/25 = 127.0$$

where $\hat{\mu}$ means 'estimate of μ'.

A good estimate of σ can be obtained by using the average range and this is shown below. Another estimate of σ could be obtained by calculating the variances within groups, and then combining these. This would be a slightly more efficient estimate of σ than the range estimate, but the gain in efficiency is quite small for samples of size 4.

Table 2.8 shows the percentage points of the distribution of the range (effectively for $\sigma = 1$, so we multiply by σ to use it). Thus, for example, for samples of size four, ranges greater than 3.98σ only occur with a probability 0.025, and only 0.1% of sample ranges are greater than 5.31σ.

Now we return to the data in Table 2.10 and we proceed as follows:

Total of 25 ranges	175.6
Average range	7.024
Constant (sample size = 4)	2.059
Estimate of σ	$7.024 \div 2.059 = 3.41$.

Based on this value of σ, and using Table 2.8, we see that only 0.1% of ranges is greater than

$$5.31\sigma = 5.31 \times 3.41 = 18.1$$

The range for group 8, at 23.8, is much greater than this. It is most unlikely that such a value could occur by chance, and there is very strong evidence that some assignable cause of variation is present in this particular sample.

Group 20, with a range of 12.4, is only $12.4/3.41 = 3.63\sigma$. This is not very unusual, as it is at the upper 5% point (Fig. 2.5). Thus deviations of range from the average of such a size could occur in 5% of occasions

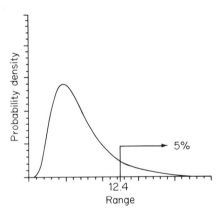

Figure 2.5 Distribution of sample ranges for samples of size 4 taken from a normal distribution with $\sigma = 3.41$.

at the upper end, and 5% of occasions at the lower end of the distribution.

Based on these results, we would be best to recalculate our estimate of σ omitting the result from group 8. (We might also omit sample 20, provided there is a good process explanation for its unusual value.) We have results as follows:

Total of 24 ranges	151.8 (175.6 − 23.8)
Average range	6.33
Constant (sample size = 4)	2.059
Estimate of σ	6.33 ÷ 2.059 = 3.07

We now find that sample 20 looks more extreme, but perhaps not so much so that it should be omitted. Thus our final estimate of σ is 3.07.

We know that in samples of size 4, the sample means will have a normal distribution with a standard error of $\sigma/\sqrt{n}$, so with $\hat{\sigma} = 3.07$, and $n = 4$, we have

$$\hat{\sigma}/\sqrt{n} = 3.07/\sqrt{4} = 1.535$$

For any normal distribution about 99.7% lies within ±3 standard deviations of the mean, so that we expect 99.7% of sample means to lie between

(overall average) ±3 × (standard error of mean of 4)

which is

$$127 \pm 3 \times 1.535 = 122.4 \text{ to } 131.6$$

If we draw lines on Fig. 2.3 at these values, we have boundaries which we expect to be crossed on only 0.3% of occasions if our population is still the same normal population. We see from Fig. 2.6

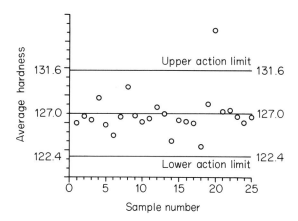

Figure 2.6 A simple Shewhart chart.

that the mean for sample 20 is well above the upper boundary, showing that there is clear evidence of the presence of some special cause of variation at this point in the process.

The boundaries are called *action boundaries*, and the way the chart is used is to take action on the process whenever a point lies outside these action boundaries. This type of chart was introduced by Walter A. Shewhart (1931), and a similar pair of action boundaries can be defined for the range chart. We shall develop this idea below.

Returning to Fig. 2.6, we see that the mean for sample 20 is well above the upper action boundary, so that we suspect the presence of a 'special cause' at this point. *Provided* investigation gives resonable grounds for a special cause, this sample should be omitted from the data used to estimate μ and σ. The reasoning is that, since a special cause was present, that sample is not representative of the population we are estimating. The recalculation of $\hat{\mu}$ and $\hat{\sigma}$ is left as an exercise. This recalculation is usually done when the chart is set up, and when the process capability is being reassessed.

Note: Some statisticians follow the method given in the British Standard, which puts the limits at ±3.09 standard errors, equivalent to the 99.8% level. There is very little to choose between the two practices.

2.9 TESTING FOR NORMALITY

Since many of the methods which follow assume normality, it is useful to have a check on this assumption. A simple test for normality is to draw a normal probability plot. (Tests for binomial and Poisson distributions are given in Chapter 10.)

Example 2.6
The data in Table 2.11 are measurements of resistance of 30 components from the same batch. In Fig 2.7 we show a histogram of the data, and Fig. 2.8 shows a cumulative distribution.

Table 2.11 Measurements of resistance of 30 components

999.1	1003.2	1002.1	999.2	989.7	1006.7
1012.2	996.4	1000.2	995.3	1009.7	993.4
998.1	997.9	1003.1	1002.6	1001.8	996.5
992.8	1006.5	1004.5	1000.3	1014.5	998.6
989.4	1002.9	999.3	994.7	1007.6	1000.9

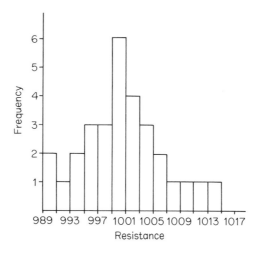

Figure 2.7 Histogram for Example 2.6.

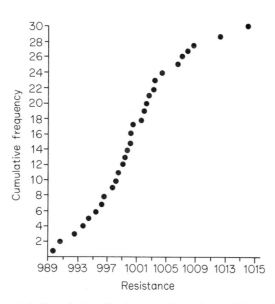

Figure 2.8 Cumulative distribution of the data of Example 2.6.

In order to see if the normal distribution fits we proceed as follows:

METHOD SUMMARY 2.1

Checking for normality – using normal probability paper

Step 1 Order the data from smallest to largest.
Step 2 Put alongside each measurement its order number, r.
Step 3 Calculate $p = (2r - 1)/2n$.
Step 4 Using special normal probability paper plot p on the vertical axis against the measurements.

Table 2.12 Calculations for normal probability plot

Observation	r	$p = (2r - 1)/2n$
989.4	1	0.01667
989.7	2	0.05
992.8	3	0.09833
993.4	4	0.1167
994.7	5	0.15
995.3	6	0.1833
996.4	7	0.2167
996.5	8	0.25
997.9	9	0.2833
998.1	10	0.3167
998.6	11	0.35
999.1	12	0.3833
999.2	13	0.4166
999.3	14	0.45
1000.2	15	0.4833
1000.3	16	0.5166
1000.9	17	0.55
1001.8	18	0.5833
1002.1	19	0.6167
1002.6	20	0.65
1002.9	21	0.6833
1003.1	22	0.7166
1003.2	23	0.75
1004.5	24	0.7833
1006.5	25	0.8167
1006.7	26	0.85
1007.6	27	0.8833
1009.7	28	0.9167
1012.2	29	0.95
1014.5	30	0.9833

The reasoning behind this test is as follows. Table 2.12 lists the cumulative frequency distribution of the observations, and if this is plotted out we get the S-shaped curve of Fig. 2.8. By plotting the observations against the value of Z_p for which the standard Normal tail probability is p we get a straight line when the data is normal. The standard deviation of the data can be calculated from the slope of the line.

Steps 1–3 are illustrated in Table 2.12 for the resistance data of Example 2.6, and the resulting probability plot is shown in Fig. 2.9.

For some other methods of testing normality see Wetherill et al. (1986).

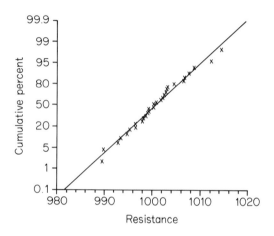

Figure 2.9 Normal probability plot for Example 2.6.

2.9.1 Discussion

The importance of getting a good fit for the distribution model used arises from the fact that in SPC we deal a lot with tail area properties of the distributions. For example, in section 2.8, the operation of the simple Shewhart chart depends on the proportion of observations beyond three standard deviations from the mean.

If non-normality is detected, some search for the reason needs to be conducted, and to ask questions such as the following:

(1) Is the non-normality due to 'outliers' or 'rogue values'?
(2) Has there been a merging of several different streams of production prior to the measurement point, so that these streams really need to be considered separately?

(3) Is the non-normality due to the fact that the measurement is down to the detectable limit?
(4) Is there a time effect, so that the process wanders in level over time, giving rise to a non-normal distribution overall.

If the basic distribution (allowing for these points) is non-normal, then a simple transformation can be tried as a means of restoring normality. See Wetherill *et al.* (1986) for a discussion, but frequently the logarithm, square root or reciprocal transformation works.

Procedures for testing the goodness of fit of binomial or Poisson distributions are dealt with in Chapter 10.

2.10* THE NORMAL APPROXIMATION TO THE BINOMIAL DISTRIBUTION

In many SPC applications, the normal distribution is used as an approximation to the binomial distribution, so that instead of calculating, say

$$\Pr(X \le 4) = \sum_{r=0}^{4} \binom{n}{r} p^r (1 - p)^{n-r}$$

the normal distribution with expectation np and variance $\{np(1 - p)\}$ is used so that we calculate

$$\Pr(X \le 4) = \int_{-\infty}^{4} \frac{1}{\sqrt{(2\pi)}\sigma} \exp\left\{-\left[\frac{X - \mu}{\sigma}\right]^2\right\} dx$$

where $\mu = np$ and $\sigma^2 = \{np(1 - p)\}$, perhaps including a 'continuity correction', to allow for the discreteness of the binomial distribution, so that the upper limit is 4.5, not 4.0.

Following this approach, a simple control chart for binomial data would be obtained by treating it as normal, putting the target at np, and the action lines at

$$np \pm 3\sqrt{\{np(1 - p)\}}.$$

A discussion of the normal approximation to the binomial distribution is given by Uspensky (1937), who gives a correction formula, and Hald (1952, 1978) carried out further studies. Hald points out that for p outside the range

$$(n + 1)^{-1} < p < n/(n + 1)$$

the binomial distribution is steadily increasing or decreasing, and the normal approximation cannot fit. Hald suggests that the normal approximation be limited to the range

$$np(1 - p) > 9$$

though he comments that this 'does not result in the same accuracy for different corresponding values of n and p determined from the formula $np(1 - p) = 9$.' (Uspensky suggests that $np(1\text{e}-p) \geq 25$.) Table 2.13 below gives some values of exact and approximate probabilities close to limits given by Hald's formula.

Table 2.13 Exact and approximate probabilities such that $\Pr(X < C) < P$; for values of n and p close to $np(1 - p) = 9$

n	p	Correct	C	Approx. with corr.	Approx. without corr.
$P = 0.05$					
909	0.01	0.0195	3	0.0312	0.0212
459	0.02	0.0476	4	0.0594	0.0421
189	0.05	0.0380	4	0.0493	0.0345
100	0.10	0.0237	4	0.0334	0.0226
$P = 0.95$					
909	0.01	0.9226	13	0.9292	0.9038
459	0.02	0.9188	13	0.9251	0.8986
189	0.05	0.9468	14	0.9540	0.9356
100	0.10	0.9274	14	0.9332	0.9088
$P = 0.01$					
909	0.01	0.0056	2	0.0140	0.0090
459	0.02	0.0051	2	0.0130	0.0083
189	0.05	0.0037	2	0.0102	0.0064
100	0.10	–		–	–
$P = 0.99$					
909	0.01	0.9883	16	0.9932	0.9894
459	0.02	0.9876	16	0.9927	0.9885
189	0.05	0.9855	16	0.9907	0.9856
100	0.10	0.9990	3	0.9940	0.9902

There are obvious difficulties in making the comparison, but there is reasonable evidence to support use of Hald's formula as a limit.

2.11* NORMAL APPROXIMATION TO THE POISSON DISTRIBUTION

This follows similar reasoning to the previous section. Instead of calculating, say

$$\Pr(X \le 4) = \sum_{r=0}^{4} e^{-\mu}\mu^r/r!$$

the normal approximation

$$\Pr(X \le 4) = \int_{-\infty}^{4} \frac{1}{\sqrt{(2\pi)}\mu} \exp\left\{\frac{(X - \mu)^2}{\mu}\right\} dx$$

is used, possibly with the 'continuity correction'. A standard result is to limit this approximation so that $\mu - 3\sqrt{\mu} \ge 0$, or $\mu \ge 9$. Table 2.14 below gives some values.

Table 2.14 Exact and approximate probabilities such that $\Pr(X < C) < P$, for various values of μ

μ	P	C	Exact	Normal approximation with corr.	without corr.
6	0.99	11	0.9799	0.9876	0.9794
6	0.95	9	0.9168	0.9235	0.8897
6	0.05	1	0.0174	0.0331	0.0206
6	0.01	0	0.0012	0.0123	0.0071
9	0.99	16	0.9889	0.9938	0.9902
9	0.95	13	0.9261	0.9332	0.9088
9	0.05	3	0.0212	0.0334	0.0227
9	0.01	2	0.0062	0.0151	0.0098
20	0.99	30	0.9865	0.9906	0.9873
20	0.95	27	0.9475	0.9532	0.9412
20	0.05	12	0.0390	0.0468	0.0368
20	0.01	9	0.0050	0.0094	0.0069

The binomial and Poisson distributions are considered further in Chapter 10. For further information see Uspensky (1937) or Hald (1952, 1978).

EXERCISES 2A

1. What model would you expect to apply in the following examples?

   (a) The number of misprints on one page of a daily newspaper.
   (b) The number of accidents per week on a particular stretch of motorway.

(c) The number of packs of a certain product which are less than the nominal weight, out of 100 produced per day.

(d) The time you take to reach work each day.

2. Obtain some data sets representing countable, attribute and continuous data from processes you are connected with. Plot the data out, and try to interpret the more extreme variations.

3. There are 16 sets of data given in Tables 2.15 and 2.16 (20 values in each set), from each of 3 distributions, A, B and C. Construct a normal probability plot for one or more of the sets for each of A, B and C, and determine whether any of these distributions is normal.

Table 2.15

A1	A2	A3	A4	A5	A6	A7	A8
2.63	3.75	3.67	1.94	1.42	4.24	3.96	3.75
4.93	2.33	2.77	3.22	3.84	2.81	3.97	2.13
3.20	2.66	3.28	2.67	4.20	2.21	2.56	3.23
3.36	2.59	2.34	4.58	3.44	4.60	2.26	3.73
2.54	2.22	3.76	3.87	1.24	1.71	3.84	2.66
2.97	1.66	3.95	3.12	2.16	3.06	4.28	3.50
4.94	2.13	3.63	0.60	1.50	3.34	3.30	2.42
4.23	3.51	3.29	2.53	1.68	3.95	4.01	3.57
1.61	2.21	4.77	3.88	3.04	3.52	2.21	3.56
2.25	1.38	1.93	2.29	2.12	2.41	0.98	2.70
4.19	3.00	3.93	3.02	3.26	5.08	3.32	1.97
2.98	2.38	0.16	2.71	1.82	3.70	2.61	3.43
3.09	3.29	1.98	2.82	2.89	3.06	2.46	3.28
2.80	2.08	3.00	2.94	4.40	2.54	1.90	4.15
5.19	2.07	2.63	2.43	2.52	1.70	4.34	3.62
1.75	2.60	2.04	3.56	3.22	2.39	3.44	2.26
3.62	3.03	4.01	3.61	3.10	3.51	1.82	2.56
1.16	2.16	4.24	3.45	2.02	3.73	4.42	1.22
2.90	2.87	1.43	4.06	2.10	3.24	1.73	3.49
1.34	2.25	3.15	2.19	1.99	2.51	2.89	3.36

Table 2.16

B1	B2	B3	B4	C1	C2	C3	C4
4.28	8.10	3.54	0.30	0.43	3.81	0.77	0.84
3.29	4.04	2.81	2.19	1.43	0.67	2.06	2.73
3.07	2.38	4.75	1.38	4.31	0.43	0.91	6.61
8.16	9.38	0.71	3.26	1.78	0.63	3.94	2.72
7.31	0.12	3.17	1.33	2.03	1.30	2.56	0.48
3.41	0.82	0.33	6.54	1.50	2.31	0.54	0.17
7.60	4.65	0.46	4.35	0.25	0.29	4.73	0.49
0.90	1.46	1.77	4.92	0.74	0.36	0.87	0.46
6.30	2.47	0.67	3.27	0.89	0.31	2.99	0.19
2.35	1.83	4.20	1.82	1.11	0.33	1.19	0.96
1.71	1.05	1.85	2.84	0.91	0.86	0.85	1.02
9.41	3.71	8.36	3.20	0.67	0.48	0.52	0.75
0.52	2.37	1.43	0.37	2.54	3.86	1.04	1.61
5.37	1.66	6.45	2.06	1.21	1.64	4.39	1.75
1.08	0.40	6.15	6.59	10.48	2.30	0.13	0.50
2.13	3.09	2.25	2.85	0.21	2.63	5.87	0.41
7.48	2.03	0.67	0.73	1.66	1.10	0.11	0.62
2.94	7.05	0.85	1.61	0.18	2.29	2.08	1.75
2.84	1.64	5.12	3.65	1.95	1.86	1.03	6.36
1.48	2.54	2.15	1.15	2.14	2.02	0.12	0.31

4. Plot the percentage points of the χ^2 distribution on normal probability paper for 5, 10 and 30 degrees of freedom.

5. How would you provide numerical measures of the quality of the service provided by the following?

   (a) The service at an industrial canteen.
   (b) Post office mail.
   (c) Telephone directory enquires.
   (d) A supermarket checkout.

6. Tins of soup are being filled on average with 377 g, the standard deviation being 1.4 g. What proportion of tins contain less than 375 g? What average fill weight is required to ensure that no more than 0.1% of tins contain less than 375 g?

7 When it is stable a process produces items that have an average

dimension of 46.75 mm and standard deviation of 0.26 mm. Upper and lower specification limits for this dimension are 46.1 mm and 47.4 mm. Assuming that the distribution of values is normal, what proportion of items will be outside specification?

8. Titanium buttons have been found to have an average measured hardness of 127.0 and a standard deviation of 3.4.

   (a) What proportion of individual buttons will have hardness measurements outside the limits (121.8, 132.2)?
   (b) If four buttons at a time are measured what is the probability that the *mean* hardness of this group will lie outside the above limits?

   What assumptions are you making, and do you think they are justifiable?

EXERCISES 2B

1. Assume that you have data available in the form of Table 2.10, with n observations per group, and k groups, and that the data is independently and normally distributed with mean μ and variance σ^2. Let action lines be placed at $A\sigma/\sqrt{n}$ from the target mean (assumed zero).

   (a) Show that the probability of action in any group is
   $$p = \phi\left(\frac{\mu\sqrt{n}}{\sigma} - A\right) + \phi\left(\frac{-\mu\sqrt{n}}{\sigma} - A\right).$$

   (b) Define the *run length* as the number of groups up to and including the first action point. Show that the distribution of run length is geometric with parameter p.
   (c) Obtain the *average run length* (ARL) for the Shewhart chart for means, when the constant $A = 3$.

2. For the geometric distribution show that
   $$Pr(R \le n) = 1 - (1 - p)^{n+1}.$$
   Hence find the values of p for which
   $$Pr(R \le n) = 0.95$$
   for $n = 10, 20, 30, 40, 50$. Compare the values of $E(R)$ for these values of p, and comment on the skewness of the distribution.

3. A large batch of items is submitted for inspection, and the items are classified as effective or defective. The proportion defective in the batch is θ. Items are sampled at random until exactly c defectives have been found. Show that the probability that this occurs at the nth item is

$$\binom{n-1}{c-1}\theta^c(1-\theta)^{n-c}$$

for $n = c$, $c + 1$, ... (Hint: the last item sampled must be a defective.)

4. Suppose that the probability that an event occurs in the interval $(t, t + \delta T)$ is $\lambda \, \delta t$, and denoted by $P_x(t)$ the probability that there have been x events up to time t. Show that

$$P_x(t + \delta T) = P_x(t)(1 - \lambda \, \delta t) + P_{x-1}(t)\lambda \, \delta t, \qquad x = 1, 2, \ldots$$

and

$$P_o(t + \delta t) = P_o(t)(1 - \lambda \, \delta t).$$

Hence show that

$$P_x(t) = e^{-\lambda t}\frac{(\lambda t)^x}{x!}$$

which is the Poisson distribution.

5. Verify some of the calcualtions in sections 2.10 and 2.11 on the normal approximation to the binomial and Poisson distributions. Extend these to lower values of n.

6. If accidents in a building are assumed to occur randomly with an average rate of 42 per year, what is the chance that there will be no accidents in April? What is the chance that there will be no more than one accident in April?

7. In a sample of size 100 from a batch with a failure rate of 15% what is the probability of

(a) exactly 18 failures?
(b) no more than 6 failures?

3
Process variation

3.1 REASONS FOR PROCESS VARIATION

For the present we shall concentrate on situations where the variable of interest is a continuous variable, and we shall deal with countable and attribute data later.

All industrial processes display variation, and there are many different reasons for it, such as:

(1) Variational noise. This is the variation we observe between product manufactured under the same conditions and specifications.
(2) Causes external to the process, such as environmental temperature, humidity, etc.
(3) Process causes. These are due to the process itself, such as build-up of waste products, ageing of a catalyst, variation of loading of a kiln etc.
(4) Assignable causes of variation. This variation may be due to the quality of batches of raw material, incorrect setting of equipment, etc.

The procedure adopted in SPC is to try to separate variation that we ordinarily expect of a process, from that which may be due to special or assignable causes. This is usually done by keeping charts for the process average level and the process spread (as outlined briefly in Chapter 2). In the following sections we describe the types of pattern we might see for charts of sample means. Somewhat similar remarks can be made about charts for process spread. We shall suppose that charts are made by plotting the means of groups of n observations, and we shall suppose that the n observations are sampled close together in time or space (or both). Sometimes observations can only be made singly, so that $n = 1$, and this happens frequently in the process industries. Much of the following discussion is relevant to both cases.

3.2 TYPES OF PROCESS VARIATION

Industrial processes display a wide variety of types of variation. In general, the component manufacturing industries have processes which display much simpler types of variation than the process industries. The following are examples.

(1) *Simple random variation*
Figure 3.1 shows the pattern of group means we would expect if our data was in fact sampled from a normal population with mean μ and standard deviation σ. Most of the observations will fall within the limits $\mu \pm 3.09\sigma$. Occasional 'special' or 'assignable' causes of variation will cause departures from this pattern.

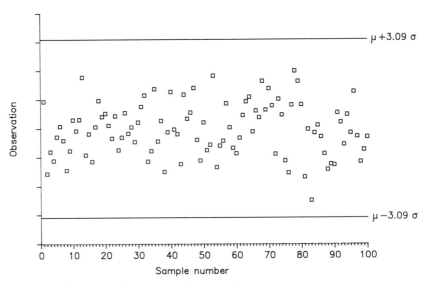

Figure 3.1 Process variation – random variation.

(2) *Short- and long-term variation – all random*
Frequently we may find that when we plot our data, the process mean varies much more than it should, based on the within-sample variation; a test for this will be given in section 3.6. There are two types of this that arise. Figure 3.2 shows a random pattern of changes in the mean, and Figure 3.3 shows some evidence of correlation between neighbouring values.

(3) *Short- and long-term variation – cycles*
Recurring cycles may be due to rotation of apparatus or machinery

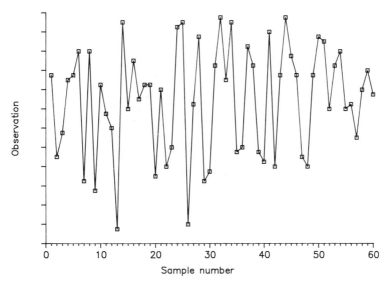

Figure 3.2 Process variation – extra variation in the mean.

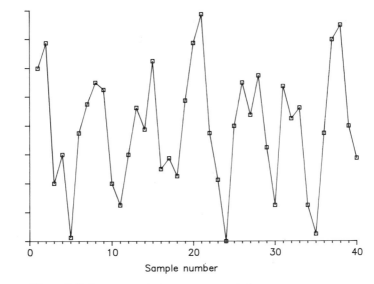

Figure 3.3 Process variation – autocorrelation present.

used in the process, environmental changes such as temperature, worker fatigue, or sometimes to the merging of subassemblies (see Fig. 3.4).

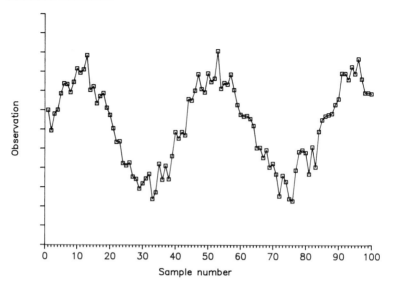

Figure 3.4 Process variation – recurring cycles.

(4) *Trends*

Trends may be due to causes such as gradual deterioration of equipment, ageing of catalysts, the accumulation of waste products (Fig. 3.5).

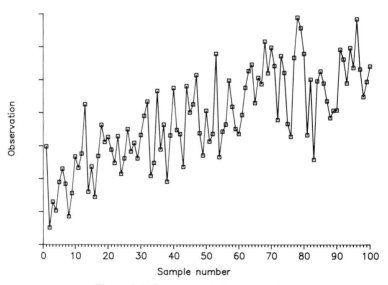

Figure 3.5 Process variation – trends.

(5) *Sudden jumps*

Sudden jumps may be due to new batches of raw material, changes in workers or equipment or modifications to the process (Fig. 3.6).

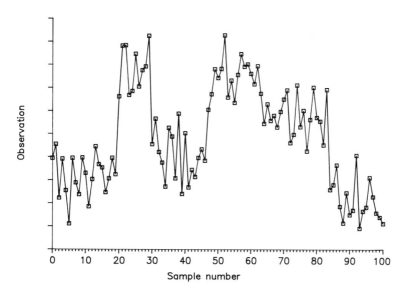

Figure 3.6 Process variation – sudden jumps.

The simple Shewhart chart given in Section 2.8 assumed simple random variation only. It is clear that some amendment to the method is needed to deal with the other types of variation.

3.3 SOME MODELS FOR PROCESS VARIATION

It is helpful to have some theoretical models on which to base our study of SPC techniques. The following subsections give a few simple models.

3.3.1 Simple random variation

The simplest situation is where we have simple normal variation, satisfying the model.

$$Model\ 1 \qquad x_{ij} = \mu + \sigma_w \varepsilon_{ij} \qquad \begin{array}{l} i = 1, 2, \ldots, k \\ j = 1, 2, \ldots, n \end{array} \qquad (3.1)$$

where n is the number of observations in a group, k is the number of groups, μ is the overall mean, σ_W^2 is the (within-group) variance, and ε_{ij} are independent $N(0, 1)$ variables. The sample means will have a distribution $N(\mu, \sigma_W^2/n)$, and Fig. 3.1 shows a typical plot of these. Evidence that special causes are present is given by values of means different to what we expect from an $N(\mu, \sigma_W^2/n)$ distribution.

3.3.2 Between- and within-group variation

Often in an industrial process, the variation of group means will be *more* than we expect from Model 1. The process parameters, such as kiln temperatures, etc., may vary slightly introducing *extra* variation, which affects the whole of each group. An appropriate model is:

$$Model\ 2 \qquad x_{ij} = \mu + \sigma_B \omega_i + \sigma_W \varepsilon_{ij} \qquad \begin{matrix} i = 1, 2, \ldots, k \\ j = 1, 2, \ldots, n \end{matrix} \qquad (3.2)$$

where σ_B^2 is the *between-group* variance, and ω_i are independent $N(0, 1)$ variates. A typical plot of group means $\bar{x}_{i.}$ is shown in Fig. 3.2. (In statistical notation a dot denotes summation over a suffix and a bar an averaging.)

For Model 2 we see that

$$V(x_{ij}) = \sigma_B^2 + \sigma_W^2 \qquad (3.3)$$

$$V(\bar{x}_{i.}) = \sigma_B^2 + (\sigma_W^2/n) \qquad (3.4)$$

These results are important for charting methods. The important feature is that increasing the group size n reduces the amount of *within-group* variation in the sample mean, but does not affect the *between-group* component.

3.3.3 Simple autocorrelated model

Often we find that for process industries, successive groups of observations are correlated, showing a pattern such as that in Fig. 3.3. This may be due to the fact that process parameters, such as pressures, temperatures, etc. vary rather slowly. A suitable model might be:

$$Model\ 3 \qquad x_{ij} = \mu + W_i + \sigma_W \varepsilon_{ij} \qquad (3.5)$$

where

$$W_i = \rho W_{i-1} + \sigma_B \omega_i \qquad (3.6)$$

and

$$W_0 = 0.$$

The parameter ρ $(-1 \leq \rho \leq 1)$ determines the correlation between groups.

The asymptotic variance of (3.6) is easily determined,

$$V(W) = \rho^2 V(W) + \sigma_B^2$$

$$V(W) = \sigma_B^2/(1 - \rho^2). \tag{3.7}$$

Therefore we find that

$$V(x_{ij}) = \frac{\sigma_B^2}{(1 - \rho^2)} + \sigma_W^2 \tag{3.8}$$

$$V(\bar{x}_{i.}) = \frac{\sigma_B^2}{(1 - \rho^2)} + \frac{\sigma_W^2}{n} \tag{3.9}$$

3.3.4 Simple Markov chain model

A simple model for data of type 5 in section 3.2 can be built up as follows. We think of the system as being in one of k states, where each state represents a given value for the mean of the process. At each sample point there may be interchange between the states, but one of these is an 'absorbing' state, representing an out of control process, which remains out of control until repaired. There is no interchange from an absorbing state.

The transition probabilities between one state and the next can be represented by a matrix called the transition matrix in which the rows represent the current state and the columns the next state:

		Next state		
	1	2	...	k
1	p_{11}	p_{12}	...	p_{1k}
2	p_{21}	p_{22}	...	p_{2k}
$\vdots$				
k	p_{k1}	p_{k2}	...	p_{kk}

Present state (rows 1, 2, ..., k)

Since there must be a transition somewhere, we have

$$\sum_{j=1}^{k} p_{ij} = 1.$$

for each i. If k is the absorbing state, $p_{kk} = 1$, and all other p_{kj} are zero.

Typically in SPC, we may expect there to be high probabilities of staying in the current state, whatever that is, so that all p_{ii} are close to one, and we may often find the remainder of the transition probability for each row i is taken up by transfers to nearby states, rather than further away ones.

A fairly realistic process model can be developed using a model of this type. Let the initial state be represented by a vector V_0, then the probability distribution of the next state is obtained by multiplying the initial state vector by the matrix of transition probabilities, so that

$$V_1 = PV_0.$$

Similarly we have

$$V_2 = PV_1, \text{ etc.}$$

It can be shown that whatever the starting state (except the absorbing state), the probability distribution of states eventually settles down to V, where V is the solution of the equation

$$V = PV.$$

From this result it is possible to calculate the variances of individual results and group means, but the calculation is not as simple as in previous cases.

3.3.5 Discussion

It is often difficult to fit a specific model to a process, particularly with more complex processes, and there are several reasons for this:

(1) There is rarely enough data collected under standard conditions.
(2) Frequently there are many variables or parameters of the process whose effects are incompletely understood. In a complex process it can be a major task to attempt to sort these effects out.
(3) Some of the most important process parameters may be impossible, expensive or time-consuming to measure.
(4) A complex process may not be stable enough to fit a simple model.

However, it is very important to have a general knowledge of the types of variation present. The only way of doing this is to collect data on important process variables and carry out analyses such as those given later in this chapter.

It would also be of interest to have theoretical results on the properties of methods under the types of variation given above which are alternatives to the simple random variation model.

3.4 SAMPLING ERROR AND MEASUREMENT ERROR

It is important to note that both sampling error and measurement error can exist, in addition to the types of variation described earlier in this chapter.

Sampling error occurs whenever a particular sample drawn does not give the same result as a sample drawn slightly differently. For example, if the product is a powder packed in bags, samples drawn from different parts of the bag may give consistently different results. If the product is produced on a conveyor belt, samples drawn from the middle or sides of the belt may give consistently different results. We shall not discuss this topic further in this volume.

Measurement error is often ignored or unrecognized. Sometimes process control systems, introduced to control variation automatically, can actually *cause* variation because they base their results on observations which have considerable measurement error in them.

The effect of measurement error can be seen as follows. Suppose we observe a variable which is normally distributed with mean μ and variance σ_0^2, but that it is observed with measurement error with variance σ_e^2. Then the actual observation will have a variance $(\sigma_0^2 + \sigma_e^2)$ (Fig. 3.7). Thus the inflation of the standard deviation σ_0 by error with standard deviation σ_e is $\sqrt{(1 + \sigma_e^2/\sigma_0^2)}$; see Table 3.1 for some values. We see that measurement error is not very serious unless $\sigma_e > \sigma_0/2$. We shall ignore measurement error in most of what follows.

A strong warning must be given at this point. Measurement error is often totally ignored, and there have been many cases in practice where

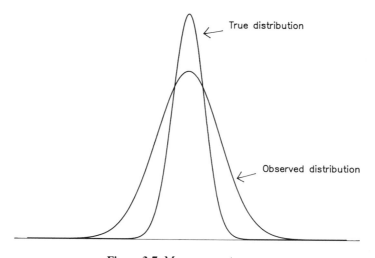

Figure 3.7 Measurement error.

Table 3.1 Inflation of standard deviation due to measurement error

σ_e/σ_0	0	0.5	0.75	1.00	2.50
Factor	1	1.12	1.25	1.41	1.58

the variation displayed by charts is mostly measurement error. The only way of being sure is to carry out an experiment. (Similar remarks can be made about sampling error.)

3.5 STUDYING PROCESS VARIATION

3.5.1 Methods of data analysis

At the end of section 3.3 we said that the only way of seeing what kind of variation is present in a process is to collect data and study it. In this section we give some good graphical techniques which can pick up the kind of variations described earlier in the chapter. Frequently it is very simple techniques which are most useful, particularly when results need to be presented to people with little statistical knowledge. We shall assume here that histograms, scatter plots, normal probability plots etc, are used as appropriate. Some other methods will be given in Chapter 4.

Once the data has been plotted, it is important to study process logs etc. in order to try to interpret the variation observed. This data analysis phase usually proves to be very productive, and frequently substantial sources of variation are detected and eliminated.

3.5.2 The use of moving-averages to smooth data

This is a method of smoothing a data plot so that cycles, trends, etc. can be seen more clearly. We describe here the *arithmetic* moving-average, or running mean. It is not necessarily the best for all purposes.

Suppose we have many successive samples, and a value (possibly a sample mean or range) for each. The method of constructing a running mean of 5 at a time is given in Method Summary 3.1.

METHOD SUMMARY 3.1

Calculating running means

Step 1 Take first 5 values.
Step 2 Find the average.
Step 3 Plot this value at the mid-time point (i.e. at the 3rd time plot).
Step 4 Drop the 1st value, include the 6th.
Step 5 Find the average.
Step 6 Plot at mid-time point (4th).
Step 7 Drop the 2nd value, include the 7th, etc.

If one smoothing operation does not appear to remove enough haphazard variation, then repeat it two or three times. Try to take care not to smooth too much, as this loses essential detail.

Example 3.1

In the manufacture of phenol, carbonyl species occur and should be kept to a minimum, certainly less than 200 ppm. The data given in Table 3.2 are from successive batches of phenol, and Figs. 3.8–10 show plots of the original data unsmoothed and after two stages of smoothing by the process outlined in Method Summary 3.1.

Table 3.2 Phenol data (ppm of carbonyl species)

139	115	120	120	126	84	76	100	100	98
80	76	96	112	69	54	61	66	35	30
35	40	35	59	66	55	30	32	29	66
46	60	55	48	48	67	125	99	79	90
90	97	101	105	95	95	145	145	150	160
175	170	170	162	162	111	101	106	99	105
107	93	103	125	119	145	147	166	155	160
115	169	163	64	118	116	99	100	107	97
99	100	99	87	70	61	60	69		

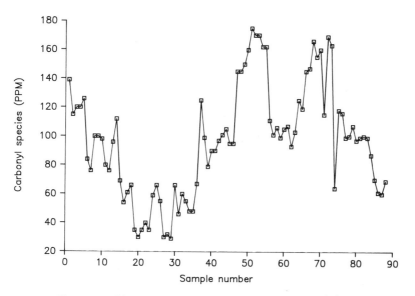

Figure 3.8 Phenol example. Plot of original carbonyl data.

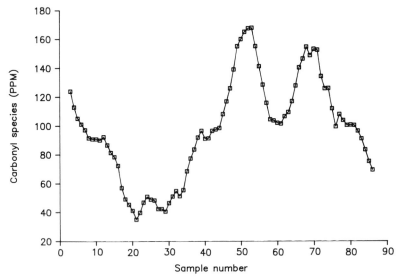

Figure 3.9 Phenol example. Plot of carbonyl data, smoothed once by 5-step moving average.

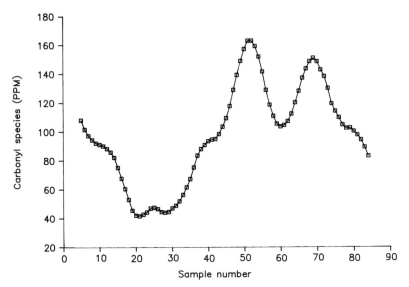

Figure 3.10 Phenol example. Plot of carbonyl data, smoothed twice by 5-step moving average.

One alternative is to smooth using running medians rather than running means. The medians are easier to calculate, and less sensitive to 'rogue' observations.

The number of sampling points over which we smooth, which was 5 in Method Summary 3.1, needs to be chosen with some care. Too large a value of this constant will result in a plot which doesn't follow trends quickly enough, whereas too small a value will result in too much scatter.

If there are n observations per sampling point, and a moving average of k means is plotted, then under normality the standard error of the moving average points is $\sigma_w/\sqrt{(kn)}$. We would want this standard error to be about half the size of any interesting difference we wished to detect. In practice, therefore, we would fix on the smallest 'interesting difference' that we want to detect, D, and put

$$D = 2\sigma_w/\sqrt{(kn)}$$

$$kn = 4\sigma_w^2/D^2$$

Frequently n is fixed from practical considerations, so this helps us to determine k. However, k must not be too large or there would be considerable delays in reaching conclusions about the data.

The moving-average plot is a good way of detecting cycles, trends or autocorrelated variation. However, some care needs to be taken over putting too much credence on the results; see Exercise 3A.5. Smoothing can easily induce patterns into otherwise random data.

3.5.3 CuSum plotting

Cumulative sum plotting is a very useful technique to highlight changes in the process average level. The idea is simply to subtract the overall mean from the data, and then cumulate the differences. As an illustration, we use the data in Table 3.3, and to make the arithmetic easier, a

Table 3.3 Weights (in grams) of capsules taken every 30 seconds from a manufacturing process that is working steadily

5.22	5.02	5.23	4.93	4.75
4.95	4.97	5.30	5.12	4.83
5.20	4.85	5.05	5.27	4.65
5.41	5.20	4.34	5.03	4.86
5.20	4.73	5.28	5.21	4.82
5.02	5.08	5.09	5.61	5.14
5.11	4.61	5.11	4.38	4.94
5.26	4.78	5.27	5.06	5.23
5.27	5.45	5.54	4.46	4.97
4.73	4.75	4.95	5.04	5.14

'reference value' of 5 has been subtracted from each observation, instead of the overall sample mean, and the first few CuSum calculations are shown in Table 3.4.

The CuSum plot is shown in Fig. 3.11; if 0.24 is added to each observation after number 25, the dotted line curve shows the resulting plot. Clearly, a change in the mean will be represented by a change in *slope* of the CuSum plot. A horizontal trace implies the overall mean (or reference value) holds. Any deviation from the reference value will be show up by a change of slope from the horizontal.

Table 3.4 Calculation of the CuSum for the first 6 values from Table 3.3 $T = 5.0$

Observation	Observation – reference value	Cumulative sum of column 2
5.22	+0.22	+0.22
4.95	−0.05	+0.17
5.20	+0.20	+0.37
5.41	+0.41	+0.78
5.20	+0.20	+0.98
5.02	+0.02	+1.00

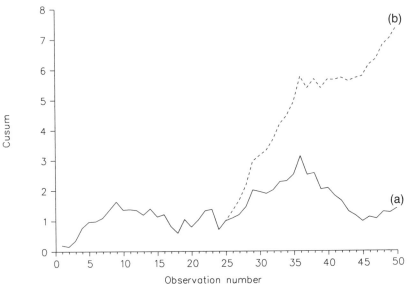

Figure 3.11 CuSum chart of Table 3.3 data; (a) original data, (b) with 0.24 added to each of the last 25 observations.

By using the CuSum plot, it is often possible to detect clearly *when* changes in the process average level occurred. This is of particular value, because an indication of when changes occurred assists considerably in diagnosing the causes of the changes.

In order to estimate the value of a changed mean, we pick two sample points, s and t, as in Fig. 3.12. We then read off the cumulative sums,

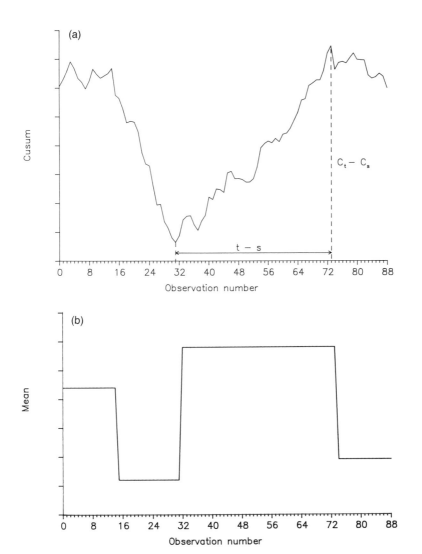

Figure 3.12 Estimating changed means from CuSum plots: (a) CuSum plot; (b) rough plot of mean values from (a). This is called a 'Manhattan diagram'.

C_t and C_s. The new value of the mean is then

$$(\text{reference value}) + (C_t - C_s)/(t - s).$$

A useful idea is to plot the values of the changed mean as a 'Manhattan diagram' – see the examples to follow. This is all summarized in Method Summary 3.2.

METHOD SUMMARY 3.2

Basic rule for CuSum plotting

Step 1   Calculate (observation − reference values).
Step 2   Plot cumulative values of these differences.
Step 3   Determine the points at which the slope changes visually.
Step 4   Plot a Manhattan diagram of the process mean values.

CuSum charts are of particular value in detecting sudden changes due to changes of operating conditions or due to new batches of raw material, etc.

(a) *Other uses of CuSums*

CuSum charts can also be used to detect changes in process spread (see below). The method is to use grouped data, and work on, say ranges of the groups. The average range is subtracted as the reference value.

For further information on CuSum plotting see Woodward and Goldsmith (1964).

3.5.4 Examining process spread

Moving averages and CuSum plots can also be used to examine process spread.

If the original data is taken in groups, then the ranges or standard deviations of these can be plotted. Moving averages or CuSum plots could then be made to see if the amount of process spread changed over time.

For 'one-at-a-time' data, we have to plot the differences of successive observations, and moving-average plots could be made of these values. If CuSum plots were to be used for plotting changes in process spread of one-at-a-time data, then the differences of successive (independent) pairs would have to be plotted in the first instance.

Changes in process spread tend to be less frequent than changes in process average level, so that rather less effort is usually put into these kinds of plot.

Yet another way of examining process spread is to chart the differences of actual observations from a 'smoothed' average level. Tukey calls the resulting plots the plots of the 'smooth' and of the 'rough'. A detailed discussion of this and other useful plotting techniques is given in Tukey (1977).

3.5.5 Conclusion

In data from complex processes, cycles, trends and autocorrelation are frequently present. In addition, sudden changes of level will be found which can be traced to new batches of raw material, changes of operating conditions, or other special or assignable causes. The first step in implementing SPC is to detect these types of variation, and eliminate them if possible. Simple methods, such as those given in this chapter, are frequently adequate. The amount of work involved in data collection and presentation may be considerable though, and the assistance from a suitable statistical or SPC computer package will often be required.

3.6 ESTIMATING THE PROCESS AVERAGE LEVEL AND VARIATION – GROUPED DATA

3.6.1 Introduction

We shall assume here that there is both within- and between-group variation, defined by σ_w and σ_B of Model 2 in section 3.3.2, and an important step is to estimate these and the process average level μ. This approach can be used even if autocorrelation is present, such as Model 3 of section 3.3.3. Once the process average level and variation are estimated we can proceed to the analysis of process capability (see Chapter 4) and the construction of charts. We shall suppose that groups of varying numbers n_i of observations are taken at frequent intervals, and we use the notation

$$\begin{array}{lll} \text{Group 1} & x_{11}, x_{12}, \ldots, x_{1n_1} & n_1 \text{ observations} \\ \quad\quad 2 & x_{21}, x_{22}, \ldots, x_{2n_2} & n_2 \text{ observations} \\ \multicolumn{3}{l}{\text{etc. for } k \text{ groups.}} \end{array}$$

It is most convenient if group sizes are equal, that is $n_1 = n_2$, etc., but in practice this is not always achievable.

A vital assumption here is that the groups of observations are all from a common source. Sometimes we have a nested sampling scheme as shown in Fig. 3.13. Here there are three groups sampled from three machines. This structure leads to a more complicated situation, and we

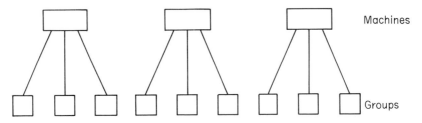

Figure 3.13 A nested sampling scheme.

shall not discuss it directly. Some of the methods below apply with modification.

3.6.2 Estimating the within-group variation

From each group we obtain the within-group standard deviation

$$s_i = \sqrt{\left\{ \sum_{j=1}^{n_i} (x_{ij} - \bar{x}_i)^2 / (n_i - 1) \right\}}$$

where

$$\bar{x}_{i\cdot} = \sum_{j=1}^{n_i} x_{ij}$$

is the sample mean of the ith group. A combined estimate of σ_w is now

$$s_w = \sqrt{\left\{ \sum_{i=1}^{k} (n_i - 1) s_i^2 \Big/ \sum (n_i - 1) \right\}} \tag{3.10}$$

which is simply the square root of the average s_i^2 if all the group sizes are equal. An alternative method when the group sizes are equal would be to use the range estimate, as set out in section 2.7.3. In making this estimate, any groups which have been identified as being subject to a 'special' cause of variation should be excluded, and they should also be excluded from the tests following in this section. These points are given in Method Summaries 3.3 and 3.4.

METHOD SUMMARY 3.3

Estimation of μ and σ_w by the 'σ' method: grouped or blocked data

Step 1   Collect at least 20 groups of n observations each; let these observations be denoted x_{ij}, $j = 1, 2, \ldots, n$; $i = 1, 2, \ldots, k$.

Step 2   Calculate the group means and variances

$$\bar{x}_{i.} = \sum_{j=1}^{n} x_{ij}/n$$

$$s_i^2 = \sum_{j=1}^{n} (x_{ij} - \bar{x}_{i.})^2/(n - 1).$$

Step 3 Calculate the overall average $\bar{\bar{x}}_{..} = \sum_{i=1}^{k} \bar{x}_{i.}/k$.

Step 4 Calculate the overall estimate s_w of σ_w,

$$s_w = \sqrt{\left[\sum_{i=1}^{k} s_i^2/k\right]}$$

Notes

(1) If the group sizes are unequal we use the following formula in Step 4.

$$s_w = \sqrt{\left[\sum_{i=1}^{k}(n_i - 1)s_i^2 \bigg/ \sum(n_i - 1)\right]}$$

where

$$s_i^2 = \sum_{j=1}^{n_i} (x_{ij} - \bar{x}_i)^2/(n_i - 1).$$

and n_i are the group sizes.

(2) Groups for which s_i is unusually large should be excluded *provided* a special cause can be found which accounts for the extra variation.

METHOD SUMMARY 3.4

Estimation of μ and σ_w by the range method: grouped or blocked data

Step 1 Collect at least 20 groups of n observations each; let these observations be denoted x_{ij}, $j = 1, 2, \ldots, n$; $i = 1, 2, \ldots, k$.

Step 2 Calculate the group means and ranges

$$\bar{x}_{i.} = \sum_{j=1}^{n} x_{ij}/n$$

$$R_i = (\text{Max}_j x_{ij}) - (\text{Min}_j x_{ij}).$$

Step 3 Calculate the overall average $\bar{\bar{x}}_{..} = \sum_{i=1}^{k} \bar{x}_{i.}/k$.

Step 4 Calculate the average range

$$\bar{R} = \sum_{i=1}^{k} R_i/k.$$

Step 5 Obtain an estimate of σ from the formula

$$\hat{\sigma}_w = \bar{R}/d_n$$

where values of d_n are the factors for converting ranges to estimates of standard deviation. These factors are given in Table 2.9 of the Appendix Tables.

Notes

(1) All groups must be of the same size.
(2) Normality is assumed.
(3) Note (2) of Method Summary 3.3 applies.

3.6.3 Estimating the between-group variation

The obvious estimate is to use the ordinary standard deviation formula on the k group means,

$$s_B = \sqrt{\left\{\sum_{i=1}^{k}(\bar{x}_{i.} - \bar{\bar{x}}_{..})^2/(k-1)\right\}} \qquad (3.11)$$

where

$$\bar{\bar{x}}_{..} = \sum\sum x_{ij}/kn$$

is the overall average. The quantity s_B will contain contributions from both between- and within-sample variation. For Model 2 of section 3.3.2 we have

$$E(s_B) \leq \sqrt{(\sigma_B^2 + \sigma_w^2/n)}$$

but this is nearly an equality.

However, the between-group variation may be affected by some special cause, which leads to the whole of one group being an outlier. Provided a special cause can be found, the group should be excluded from the calculations.

In order to estimate the component of variation due to the between-group component alone, we have to subtract the within-group component. We therefore use the formula

$$\hat{\sigma}_B = \sqrt{\{s_B^2 - s_w^2/n\}} \qquad (3.12)$$

If this quantity in the brackets is negative, we take $\hat{\sigma}_B$ to be zero. However, we obviously need a formal test of whether or not there is between-group variation, and this is given in the next section.

It is important to distinguish between the degrees of freedom in the estimates s_w and s_B. The degrees of freedom for s_w given in (3.10) is $\Sigma(n_i - 1)$ whereas the degrees of freedom for s_B is only $(k - 1)$. Thus s_w is based on a lot more information, and this factor has to be taken into account when testing for additional variation; see the next section.

3.6.4 Overall test for additional variation (all n_i equal)

If a process is in control and all of the data are sampled from a single normal distribution, then if the within-group standard deviation is σ_w, we should find that s_w estimates σ_w, but that s_B estimates $\sigma_w/\sqrt{n}$, the standard deviation of a mean. The procedure is therefore to compute the ratio

$$(ns_B^2/s_w^2) \tag{3.13}$$

and if this is greater than one, there is some evidence of the presence of additional variability, although such extra variability could be due to control actions on the process. The values in Table 3.5 give the critical values of the ratio (3.13) for the 5% probability level.

If the ratio (ns_B^2/s_w^2) is greater than the appropriate value in Table 3.5, given the group size and number of groups taken, then the extra variability is significant at the 5% probability level. Critical values for a larger range of group sizes (n) and numbers of groups (k) can be found by looking up the 5% critical value in F-tables for $(k - 1)$ and $k(n - 1)$ degrees of freedom; see the Appendix tables.

Table 3.5 Critical values of ns_B^2/s_w^2 (F-test)

Sample size (n)	No. of samples (k)											
	5	10	15	20	25	30	40	60	80	100	200	500
2	5.19	3.03	2.43	2.14	1.97	1.85	1.70	1.54	1.45	1.39	1.26	1.16
3	3.48	2.40	2.04	1.85	1.74	1.66	1.55	1.43	1.37	1.32	1.22	1.13
4	3.06	2.23	1.96	1.76	1.66	1.59	1.50	1.40	1.34	1.30	1.20	1.13
5	2.87	2.13	1.86	1.72	1.63	1.56	1.47	1.38	1.32	1.28	1.20	1.12
6	2.76	2.09	1.82	1.69	1.60	1.54	1.46	1.37	1.31	1.28	1.19	1.12
7	2.69	2.05	1.80	1.67	1.59	1.52	1.45	1.36	1.31	1.27	1.19	1.12
8	2.65	2.01	1.78	1.66	1.58	1.52	1.44	1.35	1.30	1.27	1.18	1.11
9	2.61	1.99	1.77	1.65	1.57	1.51	1.44	1.35	1.30	1.26	1.18	1.11
10	2.59	1.98	1.76	1.64	1.56	1.51	1.43	1.35	1.30	1.26	1.18	1.11

METHOD SUMMARY 3.5

Estimation of the between-group variation σ_B

Step 1 Carry out Method Summary 3.3 or 3.4 to obtain $\bar{x}_{..}$, and $\hat{\sigma}_w$.

Step 2 Calculate

$$s_B^2 = \sum_{i=1}^{k} (\bar{x}_{i.} - \bar{\bar{x}}_{..})^2 / (k - 1).$$

Step 3 Calculate the ratio $ns_B^2/\hat{\sigma}_w^2$, and see if there is significant evidence of between-group variability.

Step 4 If Step 3 gives a significant result, use as the estimate $\hat{\sigma}_B$

$$\hat{\sigma}_B = \sqrt{[s_B^2 - \hat{\sigma}_w^2/n]}.$$

Note
(1) Note (2) of Method Summary 3.3 applies.
(2) If the ratio $ns_B^2/\hat{\sigma}_w^2$ is greater than one but not significant, some account of this may have to be taken when constructing charts.

3.6.5 A worked example

Example 3.2
15 groups were taken, each of size 2, with the results given in Table 3.6. For this data the overall mean is $\bar{\bar{x}}_{..} = 26.784$ and the standard deviation

Table 3.6 Illustration of test for extra variation

Group	Data		Mean	s.d.
1	39.5	30.0	34.75	6.718
2	27.0	25.5	26.25	1.061
3	28.5	14.5	21.5	9.899
4	30.5	24.0	27.25	4.596
5	19.5	17.0	18.25	1.768
6	32.5	25.0	28.75	5.303
7	23.5	32.5	28.0	6.364
8	34.0	29.0	31.5	3.536
9	27.0	31.0	29.0	2.828
10	14.5	25.5	20.0	7.778
11	24.0	26.0	25.0	1.414
12	29.0	31.5	30.25	1.786
13	19.5	29.5	24.5	7.071
14	23.5	25.0	24.25	1.061
15	38.0	27.0	32.5	7.778

of these means is $s_B = 4.650$. The average standard deviation within groups is

$$s_w = \sqrt{[\tfrac{1}{15} (6.718^2 + 1.061^2 + \ldots + 7.778^2)]} = 5.384.$$

Thus $2s_B^2/s_w^2$ is 1.492. It is greater than 1, suggesting that there is some additional variation.

The critical value for the table $n = 2$, $k = 15$ is 2.43. Thus the additional variation is not significant in this case and could have been produced by chance. It may be that there really is some additional variation but we do not have sufficient data to be sure of this. Ideally more data would be collected to try and confirm whether there is some additional variability.

Discussion
Some processes can be modelled by the simple random variation model of Model 1 of section 3.3 when they are in control. In such a case a significant between-groups component of variation probably represents special causes of variation such as machine wear, etc. Other industrial processes, particularly in the process industries, are much more complicated and the other models of section 3.3 may apply.

In setting up control charts we need to be able to distinguish between ordinary variation of the process, about which we can do little, and 'special' causes of variation which are due to specific problems, and can be eliminated. We shall take up this discussion again in later chapters, but the test for additional variation given above is the start of the analysis. It is often useful to identify one of the models in section 3.3 which might reasonably apply in normal running.

3.6.6 Test for the presence of autocorrelation

A simple way to test for autocorrelation is to calculate the sequence of means of groups, $\bar{x}_1$, $\bar{x}_2$, . . ., and plot successive values on a scatter plot, $\bar{x}_1$ versus $\bar{x}_2$, $\bar{x}_2$ versus $\bar{x}_3$, etc. Correlation will be readily seen in the plot.

A more precise way is to calculate the autocorrelations,

$$r_s = \left\{\sum_{t=1}^{k-s} (\bar{x}_{t.} - \bar{\bar{x}}_{..})(\bar{x}_{t+s} - \bar{\bar{x}}_{..})\right\} \bigg/ \left\{\sum_{t=1}^{k} (\bar{x}_{t.} - \bar{\bar{x}}_{..})^2\right\}$$

for $s = 1$, 2, 3, . . ., where s is the lag at which the correlation is calculated. Any value outside the range $\pm 2/\sqrt{k}$ can be regarded as significant. Generally we expect higher correlations for small values of the lag.

For more details on testing for autocorrelation see Chatfield (1984) or Wetherill *et al* (1986).

3.6.7 Estimation of standard error of group means

One quantity needed to set up control or CuSum charts is the standard error of the group mean, σ_e. As we saw in section 3.3, the formula for σ_e depends on what type of model is appropriate for our problem. Most SPC methodology assumes that only simple random variation is present. While this may be valid for the component manufacturing field, it is certainly not true for the process industries. However, the first step is to estimate the within-group standard deviation, σ_w, and check for between-group variation as given in Method Summary 3.5.

If only simple random variation is present, then the standard error of a group mean is $\sigma_e = \sigma_w/\sqrt{n}$.

However, if extra variation is present, then σ_e needs to be estimated by directly calculating the standard deviation of the group means (omitting groups accounted for by special causes), which we denote s_B:

$$\hat{\sigma}_e = s_B = \sqrt{\left\{\sum(\bar{x}_{i.} - \bar{\bar{x}}_{..})^2/(k - 1)\right\}}.$$

Some care needs to be taken about this step. Clearly, if 'extra' variation is allowed for at the stage of setting up the charts, then our action lines are going to be spread out further. If this extra variation is inevitable, that is satisfactory, but otherwise our charting would be less powerful.

METHOD SUMMARY 3.6

Estimating the standard error of group means

Step 1 Estimate the within-group standard deviation σ_w by Method Summary 3.3 or 3.4.

Step 2 Use Method Summary 3.5 to test for significant between-group variation.

Step 3 If Method Summary 3.5 gives a significant result, examine the data to see if there are outlying group means for which a special cause of variation can be found. If such a cause can be found, delete these groups and recalculate.

Step 4 If there is no between-group variation the standard error of group means σ_e is estimated as

$$\hat{\sigma}_e = s_w/\sqrt{n}.$$

If there is significant between-group variation we use

$$\hat{\sigma}_e = s_B.$$

For the example worked out in section 3.6.5 the test for between-group variation is not significant, so a valid estimate of σ_e is

$$\hat{\sigma}_e = s_w/\sqrt{2} = 3.807$$

based on 15 groups $\times 1 = 15$ degrees of freedom. The estimate $s_B = 4.650$ is based on 14 degrees of freedom.

In most cases the difference between the degrees of freedom of the estimates is much greater. For example, with 15 groups and 3 observations per group s_w has 30 against 14 for s_B.

3.7 ESTIMATING THE PROCESS AVERAGE LEVEL AND VARIATION – ONE-AT-A-TIME DATA

A deeper discussion of one-at-a-time data will be given in Chapter 6, but here we give two common methods for estimating the process average level and variation. One-at-a-time data arises frequently in the process industries, where the measurement process is expensive. It also arises sometimes because there is essentially only one observation that can be made. If we are measuring the purity of a chemical produced in a batch process, both measurement errors and sampling variation due to taking different samples of the product from a batch may be negligible. The methods given in section 3.6 for estimating σ_w are not appropriate, and the following methods can be used instead.

3.7.1 Rational blocking

In some applications one-at-a-time data can be blocked by batch, shift, or some other criterion. The objective of this blocking should be such that substantial changes in process average level tend to occur between the blocks rather than within them. Under these circumstances, the within-block variation will adequately represent the process variability σ_w, and the methods of section 3.6 can be used for estimation. Defective blocking can mask changes, since a block average may then contain observations from different population means, and the estimation of σ_w is inflated. However, when it can be used, rational blocking is a convenient way of dealing with one-at-a-time data.

3.7.2 Difference of pairs method

One method of estimating σ_w which can be used is to treat the difference of successive pairs of observations as ranges of two. Following the method given in section 2.7.3 this leads to the formula

$$s_A = \left\{ \sum |d_i|/(k - 1) \right\}/1.128$$

where

$$d_i = x_i - x_{i+1}$$

and k is the number of observations. Clearly, if some observations are outlying and are found to be due to some special cause, the differences involving these can be excluded. There is further discussion of this method in Chapter 6.

METHOD SUMMARY 3.7

Estimation of μ and σ_w for one-at-a-time data

Step 1 Collect at least 50 observations; let these be denoted x_i, $i = 1, 2, \ldots, k$.

Step 2 Use the overall average to estimate μ, and put

$$\hat{\sigma}_w = \left\{ \sum_{i=1}^{k-1} |d_i|/(k - 1) \right\}/1.128$$

Notes

(1) Normality is assumed.

(2) Any points for which a special cause can be found should be excluded.

(3) Do not use the method if there is any obvious trend in the data as the estimate $\hat{\sigma}_w$ will underestimate the true variability.

Example 3.3

In the manufacture of an engineering plastic a single laminate was sampled, and put into a machine to test for strength. The results of 25 successive observations are as follows:

140.18 140.00 139.98 136.86 139.38 140.74 139.38
141.12 139.46 140.86 140.10 139.54 140.26 139.08
138.34 140.72 138.80 138.42 138.84 141.90 139.64
140.24 141.28 140.70 140.94

Following Method Summary 3.7 we have

Observation	140.18	140.00	139.98	136.86	139.38	140.74	..
Difference		-0.18	-0.02	-3.12	2.52	1.36	...

We find

$$\sum |d_i| = 30.2 \text{ and}$$

$$\hat{\sigma}_w = (30.2/24) \div 1.128 = 1.1154.$$

Charting methods

Provided a rational blocking can be used, charts for one-at-a-time data can be constructed as for grouped data, and this is discussed in Chapter 5. Other methods of charting for one-at-a-time data are given in Chapter 6.

EXERCISES 3A

1. Carry out graphical analyses and tests for extra variation on the data you collected in Exercise 2A.2.

2. The Melt Flow Index of polypropathene is measured on a single sample taken from predefined bags, so that readings are taken once per tonne, regardless of the method of shipment to the customer. The MFI specification for this grade is $4.5 \leq MFI \leq 6.5$. Table 3.7 shows MFI readings taken from several production campaigns to make the same grade of polypropathene. Carry out two 3-step moving averages of the data.

Table 3.7 Polypropathene melt flow index

Bag no.	MFI	Bag no.	MFI	Bag no.	MFI	Bag no.	MFI
1	5.75	21	4.69	41	5.73	61	5.21
2	5.30	22	4.35	42	5.68	62	5.36
3	5.21	23	5.30	43	5.52	63	4.86
4	4.91	24	5.11	44	5.57	64	5.83
5	5.45	25	5.01	45	5.49	65	5.57
6	4.98	26	5.00	46	5.21	66	5.75
7	5.36	27	5.33	47	5.77	67	6.19
8	5.43	28	4.93	48	5.69	68	5.86
9	5.18	29	4.42	49	5.44	69	5.67
10	5.47	30	4.78	50	5.67	70	5.44
11	4.96	31	4.88	51	5.49	71	5.18
12	5.01	32	4.63	52	5.75	72	5.15
13	4.73	33	5.12	53	6.06	73	5.37
14	4.67	34	4.92	54	5.68	74	5.40
15	4.34	35	5.05	55	5.57	75	5.30
16	5.95	36	5.27	56	5.80	76	4.86
17	5.54	37	5.27	57	5.50	77	4.83
18	5.48	38	5.19	58	5.38	78	4.65
19	4.85	39	5.72	59	5.26	79	4.72
20	4.78	40	5.55	60	5.31	80	4.74

3. The data given in Table 3.8 are from a single-stage continuous chemical process in which raw materials A and B are reacted together to form a product C. The reaction is exothermic and water cooling is used to control the reaction temperature to 160 °C. The raw materials A and B are both delivered by tanker from which they are run into small stock tanks. There are two stock tanks for each raw material and they are filled and emptied alternately. A full stock

Table 3.8 Data for CuSum exercise

Sample	Efficiency	Comment	Sample	Efficiency	Comment
1	45.2		34	45.8	
2	46.2		35	42.8	
3	45.5		36	45.5	
4	43.7		37	42.8	
5	47.0		38	44.5	
6	44.6		39	42.9	
7	44.2		40	45.3	
8	46.0		41	45.2	
9	44.5		42	45.4	New batch of A
10	45.1		43	45.8	
11	46.9		44	45.5	
12	44.1		45	45.5	
13	42.6		46	44.9	
14	43.9		47	44.0	
15	45.1		48	45.0	
16	45.2		49	46.4	
17	44.4		50	46.1	
18	47.6		51	42.3	
19	44.6		52	44.4	
20	46.3		53	47.0	Plant shut down
21	44.9		54	40.9	
22	43.4	New batch of B	55	42.2	
23	44.7		56	45.0	
24	44.6		57	45.3	
25	46.3		58	44.9	
26	42.2		59	47.5	
27	44.7		60	44.9	
28	45.2		61	45.4	
29	44.8		62	46.1	
30	44.0		63	46.6	
31	44.2		64	45.4	
32	45.5		65	45.3	
33	45.2		66	44.9	New batch of B

Table 3.8 (*cont.*)

Sample	Efficiency	Comment	Sample	Efficiency	Comment
67	46.4		110	46.3	
68	44.8		111	44.5	
69	45.2		112	42.5	
70	46.8		113	45.8	
71	45.5		114	43.6	
72	46.6		115	43.8	
73	47.5		116	44.5	
74	45.0		117	42.2	
75	46.8		118	46.3	New batch of A
76	44.8		119	46.1	
77	45.2		120	45.1	
78	45.7		121	46.3	
79	45.4	New batch of A	122	47.1	
80	45.0		123	45.3	
81	44.4		124	44.7	
82	44.4		125	46.5	
83	44.8		126	45.4	
84	45.4		127	47.4	
85	43.8		128	45.0	Blockage in
86	45.6		129	44.3	cooling water
87	44.6				line.
88	45.1		130	44.1	High
89	43.1				temperatures.
90	44.7		131	46.3	
91	47.4		132	45.2	
92	43.6		133	46.4	
93	44.7		134	45.5	
94	46.0		135	46.8	
95	43.9		136	44.8	
96	44.8		137	45.5	
97	46.6		138	46.0	New batch of B
98	44.6		139	45.9	
99	45.8		140	45.8	
100	44.8	New batch of B	141	46.5	
101	44.5		142	45.1	
102	43.2		143	45.6	
103	46.2		144	46.9	
104	44.7		145	45.7	
105	44.6		146	45.0	
106	43.7		147	45.3	
107	44.9		148	46.2	
108	45.9		149	47.4	
109	44.5		150	45.2	

tank contains about two weeks' supply of raw material, and each stock tank full is termed a batch. The plant occasionally has to be shut down for cleaning. The product from the plant is sampled and analysed every shift, and the last 150 observations are tabled together with an indication of when new batches of raw material were started and when other plant upsets occurred.

Plot the data on a CuSum chart (using a reference value of 45). Remembering that it is changes of inclination which indicate changes in the mean, try to interpret your graph. Also plot a Manhattan diagram.

4. Carry out a one-at-a-time estimation of σ_w on the data given in Exercise 3A.2.

5. Generate (or select from tables) 50 random normal deviates. Smooth twice using a 5-step moving average, and plot the result. Also plot the original data.

EXERCISES 3B

This exercise deals with the models of section 3.3.

1. (a) Generate 20 sets of 5 observations from one of the following:
       (i) Model 1 $\mu = 5$, $\sigma_w = 1$
       (ii) Model 2 $\mu = 5$, $\sigma_w = 1$, $\sigma_B = 0.5$
       (iii) Model 3 $\mu = 5$, $\sigma_w = 1$, $\sigma_B = 0.4$, $\rho = 0.3$
       (iv) Model 4 $\mu = 5$, $\sigma_w = 1$, $\sigma_B = 0.4$, $\rho = 0.7$
   (b) Calculate $\bar{x}$, s^2 for each group. Plot the group means and compare the results.
   (c) Obtain a combined estimate of within-group variance, s_w^2.
   (d) Obtain the variance of the 20 group means, treating these as single observations. Denote this s_B^2.
   (e) Carry out an F-test, ns_B^2/s_w^2.
   (f) Calculate s_A. Carry out a test for autocorrelation.

2. Show that two successive smoothings by 3-step moving averages is equivalent to one operation with a *weighted moving average*, with weights

$$\frac{1}{9}, \quad \frac{2}{9}, \quad \frac{3}{9}, \quad \frac{2}{9}, \quad \frac{1}{9}.$$

Similarly, explore the effect of the following smoothing operations:
(a) Two 5-step smoothings.
(b) A 3-step followed by a 5-step smoothing.

(c) A 5-step followed by a 3-step smoothing.

3. If all original observations are distributed independently $N(\mu, \sigma^2)$, find the correlation between:
   (a) Two successive points from one 3-step smoothing.
   (b) Two successive points from two 3-step smoothings.

4

Process capability

4.1 INITIAL PROCESS CAPABILITY STUDIES

In a process capability study we examine the variability in important product characteristics, and study the extent to which the process is capable of producing product which conforms to specification. The study involves considering questions such as:

(1) What are the contributions to the variability of the product?
(2) Where and why does defective quality arise in the process?
(3) Where and how can this be detected?
(4) What is the process capability index (see sections 4.3 and 4.4)?
(5) What control actions can be taken on a process?
(6) What is the effect of these actions?
(7) What type of control is appropriate, and where?

A fundamental problem to tackle is the decision as to what variables to measure, and how many charts to set up. Ideally we want to take measurements which will help us to pinpoint causes of process variation. For example, if we only take measurements at the end of the process then we may have charts with so many possible causes of variation that they are difficult to interpret and use. Also the detection of a problem at an intermediate stage of a process will not only occur earlier than detection at an end point, but can also save added-on costs to product that is not of acceptable standard. For example, in making integrated electronic networks the resistances of a sample of items are measured after printing, firing and trimming (Stage 1) and before adding connectors, inductances and condensers (Stage 2). The cost of the items is much less at Stage 1 than at Stage 2. One objective of our initial studies therefore should be to enable us to decide what to measure and plot.

There will usually be three stages in an initial process capability study:

(1) A study of the whole process as a system, and a listing of its variables.
(2) Data collection at specified points in the process.
(3) An analysis of the data.

In the first stage we would want at least an outline flow chart of the system. The variables (or parameters) of the system need to be classified as:

Input variables: These relate to the amounts, qualities and properties of input material

Process variables: These are pressures, cycle times, temperatures, etc. of the process.

Product variables: These are purity, strength, dimensional or other measurements on the product.

Other vital questions to assess at this stage, relate to the amount of control which is possible on the variables listed. It is worth noting that in some systems there are really important parameters which are very difficult to measure, and ways of doing this may have to be drawn up. In continuous processes there may be automatic controllers built in, and the presence of these must be noted. It will rarely be possible to monitor more than a small number of these variables, so a 'brainstorming' exercise needs to be carried out, and decisions made on what to observe.

The data-collecting phase may need special effort. Several variables may need to be monitored, possibly at various points in the process. If sampling can be done in groups, then groups of at least four at a time should be taken. The time frequency of the observations needs to be sufficient to study the rate and manner in which process variation occurs.

Finally, the data should be analysed using methods such as those given in the previous chapter, and the process capability established.

The procedure we have just described is sometimes rather easy to do, and this is especially true in the component manufacturing area. For the process industries, such as chemical, it can be very difficult. A typical situation in the process industries is that we may have 5–10 product variables, but 200–400 process or input variables, and often there is little hard information about the relationships between the input and process variables, such as temperatures, purity of the catalyst, and the product variables, such as hardness, tensile strength. We shall come back to this later.

After the initial process capability study we set up Shewhart or CuSum charts, and operate these for some time. As the charts are used some *special causes* of variation in the process, sometimes called *assignable causes* of variation, will be identified and either eliminated or controlled. The very operation of the charts often changes the properties of the process, so that after a while it is necessary to carry out a fresh study of process capability, and reset the charts; see Fig. 4.1.

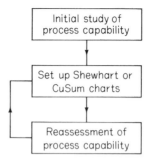

Figure 4.1 Procedure for setting up SPC.

METHOD SUMMARY 4.1

Summary of steps in a process capability analysis

The steps involved in a process capability study are as follows:

Step 1 Draw a flow chart of the process as a system.
Step 2 Determine the input, process and product variables. Be aware of important variables or parameters not measured.
Step 3 Carry out a 'brainstorming' exercise, and summarize the results in 'cause-and-effect' diagrams.
Step 4 Data acquisition.
Step 5 Graphical analyses using moving-average charts, CuSum charts, histograms, etc.
Step 6 Carry out a process capability analysis of important product variables. This should include a histogram of results over a period of time, and estimates of the process capability indices.

4.1.1 Essential conclusions from data analysis

As a result of the data analysis stage of the process capability analysis the following results or decisions are needed:

(1) What variables to chart.
(2) Some idea as to the manner in which the process goes out of control, such as by drifts or by sudden jumps, or cycles.
(3) An estimate of the standard error σ_e and of the overall mean μ.
(4) Some idea as to how quickly the process goes out of control. This will be one of the factors determining sampling frequency.

(5) Estimates of the process capability indices; see sections 4.3 and 4.4.

The essential parts of a process capability analysis are graphical and other analyses of many of the variables. The definitions of the process capability indices are complicated by the presence of the types of variation listed in section 3.2. We therefore introduce the process capability indices in the simplest situation – simple random variation only – and then indicate generalizations and complications later in the chapter.

4.2 SHEWHART CONTROL LIMITS AND SPECIFICATION LIMITS OR TOLERANCES

Let us return once more to the titanium hardness measurement data, described in section 2.8, and we shall assume that only simple random variation is present. We established in section 2.8 that the process was producing buttons with hardness measurements resulting in a normal population with mean 127.0 and standard deviation 3.07. Also, in section 2.8 we constructed a Shewhart control chart for sample means of four buttons, which controlled the sample means within

$$127.0 \pm 3 \times \frac{3.07}{\sqrt{4}}$$

i.e. 122.4 and 131.6.

If the *process* mean remains absolutely in control, virtually all *sample* means will lie within these limits, and virtually all *individual* values will lie within about 3 standard deviations of the process mean, i.e. within

$$127.0 \pm 3 \times 3.07$$

$$\rightarrow 117.8, 136.2.$$

The distribution of sample means and of individual values is shown in Fig. 4.2.

Now quite distinct from the distribution of means or of individual values, there may be specification or tolerance limits on the individual values which are fixed by physical requirements on the product. Suppose, for example, that the specification limits were set at the extreme range of the individual values set above, viz. (117.8, 136.2), then there would be about 3 items per thousand outside specification. For most (but not all) production processes this would be an acceptable quality level, and we might congratulate ourselves on having a capable and well-controlled process. Notice that the Shewhart control limits are always inside the tolerance limits, except when the sample size is 1.

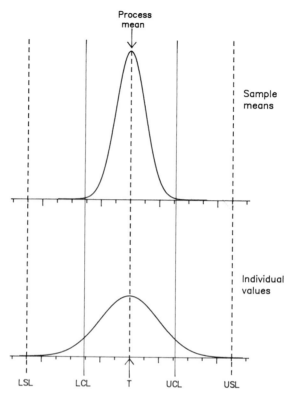

Figure 4.2 Relation between control limits and specification limits: process mean in control.

But there is no guarantee that the process mean will remain absolutely constant. Supposing it moves out to 129, say, as in Fig. 4.3. The *sample* means will now generally be higher than the target value of 127, but at each sample point there is in fact only a 4% chance of having a mean that goes outside the control limit. It could take very many samples (on average 25) before action is signalled. Meanwhile the change in process mean is also causing 1% of *individual* values to fall outside the tolerance levels. For some types of products this would be an intolerably high failure rate, especially if it goes undetected for such a long time.

Consider also the following example.

Example 4.1

Suppose we have a process with a mean of 140 and a standard deviation

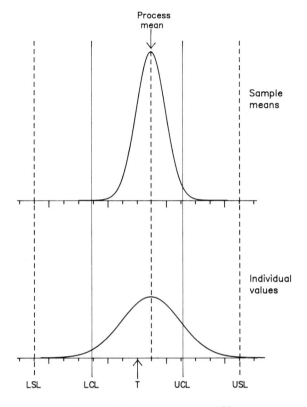

Process
mean

Sample
means

Individual
values

LSL   LCL   T   UCL   USL

Figure 4.3 Process mean at 129.

of 5.0. Specification limits are set at 130 and 150. Groups of four observations are sampled, so that the standard error of the mean is $5/\sqrt{4} = 2.5$. The upper action limits for a Shewhart $\bar{X}$-chart are set at

$$140 + 3 \times 2.5 = 147.5$$

which is well within the tolerances. However, when the mean is at 140, the number of standard deviations away of the upper specification limit is

$$(150 - 140)/5 = 2.0$$

in terms of the distribution of individual values. From Normal tables we see that 2.3% of the product is beyond this. An equal amount will lie below the low specification limit. Change in the process mean will result in less product being out of specification at one boundary, but this will be outweighed by a greater proportion being out of specification at the other.

Clearly the relationship between process variability and specification limits determines the extent of non-conformance. This is called relative capability; see the next section.

4.3 RELATIVE CAPABILITY

For the following discussion, we shall continue to assume that we are in the case of the simplest situation of section 3.2 – when our process results display random variation from a single normal population, with at most occasional 'rogue' points due to special causes. Extensions of the argument to other patterns of variation mentioned in section 3.2 will be discussed later.

Consider a process for which the specification limits are set at 110 and 146, a specification width of 36. Suppose also that the process spread $\sigma_w = 6$. Nearly all of a Normal distribution is contained within $\pm 3\sigma_w$ of the mean, so that if the process mean could be held stationary at exactly 128, the individual values would vary between

$$128 \pm 3 \times 6 = 110, 146.$$

That is, the specification limits are precisely $6\sigma_w$ wide. As discussed in the previous section, if we operated a simple Shewhart control chart centred on 128 we would be sure to get some defective product, because it is impossible to hold the process mean exactly stationary.

If in fact we had $\sigma_w = 3$ instead of $\sigma_w = 6$, then the specification limits would be $12\sigma_w$ wide. This would give us freedom to allow the process mean to vary, and yet still keep almost all of the product between the specification limits.

For a third case, suppose $\sigma_w = 9$, then the specification limits are only $4\sigma_w$ wide, and whatever we do, we shall get a considerable amount of defective product. These three cases are depicted in Fig. 4.4. We say that these three cases show medium, high and low capability respectively.

It is clear from this discussion that a rather critical quantity is the width of the specification limits with respect to σ_w. We define *capability indices* for a simple random process as follows:

Process capability index

$$C_p = (\text{allowable range})/6\sigma_w$$

The denominator of C_p is the range covering 99.7% of the distribution, and this can be used as a more general definition of C_p.

A C_p value of less than one is unsatisfactory – we have low capability. A C_p value of between 1.0 and 1.60 shows medium relative capability, and a C_p value of more than 1.60 shows high relative capability.

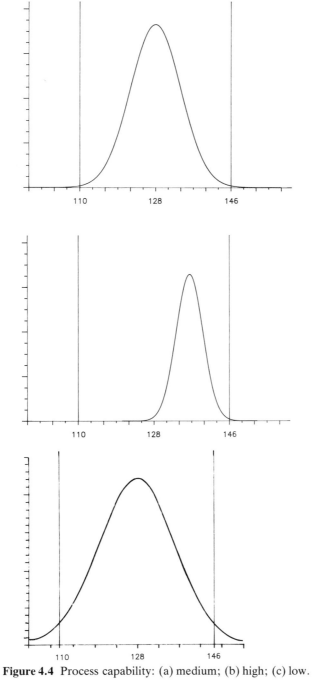

Figure 4.4 Process capability: (a) medium; (b) high; (c) low.

Example 4.2

For our titanium button example we found an estimate of μ to be 127.0, and of σ_w to be 3.07.

If specification limits are at 110 and 146 we have

$$\text{allowable range} = 146 - 110 = 36$$

$$C_p = 36/(6 \times 3.07) = 1.95$$

We should emphasize that we have been talking about standard deviations, not means. Thus, for example, even in case (b) of Fig. 4.4, we may still get bad product if the mean is not set appropriately (see Fig. 4.5). Partly for this reason, we also define a process performance index.

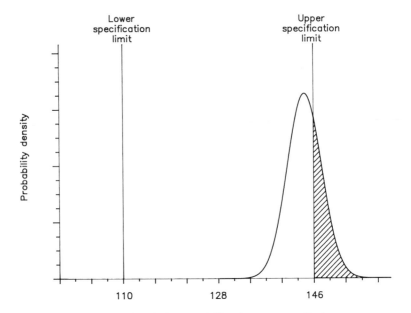

Figure 4.5 High relative capability, but uncontrolled mean.

Process performance index

$$C_{pk} = \text{Minimum of}$$

(upper specified limit − process mean)/$3\sigma_w$

and

(process mean − lower specified limit)/$3\sigma_w$

Example 4.3
For our titanium button example we have

$$\text{(upper limit} - \text{process mean)}/3\sigma = (146 - 127)/3 \times 3.07$$
$$= 2.06$$
$$\text{(process mean} - \text{lower limit)}/3\sigma = (127 - 110)/3 \times 3.07$$
$$= 1.85$$

$$C_{pk} = 1.85$$

One-sided specification limit
A very common case in industry is to have a one-sided specification limit, as when an impurity must not exceed more than a given number of parts per million. The process capability index has no meaning in such a case, and it is quite incorrect to use zero or some other artificial limit in order to achieve a 'standard' looking result. However, the process performance index is readily defined as

$$C_{pk} = \text{(specification limit} - \text{process mean)}/3\sigma_w$$

for an upper specification limit. The denominator is interpreted as half the range covering 99.7% of the distribution.

The process performance index is also more useful in more complex situations, as when the process variation exhibits cycles, regular trends, etc. See section 4.4.2.

Although these indices can be very useful in process capability studies, one should guard against putting too much reliance on them. They depend on having good estimates of the process standard deviation, and for C_{pk}, the process mean as well. Unless our process has been brought into control, our estimates of these values may have sizeable errors, or may not be stable. In addition, the process variation may not be a simple Normal distribution, and the indices will need modification; see section 4.4.1.

Further, we are depending rather heavily on the property of the Normal distribution that nearly all of it lies within $\pm 3\sigma$. Some slight deviation from Normality could wreck that. Notwithstanding these points, the coefficients C_p and C_{pk} can be useful in assessing a process, and are widely used by companies discussing quality.

Capability indices have been defined assuming Normality, but they can be generalized to situations where the data are distributed non-Normally. If we realize that 6σ represents the *actual process range* when the data are Normal, then the actual process range can be calculated for any data, however distributed. We simply cut off 1.5 in 1000 of the distribution at each end; see Fig. 4.6.

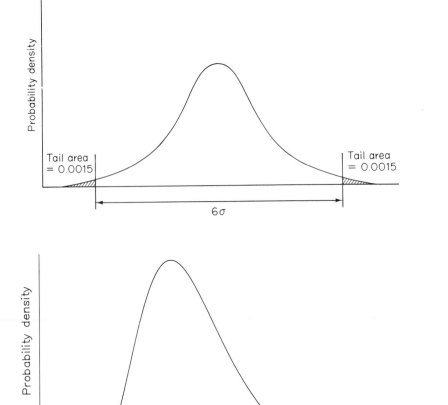

Figure 4.6 Capability indices for non-Normal data.

4.4 PROCESS CAPABILITY INDICES FOR MORE COMPLEX PROCESS MODELS

4.4.1 Between- and within-group variation

We return to the model and notation defined in section 3.6, and in addition allow measurement error of variance σ_m^2. Measurement error can only be ascertained by duplicated (blind) analyses, and we shall assume this to have been done, yielding an estimate $\hat{\sigma}_m^2$.

For Model 2 of section 3.3, with between- and within-group variances σ_B^2 and σ_w^2, we find

$$V(\bar{x}_{i.}) = \sigma_B^2 + \frac{\sigma_w^2}{n} + \frac{\sigma_m^2}{n} \tag{4.1}$$

whereas the variance of individual observations is

$$V(x_{ij}) = \sigma_B^2 + \sigma_w^2 + \sigma_m^2 \tag{4.2}$$

Now if there is measurement error σ_m^2, the estimates given in section 3.6 must be modified:

$$\hat{\sigma}_w^2 = \max \{0, s_w^2 - \hat{\sigma}_m^2\} \tag{4.3}$$

$$\hat{\sigma}_B^2 = \max \{0, s_B^2 - \frac{1}{n}(\hat{\sigma}_w^2 + \hat{\sigma}_m^2)\} \tag{4.4}$$

The capability index is redefined:

$$C_p = (\text{allowable range})/6\sqrt{(\sigma_B^2 + \sigma_w^2)} \tag{4.5}$$

and the performance index is

$$C_{pk} = \min \begin{cases} (\text{upper specification limit} - \mu)/3\sqrt{(\sigma_B^2 + \sigma_w^2)} \\ (\mu - \text{lower specification limit})/3\sqrt{(\sigma_B^2 + \sigma_w^2)} \end{cases} \tag{4.6}$$

where we use the estimates $\hat{\mu}$, $\hat{\sigma}_w^2$, $\hat{\sigma}_B^2$.

We see that in these estimates (4.3)–(4.6) the measurement error has been subtracted. This is a safe procedure only if the process average level is adequately controlled.

When we come to putting in the action lines for the control chart, we need the standard error of the mean, (4.1), which has measurement error included. This can lead on occasions to action lines for a control chart which appear to be beyond specification limits. This is a safe procedure only if we are sure of our model and estimates; alternative methods are given in Chapter 9.

The methods of this section can be used if an autocorrelated error model holds.

4.4.2 Cyclic variation

It will be sufficient to discuss the estimation of process capability indices for cyclic data; similar principles apply to other models.

Suppose we have regular or irregular cycles in the data as shown in Fig. 4.7. It is clear that because of the cycles, the overall distribution of

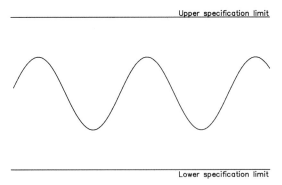

Figure 4.7 Cyclic data.

group means is not Normal, and it is *not* appropriate to use the procedures of section 3.6 to estimate σ_B^2 and σ_w^2. The overall distribution of the means will be more nearly rectangular, and the standard capability index has no meaning.

However, a performance index can be calculated, by taking the extreme positions of the cycles as estimates of μ. Since at this point we are only interested in keeping the local variation clear of the limits, only σ_w^2 is appropriate, and we revert to the performance index given in section 4.3, possibly corrected for measurement error.

It is a little unfortunate that capability indices have such a strong foothold in industry since they are fraught with difficulties as shown previously. In particular when companies report and compare capability indices, one can not be certain that C_p and C_{pk} have been calculated on the same basis. A better indicator of performance would be to record a histogram of six months' production and a calculation of the amount of non-conforming product.

4.5 HOW TO HANDLE LOW CAPABILITY PROCESSES

There are several possible ways of dealing with having a low-C_p process:

(1) Examine if there is any measurement error in the testing apparatus, so that our estimated σ_w is 'inflated'.
(2) Examine if the specification limits can be widened.
(3) Use the process as it stands, but screen out defective product using outgoing sampling inspection. This is not usually very effective.
(4) Set up a team to try to find ways of improving the process, so that σ_w is reduced.

(5) Use a control chart in the hope of improving process capability. Process variation often decreases when control charts are used.

Example 4.4

Suppose we have a process such that the lower and upper specification limits are 100 and 150, and that the process mean and standard deviation are 140 and 5.0 respectively. We have

$$C_p = (150 - 100)/5 \times 6 = 1.67$$

indicating a medium capability process. However, the process performance index is the smaller of

$$(140 - 100)/3 \times 5 = 2.67 \quad \text{and} \quad (150 - 140)/3 \times 5 = 0.67$$

so that $C_{pk} = 0.67$. This value indicates that, because of the value of the process mean a considerable amount of scrap is being produced. We can improve C_{pk} considerably by adjusting the process mean.

EXERCISES 4A

1. Carry out a process capability study on the sets of data you collected in Exercise 2A.2.

2. The observations given in Table 4.1 are measurements of tensile strength on three pieces of plastic taken once per shift. The lower and upper specification limits are 5 and 10 respectively. Carry out a process capability study.

EXERCISES 4B

1. Assuming that the original data are all independently $N(\mu,\sigma^2)$, show how to calculate 95% confidence intervals for $\hat{\sigma}_w$, and for C_p. How much data is required to estimate 95% confidence intervals for C_p to within 0.1?

Table 4.1 Tensile strength measurements for 30 shifts

Shift				Mean	s.d.
1	9.0	8.3	8.9	8.73	0.38
2	6.5	6.4	7.1	6.67	0.38
3	7.2	7.1	6.9	7.07	0.15
4	8.6	8.4	7.6	8.20	0.53
5	7.2	8.1	7.7	7.67	0.45
6	6.9	6.7	6.9	6.83	0.12
7	6.8	8.4	7.0	7.40	0.87
8	7.3	7.0	7.2	7.17	0.15
9	7.8	7.2	7.5	7.50	0.30
10	6.3	6.2	7.1	6.53	0.49
11	6.3	6.4	5.9	6.20	0.26
12	5.5	6.7	7.8	6.67	1.15
13	7.4	7.0	6.8	7.07	0.31
14	5.9	7.0	7.3	6.73	0.74
15	6.4	6.3	7.6	6.77	0.72
16	6.4	6.7	7.0	6.70	0.30
17	7.3	7.9	8.0	7.73	0.38
18	6.3	7.2	7.2	6.90	0.52
19	7.5	9.0	7.5	8.00	0.87
20	8.3	8.2	7.5	8.00	0.44
21	7.2	5.8	6.8	6.60	0.72
22	7.4	7.4	6.5	7.10	0.52
23	8.9	8.3	7.7	8.30	0.60
24	6.2	7.5	7.1	6.93	0.67
25	7.5	8.3	7.9	7.90	0.40
26	7.7	7.8	7.8	7.77	0.06
27	7.5	6.5	7.1	7.03	0.50
28	6.6	8.5	7.4	7.50	0.95
29	6.4	5.6	6.5	6.17	0.49
30	8.0	7.6	7.2	7.60	0.40

5

Basic Shewhart control charts for continuous variables

5.1 INTRODUCTION

The idea of the control chart is to operate a simple mechanism for controlling the average level and spread of a process. A minimum of two charts is required, one to control process average level and one to control process spread, but sometimes several charts are necessary. In the sections below we discuss the control of process average level and process spread separately. In addition, we limit ourselves in this chapter to data which has been selected in groups, or to one-at-a-time data which has been blocked in a suitable way; see section 3.7. More details about one-at-a-time data are given in Chapter 6. We shall also assume here that our data is subject to underlying random variation which is normally distributed; see below.

5.1.1 In control – out of control

In any production process, some variation in quality is unavoidable, and the theory behind the control chart originated by Dr W. A. Shewhart is that this variation can be divided into two categories, *random variation*, and variation due to *special* or *assignable causes*. Variations in quality which are due to causes over which we have some degree of control, such as a different quality of raw material, or new and unskilled workers are called *special causes of variation*. The random variation is the variation in quality which is the result of many complex causes, the result of each cause being slight. By and large nothing can be done about this source of variation except to modify the process.

If data from a process are such that they might have come from a single distribution (frequently Normal), having certain desired properties such as a mean in a specified range, the process is said to be *in control*. If, on the other hand, variation due to one or more special causes is present, the process is said to be *out of control*. The Shewhart control chart is a simple device which enables us to define this state of statistical control more precisely, and which also enables us to judge when it has been attained.

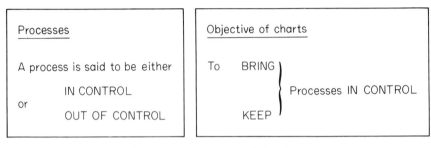

Figure 5.1 Objective of charting.

The definition of 'in control' is rather too naive, particularly for the process industries, when the models of sections 3.3.2 and 3.3.3 may be appropriate, and there may be cycles in the data. In this case the definition of 'in control' needs to be extended to cover these models, unless of course, we wish to detect and eliminate these extra sources of variation. The key point is that we are trying to find out if the process is statistically stable, or if extra sources of variation are present. Even statistically stable processes may come under investigation if they have low capability.

It is assumed, of course, that when there is evidence that special causes of variation are present, some action is initiated so that these causes can be traced and eliminated; this is usually the main aim of operating a quality control chart. Gradually, extra sources of variation are eliminated. There is now a long history of widespread industrial applications in which the control chart works, is seen to operate in this way and is of very great value.

5.1.2 Sampling risks

When operating SPC we take small samples from the process at regular intervals and plot, say, the mean and the range on a chart. As a result, we conclude that the process is either *in control* or *out of control*. If the process is out of control, this may be due to a change in process average level, or process spread, or due to a particular problem at a specified time point.

Because of the variation inherent in sampling, the average levels and the spreads as indicated by the samples will vary from sample to sample even if the true process average and spread are constant. This gives rise to two dangers when sample observations are plotted on a control chart.

When charts indicate OUT OF CONTROL we take ACTION.
Otherwise we LEAVE THEM ALONE.

Type I risk
Taking action when no change has occured.

Type II risk
Not taking action when a real change has occured.

Figure 5.2 Risks involved in charting.

These are as follows:

Type I risk: The risk that a legitimately extreme sample will give a spurious 'action' decision when no change has occurred in the process.

Type II risk: The risk that a sample will fall within the control limits although there has been a real change in the process; the change is not signalled. (The size of this risk will get smaller as the size of the change increases.)

The design of a control chart is a compromise between these two opposing risks. Different practices have grown up about the design of the charts, and the risks involved. It is usual to have

action lines at   3.09 standard errors (probability)
                3.00 standard errors (popular)

from the mean. One point beyond the action line is regarded as a signal for action. The British Standard recommendation is 3.09 standard errors, corresponding to the Normal distribution 0.001 point, and American (and some British) practices have chosen 3.00. The two practices are deeply entrenched, and there is not much between them.

Another common practice is to have

warning lines at   1.96 standard errors (probability)
                2.00 standard errors (popular)

from the mean. Two successive points beyond the warning lines is regarded as a signal for action.

The reason for the two different practices on the limits is as follows. In other charts it is standard to put the action limits at the 0.1% points, and the warning limits at the 2.5% points, and this happens in range charts, etc. It would seem inconsistent not to do this for the $\bar{X}$-chart, and this argument leads to using 1.96 and 3.09 as multipliers. However, in practice σ is nearly always unknown, and has to be estimated, and the normality assumption may not hold. In the face of these uncertainties, it seems rather pedantic to use 1.96 and 3.09, so that they are rounded off to 2 and 3. It should be noted that the use of 'popular' rather than 'probability' limits considerably reduces the average run length when the process is on target (see section 5.4). In the methods given below both 'probability' and 'popular' factors will be given.

In addition to using action and warning lines, other rules are sometimes employed, and reference will be made to these below and in Chapter 8. Considerable care has to be taken about using some of these extra rules, as they can increase the type I risk to unacceptable levels.

5.1.3 Shewhart control charts – the set-up phase

The use of Shewhart control charts can be divided into two phases:

(1) the set-up phase, which we review here,
(2) and the operational phase, which we review in section 6.6.3.

In between these two sections, we give the technical details of the different charts, how to construct and use them, and how to choose between the different options available.

The set-up phase of a Shewhart control chart is shown in Fig. 5.3. We now make some detailed comments on each of the boxes in that figure.

Box 1 Data collection. Usually special data must be collected, and rather more than is needed for routine chart operation; see Chapter 4.
Box 2 Process capability studies. These are discussed in Chapter 4. It is very desirable to identify the types of process variation which are likely to occur; see section 3.3.
Box 3 Estimation. See sections 3.6 and 3.7.
Box 4 Low capability. See section 4.5.
Box 5 Medium capability. Here we operate control charts, and expect the process to improve to a high-capability process.
Box 6 High capability. Here the process mean need not be controlled so closely; see Chapter 9.

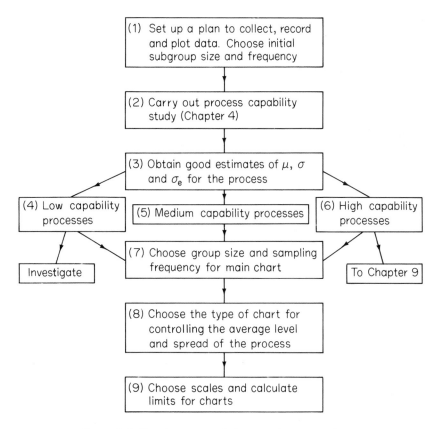

Figure 5.3 Shewhart control charts – the set-up phase.

Box 7 Group size and sampling frequency. These are discussed later. For the moment we assume either that observations are made singly, with an obvious way to group the data such as by shift, process run, etc., or that observations are taken in groups at a time. Sampling should be frequent enough to enable us to detect changes in the average process level or spread reasonably quickly.

Box 8 Choice of chart type. We describe and discuss the choice later.

Box 9 Choosing scales and calculating limits. For the Shewhart chart see sections 5.2 and 5.3.

5.1.4 An example

We shall use the following example throughout the chapter.

Example 5.1

In the manufacture of an engineering plastic, five laminates were sampled and put into a machine to test for strength. Laminates were taken once a shift from the production line, and the results in Tables 5.1 relate to 'transverse flexure strength'.

Table 5.1 Engineering plastic strength data

Shift	Observation					Mean	Median	Std dev	Range
1	140.1	139.4	143.5	141.4	136.5	140.18	140.1	2.582	7.0
2	140.0	137.4	140.8	140.5	141.3	140.00	140.5	1.528	3.9
3	138.9	139.6	141.0	141.7	138.7	139.98	139.6	1.318	3.0
4	137.1	136.0	136.0	133.7	141.5	136.86	136.0	2.875	7.8
5	143.1	141.2	138.5	137.0	137.1	139.38	138.5	2.683	6.1
6	140.5	138.7	140.2	142.0	142.3	140.74	140.5	1.461	3.6
7	139.8	141.4	137.9	137.8	140.0	139.38	139.8	1.527	3.6
8	139.5	140.5	141.0	142.1	142.5	141.12	141.0	1.213	3.0
9	137.8	142.5	138.5	140.3	138.2	139.46	138.5	1.950	4.7
10	144.1	142.3	138.0	140.8	139.1	140.86	140.8	2.442	6.1
11	140.3	139.7	143.5	138.0	139.0	140.10	139.7	2.085	5.5
12	141.2	139.4	139.2	138.9	139.0	139.54	139.2	0.948	2.3
13	140.4	138.4	139.2	140.1	143.2	140.26	140.1	1.822	4.8
14	139.2	139.4	137.9	141.4	137.5	139.08	139.2	1.532	3.9
15	137.7	135.8	138.5	141.6	138.1	138.34	138.1	2.096	5.8
16	137.7	141.9	140.9	141.7	141.4	140.72	141.4	1.730	4.2
17	137.6	138.9	139.1	141.8	136.6	138.80	138.9	1.961	5.2
18	137.8	136.6	139.6	139.0	139.1	138.42	139.0	1.213	3.0
19	140.5	138.2	139.8	136.1	139.6	138.84	139.6	1.744	4.4
20	141.0	143.3	141.7	143.0	140.5	141.90	141.7	1.223	2.8
21	137.6	137.3	141.2	138.8	143.3	139.64	138.8	2.558	6.0
22	138.5	141.4	142.5	138.7	140.1	140.24	140.1	1.723	4.0
23	143.1	138.6	142.1	140.5	142.1	141.28	142.1	1.764	4.5
24	140.0	138.5	142.5	142.2	140.3	140.70	140.3	1.657	4.0
25	140.9	143.1	138.3	142.8	139.6	140.94	140.9	2.055	4.8
Totals						3496.76	3494.4		114.0

Estimation of μ and σ from the data in Table 5.1

Case (i): 'σ' method

$$\bar{X} = 3496.76/25 = 139.87$$
$$\hat{\sigma}_w = \sqrt{\{(2.582^2 + 1.528^2 + \cdots + 2.055^2)/25\}}$$
$$= \sqrt{(89.6516/25)} = 1.8937$$

Case (ii): range method

$$\overline{\overline{X}} = 3496.76/25 = 139.87$$
$$\overline{R} = (7.0 + 3.9 + \cdots + 4.8)/25 = 114/25 = 4.56$$
$$n = 5, d_n = 2.326,$$

so that

$$\hat{\sigma}_w = 4.56/2.326 = 1.9605$$

A test for the presence of extra variation is not significant, and the standard error of the mean is

$$\sigma_e = \sigma_w/\sqrt{n}$$

which is estimated as

$$\hat{\sigma}_e = \hat{\sigma}_w/\sqrt{n} = 1.9605/\sqrt{5} = 0.8768$$

for the range estimate of σ_w.

Note: It will be found that when control charts are plotted, sample 4 is beyond the action limits. Any such points should be omitted and the calculations redone *provided* a special cause of variation is found (see section 5.2.2).

5.2 CONTROL CHARTS FOR AVERAGE LEVEL

In this section we set out how to construct and use an $\overline{X}$-chart for controlling the average level of a process. Alternative charts will be discussed in the next chapter.

5.2.1 $\overline{X}$-charts: chart construction

The construction of an $\overline{X}$-chart relies on having good estimates $\hat{\mu}$ of the process average level and $\hat{\sigma}_e$ of the standard error of the group means. These estimates are derived either from data from process capability studies, or from fresh data. If data from process capability studies is used we must make quite sure that conditions have not changed in the interval since the studies were carried out. Fresh data may be more representative of current process performance but at least 20 groups or blocks of data should be collected. Sometimes we may be given target values of μ and σ_e to use for chart construction. We shall assume that the sample size n and sampling interval have been chosen. Further advice on choosing these quantities is given later. The construction of an $\overline{X}$-chart follows the reasoning given in section 5.1.2, and is set out in Method Summary 5.1.

METHOD SUMMARY 5.1

Construction of $\bar{X}$-chart

Step 1 Obtain estimates of the process average level, $\hat{\mu}$, and the process variability, and also obtain the estimated standard error of group means, $\hat{\sigma}_e$.

Step 2 Choose the scale of the chart so that $\hat{\mu}$ is near the centre, and so that the scale covers approximately $\pm 4\hat{\sigma}_e$ from $\hat{\mu}$, where n is the sample size at each sampling point.

Step 3 Mark the action lines at $\hat{\mu} \pm 3.09\hat{\sigma}_e$ (probability); $\hat{\mu} \pm 3\hat{\sigma}_e$ (popular)

Step 4 Mark the warning lines at $\hat{\mu} \pm 1.96\hat{\sigma}_e$ (probability) $\hat{\mu} \pm 2\hat{\sigma}_e$ (popular)

5.2.2 Illustration of construction methods given in section 5.2.1

Here we construct a chart using the data of Example 5.1 as fresh data from our process. The procedure is the same whether the σ or 'range' methods are used to estimate σ. We shall use the range-method estimate:

Step 1 From section 5.1.4, $\bar{X} = 139.87$, and $\hat{\sigma}_e = 0.8768$.

Step 2 Centre the chart at, say 140. The scale should cover $140 \pm 4\hat{\sigma}_e$, or about 136 to 144.

Step 3 Action limits:
$139.87 \pm 3.09 \times 0.8768 = 137.16, 142.58$ (probability)
$139.87 \pm 3 \times 0.8768 \quad = 137.24, 142.50$ (popular)

Step 4 Warning limits:
$139.87 \pm 1.96 \times 0.8768 = 138.15, 141.59$ (probability)
$139.87 \pm 2 \times 0.8768 \quad = 138.12, 141.62$ (popular)

The chart is shown in Fig. 5.4, with the data plotted. Since the process is found to be out of control at group 4, a search for a special cause of variation should be undertaken. If a special cause is found, group 4 should be omitted and the calculations repeated. This is left as an exercise.

5.2.3 $\bar{X}$-charts: interpretation

It is important to use charts for control of average level and spread of a process together, and section 5.5 deals with this. In this section we consider some of the basic rules for interpreting the $\bar{X}$-chart.

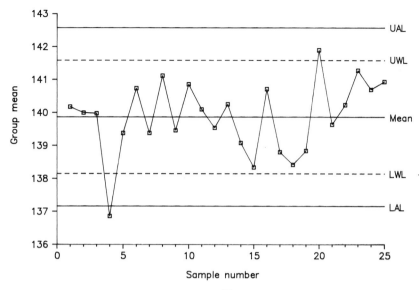

Figure 5.4 $\bar{X}$ chart

(a) *Assumptions of $\bar{X}$-chart*
The method assumes

(1) that the distribution of the data is Normal, or at least approximately so;
(2) that the group sizes are equal;
(3) that all groups will be weighted equally;
(4) that the observations are independent.

The action to be taken when these assumptions do not hold is set out in section 5.5. Normality is not usually very important.

(b) *Basic rules for $\bar{X}$-chart*
The $\bar{X}$-chart is regarded as showing evidence that a *special* or *assignable cause* of variation is present when either of the following hold:

(1) one point is outside the action limits;
(2) two successive points are outside the same warning limit.

Either of these show evidence of an assignable cause *provided* checking shows that it was not due to miscalculation. These are illustrated in the Fig. 5.5(a) and (b).

Some others also use the following rules but these drastically affect the properties of the chart:

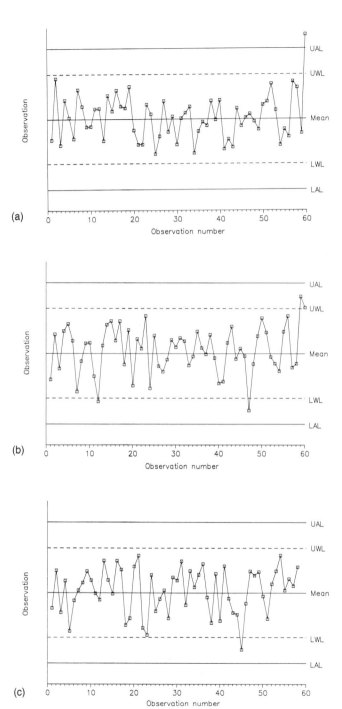

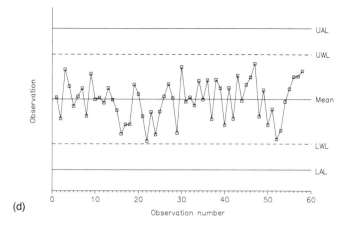

(d)

Figure 5.5 Assignable causes of variation: (a) action signal by rule (1); (b) action signal by rule (2); (c) action signal by rule (3); (d) action signal by rule (4).

(3) seven successive points on one side of the mean;
(4) seven successive points either increasing or decreasing.

A discussion of the value of these extra rules is given in Chapter 8. The chief problem is that these rules drastically increase the chance of false alarms – type 1 errors.

5.3 CHARTS FOR CONTROL OF (WITHIN-GROUP) PROCESS SPREAD

5.3.1 Range charts – construction

There are two ways of setting up the range chart – the 'range' method and the 'σ' method. If process capability data are used to get an estimate of σ_w, then this is fed into the appropriate step of the σ method. These methods are set out below.

METHOD SUMMARY 5.2

Construction of a range chart by the range method

Step 1 Obtain the average range $\bar{R}$ either from process capability studies data, or from at least 20 groups of fresh data.

Step 2 Choose the scale of the range chart so that the range goes down to zero, and up to about twice the largest range observed in the trial data sets.

Step 3 Mark the action and warning limits on the chart:

Lower action limit:	$D_1\bar{R}$
Upper action limit:	$D_2\bar{R}$
Lower warning limit:	$D_3\bar{R}$
Upper warning limit:	$D_4\bar{R}$

where the D_1, D_2, D_3 and D_4 values are given in Table 5.2 and in the Appendix tables.

Notes 1. Step 1 is as for the $\bar{X}$-chart – the same data are used.
2. The factors given in Table 5.2 are obtained from the distribution of the range in Normal samples, and from the conversion factors from range to estimates of σ.

Table 5.2 Factors for constructing range charts from an average range D_1, D_2, D_3, D_4

Group size	Action lines		Warning lines	
n	D_1	D_2	D_3	D_4
2	0.00	4.12	0.04	2.81
3	0.04	2.99	0.18	2.17
4	0.10	2.58	0.29	1.93
5	0.16	2.36	0.37	1.81
6	0.21	2.22	0.42	1.72
7	0.26	2.12	0.46	1.66
8	0.29	2.04	0.50	1.62
9	0.33	1.99	0.52	1.58
10	0.35	1.94	0.54	1.55

Note: The action and warning lines are obtained by multiplying these factors by the average range. The action lines use D_1 and D_2, and the warning lines use D_3 and D_4.

METHOD SUMMARY 5.3

Construction of a range chart by the 'σ' method

Step 1 Obtain an estimate of σ_w either from process capability studies data, or from at least 20 groups of fresh data (*Note*: Use σ_w, not σ_e)

Step 2 Use the factors from Table 5.3, and multiply by $\hat{\sigma}_w$ to find where to plot the action and warning limits. The scale should be chosen to extend to about 50% greater than the upper action limit.

Note Step 1 is as for the $\bar{X}$-chart – the same data are used.

Table 5.3 Factors for constructing range charts from an estimate of σ (D_5, D_6, D_7, D_8)

Group size n	Action lines D_5	D_6	Warning lines D_7	D_8
2	0.00	4.65	0.04	3.17
3	0.06	5.06	0.30	3.68
4	0.20	5.31	0.59	3.98
5	0.37	5.48	0.85	4.20
6	0.53	5.62	1.07	4.36
7	0.69	5.73	1.25	4.49
8	0.83	5.82	1.41	4.60
9	0.97	5.90	1.55	4.70
10	1.08	5.97	1.67	4.78

Note: The action and warning lines are obtained by multiplying these factors by an estimate of σ. The action lines are D_5 and D_6, and the warning lines use d_7 and D_8.

5.3.2 Illustration of construction methods for range chart

Here we use the range method as set out in Method Summary 5.2.

Step 1 $\bar{R} = 114.0/25 = 4.56$
Step 3 Factors from Table 5.2 are for $n = 5$, so we have

Lower action limit:	$0.16 \times 4.56 = 0.73$
Upper action limit:	$2.36 \times 4.56 = 10.76$
Lower warning limit:	$0.37 \times 4.56 = 1.69$
Upper warning limit:	$1.81 \times 4.56 = 8.25$

The chart for Example 5.1 data is shown in Fig. 5.6.

5.3.3 Range charts – interpretation

(a) *Assumptions of the range chart*
The method assumes

(1) that the distribution of the data is Normal;
(2) that the group sizes are equal;
(3) that all groups will be weighted equally;
(4) that the groups are independent of each other;
(5) that all between-group variation is due to special causes.

The last point is particularly important. Since the methods plot *within-group* ranges or standard deviations, between-group variability is

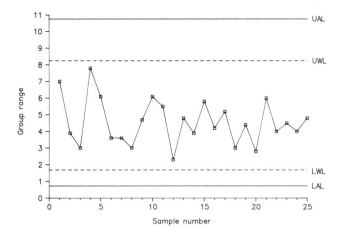

Figure 5.6 Construction of a range chart.

not detected. Methods for doing this will be discussed in the next chapter.

Normality can be quite critical for the range chart, and also lack of independence between groups. Sometimes lack of Normality can be corrected by use of a simple transformation.

(b) *Basic rules for the range chart*

These rules are the same as for the $\bar{X}$-chart, given in section 5.2.3; see Fig. 5.7. Larger ranges mean an increase in the process spread. A range below the lower action limit may indicate one of the following:

(1) The process spread has reduced and the charts may need rescaling.

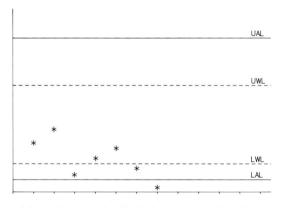

(a) Action at point 7 – below lower action limit

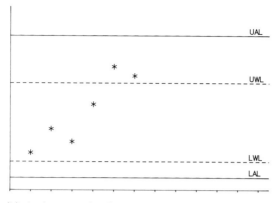

(b) Action at point 6 – above upper warning limit

Figure 5.7 Illustration of use of range chart.

(2) The measurement apparatus has jammed.
(3) There is a mistake in the calculations.

5.3.4 Standard deviation charts

These are very similar to the range charts, except that standard deviations are calculated and plotted for each group. That is, we follow

Table 5.4 Factors for constructing deviation charts from an estimate of standard deviation (D_9, D_{10}, D_{11}, D_{12})

Group size	Action lines		Warning lines	
	D_9	D_{10}	D_{11}	D_{12}
2	0.00	3.29	0.00	2.24
3	0.00	2.63	0.16	1.92
4	0.09	2.33	0.27	1.77
5	0.15	2.15	0.35	1.67
6	0.21	2.03	0.41	1.60
7	0.25	1.93	0.45	1.55
8	0.29	1.86	0.49	1.51
9	0.33	1.81	0.52	1.48
10	0.36	1.76	0.55	1.45
11	0.38	1.72	0.57	1.43
12	0.41	1.69	0.59	1.41

Note: The action and warning lines are obtained by multiplying these factors by an estimate of σ_w.

the 'σ' method of Section 5.3.1 above, but then use Table 5.4 to get the factors:

lower action limit:	$D_9\hat{\sigma}_w$
upper action limit:	$D_{10}\hat{\sigma}_w$
lower warning limit:	$D_{11}\hat{\sigma}_w$
upper warning limit:	$D_{12}\hat{\sigma}_w$

The interpretation and use of the standard deviation chart is the same as for the range chart. It is more efficient than the range chart, and particularly so if the group size is larger than about 8.

The factors in Table 5.4 are obtained from the distribution of standard deviations in Normal samples.

5.3.5 Control of between-group spread

If the test for extra variation set out in section 3.6.3 shows extra variation present, then this variation also needs controlling. Clearly, the methods given in section 5.3.1–4 *only control the within-group variation*.

Control of between-group variation can be affected by calculating a moving-range chart or a moving-standard-deviation chart, based on the group means. This is set out in the next chapter, along with other similar types of control chart. The commonly used method is to operate an $\bar{X}$ and R or s chart, as set out above, but for the process industries this needs to be supplemented by methods given in the next chapter.

5.4 THE AVERAGE RUN LENGTH

In order to design our charts in a more precise way, and in order to compare properties of alternative charts we need to introduce the concept of *run length*. The run length is the number of observations plotted on the charts until an 'out of control' signal is given. Run lengths are usually calculated assuming that observations are sampled independently from a specific population, and here we assume that there is simple random variation only.

Suppose we operate a Shewhart $\bar{X}$-chart where $\sigma = 1$ and we use a group size of 4, sampled, say every 10 minutes. Suppose also that the target mean is zero, and this is made the centre of the $\bar{X}$-chart, but that the process mean is 1. How many groups will be sampled before a signal is given that the mean is off target? Figure 5.8 shows the control charts for three computer simulations of the randomly generated groups that could result from this situation. The number of groups to an 'out of control' signal is called the *run length*.

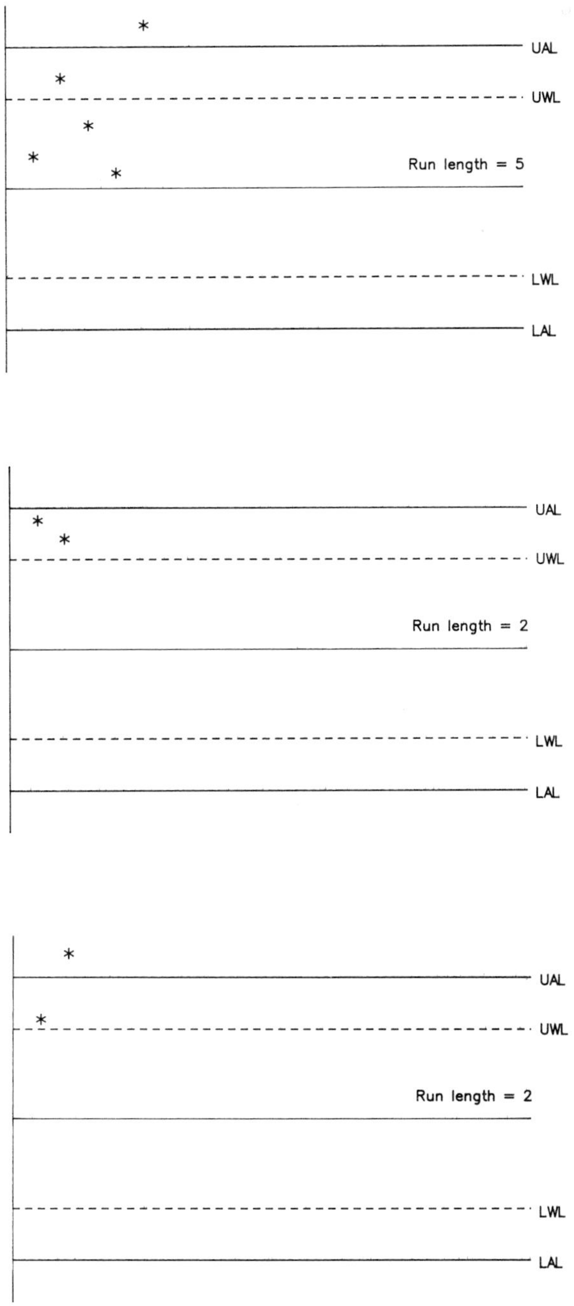

Figure 5.8 Simulation of an $\bar{X}$ chart.

The actual run length observed on any trial will obviously differ due to random variation. The average of the three trials we have seen is 3. For our example this means that an average 30 minutes' production would elapse before this change in process mean was discovered. The long run average – taken over a very large number of trials – can be calculated theoretically and this is called the *average run length* (ARL). Some of the theory is given in the next section and in Chapter 8.

It is helpful to carry out some simulation trials in order to see how the run length varies, and the exercises at the end of the chapter set this out.

The ARL curves will tell us how many groups, on average, will have to be sampled, before a given change in the process mean is detected. Figure 5.9 shows the ARL curve of the $\bar{X}$-chart, see also Table 5.5.

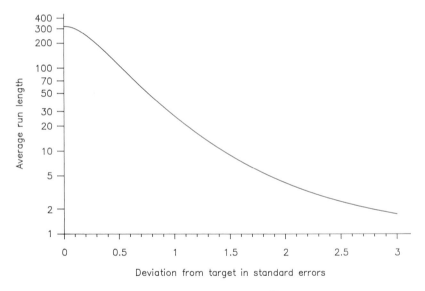

Figure 5.9 ARL curve of the $\bar{X}$ chart.

We see from Table 5.5 that if the true mean of the process differs from the target value by the amount $\sigma/\sqrt{n}$, so that $\theta/(\sigma/\sqrt{n})$ is 1.0, then on average 26.35 groups will be sampled until an 'out of control' signal is given. We see that $\theta/(\sigma/\sqrt{n})$ has to be about 2.5 before the ARL is reduced to 2.47. We can use ARL charts to study the properties of any scheme we propose, and to help guide us on a choice of sample size and sampling frequency.

Table 5.5 ARL for deviations of various sizes θ from the target value

Deviation in standard error units $\theta/(\sigma/\sqrt{n})$	ARL	
	Probability limits	Popular limits
0	320	278
0.5	108.03	100.60
1.0	26.35	25.61
1.5	8.92	8.78
2.0	4.14	4.07
2.5	2.47	2.41

Example 5.2
Suppose we know $\sigma = 1$, and that we wish to detect a change in the mean of 0.5 units within about 20–25 minutes. If we sample every 5 minutes, we want an ARL of about 4 or 5 at $\theta = 0.5$. From Table 5.5 we see that we must have $\theta/(\sigma/\sqrt{n})$ at about 2.0, so

$$0.5\sqrt{n} = 2$$
$$n = 16$$

This is a large group, and we may wish to investigate sampling more frequently than every 5 minutes, if this is practicable. Otherwise we may have to consider relaxing our requirements.

5.5 SPECIAL PROBLEMS

The charting methods given in this chapter are based on certain assumptions. The action to be taken when these are not valid is as explained in Sections 5.5.1–2.

5.5.1 Non-normality

Basically, non-normality does not matter much for controlling process average level, provided the group size is at least four, but it can affect charts for control of spread markedly. Frequently investigations will show that non-normality is due to some way in which the process is operated, such as due to the merging of streams, and this can be corrected. Failing this, it is often possible to transform data to normality by using a simple transformation such as logarithm, square root, etc.

If there is non-normality and this cannot be corrected or transformations used, then the methods given are readily transferred to another distribution. The procedure involved would be to collect sufficient data to fit a distribution, and then fit action and warning lines at the appropriate percentage points.

5.5.2 Unequal numbers in groups

If the numbers in the groups change, it is a simple matter to change the limits, as shown in Fig. 5.10.

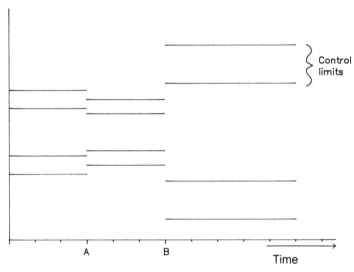

Figure 5.10 Change of group size.

5.5.3 Correlation

It is clear that if successive group means are correlated, as for example in model 3 of section 3.3, the Shewhart chart could be affected markedly. Vasilopoulos and Stamboulis (1978) have shown how to alter the decision limits for a simple autoregressive model. However, the extra variation caused by an autoregressive model would be likely to be detected by the test of section 3.6.4. This would lead to $\hat{\sigma}_e$ being based on variation between group means rather than on the within-group estimate. The procedures given above can therefore cope with autocorrelation with one exception. The use of warning limits should be discontinued in the presence of autocorrelation – positive autocorrelation will lead to too many false alarms.

A thorough study of this aspect of Shewhart charts does not seem to have been attempted.

5.6* SOME THEORETICAL RESULTS FOR SHEWHART CHARTS

5.6.1 Shewhart chart with action lines only

In this section we assume simple random variation only, and derive some theoretical results on the average run length. Further results will be given in Chapter 8.

First we deal with a Shewhart chart for means with action lines only, as set out in section 2.8. Suppose we take observations in groups of n at a time, which we denote X_{ij}, $j = 1, 2, \ldots, n$, $i = 1, 2, \ldots$. The group means $\bar{X}_i = \Sigma_j X_{ij}/n$ are plotted on a chart with upper and lower action limits at x_{UA}, x_{LA}. If all observations are independently and identically distributed with an $N(\mu, \sigma^2)$ distribution, then the probability of being outside the action limits is

$$
\begin{aligned}
p &= \int_{-\infty}^{x_{LA}} \frac{\sqrt{n}}{\sqrt{(2\pi)}\sigma} \exp\{-n(x - \mu)^2/2\sigma^2\}dx \\
&+ \int_{x_{UA}}^{\infty} \frac{\sqrt{n}}{\sqrt{(2\pi)}\sigma} \exp\{-n(x - \mu)^2/2\sigma^2\}dx \\
&= \Phi\left(\frac{x_{LA} - \mu}{\sigma/\sqrt{n}}\right) + \Phi\left(\frac{\mu - x_{UA}}{\sigma/\sqrt{n}}\right)
\end{aligned} \tag{5.1}
$$

It is clear that the distribution of run length R is geometric with parameter p, see section 2.5. This means that the ARL is

$$\text{ARL} = E(R) = 1/p$$

and the variance of the run length distribution is

$$V(R) = (1 - p)/p^2$$

If the chart is set up in the standard way using the exact μ and σ, then $p = 0.002$, so that

$$E(R) = 500 \quad \text{and} \quad V(R) = 249\,500$$

and the standard deviation of R is 499.5. The highly skewed nature of the geometric distribution needs to be taken note of, and Table 5.6 illustrates this. If charts are being designed using ARL as a basis, this point about the shape of the run-length distribution needs to be watched carefully.

Table 5.6 Illustrations of the geometric distribution

| | | | | Percentage points | |
p	Mean	Variance	50%	90%	95%
0.1	10	90	7	22	29
0.05	20	380	14	45	59
0.01	100	9900	69	230	299
0.005	200	39800	139	460	598
0.001	1000	999000	693	2302	2995

5.6.2 Shewhart chart with warning lines

We now consider the modified Shewhart chart with warning lines, operated by the rules set out in section 5.2.3. That is, action is taken when one point is outside the action line or two successive points outside the warning lines. Let p_0, p_1 and p_2 be the probability of sample means falling in the regions shown in Fig. 5.11, and let the run lengths from points within these regions be L_0, L_1 and L_2.

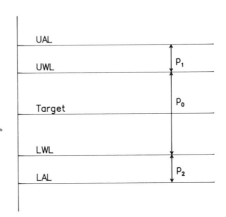

Figure 5.11 Shewhart chart with warning lines.

By taking one observation, we easily generate the following equations:

$$L_0 = 1 + p_0 L_0 + p_1 L_1 + p_2 L_2$$
$$L_1 = 1 + p_0 L_0 + p_2 L_2$$
$$L_2 = 1 + p_0 L_0 + p_1 L_1$$

We then easily obtain

$$L_0 = (1 + p_1 + p_2 + p_1p_2)/(1 - p_0 - p_1p_2 - p_0p_1 - p_0p_2 - p_0p_1p_2) \tag{5.2}$$

In this expression, the ps are functions like (5.1) when the data are IID normal. However, it is relatively easy to work out the ARL for any distribution, so long as the Xs are independent and identically distributed. Some values of the ARLs for the standard chart with boundaries at $\pm 3.09\sigma/\sqrt{n}$ and $\pm 1.96\sigma/\sqrt{n}$ ('probability' limits), and $\pm 3\sigma/\sqrt{n}$ and $\pm 2\sigma/\sqrt{n}$ ('popular' limits) are given in Table 5.5.

In Table 5.7 we show the ARL for the standard (probability) boundaries, and the ARLs which apply if the estimate of σ is under- or overestimated by 10%. This table clearly shows a very dramatic effect, and shows the importance of obtaining a good estimate of σ.

Table 5.8 shows the ARLs which apply to the standard (probability)

Table 5.7 ARLs for standard (probability) boundaries for errors in $\hat{\sigma}$

Mean	1 (exact)	$\hat{\sigma}/\sigma$ 0.9	1.10
0	320.00	125.95	884.00
0.25	222.85	93.91	571.79
0.50	108.03	50.92	247.34
0.75	51.50	26.86	106.40
1.00	26.35	15.06	49.49
1.50	8.92	5.97	14.12
2.00	4.14	3.12	5.72
2.50	2.46	2.02	3.09
3.00	1.75	1.52	2.05

Table 5.8 ARLs for standard (probability) boundaries with a χ^2 distribution

Mean	20	D.F. of χ^2 60	120	∞
0	146.53	219.79	259.06	320.00
0.25	89.18	124.35	146.76	222.85
0.50	54.44	68.70	77.14	108.03
0.75	33.65	38.88	41.76	51.50
1.00	21.18	22.81	23.66	26.35
1.50	9.09	8.98	8.94	8.92
2.00	4.49	4.33	4.27	4.14
2.50	2.62	2.55	2.53	2.46
3.00	1.80	1.78	1.77	1.75

scheme if the points plotted have a χ^2 rather than a normal distribution; see also Fig. 5.12. The coefficients of skewness are

$$20 \text{ d.f} : 0.63 \qquad 60 \text{ d.f} : 0.37 \qquad 120 \text{ d.f} : 0.26$$

While the effect of skewness is not as severe as the effect of errors in $\hat{\sigma}$, there is still a very strong effect, even for quite small skewness in the distribution. This leads us to conclude that severe skewness of the original population could be important if the group size is small.

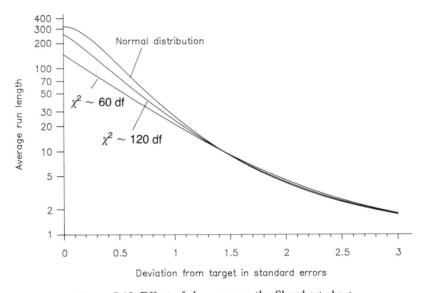

Figure 5.12 Effect of skewness on the Shewhart chart.

5.6.3 The position of the warning lines

By using equation (5.2) we can vary the values of p_0 and p_1 to get the same ARL when the process is on target. There are two limiting cases:

(1) No 'warning' region. Here we have

$$p_0 = (L_0 - 1)/L_0$$

where L_0 is the ARL when the process is on target. This leads to boundaries at a distance 2.955 standard errors from the target, for $L_0 = 320$.

(2) No 'action' region, but simply a warning region. Here we have

$$p_1 = \{1 + \sqrt{(1 + 8L_0)}\}/4L_0$$

which gives $p_1 = 0.0403$ for $L_0 = 320$, and this is at 1.747 standard errors from the target.

Table 5.9 gives the ARL for these two limiting cases and for some intermediate ones. We see that broadening the warning region increases the ARL at large distances from the target, and reduces the ARL for small distances from the target. In fact broadening the warning region a little from the standard position improves the ARL curve for small deviations without paying too high a price at high deviations. This is evidence that the warning region should not be set narrower than the standard (probability) positions. In fact the standard British chart achieves a good result at high deviations from the target, and perhaps the price being paid for this is too high.

Table 5.9 Shewhart chart with warning lines: Position of the boundaries

	Values of p_0, p_1 and position of action limits (see Fig. 5.11)					
Prob(action)	0.0032	0.002	0.0015	0.001	0.0005	0
p_0	0.9968	0.9500	0.9407	0.9327	0.9257	0.9194
p_1	0	0.0240	0.0289	0.0331	0.0368	0.0403
Warning line	2.955	1.96	1.92	1.83	1.78	1.75
Action line	2.955	3.09	2.03	3.29	3.48	∞

	ARL					
Mean						
0	320.00	320.00	320 00	320.00	320.00	320.00
0.25	244.59	222.85	217.67	213.83	211.25	210.80
0.50	136.69	108.03	102.70	99.03	96.73	96.67
0.75	72.32	51.50	48.42	46.42	45.27	45.56
1.00	39.49	26.35	24.77	23.80	23.30	23.71
1.50	13.73	8.92	8.52	8.31	8.27	8.66
2.00	5.89	4.14	4.05	4.03	4.08	4.45
2.50	3.08	2.46	2.46	2.50	2.58	2.96
3.00	1.93	1.75	1.77	1.82	1.91	2.36

If Shewhart charts are to be used, rather than CuSum charts, then several sets of boundaries could easily be prepared, which have good properties at different deviations of the mean from the target. However, it would be reasonable to argue from the results of Table 5.9 that the differences are small.

5.6.4 A modified scheme

Page (1955) studied the effect of variations in the type of rule used in the Shewhart chart, but only a limited number of calculations were reported.

The following rule is suggested: Take action if one point is outside the action limits, or two out of three points outside the same warning limit.

The ARL function for this rule can be derived in a similar way to the method used in section 5.6.2, and we have the formula

$$L_0 = \frac{1 + (1 + p_0)(p_1 + p_2) + 2p_1 p_2 (1 + p_0)^2}{\{1 - p_0 - p_1 p_2 (1 + p_0)^2 + p_0 p_1 p_2 (1 - p_0^2) - p_0^2 (p_1 + p_2)\}}$$

After some calculation, it was found that warning and action boundaries at ± 2.17 and ± 3.04 standard errors gave the following results:

Mean	0	0.25	0.5	1	1.5	2	2.5	3
ARL	320	226.1	111.3	27.2	9.2	4.2	2.5	1.8

This shows no improvement over the previous boundaries.

We therefore reach the conclusion that the standard positions for the boundaries is a satisfactory compromise. For significant improvements it is desirable to run a Shewhart chart in combination with a moving-average chart, or else a snub-nosed CuSum scheme.

5.7* CHARTS FOR CONTROL OF PROCESS SPREAD

The theory for obtaining properties of charts for control of process spread follows the methods described above for control of process average level. The ARL formula is the same (5.2), but the p_is involve the distribution of the range or standard deviation. Much less work has been done in this area. A comparison of range and standard deviation is given by Tuprah and Ncube (1987). Some of their results are given in Table 5.10 below. Tables showing the effect of non-normality or correlation do not seem to be available.

Table 5.10 ARL values for Shewhart control charts with warning lines

k	5		10		15		20	
	R-chart	S-chart	R-chart	S-chart	R-chart	S-chart	R-chart	S-chart
UWL	3.97	1.5829	4.577	1.3984	4.984	1.3213	5.1060	1.278
UAL	5.00	1.9702	5.530	1.6463	5.800	1.518	5.9920	1.443
σ								
1.0	200.00	200.00	200.00	200.00	200.00	200.00	200.00	200.00
1.1	63.40	60.00	50.00	41.70	43.80	32.40	39.90	26.50
1.2	27.20	25.10	18.40	14.40	14.90	10.00	12.80	7.60
1.3	14.40	13.20	9.00	6.90	7.00	4.70	5.90	3.60
1.4	8.90	8.20	5.30	4.10	4.10	2.90	3.50	2.20
1.5	6.20	5.70	3.70	2.80	2.80	2.10	2.40	1.70
1.6	4.60	4.30	2.80	2.30	2.20	1.70	1.90	1.40
1.7	3.60	3.40	2.20	1.90	1.80	1.40	1.60	1.20
1.8	3.00	2.80	1.90	1.60	1.50	1.30	1.40	1.10
1.9	2.60	2.40	1.70	1.40	1.40	1.20	1.20	1.10
2.0	2.30	2.20	1.50	1.30	1.30	1.10	1.20	1.00

UWL is the Shewhart upper warning line, and UAL is the Shewhart upper action line.

EXERCISES 5A

1. *Simulation exercises*. This exercise can be carried out by a group of five people, each of whom selects one of the numbered data sets given in Appendix B. The objective of the exercise is to investigate the variation in run lengths which occur as a result of the preceding rules, and the same data sets will be used in Chapter 7 to compare average run lengths of Shewhart and CuSum charts. (However, better results may be obtained by using a group of at least a dozen people).

   Suppose that you are manager of a process, and you wish to set up Shewhart $\bar{X}$-charts on the basis of one of the initial data sets marked I1, I2 etc. Having set up your chart, now run the corresponding data sets A, B, C, D through your chart until action is given or until the end of the dataset. Record the run length to (and including) the action point, and try to estimate from the plots where the processes changed.

2. Set up Shewhart $\bar{X}$ and range charts for the data set you collected in Exercise 2A.2.

3. Design some simple simulation trials to estimate the effect of

autocorrelation and non-normality on the ARL properties of the Shewhart $\bar{X}$ chart, range chart and standard deviation charts.

4. Assuming that there is no extra variation, the estimate of $\hat{\sigma}_e$ for the chart for means is $\hat{\sigma}/\sqrt{n}$. The action and warning lines are then placed at:

	Popular limits	Probability limits
Action lines	$\bar{x} \pm A\hat{\sigma}$	$\bar{x} \pm A_{0.001}\hat{\sigma}$
Warning lines	$\bar{x} \pm A_1\hat{\sigma}$	$\bar{x} \pm A_{0.025}\hat{\sigma}$

where $A = 3/\sqrt{n}$, $A_1 = 2/\sqrt{n}$, $A_{0.025} = 1.96/\sqrt{n}$, and $A_{0.001} = 3.09/\sqrt{n}$.

If the charts are to be constructed directly from the average range, the corresponding limits are placed at

$$\bar{x} \pm A'\bar{R}, \qquad \bar{x} \pm A_1'\bar{R}$$

for the popular action and warning lines, where

$$A' = 3/d_n\sqrt{n}, \qquad A_1' = 2/d_n\sqrt{n},$$

and $\bar{R}$ is the average range within groups.

Calculate a table of values of A, A_1, $A_{0.025}$, $A_{0.001}$, and the corresponding A', A_1', $A_{0.025}'$, $A_{0.01}'$ for n from 1 to 10 in unit steps. Tables of these values occur in standard works on quality control.

EXERCISES 5B

1. Set up a Shewhart $\bar{X}$-chart with action and warning lines, and use $n = 1$, $\sigma = 1$, $\mu = 0$. Select data from a table of random normal deviates, add 1.5 to each number, and plot. Terminate when action is signalled and count the run length. Repeat a few times. Calculate the average and variance of the run length.

2. Suppose you want to operate a Shewhart chart with action lines only, but achieve the same in-control ARL as in the standard chart with probability limits, which is 320. What distance should the action boundaries be from the target? Calculate the ARL function, and compare it with the results given in section 5.4.

3. Suppose you are going to use a Shewhart chart with warning lines, but modify the rules so that action is taken when one point is outside the action limits, or two successive points outside either warning limit. Obtain the formula corresponding to (5.2) in section 5.6.2. Calculate the ARL function and compare your results with those in section 5.4.

4. In a certain industrial process, it is known that $\sigma = 4$, and it is desirable to detect a difference in mean of 4 units in about 60 minutes. Currently sampling is every 15 minutes.
   (a) What group size should be used?
   (b) Approximately how frequently must the sampling be performed if the producer wishes to be 90% sure of picking up the change in one hour?

5. Show that for an on target mean, formula (5.2) reduces to

$$L_0 = (1 + p_1)/(1 - p_0 - p_1 - p_0 p_1),$$

hence verify the formula in section 5.6.3(2).

6. Design Shewhart control charts with both action and warning lines, with in-control ARLs of 200 and 500. How will you decide the position of the warning lines?

6

Extensions to Shewhart charts for one-at-a-time data

6.1 ONE-AT-A-TIME SAMPLING

6.1.1 Circumstances giving rise to one-at-a-time sampling

One-at-a-time data arises frequently in practice, especially in the process industries. In the component manufacturing field, many individual components are produced, and each stands on its own merits. It is then easy to sample a group of n at a time to get information about the process average level and process spread. In continuous processes typically a rather different situation applies. The instantaneous variation of the chemical, fluid, etc., may be quite small, but the process varies gently in time for many reasons often incompletely understood. For a process of this type, selecting a group of observations close together in time will only represent measurement or sampling error, which may be negligible. In order to be able to get close control of such a process over time, it is necessary to use rational blocking or moving averages. Charts of individual values will not detect the kind of slow drifts experienced. In this chapter the construction of 'moving' type charts is described, but there are some preliminary points to settle first.

It is convenient to think first in terms of Model 2 of section 3.3, where there is both between- and within-group variation, with variances σ_B^2 and σ_w^2 respectively. Here σ_B^2 represents variation in the process average level over time, and σ_w^2 the local or sampling variation. The variance of a group of n observations taken at one point in time is

$$V(\bar{x}_{i.}) = \sigma_B^2 + \sigma_w^2/n \qquad (6.1)$$

whereas the variance of a mean of n observations sampled singly over a period is

$$V(\bar{x}_{i.}) = (\sigma_B^2 + \sigma_w^2)/n \qquad (6.2)$$

showing that one-at-a-time sampling is more efficient. However, two points should be made. Firstly local variation, σ_w^2, may well be crucially important, rather than variation of the process average level over time since in some cases the latter might be subject to some rough control. At least *two* observations need to be sampled at a time even to estimate σ_w^2, and rather more than two observations are really needed.

Secondly, the cost of sampling a group of observations is often much less than the cost of obtaining the same number of single observations. The sampling cost is made up of staff costs, machinery costs, cost of disturbance to the production line etc., and the actual cost of using these facilities to obtain, say, five observations rather than one, is often much less than five times the cost of a single observation.

The key reason why observations are often sampled in groups for SPC is that control of process spread is critical, and grouped observations are necessary to estimate process spread. In the process industries, or in other applications where there is substantial *between*-group variability, one-at-a-time sampling is often more appropriate. Control of process spread can then be achieved through a moving-range or moving-stan-dard-deviation chart; see section 6.4.

For the process industries, Model 3 of section 3.3.3 may be more appropriate than Model 2, and here the gain for one-at-a-time sampling is less obvious. Correlation between observations tends to produce a result closer to the 'grouped' observations variance (6.1) than (6.2).

6.1.2 Some alternative charting methods

If the group size is small, or perhaps one, the charting methods given in Chapter 5 cannot be used effectively. For example, although we can construct a Shewhart chart for group size $n = 1$, the limits are very wide, so that the chart has little power. Some alternative approaches when the group size is small or one are as follows.

(1) *Rational blocking*
    In this method we artificially block the data by shift, batch, day etc. as described in section 3.7.1. We hope to have some rational method of doing this, so that special causes of variation occur between rather than within groups. Once blocked data has been achieved, the charting methods of Chapter 5 can be used. Although this is a very simple way of getting round the problem, an unfortunate choice of blocking can mask changes, and inflated estimates of spread can also result, leading to wide limits.
(2) *Moving-averages, moving ranges*
    The alternative to rational blocking is to use moving averages or moving ranges. Two types of moving-average chart are given later in

this chapter. The disadvantage of any moving-average chart is that action is necessarily delayed by the averaging.

A key problem with one-at-a-time data is the estimation of the standard error σ_e of the points being plotted, and this was discussed briefly in section 3.7. In the next section we consider the problem of estimating σ_e for one-at-a-time data again. There is obviously no way of estimating σ_w directly unless observations are replicated, at least for a period, although the 'estimation by differences' method given in section 3.7.2 may get close to it. On the other hand, other methods given below give results much closer to σ_e directly. Because of the confusion about what is being estimated, the suffixes σ_w, σ_B, σ_e will be dropped while the methods are presented.

The underlying problem here is much deeper than the following discussion suggests. An approach based on a more appropriate model needs to be tried. However, the methods given below give satisfactory results in practice.

6.2 ESTIMATION OF σ FOR ONE-AT-A-TIME DATA

In this section we consider again the estimation of σ for one-at-a-time data, and take this on from section 3.7. In order to illustrate the methods we use the data of section 5.1.4, and treat the group means as if they were single observations. (This will enable us to get charts which we can easily compare with those in Chapter 5.)

If a rational blocking exists, a σ estimate based on this should be calculated. However, it may be useful to compare it with estimates given below. Any large discrepancy merits investigation.

Example 6.1 Engineering plastic strength data

In the manufacture of an engineering plastic, a single laminate was sampled and put into a machine to test for strength. The laminates were taken five times a shift from the production line, and the results in Table 6.1 relate to 'transverse flexure strength'. In the following sections we use the column of means as if they were single observations.

6.2.1 The overall σ estimate

One easy estimate of σ is simply to use all of our data together, and calculate the overall standard deviation to get $\hat{\sigma}$. Clearly, any points representing special causes should be omitted, and the easiest way of finding this out is to set up trial charts based on all the data. Any point out of control should be investigated with a view to omitting it.

Table 6.1 Engineering plastic strength data

Shift						Mean	Median	Std dev	Range
1	140.1	139.4	143.5	141.4	136.5	140.18	140.1	2.582	7.0
2	140.0	137.4	140.8	140.5	141.3	140.00	140.5	1.528	3.9
3	138.9	139.6	141.0	141.7	138.7	139.98	139.6	1.318	3.0
4	137.1	136.0	136.0	133.7	141.5	136.86	136.0	2.875	7.8
5	143.1	141.2	138.5	137.0	137.1	139.38	138.5	2.683	6.1
6	140.5	138.7	140.2	142.0	142.3	140.74	140.5	1.461	3.6
7	139.8	141.4	137.9	137.8	140.0	139.38	139.8	1.527	3.6
8	139.5	140.5	141.0	142.1	142.5	141.12	141.0	1.213	3.0
9	137.8	142.5	138.5	140.3	138.2	139.46	138.5	1.950	4.7
10	144.1	142.3	138.0	140.8	139.1	140.86	140.8	2.442	6.1
11	140.3	139.7	143.5	138.0	139.0	140.10	139.7	2.085	5.5
12	141.2	139.4	139.2	138.9	139.0	139.54	139.2	0.948	2.3
13	140.4	138.4	139.2	140.1	143.2	140.26	140.1	1.822	4.8
14	139.2	139.4	137.9	141.4	137.5	139.08	139.2	1.532	3.9
15	137.7	135.8	138.5	141.6	138.1	138.34	138.1	2.096	5.8
16	137.7	141.9	140.9	141.7	141.4	140.72	141.4	1.730	4.2
17	137.6	138.9	139.1	141.8	136.6	138.80	138.9	1.961	5.2
18	137.8	136.6	139.6	139.0	139.1	138.42	139.0	1.213	3.0
19	140.5	138.2	139.8	136.1	139.6	138.84	139.6	1.744	4.4
20	141.0	143.3	141.7	143.0	140.5	141.90	141.7	1.223	2.8
21	137.6	137.3	141.2	138.8	143.3	139.64	138.8	2.558	6.0
22	138.5	141.4	142.5	138.7	140.1	140.24	140.1	1.723	4.0
23	143.1	138.6	142.1	140.5	142.1	141.28	142.1	1.764	4.5
24	140.0	138.5	142.5	142.2	140.3	140.70	140.3	1.657	4.0
25	140.9	143.1	138.3	142.8	139.6	140.94	140.9	2.055	4.8
Totals						3496.76	3494.4		114.0

This estimate of σ will obviously be inflated by a considerable amount of 'between-sample' variation, if any is present. As such, it is a useful upper boundary in guiding us to what $\hat{\sigma}$ to use.

For the data given in Table 6.1, we find that the overall $\hat{\sigma}$ is 1.110, if the group means are treated as if they were single observations.

If there are marked changes of level, so that the data can be split into two or more segments, then the segments should be treated separately, and the $\hat{\sigma}$ estimates combined using the formula (3.10).

6.2.2 Use of moving ranges

In section 3.7.2 we obtained an estimate of σ for one-at-a-time data by treating differences of successive observations as if they were ranges of two observations. This method is readily extended and we could get another estimate by using ranges of successive groups of three observations, or of four observations, etc. The method is set out in Method Summary 6.1, and the results can be plotted as shown in Figure 6.1.

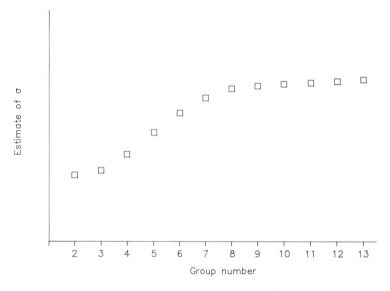

Figure 6.1 Example of moving-range estimates of σ.

If ranges of two are used to get an estimate of σ (successive differences), there will probably not be much 'between-sample' variation in the estimate of σ, but if we use ranges of three or more to estimate σ, the estimate will tend to be inflated. Therefore if a plot of $\hat{\sigma}$ against the number of points in the moving-range (2, 3, 4 etc.) is relatively flat, there is little evidence of between-sample variation. If the curve is sharply rising, as in Fig. 6.1, some examination should be made for the causes of the extra between-sample variation. This may lead to considerable difficulty in deciding which estimate to use in setting up Shewhart charts, and we discuss this below.

METHOD SUMMARY 6.1

Estimation of σ by moving-ranges of k points

Step 1 Calculate the moving-ranges for groups of size k (for $k = 2$, 3, 4, . . .). Use at least 25 observations, and preferably 50 or 100.

Step 2 Sum the absolute values of the ranges and divide by the number of ranges (not observations).

Step 3 Divide the result of Step 2 by the appropriate factor from Table 2.9.

Step 4 Tabulate the results for groups of size 2, 3, 4, ... as in Table 6.2.

Notes

(1) Differences due to special causes should be excluded. This can be done by constructing a trial Shewhart chart.

(2) This method should not be used if there is an obvious trend in the data which can be attributed to ageing of a catalyst, machine wear, etc.

(3) If there are missing observations, groups containing these should be deleted.

(4) You will get a different estimate if you re-sample using a different time interval.

Table 6.2 Moving-range estimate of σ

Size of moving range	2	3	4	5	6	7
$\hat{\sigma}$	1.115	1.102	1.133	1.110	1.111	1.104

Size of moving range	8	9	10	11	12
$\hat{\sigma}$	1.098	1.089	1.091	1.094	1.086

6.2.3 Examples

Example 6.2 Engineering plastic strength data

The above procedure was carried out for shift means of the example strength data of Table 6.1, and the estimates of σ are shown in Table 6.2. These estimates are flat, so there is no evidence of the presence of any between-sample variation. The overall $\hat{\sigma}$ is 1.110 which is about the same. One reason for this is that the data were generated by artificially sampling a Normal distribution.

Example 6.3 Water content of antifreeze data
The data in Table 6.3 below represent the water content of successive batches of antifreeze, and a plot of the data is given in Fig. 6.2. The results of the moving-range estimates of σ are given in Table 6.4.

Table 6.3 Water content (in ppm) of batches of antifreeze

2.23	2.53	2.62	2.63	2.58	2.44	2.49	2.34	2.95
2.54	2.60	2.45	2.17	2.58	2.57	2.44	2.38	2.23
2.23	2.54	2.66	2.84	2.81	2.39	2.56	2.70	3.00
2.81	2.77	2.89	2.54	2.98	2.35	2.53		

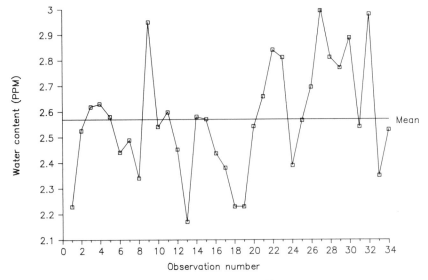

Figure 6.2 Analysis of antifreeze.

Table 6.4 Estimates of σ for antifreeze data

Size of moving range	2	3	4	5	6	7
$\hat{\sigma}$	0.179	0.190	0.196	0.202	0.202	0.204

Size of moving range	8	9	10	11	12
$\hat{\sigma}$	0.207	0.212	0.213	0.214	0.217

The overall $\hat{\sigma} = 0.220$. The moving-range estimates increase steadily, representing the fact that more between-sample variation is included in $\hat{\sigma}$ as the 'size' of the moving range increases, 2, 3, 4, ... Clearly, as the size increases further, we would expect $\hat{\sigma}$ to settle down at a value close to the overall $\hat{\sigma}$.

6.2.4 Discussion

The fact is that the estimation of σ for one-at-a-time data has not been thoroughly studied. Some national and international standards give the method of successive differences described in section 3.7.2, and this is what has been used in the past. If there is no evidence of additional long-term variation, as in our first example, this is the preferred method.

In the second example moving-range estimates for sizes 2, 3, 4, . . . gave increasing estimates of σ. This is presumably because there are relatively long-term changes occurring to or within the production process, and the extent of these is more likely to be seen in a range of 4 or 6 successive points than in only 2. It is also clear from this that if the successive difference method is used, but sampling points are set much further apart in time, then this also will lead to an inflated estimate of σ.

For data such as Example 6.3, where there is considerable between-sample variation, it will be necessary to think carefully about what $\hat{\sigma}$ to use to set up a Shewhart or a CuSum chart to control *process average level*. The choice may lie between

(1) Regarding current overall variability as acceptable, and setting up charts using a large estimate of σ. This method will tend to lose power in detecting changes.
(2) Regarding the short-term variability as an achievable goal, setting up charts using a small estimate of σ, and identifying and removing the causes of long-term variability. This method may lead to frequent false alarms.

The advice of a statistician may be very helpful, but will not entirely remove the need to make this choice.

Charts for control of *spread* are generally less problematic, as a σ estimate can be used which is appropriate to the time span over which variability is being calculated, and this is generally fairly short. However, the above arguments may still apply if σ estimates increase rapidly for different sizes of the moving-range group.

6.3 DETAILS OF FURTHER CONTROL CHARTS FOR CONTROL OF PROCESS AVERAGE LEVEL

In Chapter 5 we only studied the straightforward $\bar{X}$ and R or σ charts. The purpose of this section is to give some details of further types of control chart which have been mentioned earlier in this chapter. Moving-average and moving-range charts are especially useful for one-at-a-time data.

The construction methods given below apply for groups of size n, but for one-at-a-time data put $n = 1$ throughout. We shall assume that the process capability study has been carried out, and that estimates of the process variability are available. We shall denote the group means by $\bar{X}_1, \bar{X}_2, \ldots$ and the estimate of standard error of the $\bar{X}_i$ is denoted $\hat{\sigma}_e$ (see section 3.6.7). If we have one-at-a-time sampling, $\hat{\sigma}_e$ is simply an estimate of σ obtained by the methods outlined in section 6.2. The following subsections assume that this estimate $\hat{\sigma}_e$ is available.

6.3.1 Moving-average charts

In the moving-average chart, we plot the averages of the last k groups of size n, as shown in Fig. 6.3. The points on the time axis represent times at which groups of size n are taken. For a moving average of 3s, these averages are represented at the middle of the three points, as shown. For a moving average of 4s, the averages fall half-way between two time points at which groups are sampled. The points for moving averages of 4s are recorded at the centre points of the lines shown in Fig. 6.3; some example calculations are given in Table 6.5.

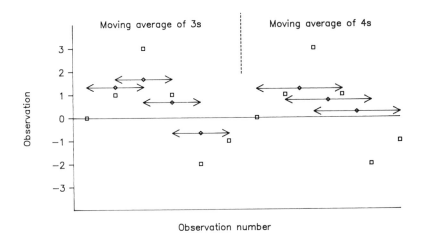

Figure 6.3 Moving averages.

Table 6.5 Calculation of moving averages

Sample No.	Mean	Moving averages of 3s			Moving Average	Moving averages of 4s				Moving Average
1	140.18	—	140.18	140.00	—	—	140.18	140.00	140.00	—
2	140.00	140.18	140.00	139.98	140.05	140.18	140.00	139.98	139.98	139.25
3	139.98	140.00	139.98	136.86	138.95	140.00	139.98	136.86	136.86	139.05
4	136.86	139.98	136.86	139.38	138.74	139.98	136.86	139.38	139.38	139.24
5	139.38	136.86	139.38	140.74	138.99	136.86	139.38	140.74	140.74	139.02
6	140.74	139.38	140.74	139.38	139.83	139.38	140.74	139.38	139.38	140.16
7	139.38	140.74	139.38	141.12	140.41	140.74	139.38	141.12	141.12	—
8	141.12	139.38	141.12	—	—	139.38	140.74	—	—	—

Points are lost at the start and finish of a moving-average chart, because there is not enough data to complete the chart. If desired, these missing points could be filled in with the averages of the points available at the ends, but if this is done, *the action limits calculated below should be disregarded for these points*. In a moving-average chart, only action lines are used because successive moving averages are highly correlated.

The usual method of constructing charts, given below, ignores the dependence between successive moving averages.

6.3.2 Construction of a moving-average chart

Following the discussion in section 6.3.1 the method is set out in Method Summary 6.2.

METHOD SUMMARY 6.2

Construction of a moving-average chart

Step 1 (Grouped or blocked data) Obtain estimates of the process average level, $\hat{\mu}$, and process variability, and also obtain the estimated standard error of group means $\hat{\sigma}_e$.

Step 1 (One-at-a-time data) Obtain an estimate of the process average level, $\hat{\mu}$. Also obtain an estimate of the process variability using Method Summary 6.1, and choose a suitable $\hat{\sigma}_e$ for charting.

Step 2 Choose the scale of the chart so that $\hat{\mu}$ is near the centre, and so that the scale covers approximately $\pm 4\hat{\sigma}_e/\sqrt{(k)}$.

Step 3 Mark the action lines at $\hat{\mu} \pm 3.09\hat{\sigma}_e/\sqrt{(k)}$.

Note

(1) This assumes that all groups are of the same size.

An alternative to disregarding the first few points is to plot the moving averages of 2, 3, ... points, etc., until k points are available. If this method is used the corresponding action lines have to be recalculated at each point until k points are available.

Example 6.4 Illustration of moving-average chart

Step 1 Suppose we are given $\mu = 140$, $\sigma = 2$, $n = 5$, $k = 3$, then
$\sigma_e = 2/\sqrt{5} = 0.89$.

Step 2 Scale chart to cover $140 \pm 4\sigma_e/\sqrt{(k)} = 140 \pm 4 \times 0.89/\sqrt{3}$
$$= 137.94, 142.06.$$

Step 3 Action lines: $140 \pm 3.09 \times 0.89/\sqrt{3} = 138.4, 141.6$

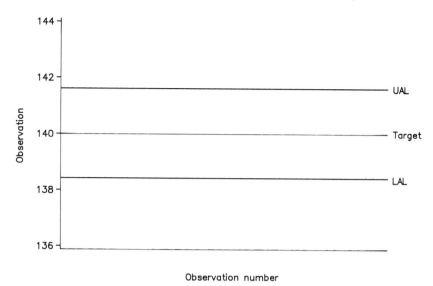

Figure 6.4 Construction of a moving-average chart.

6.3.3 Moving-average charts: interpretation and use

The points given in section 5.2.3 for $\bar{X}$-charts are all applicable here, except that there are no warning limits.

Moving-average charts are usually used particularly when 'groups' have to be of size one or two, so that the resulting control limits are wide. The disadvantage is that because averages are taken over a period of time, there may be a delay before lack of control is detected. Furthermore, suppose we are averaging over four groups, then if just one of the group means is out of control, this can easily be swamped by averaging with three other group means which are in control.

Moving-average charts can be used successfully if the following conditions are all satisfied:

(1) The group size is limited for some reason.
(2) The true mean changes rather slowly.
(3) The process spread is fairly stable.

The construction method given above ignores the correlation between successive moving-averages. It assumes that if the standard error of a point is σ_e, then the moving average of k of these points will overall have a Normal distribution with standard error $\sigma_e/\sqrt{k}$. However, correlation considerably affects run-length properties, and this is discussed in section 6.7.2.

6.3.4 Exponentially weighted moving-average charts (EWMA charts)

The exponentially weighted moving-average chart is particularly useful either when we have one-at-a-time data, or else when great precision is needed to detect small changes. Basically the method is to form a new moving-average at each sampling point by calculating a weighted average of the new value and the previous moving-average. Therefore in the exponentially weighted moving-average chart all of the past data has some effect on the current value, but it rapidly loses influence. The details are given in Method Summary 6.3 (we assume that an estimate of σ_e is available). The implied weights on observations are given in Table 6.7.

METHOD SUMMARY 6.3

Construction of exponentially weighted moving-average charts

Step 1 (Grouped or blocked data) Obtain estimates of the process average level, $\hat{\mu}$, and process variability, and also obtain the estimated standard error of group means $\hat{\sigma}_e$.

Step 1 (One-at-a-time data) Obtain an estimate of the process average level, $\hat{\mu}$. Also obtain an estimate of the process variability using Method Summary 6.1, and choose a suitable $\hat{\sigma}_e$ for charting.

Step 2 Choose a value for p in the range 0.1–0.5. This is the amount of weight put on the current value.

Step 3 Choose a starting value, k_0, as either the overall mean or a target value.

Step 4 Calculate and plot the moving average k_i using the formula

$$k_i = p\bar{X}_i + (1 - p)k_{i-1}$$

where the $\bar{X}_i$ are group means, or for one-at-a-time data, single values.

Step 5 Use action limits only, and place them at

$$\mu \pm A_1\hat{\sigma}_e$$

where the A_1 values are given in Table 6.6.

We see from Table 6.7 that with $p = 0.5$ the weight on a group drops down markedly after 3 or 4, but with $p = 0.1$, the weights decrease rather slowly. The choice of p in any particular case depends on how much weight is required on past group means.

Table 6.6 Factors for constructing exponentially weighted moving-average charts from an estimate of $\sigma(A_1)$

p	Group size 1	2	3	4	5	6	7	8
0.05	0.495	0.350	0.286	0.247	0.221	0.202	0.187	0.175
0.10	0.709	0.501	0.409	0.355	0.317	0.289	0.268	0.250
0.15	0.880	0.622	0.508	0.440	0.394	0.359	0.333	0.311
0.20	1.030	0.728	0.595	0.515	0.461	0.420	0.389	0.364
0.25	1.168	0.826	0.674	0.584	0.522	0.477	0.422	0.413
0.30	1.298	0.918	0.750	0.649	0.581	0.530	0.491	0.459
0.35	1.423	1.006	0.822	0.712	0.637	0.581	0.538	0.503
0.40	1.545	1.093	0.892	0.773	0.691	0.631	0.584	0.546
0.45	1.665	1.177	0.961	0.833	0.745	0.680	0.629	0.589
0.50	1.784	1.262	1.030	0.892	0.798	0.728	0.674	0.631

Notes: (1) The action lines are obtained by multiplying these factors by an estimate of σ.
(2) The first 6 observations should be ignored when making decisions about in or out of control.
(3) The values are $3.0902\sqrt{\{p/n(2-p)\}}$.

Table 6.7 Implied weights for exponentially weighted moving averages

p	Current observation	Number of previous observations 1	2	3	4	5
0.5	0.5	0.25	0.125	0.0625	0.0312	0.0156
0.2	0.2	0.16	0.128	0.1024	0.0819	0.0655
0.1	0.1	0.09	0.081	0.0729	0.0656	0.0590

Exponentially weighted moving-average charts are particularly useful with processes which have slowly drifting means, rather than those which are liable to sudden jumps.

6.3.5 Exponentially weighted moving-averages: starting-up problems

The factors given in Table 6.6 are based on the asymptotic variance of m_i. If we write the asymptotic variance $V(k)$, then we have

$$V(k) = p^2 V(\bar{X}_i) + (1-p)^2 V(k)$$

leading to

$$V(k) = \frac{p}{(2-p)} V(\bar{X}_i) = \frac{p\sigma^2}{n(2-p)}. \tag{6.3}$$

However, if we start with a fixed k_0, then we have

$$V(k_1) = p^2\sigma^2/n$$

$$V(k_2) = [p^2 + p^2(1 - p)^2]\sigma^2/n$$

$$V(k_3) = [p^2 + p^2(1 - p)^2 + p^2(1 - p)^4]\sigma^2/n, \text{ etc.}$$

The convergence of these to the asymptotic formula given above can sometimes be rather slow, see Table 6.8, especially if p is rather small.

Table 6.8 Tendency of standard error of k_i to the asymptotic formula

	Standard error of k_i at observation					
p	2	4	6	8	10	Asymptotic
0.05	0.069	0.093	0.109	0.120	0.128	0.160
0.10	0.135	0.173	0.194	0.207	0.215	0.229
0.20	0.256	0.304	0.322	0.329	0.331	0.333
0.30	0.366	0.408	0.417	0.419	0.420	0.420

Owing to this feature, it is unwise to take much notice of an out of control signal given within the first few observations when starting up an EWMA chart.

6.4 CONTROL OF PROCESS SPREAD

6.4.1 Moving-range charts

We have already discussed moving ranges in section 6.2, and a plot of moving ranges can be made in order to control process spread. For one-at-a-time data, a moving-range chart or a moving-standard-deviation chart is the *only* way of controlling process spread. However, one of these charts may be useful with grouped data, as an extra chart, if there is a substantial between-group variation. In this case we plot the moving range of the group means.

METHOD SUMMARY 6.4

Construction of moving-range chart

Step 1 Determine k, the number of sampling points the range is taken over. This is often determined by practical considerations.

Step 2 (One-at-a-time data) Obtain an estimate $\hat{\sigma}$ of the process spread by using moving ranges of k points; see Method Summary 6.1.

Step 2 (Grouped or blocked data) Obtain an estimate $\hat{\sigma}_e$ of the standard error of group means; see Method Summary 3.6.

Step 3 Choose the scale of the moving-range chart so that the range goes down to zero, and up to about twice the largest range observed.

Step 4 Mark the action limits on the chart:

Lower action limit $D_5\hat{\sigma}$
Upper action limit $D_6\hat{\sigma}$

where D_5 and D_6 are given in Table 5.3.
There are *no* warning limits on a moving-range chart.

The interpretation of a moving-range chart is as for a range chart; see section 5.3.3. A crucial point is the choice of k, the number of sampling points that the range is taken over. As k increases, more between-sample variation will inflate the ranges. The choice of k is determined by practical considerations of the type of variation it is intended to control.

We notice again that this construction ignores the dependence between successive moving ranges.

6.4.2 Moving-standard-deviation charts

Instead of using moving ranges, we could use moving standard deviations, and otherwise the procedure is as given in section 6.4.1. Again only action lines are used, and the factors D_9 and D_{10} from Table 5.4 are used. The quantities plotted are the moving standard deviations.

There is very little to choose between a moving-range chart and a moving-standard-deviation chart, except that the former are more clearly understood by process staff.

6.5 CHOICE OF CHARTING METHOD

6.5.1 Choice between charts for control of average level

Here we summarize some of the advantages and disadvantages of the alternative Shewhart charts for controlling the average level of a process. In Chapter 7 we introduce CuSum charts, and then give some discussion about an overall choice of chart. In the process industries, where both sudden movements and sudden drifts occur, there is value in keeping both an $\bar{X}$ chart and a moving-average chart.

$\bar{X}$ *charts*
Advantages   (1) Good at detecting sudden jumps in average level
               (2) Well used and reliable
               (3) Easy to understand
Disadvantages (1) Rather slow to detect drifts in average level
               (2) Not very good at picking out small changes in average level.

Moving-average charts
Advantages   (1) Better than $\bar{X}$ charts at detecting slow drifts
               (2) Can be used when group size n is small, and when $n = 1$
Disadvantages (1) Delays in responding to sudden jumps in average level.

Exponentially weighted moving-average charts
Advantages   (1) Good at detecting slow drifts
               (2) Can be used with small group sizes, and when $n = 1$
Disadvantages (1) Delays in responding to sudden jumps.

For one-at-a-time, individual charts ($n = 1$ in the methods given in Chapter 5) are sometimes used, for example when data is infrequent, and moving averages would cause undue delay. A moving-average chart or EWMA chart should then be used as well.

6.5.2 Charts for control of process spread

If the data is one-at-a-time, then the moving-range chart is the only one usable. If the data is grouped or blocked, ordinary range or standard deviation charts should be used. However, even in this case, a moving-range chart based on group averages will help to keep control of between-sample variation, if there is any.

The choice of charting method will be discussed again after CuSum charts have been explained; see Chapter 7.

6.6 PRACTICAL USE OF SHEWHART AND MOVING-AVERAGE CHARTS

6.6.1 Relation between 'control' and process capability

A process is said to be 'in control' if there is no evidence from either the chart for control of average level or the chart for control of process spread that assignable causes of variation may be present. It is important to note that we can have a process in control, but producing defective quality material because of low relative capability (see Fig. 6.5). The reverse can be true when the process is of high capability.

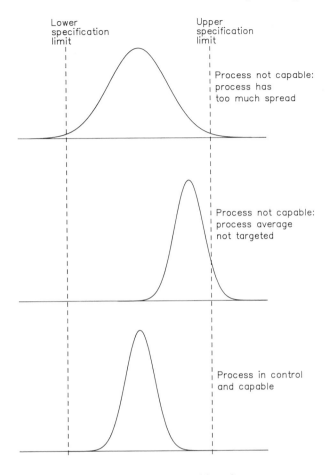

Figure 6.5 Control and capability of processes.

6.6.2 Out of control!

When the charts show an 'out of control' point which is not due to miscalculation, we may have evidence from either or both of the charts for average level and the chart for process spread. Apart from the specific rules given in previous sections, there may be other obviously non-random patterns in the plots. For example, we may have too much clustering of the data in the centre of the chart, or too much clustering towards the extremes. Alternatively, we may observe 'cycles' in the charts.

The great value of the charts is that they show when to set up procedures to look for special causes of variation (which may involve stopping the process) and when to leave the process alone. By seeing whether there is evidence of a shift in level, or spread, or both, and by seeing whether this is a sudden change or a steady drift, we can get some clues as to the possible cause. The step of 'problem-hunting' for special causes of variation is expensive and time-consuming – but not so expensive as bad product!

In some industries, indications of when to leave a process alone are as valuable as indications of when to search for a special cause.

6.6.3 Shewhart and moving-average control charts – the operational phase

Here we continue the discussion started in section 5.1.3, and assume that the 'set-up' phase of Shewhart control charts has been completed. Figure 6.6 shows the flow of the operational phase.

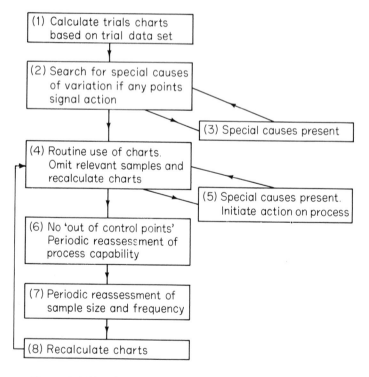

Figure 6.6 Shewhart control charts – the operational phase.

Box 1 We assume that at least 20 groups of observations are available (or at least 50 observations for one-at-a-time data), and that trial limits are calculated as given in sections 5.2, 5.3, 6.3 and 6.4.

Boxes 2 and 3 If any of the 'trial' groups shows an out of control signal on any of the charts and a special cause of variation is found to be present, then this group should be omitted and the limits recalculated. We should beware of discarding data we simply do not like, but by omitting groups where a special cause is known we will get a better estimate of the underlying process spread. In particular, the process spread should be in control before we can proceed much further.

Box 4 Once satisfactory limits are established, we use the charts as specified.

Box 5 If a special cause of variation is present, we must initiate action on the process.

Boxes 6–8 If there are no 'out of control' points, periodic checks should be made on the process, to examine the process capability, and to see if the limits need recalculating. Occasionally, we need reviews of the choice of sample size and frequency.

6.7* PROPERTIES OF EWMA AND MA CHARTS

6.7.1 The average run length of EWMA charts

We shall operate the EWMA scheme of section 6.3.4, with $m_0 = u$, a target value of zero, and $\sigma^2 = 1$. Action limits are placed at $\pm h$. Then the first observation leads to

$$m_1 = (1 - p)u + px_1.$$

If this is beyond $\pm h$, a decision is reached, but otherwise a point in the continuation region is reached. In this way, the ARL function $L(u)$ is seen to satisfy

$$L(u) = \Pr\{|(1 - p)u + px| > h\}$$

$$+ \int_{\{|(1-p)u+px|<h\}} \{1 + L((1 - p)u + px)\}f(x)\,dx$$

which is

$$L(u) = 1 + \frac{1}{p}\int_{-h}^{h} L(y)f\left(\frac{y - (1 - p)u}{p}\right)dy. \qquad (6.4)$$

This is a Fredholm integral equation of the second kind. Crowder (1987) has tabulated the solutions of this equation. He also showed how to extend the methods to obtain other properties of the run-length distribution.

Crowder (1987) showed an interesting property of EWMA schemes. Notwithstanding a design which gives a long ARL when on target, there can still be a substantial probability of a false signal within the first few observations. This is the 'starting problem' discussed in section 6.3.5. Unfortunately, the theory given above goes through most easily when a constant action limit is used.

6.7.2 Properties of moving-average (MA) charts

To get ARLs of MA charts we adopt the following procedure. A moving-average scheme of k points is used, and a single action limit put at h. The target is taken as zero, and observations X_i are assumed to be $N(0, 1)$.

Now define

$$y_k = (x_1 + \cdots + x_k)/k$$

$$y_{k+1} = (x_2 + \cdots + x_{k+1})/(k + 1)$$

so that the ARL of a one-sided scheme is

$$L = P(y_k > h) + 2P(y_k < h, \, y_{k+1} > h) + \cdots$$
$$+ \, kP(y_k < h, \, \ldots, \, y_{2k-1} < h, \, y_{2k} > h)$$
$$+ \, (k + 1)P(y_k < h, \, \ldots, \, y_{2k} < h, \, y_{2k+1} > h),$$

then it can be shown (Kuhbier, personal correspondence) that this can be rewritten as follows. Define

$$p_1 = P(y_k < h)$$
$$p_2 = P(y_k < h, \, y_{k+1} < h)$$
$$\vdots$$
$$p_k = P(y_k < h, \, \ldots, \, y_{2k-1} < h)$$

then the ARL is

$$L = (1 - p_1) + 2(p_1 - p_2) + \cdots + k(p_{k-1} - p_k)$$
$$+ \, \frac{p_k}{p_{k-1} - p_k}((k + 1)p_{k-1} - kp_k). \tag{6.5}$$

This formula involves a great deal of computing, so it is not a practical method for large values of k. The method can be extended, in principle, to cover observations which are not independent, but come from an autoregressive process, but again there are computational problems. An approximation is given by Lai (1974), but this also involves the calculation of multivariate normal integrals.

The formula (6.5) can be extended to deal with the two-sided case, but the computational problems are then worse. It seems likely that the formula given by De Bruyn (1968) for combining the ARL of two one-sided schemes can be used as an approximation,

$$\frac{1}{L} = \frac{1}{L^u} + \frac{1}{L^l}$$

where L^u and L^l are the ARLs for the upper and lower boundaries.

There are a number of practical situations where moving-average charts might be useful, and some quicker, more approximate method of obtaining ARLs would be invaluable.

6.7.3 Properties of moving-range and moving-standard-deviation charts

'Moving' charts for control of process spread are likely to be very sensitive to the assumptions of normality, independence, etc., and to the presence of autocorrelation. There is need for a thorough study of this type of chart.

EXERCISES 6A

1. The melt flow index of a plastic is measured on a single sample taken from pre-defined bags, so that readings are taken once per tonne, regardless of the method of shipment to the customer.

   The MFI specification for this grade is $4.5 \leq \text{MFI} \leq 6.5$.

   Table 6.9 gives MFI readings taken from several production campaigns to make the same grade of the product. Finish the calculations and set up control charts to control process average level and process spread.

2. Use the data sets in Appendix B to set up and plot moving-average charts. Use the means given as if they were single observations. Set up the chart using the 'I' datasets, then run the corresponding datasets A, B, C, D until action is given, or until the end of the data set. Count the run lengths as the number of the original means used. Compare your results with those you obtained in Exercise 5A.1.

Table 6.9 Melt Flow Index

Bag No.	MFI	Mov. Av. 3 point	Smoothed Twice	Bag No.	MFI	Mov. Av.	Smoothed Twice
1	5.75			41	5.73	5.65	5.65
2	5.30	5.42		42	5.68	5.64	5.63
3	5.21	5.14	5.25	43	5.52	5.59	5.59
4	4.91	5.19	5.15	44	5.57	5.53	5.51
5	5.45	5.11	5.19	45	5.49	5.42	5.48
6	4.98	5.26	5.21	46	5.21	5.49	5.49
7	5.36	5.26	5.28	47	5.77	5.56	5.56
8	5.43	5.32	5.31	48	5.69	5.63	5.60
9	5.18	5.36	5.30	49	5.44	5.60	5.59
10	5.47	5.20	5.24	50	5.67	5.53	5.59
11	4.96	5.15	5.08	51	5.49	5.64	5.65
12	5.01	4.90	4.95	52	5.75	5.77	5.74
13	4.73	4.80	4.76	53	6.06	5.83	5.79
14	4.67	4.58	4.79	54	5.68	5.77	5.76
15	4.34	4.99	4.95	55	5.57	5.68	5.69
16	5.95	5.28	5.31	56	5.80	5.62	5.62
17	5.54	5.66	5.41	57	5.50	5.56	5.52
18	5.48	5.29	5.33	58	5.38	5.38	5.42
19	4.85	5.04	5.03	59	5.26	5.32	5.32
20	4.78	4.77	4.81	60	5.31	5.26	5.29
21	4.69	4.61	4.72	61	5.21	5.29	5.23
22	4.35	4.78	4.77	62	5.36	5.14	5.26
23	5.30	4.92	4.95	63	4.86	5.35	5.30
24	5.11	5.14	5.03	64	5.83	5.42	5.50
25	5.01	5.04	5.10	65	5.57	5.72	5.66
26	5.00	5.11	5.08	66	5.75	5.84	5.83
27	5.33	5.09	5.03	67	6.19	5.93	5.89
28	4.93	4.89	4.90	68	5.86	5.91	
29	4.42	4.71	4.77	69	5.67		
30	4.78	4.69	4.72	70	5.44		
31	4.88	4.76	4.78	71	5.18		
32	4.63	4.88	4.84	72	5.15		
33	5.12	4.89	4.93	73	5.37		
34	4.92	5.03	5.00	74	5.40		
35	5.05	5.08	5.10	75	5.30		
36	5.27	5.20	5.17	76	4.86		
37	5.27	5.24	5.28	77	4.83		
38	5.19	5.39	5.37	78	4.65		
39	5.72	5.49	5.52	79	4.72		
40	5.55	5.67	5.60	80	4.74		

EXERCISES 6B

1. Most one-at-a-time data in the process industries is autocorrelated. Set up a simple simulation study to examine the effect of autocorrelation on the methods given in section 6.2 for estimating σ.

2. Use the variance results given in section 6.3.5 to work out improved boundaries for use at the start of an EWMA chart, instead of using the asymptotic variance throughout.

3. Set up a simulation experiment to determine the ARL curve of moving-average and EWMA charts. Take care to define your starting rule carefully, until the asymptotic boundaries are reached. If the run-length distribution is approximately geometric, how many trials will be needed to determine the ARL to within 1%? (It is suggested that you only try those situations where the ARL is short; for example, when the mean has shifted one or two standard errors from the target.)

7

Cumulative sum techniques for continuous variables

7.1 INTRODUCTION

7.1.1 The value of CuSums

In the 1960s an alternative to the Shewhart chart was devised based on cumulative sum plotting, and we have already introduced this method in Chapter 3. Basically, it is simply a different way for deciding when a process is or is not in control. Practical use of CuSums is therefore in the same context as Shewhart charts, and the 'set-up phase' described in section 5.1.3, and the need to periodically reassess process capability (section 6.6.3), apply as before.

CuSum charting has been used a great deal in industry, and some published examples are given, for example, in Woodward and Goldsmith (1964). Changes of mean are shown up in CuSum charts by *changes of inclination* of the chart, and it is this which gives CuSum charts their greater visual impact. For example, Fig. 7.1 shows again the CuSum plot of the example in section 3.5.3, with 0.24 added to the last 25 observations, and there is very clear evidence of a change in the mean at about observation 25. Figure 7.2 shows the same data, plotted on a standard Shewhart chart, and there is no evidence of a change.

In Chapter 3 we were using CuSums on past data, but in this chapter we are using CuSums on new data, in order to detect changes. With past data there is no problem over scaling the chart, as we can simply scale appropriately. With new data, some convention on scaling is necessary and we discuss this next. An estimate of σ_e is needed, and this may be relatively straightforward, if it is appropriate to use $\hat{\sigma}_w/\sqrt{n}$, or may involve the use of one of the methods of estimation discussed in Chapter 3 or 6. We shall assume that an estimate of σ_e of the standard error of the points is available.

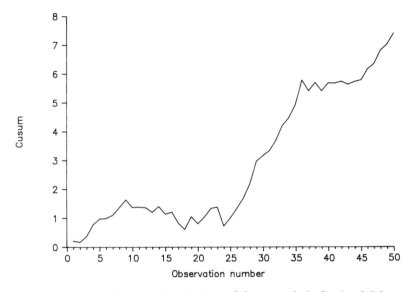

Figure 7.1 A CuSum plot for the data of the example in Section 3.5.3.

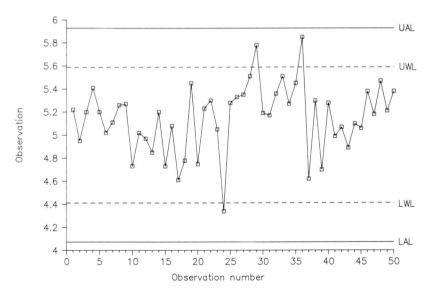

Figure 7.2 A time plot of the capsule weights given on page 51 but with 0.24 g added to each of the last 25 observations.

7.1.2 Choice of scale for plotting a CuSum

Visual interpretation of CuSum charts is very important. To make this as easy as possible we require a good choice for the relationship between the scales of the horizontal and vertical axes. The following is recommended for most applications, although there may sometimes be good reasons for choosing other relationships. The idea behind this rule is that inclinations of 45° are easiest to see, so we try and arrange that shifts likely to be of importance, that is shifts of the mean of about $2\sigma_e$, have an inclination of about 45°. The rule is set out in Method Summary 7.1 (Fig. 7.3).

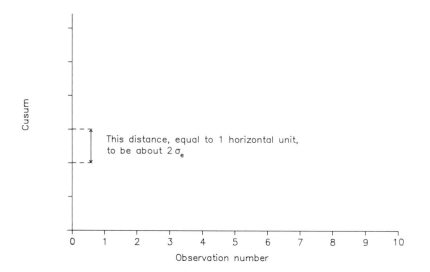

Figure 7.3 Scaling a CuSum chart.

METHOD SUMMARY 7.1

Scaling a CuSum plot

Step 1   Choose any convenient interval for the horizontal axis (sample index number, days, batches, etc.)

Step 2   Mark off one unit of this interval on the vertical scale (cumulative sum).

Step 3   Let this distance represent approximately $2\sigma_e$ units, where σ_e is the standard error of the observations on which the CuSum is calculated. (Since it is important that the scale

should be easy to use, then in practice this distance
represents a round number between $1\sigma_e$ and $3\sigma_e$ units.)

Even with a good choice of scale there are sometimes problems in
plotting when the CuSum plot moves off the top or the bottom of the
chart. The absolute position of the chart is not important; it can all be
shifted up or down on the page without affecting its properties or the
conclusions to be drawn. So for some appropriate earlier sampling point
define a new starting point for the CuSum (this may or may not be
zero). Calculate and plot all subsequent values from this point, in
parallel with the original (see Fig. 7.4). Drop the original plot when this
seems appropriate. Alternatively, the plot may be drifting because the
target value used for calculation is not the same as the process mean. In
this case it may be that a different target value should be used.
However, this depends on the use to which the plot is to be put.

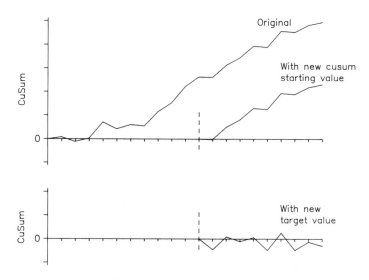

Figure 7.4 Coping with CuSums going off the chart.

7.1.3 V-masks for CuSums to control process average level

Shewhart charts are used with a simple *decision rule* (the action and
warning lines) to see when the process is out of control, requiring
corrective action, and when the process should be left alone.

CuSums can also be used with decision rules to decide when a shift in
process average has occurred. The simplest CuSum decision rule uses a

truncated V-mask. The International Standard suggests a 'standard mask', but others can be constructed, and their design will be discussed later. The mask is shown in Fig. 7.5. The datum point A is placed on the latest CuSum value, and an out of control signal is given when the previous trace crosses the arms of the mask. The vertical half-distance, AB or AC is termed the *decision interval*, $H = h\sigma_e$. The two sloping lines, BD, CE, are the *decision lines*. They may be extended indefinitely beyond D or E if required.

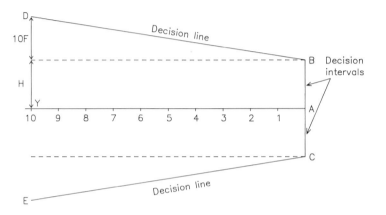

Figure 7.5 Truncated V-mask for CuSum charts.

In the standard V-mask $h = 5$ and $f = \frac{1}{2}$, so that the decision interval H is $5\sigma_e$. The slope of the arms is then determined by setting the distance $F = \frac{1}{2}\sigma_e$, so that $DY = YE = 10\sigma_e$, where Y is 10 sample intervals before the datum point A. Other possible choices for h and f will be discussed later.

Notice that a line of constant slope less than that of the arms of the mask will never cross the mask, so that the slopes of the arms relate to minimum 'interesting' changes in the mean. The 'decision interval' H allows for some random scatter about the plot.

METHOD SUMMARY 7.2

Setting up a CuSum V-mask

Step 1   Scale your plot as in Method Summary 7.1.

Step 2   Draw a vertical line equal to a distance $2H$ on your chosen scale. Draw a horizontal line through the middle of this.

Step 3   Move back 10 steps, and draw a vertical line of length

$(2H + 20F)$, centred on the same horizontal line as in Step 2.

Step 4   Join up your points to make a V-mask. Transfer this to a piece of acetate sheet for use as you plot data.

Using the V-mask

The method of using the V-mask is given in Method Summary 7.3; see Fig. 7.6. Obviously the shift in mean may have occurred some time before it is signalled. Estimation of the point of change and of its magnitude can be made from the CuSum chart, by simply looking to see when the chart changed its slope.

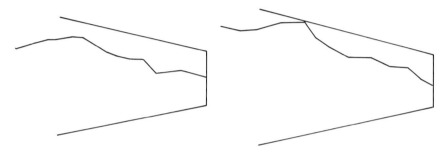

Figure 7.6 Use of a V-mask.

METHOD SUMMARY 7.3

Using a CuSum V-mask

Step 1   Plot the latest points on your graph, using Method Summary 3.2, with the estimated mean as reference value.

Step 2   Put the centre point of the truncated V-mask on the latest datum.

Step 3   If the lower arm (or its extension) crosses the trace, an increase in mean is signalled.

Step 4   If the upper arm (or its extension) crosses the trace, decrease in mean is signalled.

7.1.4 Average run lengths and comparison of charts for control of process average level

If a large change in mean occurs it will cause a large average change in gradient of the CuSum, which in turn will lead to a rapid decision. A smaller change in mean will generally have to persist for much longer before it is detected. If the process is on target all the time only a very unusual pattern of random behaviour will cause the CuSum to cross the decision lines, so that the average run length will be large. The ARL curve of the standard CuSum scheme is given in Fig. 7.7. (For the SN reference in the chart see the reference to the 'snub-nosed' scheme below.)

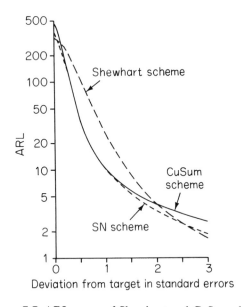

Figure 7.7 ARL curve of Shewhart and CuSum chart.

As there are many possible choices of the parameters h and f of the V-mask, leading to different ARL curves, it is difficult to compare CuSum and Shewhart schemes precisely. However, the standard CuSum V-mask can be thought of as a good equivalent to the ordinary Sherwhart chart with either 'probability' or 'popular' limits. Figure 7.7 also shows the ARL curve for the Shewhart chart with probability limits. The comparison between these ARL curves is a good general summary of the comparison between Shewhart and CuSum charts. The following observations are useful.

If the process mean is:

(1) on target, the Shewhart chart is more likely to signal a warning than a CuSum chart;

(2) between about $\frac{1}{2}\sigma_e$ and $1\frac{1}{2}\sigma_e$ from the target, the CuSum chart detects this much more quickly than the Shewhart chart;
(3) more than 3σ from the target, the Shewhart chart often detects this more quickly than CuSum chart. (It may take at least two or three observations on a CuSum to spot a slope, whereas one very bad point can signal action on a Shewhart chart.)

Clearly the CuSum chart has much better properties than the Shewhart chart *except* for very large changes in mean. However, this can itself be compensated for by using different shapes for the V-mask; see section 7.1.5.

7.1.5 Alternative shapes for the mask

Bissell (1979) showed that some improvement in the ARL properties of the CuSum scheme can be obtained by using a semi-parabolic mask, shown in Fig. 7.8; see Table 7.1. The ARL curve in Fig. 7.7 shows greatly improved properties.

Rowlands *et al.* (1982) showed that a much simpler and almost equivalent procedure is to superimpose two or more V-masks, as shown in Fig. 7.9, leading to a snub-nosed V-mask. They conclude their studies by showing that superimposing two masks is enough to achieve nearly optimal results. Some of the results in Table 7.2 are drawn from Rowlands *et al.* (1982). We see that the ordinary V-mask gives very good ARL properties over a limited range of values for shifts of the mean. The semi-parabolic mask has good properties over a wider range, but the snub-nosed scheme is as good, and is easier to operate; see section 7.1.7. The snub-nosed scheme (2), which superimposes ($h = 5$, $f = 0.5$) with ($h = 2.05$, $f = 1.3$) is a good equivalent of the ordinary Shewhart charts for ordinary use. Alternatively, the snub-nosed scheme (3) has a slightly higher on-target ARL.

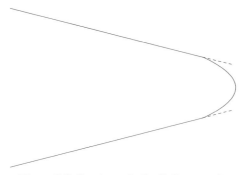

Figure 7.8 Semi-parabolic CuSum mask.

Table 7.1 ARL values for some CuSum and Shewhart schemes

Shift in average from target (units of σ_e)	Shewhart charts		CuSum schemes		SN	Snub-nosed V-mask		
	Probability limits	Popular limits	(1)	(2)		(1)	(2)	(3)
0	320.0	278.0	232	232	232	232	300	350
0.5	108.0	100.6	30.0	58	36	32	36	37
1.0	26.4	25.6	9.0	13.1	9.8	9.3	10.1	10.2
1.5	8.9	8.8	5.1	5.2	5.2	5.0	5.3	5.4
2.0	4.1	4.1	3.6	3.0	3.3	3.3	3.3	3.4
2.5	2.46	2.41	2.77	2.16	2.25	2.31	2.34	2.5
3.0	1.75	1.70	2.31	1.69	1.70	1.76	1.83	1.90
3.5	1.39	1.35	2.03	1.40	1.39	1.46	1.49	1.54
4.0	1.19	1.17	1.82	1.21	1.19	1.23	1.26	1.30

Notes: (1) CuSum scheme (1) is $h = 4.31$, $f = 0.5$.
(2) CuSum scheme (2) is $h = 2.07$, $f = 1.1$.
(3) The snub-nosed V-mask scheme (1) superimposes ($h = 4.66$, $f = 0.5$) with ($h = 1.89$, $f = 1.4$).
(4) The snub-nosed V-mask scheme (2) superimposes ($h = 5$, $f = 0.5$) with ($h = 2.05$, $f = 1.3$).
(5) The snub-nosed V-mask scheme (3) superimposes ($h = 5$, $f = 0.5$) with ($h = 2.2$, $f = 1.3$).

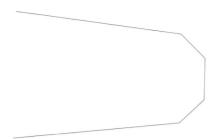

Figure 7.9 Snub-nosed V-mask.

Table 7.2 Parameters for constructing a semi-parabolic CuSum mask

Distance from datum (sample intervals) i	Half-width of mask at i (units of σ_e) Y	
0	1.25	
1	3.1	
2	4.65	$Y = 1.25 + 2i - 0.15i^2$
3	5.9	
4	6.85	
5	7.5	
6	8.0	
7	8.5	
8	9.0	$Y = 5 + 0.5i$
9	9.5	
10	10.0	
15	12.5	
20	15.0	

Note: The equations may be used for construction of the mask if required.

7.1.6 Sample size and sampling frequency

All the above discussion has been in terms of σ_e, the standard error of sample means. The sample of size n is drawn at intervals from the process, and provided there is no additional between-group variability the value of n determines the actual sensitivity of the CuSum, since,

$$\sigma_e = \frac{\sigma_w}{\sqrt{n}}$$

σ_w being the standard deviation of process variability.

In addition, it must be said that all ARL values above depend quite critically on the assumption that the sample means have a Normal distribution. There is no guarantee that this is indeed true for the individual values from the process, but we stated in Chapter 2 that the central limit theorem operates to confer normality on averages. To ensure this it is thought that there should be a minimum of 4 in the sample, or more if it is known that there is evidence of appreciable non-normality in the distribution of individual observations. With this as a lower bound, we can choose a sample size based on the following reasoning. The ARL at $1.5\sigma_e$ is seen to be about 6 on Fig. 7.7. If we choose n so that $1.5\sigma_e$ is the smallest change of importance, this will give us an ARL of about 6.

Let M be the actual change in level of mean that is important. Then choose n so that

$$M \simeq 1.5\sigma_e$$

that is

$$n \simeq \left[\frac{1.5\sigma_w}{M}\right]^2$$

Let the minimum length of time for which such a change might persist, or the time for which it is tolerable, be D. Choose a sampling interval $\leqslant D/6$. Clearly, either or both of these requirements may need modifying depending on cost and practicality.

For one-at-a-time data, or data where there is substantial between-group variability, the only flexibility we might have is in the sampling frequency. If we assume that a change of $1.5\sigma_e$ has an ARL of about 6, we can adjust the sampling frequency accordingly. Extra care needs to be taken over non-normality for one-at-a-time data.

7.1.7 The decision interval scheme for a CuSum

The plotted CuSum using a V-mask is an excellent visual device. However, it may be necessary to computerize the maintenance of CuSums, and the decision-interval scheme allows this and is *exactly* equal to the plotted CuSum above. (For the snub-nose CuSum scheme, two of the following decision interval schemes have to be superimposed.) The procedure is detailed in Method Summary 7.4.

The scheme works for a one-sided test, so two decision interval schemes must be operated to check for increases or decreases in the mean. The basic idea is to cumulate a sum using a specially chosen reference value, and ignore negative values of this score (for increases in the mean). That is, we calculate

$$S_{i+1} = \max\{0, S_i + (\text{obs.} - \text{reference})\}.$$

In the description of Method Summary 7.4, the decision interval, h and slope, f, are as defined in section 7.1.3, but the use of these parameters is slightly different.

METHOD SUMMARY 7.4

Decision interval CuSum schemes

Step 1 Set $K_1 = T + F$
Set $K_2 = T - F$
where T is the reference value used for a CuSum plot, and $F = f\sigma_e$ is the slope of the arms of the V-mask.

To detect increases in process average level:

Step 2 Set CuSum C1 at zero.

Step 3 Accumulate the CuSum using K_1 as reference value.
If the CuSum becomes *negative* return to Step 2.
If the CuSum reaches or exceeds the decision interval $H = h\sigma_e$ this constitutes an *action* signal.

To detect decreases in process average level:

Step 4 Set CuSum C2 at zero.

Step 5 Accumulate the CuSum using K_2 as reference value.
If the CuSum becomes *positive* return to Step 4.
If the CuSum reaches or falls below the value $-H$ this constitutes an *action* signal.

CuSums for increase and for decrease in the mean can be run simultaneously.

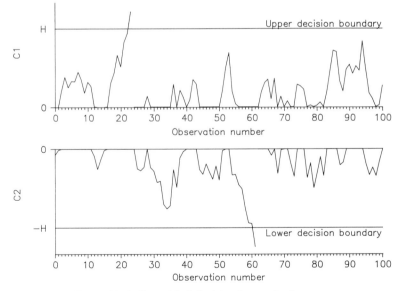

Figure 7.10 Two-sided decision interval scheme.

If a two-sided decision interval scheme is calculated and plotted, it will look something like Fig. 7.10. A worked example for a one-sided scheme will clarify it.

Worked example

As an example we return to the data given in Table 3.3, but with 0.24 added to the last 25 values. The target value for this data was 5.0 and the standard deviation 0.3. Some of the calculations are given in Table 7.3; check these values. The plot for detecting increases in the mean is shown in Fig. 7.11; the plot for detecting decreases in the mean can also be made but does not signal action.

Clearly the ordinary CuSum plot has the better visual impact, but the decision interval scheme is easier on a computer. One solution is to use the decision interval scheme until action is signalled, and then get a retrospective plot of the last 50 or 100 data points.

Table 7.3 Calculations for the decision interval scheme

$$
\left.\begin{array}{l} T = 5.0 \\ \sigma_e = 0.3 \\ h = 5 \\ f = \frac{1}{2} \end{array}\right\} \quad \rightarrow \quad \left\{\begin{array}{l} K_1 = 5.15 \\ K_2 = 4.85 \\ H = 1.5 \end{array}\right.
$$

Observation	C1	C2
5.22	0.07	0
4.95	0	0
5.20	0.05	0
5.41	0.31	0
5.20	0.36	0
5.02	0.23	0
5.11	0.19	0
5.26	0.30	0
5.27	0.42	0
4.73	0	−0.12
5.02	0	0
4.97	0	0
4.85	0	0
5.20	0.05	0
4.73	0	−0.12

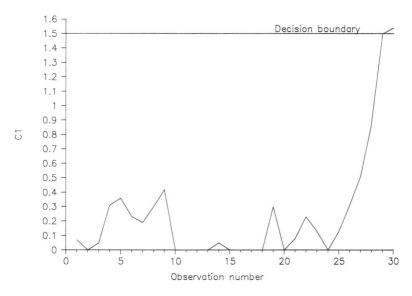

Figure 7.11 Decision interval CuSum plot for the data of page 51, with 0.24 added to the last 25 data points.

7.1.8 Equivalence of CuSum plot and decision interval CuSum schemes

In order to see the equivalence, consider a trace which crosses the lower arm of the V-mask, as in Fig. 7.12.

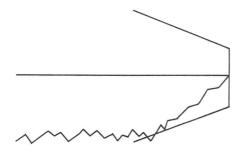

Figure 7.12 Intersection of lower arm of V-mask.

The arm of the V-mask has slope F. If the increment to the CuSum plot $(x - T)$ is less than F, this is less than the slope of the V-mask and there will never be a signal. On the decision interval scheme (for increases in the mean), there will never be any signal if $(x - K_1)$ remains negative. These statements are equivalent if $K_1 = T + F$.

A signal is given on the CuSum plot if for any s,

$$\sum_{t-s}^{t}(x - T) > sF + H.$$

This is equivalent to

$$\sum_{t-s}^{t}(x - T - F) > H$$

which is the rule used in the decision interval scheme. The two schemes are therefore exactly equivalent (the result for schemes for decreases in the mean follow in a similar way).

The above argument can be extended to see intuitively why the V-mask works. A change of mean level means a change in inclination of the trace. The V-mask detects changes of slope, but the decision interval allows for a certain amount of random scatter about the trace. For a large change in the mean, the slope of the trace will be steep, and only a few observations will be required to reach an action point. If the change in the mean is small, the slope of the trace will be low, and a large number of observations are required to reach action.

7.1.9 Comparison of CuSum with some other charting methods

Table 7.4 shows a comparison of ARLs of CuSum schemes with exponetially weighted moving-average or arithmetic running-mean charts. In fact the EWMA chart with $p = \frac{1}{4}$ and the running-mean chart with $k = 4$ are not the best ones possible, but are the ones available in the paper by Roberts (1966). It is in fact possible to construct such charts with similar ARL properties to CuSum charts at specified deviations of the mean from target, but p or k must be chosen in advance. With the CuSum chart, no such prior choice is necessary, and the plot works well for a range of deviations of the mean from target.

Table 7.4 ARL values for given deviations from the target value

Deviation from target value (multiples of $\hat{\sigma}_e$)	EWMA (Geometric mean) $p = \frac{1}{4}$	Arithmetic running mean $k = 4$	CuSum schemes $h = \pm 2.0\sigma$ $f = \pm 1.31\sigma$	$h = \pm 5.0\sigma$ $f = \pm 0.50\sigma$
0	480.0	480.0	480.0	480.0
0.5	46.0	72.0	117.0	37.0
1.0	5.3	5.8	6.9	5.9
2.0	3.6	3.7	3.7	4.3
2.5	2.7	2.9	2.4	3.5

7.1.10 Summary of the advantages and disadvantages of CuSum

(a) *Advantages*
(1) Improvement in efficiency over Shewhart in region $0.5\sigma_e$ to $2.0\sigma_e$. ARL properties above $2\sigma_e$ greatly improved by using semi-parabolic or snub-nosed mask.
(2) Change in mean detected visually by change in slope.
(3) Point of change located easily – useful in determining cause of change.
(4) Use when measurement is moderately/very expensive and simplicity is not so important.
(5) Can be used when observations are available singly.

(b) *Disadvantages*
(1) More complex to use.
(2) If there are lots of charts either different V-masks are required, or inconvenient scales will be used for some charts.
(3) When the process mean changes, then either the CuSum runs off the chart, or else the target value is changed and the chart is discontinuous. In either case other changes are less obvious. (This can be a problem with the analysis of past data.)
(4) Changes in the process mean are detected most easily when the CuSum is usually running level. If the CuSum shows a small change in the mean, and no adjustment is made, changes are less easy to spot.
(5) Do not use CuSum when measurements are cheap and extreme simplicity is required (saved cost of CuSum may 'buy' increased sample size/frequency).

7.2 CuSum CHARTS FOR CONTROL OF AVERAGE LEVEL

7.2.1 Parameters for the six alternative standard CuSum decision rules

The basic CuSum scheme, with $h = 5$, $f = 0.5$ is a very good one to use if we wish to detect changes in mean of between $0.75\sigma_e$ and $1.5\sigma_e$ from the target value quickly, and yet have long ARLs (say 700–1000) when the process is actually on target. But in practice we may be more concerned about a different size of departure from target, or may be prepared to accept more frequent false alarms in order to achieve earlier detection of real change.

We shall define the following:

L_a is the ARL when the process is running at a mean of μ_a, the acceptable quality level (process average/target value);

L_r is the ARL when the process is at the rejectable quality level μ_r;

$\mu_r - \mu_a$ is then the critical shift from the target value.

The International Standard gives six alternative sets of h, f which optimize the performance of the chart for critical shifts of different sizes. Half of these – the C1 schemes – ensure that L_a is quite high, while the other half – C2 schemes have a much lower ARL when the process is actually on target. The parameters are shown in Table 7.5, and the masks are shown in Fig. 7.13.

Table 7.5 CuSum parameters for alternative decision rules

Critical shift from target, in units of standard error (σ_e)	C1 schemes (L_a 700–1000)		C2 schemes (L_a 140–200)	
	h	f	h	f
(a) < 0.75	8	0.25	5	0.25
(b) 0.75 to 1.5	5	0.50	3.5	0.5
(c) > 1.5	2.5	1.0	1.8	1.0

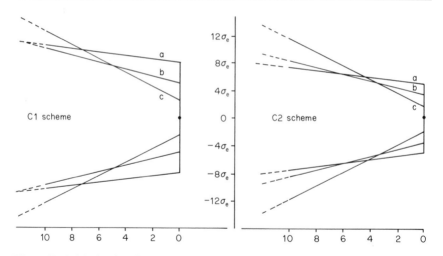

Figure 7.13 Masks for C1 and C2 schemes. Extracts from British Standards are reproduced with the permission of BSI.

A comparison of ARLs is made among the three C1 schemes and with S1 (Shewhart chart with action and warning limits at $3.09\sigma_e$ and $1.96\sigma_e$ respectively). The three C2 schemes are compared among themselves and with S2 (Shewhart chart with action and warning limits of $2.65\sigma_e$ and $1.65\sigma_e$ respectively). These are shown in Table 7.6. The

Table 7.6 Average run length data for alternative decision rules. Extracts from British Standards are reproduced with the permission of BSI

Shift from targets in units of σ_e	C1 scheme					C2 scheme			
	(a)	(b)	SPM	(c)	S1	(a)	(b)	(c)	S2
0	730	930	(470)	715	640	140	200	170	167
0.25	85	140	(113)	205	256	38	55	68	76
0.5	29	38	(35)	68	126	17	22	30	38
0.75	16.4	17	(16.5)	27	52	10.5	11.5	15	20
1.0	11.4	10.5	(10)	13.4	26	7.4	7.4	8.8	11
1.5	7.1	5.8	(5.3)	5.4	8.9	4.7	4.3	4.0	5.0
2.0	5.2	4.1	(3.4)	3.25	4.15	3.5	3.0	2.5	2.8
2.5	4.2	3.2	(2.3)	2.3	2.46	2.8	2.4	1.9	1.86
3.0	3.5	2.6	(1.74)	1.85	1.75	2.4	2.0	1.5	1.44
4.0	2.6	1.9	(1.21)	1.32	1.19	1.9	1.5	1.12	1.09

ARL, given in this table are calculated on a one-sided basis. The boxed regions show the regions in which the ARLs are good relative to the others.

In section 7.4, as an appendix to this chapter, nomograms are included for designing other CuSum schemes with specific characteristics. However, it is anticipated that the six given above will probably be sufficient for a majority of cases, and that in practice C1 (b) will often be found to be the most useful. If so, there is the great advantage that, provided scaling is carried out as described in section 7.1.2, the masks used for different charts will be very similar or identical. Users will then develop a feel for the look of an in-control chart which is very useful in diagnosing trouble.

7.2.2 Summary of steps for setting up CuSum charts for control of average level

We shall assume that the set-up phase (see section 5.1) has been completed to the point where we have decided to use a CuSum chart and need to select and set up the particular chart for use.

METHOD SUMMARY 7.5

Setting up CuSum charts

Step 1 Obtain data from the capability study or as fresh data. Inspect the data for special causes of variation. Test for Normality.

Step 2 Estimate σ_e, the standard error of group means (if these are plotted) or of individual values. See sections 3.6, 3.7 and 6.2 for a full discussion.

Step 3 Choose a suitable reference value T, using one of
(1) the value of $\hat{\mu}$ obtained from the data of Step 1;
(2) an (achievable) target value.

Step 4 Choose one of the six standard sets of parameters h and f (see section 7.2.1). If in doubt use the standard scheme $h = 5$, $f = 0.5$.

Step 5 Choose between a CuSum plot or a decision interval scheme. The two schemes are exactly equivalent in their ARL properties.

Step 6a CuSum plot.
Set up the scale of the chart (section 7.1.2) and draw the V-mask (section 7.1.3) using $\hat{\sigma}_e$, h and f.
Calculate and plot the CuSum with reference value T.

Step 6b   Decision interval scheme

Calculate the CuSum C1 with reference value $K_1 = T + f\hat{\sigma}_e$. Keep it non-negative.

Calculate the CuSum C2 with reference value $K_2 = T - f\hat{\sigma}_e$. Keep it non-positive.

Action is signalled if the size of either reaches or exceeds $h = h\sigma_e$.

Note

A degree of non-normality is not critical with grouped data, but more serious with one-at-a-time data

---

(a) *Chart interpretation*

When the plot goes over the lower (or upper) arm of the V-mask, there is evidence that the process average level has increased (or decreased). A search for an assignable cause of variation should then be made.

The time at which the process started to change is seen on the chart, and the slope of the chart shows the new process average.

Erratic behaviour of the chart probably indicates that the process spread has increased.

(b) *Replotting*

Periodically it will be necessary to revise a CuSum chart because of a change in the process average level or the process spread.

7.2.3 Observations one-at-a-time

CuSum charts are particularly valuable for the case where observations occur one at a time, such as one per shift, one per hour, etc. In that case our usual estimate of σ cannot be used, but the methods given in sections 3.7 and 6.2 can be used to estimate σ_e. Fig. 7.14 shows a typical example of one-at-a-time data; in this case oil content has been determined for successive batches of product.

7.3 CuSum CHARTS FOR CONTROL OF PROCESS SPREAD

7.3.1 The distribution of ranges or standard deviations

As with the Shewhart charts for control of process spread, there is both a range and standard deviation method available here, but there is also a third method, based upon a transformation.

The difficulty with CuSum charts for process spread is that for realistic sample sizes the distribution of range or standard deviation estimates is skew, as shown in Fig. 7.15.

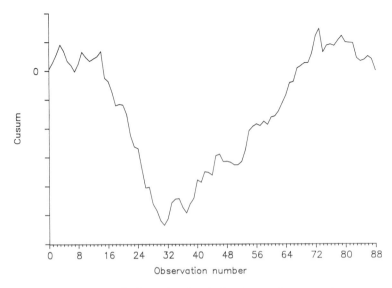

Figure 7.14 CuSum plot for single observation example.

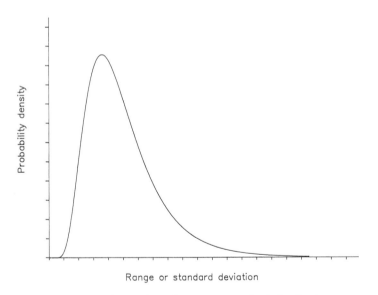

Figure 7.15 Distribution of range or standard distribution.

This means that, if we consider differences of range from its average, then the increases in this range are much larger than the decreases. As a result of this, we ought really to use CuSum charts with asymmetrical arms. However, as *increases* in σ are what we are looking for, usually only the *lower* arm is used; see Fig. 7.16. If we do use a *symmetrical* mask based on the parameter values to follow, then tests for decreases in σ as shown by the mask are somewhat conservative, especially for very small group sizes.

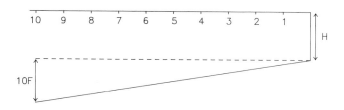

Figure 7.16 Mask for range chart.

As with Shewhart charts, non-Normality has a much greater effect on charts for range or s.d. than it does on $\overline{X}$-charts, and a test for Normality of the original data is important before setting up the charts.

The three methods are described first, then we discuss the choice.

7.3.2 CuSum scheme for ranges

METHOD SUMMARY 7.6

CuSum scheme for ranges

Step 1 Collect at least 20 groups of n observations each, where n is usually between 4 and 6. Test the data for Normality, using a Normal plot or otherwise.

Step 2a Calculate the range of each group, and the average range over the groups.

$$\overline{R} = (\text{sum of group ranges})/(\text{no. of groups}).$$

Use this as the target value R_T.

Step 2b Alternatively, estimate the within-group standard deviation, $\hat{\sigma}_w$ and set $R_T = d_n \hat{\sigma}_w$; see Table 2.9 for values of d_n.

Step 3 Choose whether to use a C1 or a C2 scheme. (See Table 7.8 for ARL properties.)

Step 4a Scale the vertical axis so that one horizontal unit represents approximately $a_n R_T$. Construct a mask (lower arm only) with parameters

$$H = hR_\mathrm{T} \qquad \text{decision interval}$$

$$F = fR_\mathrm{T} \qquad \text{slope of decision line}$$

where a_n, h and f are taken from Table 7.7. Use R_T as the reference value for the CuSum.

Step 4b Alternatively, operate a one-sided decision interval scheme, (see section 7.1.6) with parameters

$$H = hR_\mathrm{T} \qquad \text{decision interval}$$

$$F = kR_\mathrm{T} \qquad \text{reference value}$$

where h and k are taken from Table 7.7.

Notes

(1) Group sizes must be constant to run this chart.
(2) Normality should be checked periodically.

Table 7.7 CuSum schemes for range in samples from a Normal population. Extracts from British Standards are reproduced with the permission of BSI

Sample size, n		2	3	4	5	6	8	10
d_n		1.128	1.693	2.059	2.326	2.534	2.847	3.078
a_n		1.5	1.0	0.85	0.75	0.65	0.55	0.5
C1	h	2.5	1.75	1.25	1.0	0.85	0.55	0.5
	k	1.85	1.55	1.5	1.45	1.45	1.4	1.35
	f	0.85	0.55	0.5	0.45	0.45	0.4	0.35
C2	h	2.5	1.75	1.25	1.0	0.85	0.55	0.5
	k	1.55	1.35	1.3	1.3	1.3	1.25	1.25
	f	0.55	0.35	0.3	0.3	0.3	0.25	0.25

Table 7.8 ARL data for CuSum range schemes. Extracts from British Standards are reproduced with the permission of BSI

Sample size	Type of scheme	ARLs for mean range at stated multiples of $\bar{k}$							
		1.0	1.12	1.25	1.6	2.0	2.5	3.2	4.0
2	C1	779	170	66	16	7.2	4.3	3.0	2.3
	C2	170	63	30	10	5.5	3.6	2.7	2.1
3	C1	893	165	49	9.6	4.5	2.8	2.0	1.6
	C2	196	52	21	6.5	3.6	2.4	1.8	1.5
4	C1	918	145	39	7.1	3.3	2.1	1.6	1.30
	C2	157	39	15	4.7	2.7	1.9	1.46	1.24

Table 7.8 (*cont.*)

Sample size	Type of scheme	ARLs for mean range at stated multiples of $\bar{k}$							
		1.0	1.12	1.25	1.6	2.0	2.5	3.2	4.0
5	C1	771	116	30	5.6	2.7	1.8	1.36	1.16
	C2	179	39	14	4.0	2.3	1.6	1.30	1.13
6	C1	942	131	31	5.0	2.4	1.6	1.26	1.10
	C2	204	40	13	3.6	2.0	1.45	1.20	1.07
8	C1	893	111	25	4.0	2.0	1.37	1.13	1.04
	C2	162	29	10	2.8	1.7	1.26	1.09	1.02
10	C1	635	77	17	3.2	1.7	1.22	1.07	1.01
	C2	184	30	9.2	2.6	1.52	1.17	1.05	1.01

(a) *Interpretation of the chart*

For a CuSum plot scheme, there is evidence that the process spread has increased when the lower arm of the mask cuts the plot on chart. A search for an assignable cause of variation should then be made.

(b) *Assumptions*

This chart assumes:

(1)   that the underlying distribution is Normal;
(2)   that the groups are of equal size;
(3)   that points are weighted equally.

All methods of control of process spread are sensitive to Normality. Periodically, a Normal plot should be made, by the method given in Chapter 2. If there is any doubt, a statistician should be consulted. It could be that a simple transformation of the data, such as square root or logarithm, will render the data Normal.

It is difficult to take account of varying group sizes in a CuSum plot, and this is one of the limitations of the scheme.

7.3.3 CuSum scheme for standard deviations

METHOD SUMMARY 7.7

CuSum scheme for standard deviations

Step 1   Collect at least 20 groups of n observations each, where n is usually between 4 and 6. Test the data for Normality.

Step 2   Calculate the standard deviation s_i for each group. Calculate the estimate of σ_w, using the formula

$$\hat{\sigma}_w = \sqrt{[(\textstyle\sum(n_i - 1)s_i^2)/(\sum(n_i - 1))]}.$$

Step 3   Choose between the C1 and C2 schemes. (A table of ARL properties is given in Table 7.10.)

Step 4a   Scale the vertical axis so that one horizontal unit represents approximately $a_n \hat{\sigma}_w$. Construct a mask (lower arm only) with parameters

$$H = h\hat{\sigma}_w \qquad\qquad \text{decision interval}$$

$$F = f\hat{\sigma}_w \qquad\qquad \text{slope of decision line}$$

where a_n, h and f are obtained from Table 7.9. Use $\hat{\sigma}_w$ as the reference value for the CuSum.

Step 4b   Alternatively, operate a decision interval scheme (see section 7.1.6), with parameters

$$H = h\hat{\sigma}_w$$

$$K = k\hat{\sigma}_w$$

where h and k are taken from Table 7.9.

Notes
(1) Group sizes can vary a little.
(2) Normality should be checked periodically.

Table 7.9 CuSum schemes for standard deviation in samples from a Normal population. Extracts from British Standards are reproduced with the permission of BSI

Sample size, n	2	3	4	5	6	8	10	12	15	20
a_n		1.5	1.0	0.85	0.75	0.65	0.55	0.5	0.45	0.4	0.35
C1 h		2.0	1.6	1.15	0.9	0.8	0.6	0.5	0.4	0.35	0.3
C1 k		1.5	1.35	1.35	1.35	1.32	1.3	1.3	1.3	1.27	1.23
C1 f		0.5	0.35	0.35	0.35	0.32	0.3	0.3	0.3	0.27	0.23
C2 h		2.0	1.6	1.15	0.9	0.8	0.6	0.5	0.4	0.35	0.3
C2 k		1.25	1.15	1.2	1.2	1.2	1.2	1.2	1.2	1.18	1.16
C2 f		0.25	0.15	0.2	0.2	0.2	0.2	0.2	0.2	0.18	0.16

Table 7.10 ARL data for deviation schemes. Extracts from British Standards are reproduced with the permission of BSI

Sample size	Type of scheme	ARLs at stated multiples of the set standard deviation							
		1.0	1.12	1.25	1.6	2.0	2.5	3.2	4.0
2	C1	920	190	72	16	7.4	4.4	3.0	2.3
	C2	185	67	32	10	5.6	3.7	2.6	2.1
3	C1	920	160	48	9.4	4.4	2.8	2.0	1.6
	C2	155	43	19	6.7	3.7	2.4	1.8	1.5
4	C1	840	130	35	6.6	3.2	2.1	1.5	1.28
	C2	180	41	16	4.7	2.6	1.8	1.4	1.23
5	C1	820	110	28	5.2	2.6	1.7	1.31	1.14
	C2	155	33	12	3.7	2.2	1.5	1.24	1.11
6	C1	850	99	23	4.3	2.2	1.5	1.20	<1.1
	C2	190	33	11	3.3	1.9	1.4	1.15	<1.1
8	C1	720	74	17	3.2	1.7	1.25	<1.1	→1
	C2	180	27	8.7	2.6	1.55	1.19	<1.1	→1
10	C1	930	78	15	2.8	1.5	1.15	→1	→1
	C2	200	25	7.6	2.2	1.4	1.10	→1	→1
12	C1	840	67	13	2.3	1.33	<1.1	→1	→1
	C2	170	21	6.3	1.9	1.23	<1.1	→1	→1
15	C1	860	56	9.7	2.0	1.20	<1.1	→1	→1
	C2	170	18	5.2	1.6	1.13	→1	→1	→1
20	C1	810	40	6.9	1.6	<1.1	→1	→1	→1
	C2	166	17	4.6	1.37	<1.1	→1	→1	→1

7.3.4 CuSum scheme for standard deviations based on transformations

BS 5703, Part 3, section 7.5.2, gives a CuSum method for standard deviations based on the transformation

$$y = (s/\sigma)^{0.625}$$

which turns out to be nearly Normal for group sizes $n = 3$–20. See BS 5703 for values of the constants for charting.

7.3.5 Choice between plotting methods

The gain in efficiency by using CuSums for control of process spread is less than that for control of process average level, and Table 7.11 shows

Table 7.11 Average run length at different multiples of R_T for ranges in groups of size 4

Scheme	Multiples of R_T				
	1.0	1.12	1.25	1.6	2.0
C1	918	145	39	7.1	3.3
S1	640	138	44	8.1	3.4
C2	157	39	15	4.7	2.7
S2	166	49	20	5.2	2.7

a comparison of Shewhart and CuSum schemes for selected parameters. However, there is a substantial gain in visual interpretation. In addition, CuSum schemes enable us to estimate local averages, and to see more clearly when a given change in the process spread started.

For hand plotting, ranges have the advantage of simplicity. The standard deviation scheme is slightly more efficient, but more prone to errors in calculation for hand plotting.

7.3.6 Control of process spread with one-at-a-time data

For one-at-a-time data, suppose the observations are x_1, x_2, x_3, ..., then we *arbitrarily* break the data into *independent groups*, and obtain ranges or standard deviations of the groups. For example, if our data is

$$1.2 \quad 4.6 \quad 3.8 \quad 2.9 \quad 1.7 \quad 3.2$$

then for groups of size 2, and when using ranges, we have

	observations	4.6	3.8	3.2	*Note*
		$\underline{1.2}$	$\underline{2.9}$	$\underline{1.7}$	Independent groups!
		3.4	0.9	1.5	

and then proceed as in section 7.3.2. We would usually use group sizes in the range 2–6. A similar procedure holds for using standard deviations of the groups.

For grouped data where there is between-group variation an additional chart for spread should be set up using the method discussed above for one-at-a-time data, working on the group means.

7.4* NOMOGRAM FOR CuSums

The six sets of CuSum decision parameters (h, k) given Table 7.5 will be sufficient for most purposes. If other choices are required, Fig. 7.17 gives a nomogram, reprinted from Goel and Wu (1971), which should

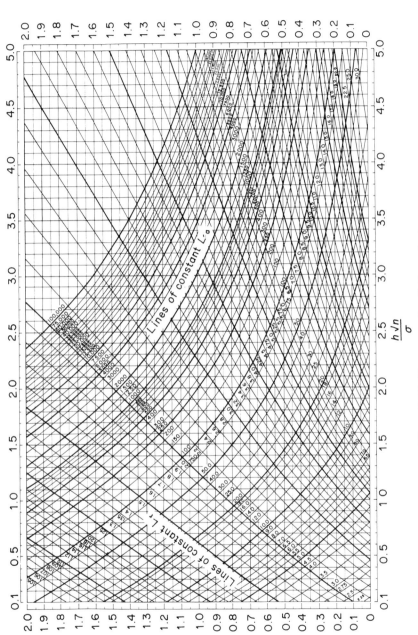

Figure 7.17 Nomogram for CuSum charts.

be used as given below. Suppose the observations are normally distributed with an unknown mean μ and a known or estimated standard deviation σ. The observations are sampled in groups of size n so that the standard error of the mean $\bar{x}$ is $\sigma/\sqrt{n}$.

METHOD SUMMARY 7.8

Design of one-sided CuSum scheme

Step 1   Choose an acceptable quality level (AQL), μ_a, and a desired ARL at this level, L_a. Also choose a rejectable quality level, μ_r, and a desired ARL at this level, L_r.

Step 2   Set the reference value $K = (\mu_a + \mu_r)/2$.

Step 3   Enter the contour nomogram at the intersection of L_a and L_r, and read off h' and f' from the vertical and horizontal axes.

Step 4   Calculate the implied value of $n' = (4f'^2\sigma^2)/(\mu_a - \mu_r)^2$. Round this up or down to an interger value n, and recalculate f, where

$$f = |\mu_a - \mu_r|\sqrt{n}/2\sigma.$$

Step 5   Re-enter the contour nomogram at this value of f, and read off a series of possibilities for L_a and corresponding h.

Step 6   Decide on a particular set of (h, f) to use from the sets of values arising from the two methods of rounding in Step 4.

Example 7.1

Suppose $\mu_a = 2.5$, $L_a = 600$, $\mu_r = 0$, $L_r = 6$ and $\sigma = 3.5$. Then $K = 1.25$, and we have $h' = 3.58$, $f = 0.67$. This leads to

$$n' = (4 \times 0.67^2 \times 3.5^2)/2.5^2 = 3.52.$$

For $n = 3$, $f = 0.62$ and we could have $L_a = 600$ with $h = 3.87$ and $L_r = 6.7$, or we could have $L_r = 6$ and $h = 3.32$, $L_a = 300$. A decision must be made between these values.

If the ARLs at the AQL and the RQL are not pre-specified, then the next Method Summary gives a suitable procedure.

METHOD SUMMARY 7.9

Design of one-sided CuSum scheme from limited information

Step 1   Given μ_a, μ_r and σ, calculate

$$f = |\mu_a - \mu_r|\sqrt{n}/2\sigma$$

for several suitable values of n (integral).

Step 2 Enter the nomogram at these values of f and tabulate alternative schemes.

Step 3 Choose between the sets of (h, f, n) given.

Example 7.2

For the values $\mu_u = 2.5$, $\mu_r = 0$, $\sigma = 3.5$ as in Example 7.1, the values in Table 7.12 can be obtained. A choice must be made between these options.

Table 7.12 Illustration of Method Summary 7.9

n	$f = |\mu_u - \mu_r|\sqrt{n}/2\sigma$	L_u	L_r	h
1	0.357	100	9.4	3.58
		200	11.7	4.41
2	0.505	100	6.0	2.83
		200	7.3	3.46
		300	8.0	3.89
3	0.619	100	4.6	2.44
		200	5.5	2.98
		300	6.0	3.32
		400	6.4	3.57

METHOD SUMMARY 7.10

Calculation of ARL curve of a one-sided CuSum scheme

Step 1 Given h, n, σ and reference value K, draw a vertical line at h, and obtain the L_a, L_r corresponding to

$$f = d\sqrt{n}/\sigma$$

for a series of values of d.

Step 2 For a scheme for detecting increases in the mean, the ARL is L_a at $(K - d)$ and L_r at $(K + d)$.

Example 7.3

For $h = 2.5$, $n = 1$, $\sigma = 1$, $K = 1$, the following ARL values are obtained:

μ	0	0.5	1.0	1.5	2.0
ARL	700	70	13.4	5.4	3.2

In order to use the nomogram, calculate the ARL of a two-sided CuSum scheme, using the formula

$$\frac{1}{L} = \frac{1}{L_u} + \frac{1}{L_l}$$

where L_u and L_l are the ARLs of the upper and lower schemes.

Although this nomogram has a limited range of h values, it is very accurate. For other nomograms, some with greater range, see Bissell (1969), BS 5703, and Kemp (1962).

EXERCISES 7A

1. Construct a standard V-mask from the initial data set used for the simulation exercise of Chapter 5.

   Continue the plot of a CuSum for the means of run A from that same process, applying the V-mask to each point as it is plotted. Stop when action is signalled, and note the run length. Look back at your CuSum plot and try to determine the point at which the chart first seemed to slope up or down (*not* necessarily the corner point).

   Repeat the above for process runs B, C and D. Compare the run lengths for each process run with those obtained for a Sherwhart $\bar{X}$ chart in Chapter 5. For a class exercise, compare the average run lengths. How much easier is it to detect the point of change with CuSum charts?

2. Carry out the decision interval scheme calculations for process run A of the data sets in Appendix B.

3. Draw the standard snub-nosed V-mask, and try it on the first few results from Set A of Question 1. Compare your results. For the first set, work out how to carry out this procedure by operating two parallel decision interval schemes.

4. The data in Table 7.13 were obtained one-at-a-time from a process.

Table 7.13

10.1	9.9	10.2	9.1	10.3	9.4	10.1	9.9	10.6	9.5	9.6	9.3	9.9	
9.2	10.2	8.7	9.8	10.4	11.1	10.2	10.1	10.5	9.2	10.1	10.8	10.3	
10.0	9.2	10.5	10.1	9.7	9.6	7.9	11.0	10.3	10.7	10.6	9.5	11.6	
11.7	10.1	9.3	10.7	9.2	8.8	9.4	11.2	9.4	8.8	11.9	9.3	11.8	
8.6	10.2	12.0	9.7	10.9	9.1	10.7	13.3	9.7	9.1	10.2	11.5	10.7	
8.3	11.9	7.0	8.0	11.5	8.7	9.8	7.6	11.6	10.6	7.1	9.8	9.1	
10.5	7.5	8.9	8.6	8.8	9.3	11.7	9.6	7.9	10.4	10.5	9.0		

The s.d. of this process when in control is estimated to be $\hat{\sigma}_w = 0.8$. Set up a CuSum decision interval scheme for ranges of 2 or 3 or 4 or 5 at a time, and determine when the process goes out of control.

5. Set up a CuSum scheme for standard deviation of groups of 2, 3, 4 or 5 at a time for the data given in Question 4.

EXERCISES 7B

1. Given $\mu_a = 120$, $L_a = 500$, $\mu_r = 124$, $L_r = 4$, $\sigma = 4$, determine a one-sided CuSum scheme.

2. If $\sigma = 1$ in Question 1, how closely can the requirements be achieved?

3. Given $n = 1$, $\sigma = 1$, find two-sided CuSum schemes corresponding to

   (a) $\mu_a = 0$, $L_a = 200$, $\mu_r = 2$, $L_r = 3$

   (b) $\mu_a = 0$, $L_a = 400$, $\mu_r = 2$, $L_r = 3$.

   Discuss the use of these and Example 7.3 as alternatives to a standard Shewhart chart, in place of the 'standard' V-mask.

4. Design a set of simulation trials to verify the ARL results for the snub-nosed V-mask given in section 7.1.5.

8*

Further theoretical results on control charts for continuous variables

8.1 INTRODUCTION

In this chapter we give some further theoretical results on properties of the charting methods. The derivation of run length properties of CuSum schemes is given, but it is convenient first to discuss some methods which give further information on the properties of Shewhart charts.

In practice there are several factors affecting the choice of charting methods:

(1) The run length distribution and average run length curve under simple distribution shift or scale changes. There is some evidence that most run length distributions are close to geometric, so that interest centres on the ARL curve.

(2) Ease of use and interpretation. Control charts have to be used by factory staff, management, and others who are not trained statistically. Some charts, such as the CuSum, are not used as frequently as they might be because of the complexities of use and interpretation. For a similar reason, extra rules to improve the power of the Shewhart chart are also less frequently used than they might be.

(3) Sensitivity to departures from assumptions. Most charting methods assume independent and identically distributed normal random variables. While the $\bar{X}$ chart is reasonably robust to departures from normality, charts for control of process spread are not, and when there are specification limits (see Chapter 9) normality can be important. Further, there are often serial correlations or cyclic patterns in industrial data, and the effects of these need to be investigated.

(4) The power of various charts to detect more complex patterns than simple shift or scale changes.

It is perhaps surprising that there are a number of gaps in our current knowledge of these points.

8.2 THE EFFECT OF DEPARTURES FROM ASSUMPTION ON MOMENTS OF $\bar{x}$ AND s^2

Suppose we have independent random variables X_1, X_2 ..., with $E(X) = \mu$, $V(X) = \sigma^2$, and coefficients of skewness and kurtosis γ_1 and γ_2. (For an explanation see the references listed in section 2.2.) We now define

$$\bar{X} = \sum_1^n (X_i - \mu)/n$$

then it is easy to show that

$$E(\bar{X}) = 0 \qquad V(\bar{X}) = \sigma^2/n \qquad \gamma_1(\bar{X}) = \gamma_1/\sqrt{n} \qquad \gamma_2(\bar{X}) = \gamma_2/n$$

This simply restates the well-known central limit theorem property that when we are dealing with sample means, non-normality of the original distribution doesn't matter much. However, care has to be taken due to the small sample sizes used in SPC work.

We also find that for the sample variance

$$s^2 = \sum (X_i - \bar{X})^2/(n - 1)$$

then

$$E(s^2) \; \sigma^2$$

and

$$V(s^2) = \frac{2\sigma^4}{(n - 1)}\left(1 + \frac{\gamma_2(n - 1)}{2n}\right) \tag{8.1}$$

so that kurtosis can considerably inflate the variance of s^2, and this effect does *not* disappear as sample sizes increase.

If now we assume that successive observations have a correlation ρ, then we find

$$E(\bar{X}) = 0$$

$$V(\bar{X}) = \frac{\sigma^2}{n}\left[1 + 2\rho\left(1 - \frac{1}{n}\right)\right] \tag{8.2}$$

and

$$E(s^2) = \sigma^2(1 - 2\rho/n) \tag{8.3}$$

Thus when we have positive autocorrelation, the variance of the mean is inflated, whereas the sample variance gives an underestimate of σ^2.

The general conclusions for charting are as follows.

(a) *Control of process average level*

Skewness and kurtosis are likely to have very little effect, even with samples of sizes as small as 5. Positive autocorrelation will lead to too many false positives, when boundaries are based on independence.

(b) *Control of process spread*

Kurtosis of the original distribution can have a large effect on $V(s^2)$. Positive autocorrelation will lead to far too many false positives in range or standard deviation charts.

It should be noted that if we are dealing with charts for specification limits, see Chapter 9, then non-normality will be very important. The properties of charts for specification limits depend on the distribution of *individual* values, rather than of process means.

8.3 SHEWHART CHARTS – MARKOV CHAIN APPROACH

The methods given in section 5.6 can be used to obtain ARL results for Shewhart charts for a variety of distributions. In order to obtain more detailed results on run length properties, a different approach is necessary. The following method, given by Brook and Evans (1972) is of interest, and it leads on to methods usable for a study of CuSum chart properties.

8.3.1 Shewhart chart with warning lines

A Shewhart chart with warning lines can be represented as a simple Markov chain with four states:

State 0: Current point is in the main plotting region.
State 1: Current point is in the lower warning region, and the previous point was not.
State 2: Current point is in the upper warning region and the previous point was not.
State 3: Current point signals action by either one point outside the action limits or two successive points in the same warning region.

State 3 is said to be an absorbing state since at this point the procedure stops (with action being signalled).

The probabilities of points falling in three of the regions is as shown in Fig. 5.9. These probabilities will depend on the specific distribution being assumed.

The transition matrix can now be written:

		\multicolumn{4}{c}{Final state}			

		Final state				
		0	1	2	3	
Initial	0	p_0	p_1	p_2	p_3	
state	1	p_0	0	p_2	$(p_1 + p_3)$	(8.4)
	2	p_0	p_1	0	$(p_2 + p_3)$	
	3	0	0	0	1	

We write this transition matrix as $\mathbf{P}$, and we denote the probability distribution of states at step n as $\mathbf{S}_{(n)}$. This consists of four elements – one for each state – which we label as follows:

$$\mathbf{S}_{(n)} = (S_{(n)_0}, S_{(n)_1}, S_{(n)_2}, S_{(n)_3}).$$

Then we have

$$\mathbf{S}_{(n)} = \mathbf{P}\mathbf{S}_{(n-1)} = \mathbf{P}^n\mathbf{S}_{(0)} \qquad (8.5)$$

where $\mathbf{S}_{(0)}$ is the distribution of initial states. If X is the number of steps to an action signal, then

$$\Pr(X \leq x) = S_{(x)_3}.$$

For example, suppose we start in State 0, so that $\mathbf{S}_{(0)} = (1, 0, 0, 0,)$, and suppose that the distribution of observations is exactly on target, then

$$p_0 = 0.95, \; p_1 = p_2 = 0.024, \; p_3 = 0.002,$$

where p_3 is the probability of a point falling in the action region, and by using (8.5) we have

$S'_{(1)} = (0.950, 0.024, 0.024, 0.002)$ $\Pr(X \leq 1) = 0.002000$

$S'_{(2)} = (0.948, 0.023, 0.023, 0.005)$ $\Pr(X \leq 2) = 0.005148$

$S'_{(3)} = (0.945, 0.023, 0.023, 0.008)$ $\Pr(X \leq 3) = 0.008260$

etc.

This particular calculation is tedious, and liable to numerical errors for large run lengths.

Another way of doing the calculations is as follows. If we always have the absorbing states as the last state, then we can partition $\mathbf{P}$

$$\mathbf{P} = \begin{bmatrix} \mathbf{R} & \mathbf{p} \\ \mathbf{0}' & 1 \end{bmatrix} \qquad (8.6)$$

and since the rows of **P** add to unity we have

$$p = (I - R)1 \tag{8.7}$$

from which it follows that

$$P^r = \begin{bmatrix} R^r & (I - R^r)1 \\ 0 & 1 \end{bmatrix} \tag{8.8}$$

Therefore if we write

$$F_r = (I - R^r)1 \tag{8.9}$$

then the first element of F_r gives the cumulative probability for runs of length r starting from State 0. The results of some calculations performed on this basis are shown in Table 8.1. This demonstrates the highly skewed nature of the distribution, and also the closeness of the approximating geometric distribution.

Table 8.1 Run length distribution for the Shewhart chart (probability limits)

Run length	Prob {run length < r} Shift in mean (standard error units)			Geometric distribution Shift in mean (standard error units)		
	0	0.5	1.0	0	0.5	1.0
20	0.0597	0.1670	0.5368	0.0607	0.1697	0.5387
40	0.1168	0.3089	0.7893	0.1177	0.3107	0.7872
60	0.1705	0.4267	0.9042	0.1712	0.4277	0.9019
80	0.2209	0.5244	0.9564	0.2215	0.5248	0.9547
100	0.2682	0.6054	0.9802	0.2687	0.6055	0.9791
150	0.3743	0.7526	0.9972	0.3747	0.7522	0.9970
200	0.4650	0.8449	0.9996	0.4653	0.8443	0.9996
250	0.5426	0.9028	0.9999	0.5427	0.9022	0.9999
300	0.6089	0.9391		0.6090	0.9386	
350	0.6657	0.9618		0.6656	0.9614	
400	0.7141	0.9761		0.7141	0.9758	
500	0.7910	0.9906		0.7909	0.9904	
600	0.8472	0.9963		0.8471	0.9962	
1000	0.9564	0.9999		0.9563	0.9999	

8.3.2 Expectation and variance of run length distributions

The Markov chain approach of the previous section can be extended to evaluate the expectation and variance of the run length distribution directly. Write the factorial moments of the run length, starting from a state i, as

$$\mu_i^{(s)} = E\{X_i(X_i - 1) \ldots (X_i - s + 1)\} = E\{X^{(s)}\}$$

Now a run length of r is the same as a step of one followed by a run-length of $(r - 1)$, so that

$$\mu_i^{(s)} = \sum_{r=s}^{\infty} r^{(s)} \Pr(X_i = r)$$

$$= \sum_{r=s}^{\infty} r^{(s)} \sum_{j=0}^{H-1} p_{ij} \Pr(X_i = r - 1),$$

where p_{ij} is the transition probability of going from state i to state j in one step. The absorbing state is taken as H and state 1 as the initial state. Now we have

$$r^{(s)} = (r - 1)^{(s)} + sr^{(s-1)}$$

so that

$$\mu_i^{(s)} = \sum_{j=0}^{H-1} p_{ij} \{\mu_j^{(s)} + s\mu_j^{(s-1)}\}.$$

In matrix form this equation is

$$(\mathbf{I} - \mathbf{R})\boldsymbol{\mu}^{(s)} = s\mathbf{R}\boldsymbol{\mu}^{(s-1)} \tag{8.10}$$

For $s = 1$ we have

$$(\mathbf{I} - \mathbf{R})\boldsymbol{\mu} = \mathbf{1}$$

so that the first element of $(\mathbf{I} - \mathbf{R})^{-1}\mathbf{1}$ is the average run length starting from the initial state.

Once $\boldsymbol{\mu}$ has been evaluated, (8.10) can be used to calculate other moments. We write (8.10)

$$\boldsymbol{\mu}^{(s)} = s\{(\mathbf{I} - \mathbf{R})^{-1}\mathbf{R}\}\boldsymbol{\mu}^{(s-1)}$$

$$= s\{(\mathbf{I} - \mathbf{R})^{-1} - \mathbf{I}\}\boldsymbol{\mu}^{(s-1)} \tag{8.11}$$

This last equation is easy to calculate; to get the next moment a simple matrix multiplication is required and multiplication by a constant.

The material in sections 8.3.1 and 8.3.2 can be used in a very general setting, and the properties of many types of SPC scheme can be evaluated using these results.

The results in Table 8.2 demonstrate that the standard deviation is approximately what we would expect if the actual run length distribution were exactly geometric.

Table 8.2 Expectation and variance of run length distribution for the Shewhart $\bar{X}$ chart with warning lines (probability limits)

Mean	Expectation	Std. deviation	Std. deviation if geometric
0	320.00	319.15	319.49
0.5	108.03	107.09	107.53
1.0	26.35	25.39	25.85
1.5	8.92	7.97	8.40
2.0	4.14	3.23	3.61
2.5	2.46	1.59	1.90
3.0	1.75	0.91	1.14

8.3.3 Supplementary runs rules

Champ and Woodall (1987) have used a Markov chain model to calculate the ARL of a Shewhart chart using supplementary rules. The procedure is as follows.

The rules are all expressed in the form that k_i of the last m_i observations fall in the range (a_i, b_i), assuming unit variance, and a zero mean when on target. This is denoted $T(k_i, m_i, a_i, b_i)$, and is called the rule C_i. Many of the suggested ways of operating a Shewhart chart can be expressed as using a combination of the rules, $C_i \cup C_j \cup C_k, \cdots$. The rules considered are shown in Table 8.3.

Table 8.3 Champ and Woodall's rules

Rule 1:	$C_1 = \{T(1, 1, -\infty, -3), T(1, 1, 3, \infty)\}$.
Rule 2:	$C_2 = \{T(2, 3, -3, -2), T(2, 3, 2, 3)\}$.
Rule 3:	$C_3 = \{T(4, 5, -3, -1), T(4, 5, 1, 3)\}$.
Rule 4:	$C_4 = \{T(8, 8, -3, 0), T(8, 8, 0, 3)\}$.
Rule 5:	$C_5 = \{T(2, 2, -3, -2), T(2, 2, 2, 3)\}$.
Rule 6:	$C_6 = \{T(5, 5, -3, -1), T(5, 5, 1, 3)\}$.
Rule 7:	$C_7 = \{T(1, 1, -\infty, -3.09), T(1, 1, 3.09, \infty)\}$.
Rule 8:	$C_8 = \{T(2, 3, -3.09, -1.96), T(2, 3, 1.96, 3.09)\}$.
Rule 9:	$C_9 = \{T(8, 8, -3.09, 0), T(8, 8, 0, 3.09)\}$.

For example, rule C_2 states that two out of the last three observations fall in the ranges $(-3, -2)$ or $(2, 3)$. As rules of the type C_2 are used, the authors define a vector

$$\mathbf{W}_i = (W_{i,1}, \ldots, W_{i,m_{i-1}})$$

where

$$W_{ij} = 1 \text{ if the } j\text{th previous observation was in } (a_i, b_i),$$
$$= 0 \text{ otherwise.}$$

They also define

$$\mathbf{X}_i = (X_{i,1}, \ldots, X_{i,m_i-1})$$

where $X_{i,j} = W_{i,j}$ if $\Sigma_{h=1}^{j}(1 - W_{i,h}) < m_i - k_i + 1$ so that the $X_{i,j}$ have 1s only where an observation can contribute to an out of control signal. Then for t rules, a vector

$$\mathbf{X}_i, \ldots, \mathbf{X}_t$$

represents the transient states.

From this basis, the methods follow those of Brook and Evans (1972), to obtain ARLs and some other properties of run length distributions. The calculations are all performed using independent, identically distributed normal random variables, and it is to be noted that some commonly occurring rules, such as seven points increasing or decreasing, are not covered by these methods.

Table 8.4 shows the results, and some important features stand out. In particular, a combination of rules such as C_7 or C_9 dramatically increases the false alarm rate. As these rules are popular in some circles, this point needs to be noted.

Table 8.5 shows how the ARLs of Table 8.4 compare with a simple Shewhart chart with action boundaries only, set so as to give the same false alarm rate when the process is on target. We see that employment of these extra rules can considerably increase the power of the charts to detect moderate changes, sometimes at the cost of *reduced* power to detect large changes. Again we see that the rules C_7 and C_9, highlighted above, behave particularly badly in this respect.

8.4 CUMULATIVE SUM CHARTS

8.4.1 Exact theory

In order to work out properties of CuSum charts we use the decision interval scheme of section 7.1.7, which we note is exactly equivalent to the CuSum plot scheme.

Another point is that if we operate decision interval schemes for both upper and lower sides, then we can show that

$$\frac{1}{(\text{ARL})_{\text{combined}}} = \frac{1}{(\text{ARL})_{\text{upper}}} + \frac{1}{(\text{ARL})_{\text{lower}}} \qquad (8.12)$$

This enables us to study the ARL of a one-sided scheme separately.

Table 8.4 ARLs for Shewhart control charts with supplementary runs rule

Shift d									Control charts							
	C_1	C_7	C_{12}	C_{78}	C_{15}	C_{13}	C_{14}	C_{79}	C_{16}	C_{123}	C_{156}	C_{124}	C_{789}	C_{134}	C_{1456}	C_{1234}
0.0	370.40	499.62	225.44	239.75	278.03	166.05	152.73	170.41	349.38	132.89	266.82	122.05	126.17	105.78	133.21	91.75
0.2	308.43	412.01	177.56	185.48	222.59	120.70	110.52	120.87	279.53	97.66	208.44	89.14	91.19	76.01	96.37	66.80
0.4	200.08	262.19	104.46	106.15	134.17	63.88	59.76	63.80	165.48	52.93	119.47	48.71	49.19	40.95	51.94	36.61
0.6	119.67	153.86	57.92	57.80	75.27	33.99	33.64	35.46	89.07	28.70	63.70	27.49	27.57	23.15	29.01	20.90
0.8	71.55	90.41	33.12	32.75	42.96	19.78	21.07	22.09	48.40	16.93	34.96	17.14	17.14	14.62	17.94	13.25
1.0	43.89	54.55	20.01	19.70	25.61	12.66	14.58	15.26	27.74	10.95	20.43	11.73	11.71	10.19	12.19	9.22
1.2	27.82	34.03	12.81	12.62	16.06	8.84	10.90	11.42	17.05	7.68	12.83	8.61	8.59	7.66	8.90	6.89
1.4	18.25	21.97	8.69	8.58	10.60	6.62	8.60	9.05	11.28	5.76	8.65	6.63	6.62	6.08	6.84	5.41
1.6	12.38	14.68	6.21	6.16	7.36	5.24	7.03	7.44	7.98	4.54	6.22	5.27	5.27	5.01	5.42	4.41
1.8	8.69	10.15	4.66	4.64	5.36	4.33	5.85	6.24	5.97	3.73	4.71	4.27	4.27	4.24	4.39	3.68
2.0	6.30	7.25	3.65	3.65	4.07	3.68	4.89	5.25	4.67	3.14	3.72	3.50	3.52	3.65	3.61	3.13
2.2	4.72	5.36	2.96	2.98	3.22	3.18	4.08	4.41	3.78	2.70	3.04	2.91	2.94	3.17	3.01	2.70
2.4	3.65	4.08	2.48	2.51	2.64	2.78	3.38	3.67	3.14	2.35	2.55	2.47	2.50	2.77	2.54	2.35
2.6	2.90	3.20	2.13	2.17	2.22	2.43	2.81	3.05	2.64	2.07	2.19	2.13	2.16	2.43	2.19	2.07
2.8	2.38	2.59	1.87	1.91	1.93	2.14	2.35	2.54	2.26	1.85	1.91	1.87	1.91	2.14	1.91	1.85
3.0	2.00	2.15	1.68	1.71	1.70	1.89	1.99	2.14	1.95	1.67	1.70	1.68	1.71	1.89	1.70	1.67

Table 8.5 Ratios of ARLs: Shewhart chart to the corresponding Shewhart chart with supplementary runs rules (shown in parentheses)

Shift d	3.00 C_1	3.09 C_7	2.84 C_{12}	2.86 C_{78}	2.91 C_{15}	2.74 C_{13}	2.71 C_{14}	2.75 C_{79}	2.98 C_{16}	2.67 C_{123}	2.89 C_{156}	2.64 C_{124}	2.66 C_{789}	2.59 C_{134}	2.67 C_{1456}	2.54 C_{1234}
									Shewhart control limit c							
0.0	1.00	1.00	0.98	0.98	1.00	0.98	0.97	0.98	0.99	0.99	0.97	0.99	0.98	0.98	0.99	0.98
0.2	1.00	1.00	1.06	1.08	1.04	1.15	1.15	1.19	1.04	1.16	1.05	1.17	1.18	1.19	1.18	1.18
0.4	1.00	1.00	1.21	1.26	1.15	1.49	1.47	1.54	1.14	1.49	1.22	1.50	1.52	1.56	1.52	1.53
0.6	1.00	1.00	1.34	1.42	1.25	1.77	1.66	1.74	1.27	1.76	1.40	1.71	1.75	1.80	1.74	1.77
0.8	1.00	1.00	1.45	1.54	1.33	1.92	1.68	1.76	1.40	1.91	1.55	1.76	1.80	1.84	1.80	1.82
1.0	1.00	1.00	1.52	1.61	1.39	1.93	1.57	1.63	1.51	1.92	1.66	1.68	1.72	1.75	1.72	1.75
1.2	1.00	1.00	1.54	1.63	1.43	1.83	1.40	1.44	1.56	1.84	1.71	1.55	1.58	1.58	1.59	1.61
1.4	1.00	1.00	1.54	1.62	1.44	1.68	1.22	1.25	1.55	1.70	1.70	1.40	1.43	1.40	1.43	1.45
1.6	1.00	1.00	1.50	1.56	1.43	1.50	1.07	1.07	1.49	1.55	1.63	1.27	1.29	1.24	1.30	1.31
1.8	1.00	1.00	1.44	1.49	1.40	1.33	0.94	0.94	1.41	1.39	1.54	1.17	1.19	1.10	1.18	1.18
2.0	1.00	1.00	1.37	1.41	1.35	1.18	0.86	0.84	1.31	1.27	1.44	1.09	1.10	0.99	1.10	1.08
2.2	1.00	1.00	1.29	1.32	1.30	1.07	0.80	0.78	1.21	1.16	1.34	1.04	1.04	0.91	1.04	1.01
2.4	1.00	1.00	1.22	1.24	1.24	0.98	0.78	0.75	1.13	1.08	1.25	1.00	1.00	0.85	1.00	0.96
2.6	1.00	1.00	1.16	1.16	1.19	0.93	0.78	0.74	1.08	1.02	1.18	0.97	0.96	0.81	0.97	0.92
2.8	1.00	1.00	1.11	1.10	1.13	0.89	0.80	0.76	1.03	0.98	1.13	0.95	0.94	0.80	0.95	0.90
3.0	1.00	1.00	1.05	1.05	1.10	0.88	0.82	0.78	1.01	0.95	1.08	0.93	0.92	0.80	0.94	0.89

The decision interval scheme can be considered as a sequence of sequential probability ratio tests; (for a description of and references to this see Wetherill and Glazebrook (1986)). Let the variable z denote the distance from the lower boundary of the scheme, so that the two boundaries are at $z = 0$ and $z = H$. A single test is defined as a path starting at a value z satisfying $0 \leq z < H$, and ending at the upper or lower boundary; in the degenerate case the path may be one point only. For such a test let

$$P(z) = \text{probability that a test starting at } z \text{ ends at } z < 0$$

$$N(z) = \text{average sample number of a test starting at } z.$$

The decision interval scheme is a series of such tests, and terminates with the first test to cross the upper boundary. Let $L(z)$ denote the ARL of a decision interval scheme in which the first test starts at the point z, but all subsequent tests start at the lower boundary.

We have usually discussed only CuSum schemes in which the observations are normally distributed, but to be general we denote the probability density function of the observations by $f(x)$, and cumulative distribution by $F(x)$. The CuSum scheme proceeds by observing x, and if the current score is z, the new score is

$$\begin{array}{ll} z + x - K & \text{if } x \geq K - z \\ 0 & \text{if } x \leq K - z. \end{array}$$

or

We begin by considering a single test starting from a score z, and obtain a formula for $P(z)$. If one observation is taken, there are three possibilities, as indicated in Table 8.6.

Table 8.6 Score used in derivation of ARL formula

Observation	New score	Outcome
(1) $x \leq K - z$	0	Test ends at lower boundary
(2) $K - z \leq x \leq H + K - z$	$z + x - K$	Test in progress
(3) $x \geq H + K - z$	H	Test ends at upper boundary

The probability of the first event is $F(K - z)$. If the second event happens, there is a further probability $P(y)$, for every $y = z + x - K$, $0 < y < H$, ending at the lower boundary. The last event is irrelevant to $P(z)$. Therefore we have the equation

$$P(z) = F(K - z) + \int_0^h P(y)f(y + K - z)\,dy \qquad (8.13)$$

In a similar way we can obtain the equations

$$N(z) = 1 + \int_0^h N(y)f(y + K - z)\,dy \qquad (8.14)$$

and

$$L(z) = 1 + L(0)F(K - z) + \int_0^h L(y)f(y + K - z)\,dy \qquad (8.15)$$

Equations (8.13) and (8.14) have been described by Page (1954), and Page (1961) and Kemp (1958) gave numerical methods for solving them.

The ARL of the decision interval scheme is $L(0)$, and once $P(0)$ and $N(0)$ are obtained by solving (8.18) and (8.19), $L(0)$ can be obtained from the formula

$$L(0) = N(0)/\{1 - P(0)\} \qquad (8.16)$$

instead of by solving (8.15) directly. This formula can be derived as follows. In a decision interval scheme the number of sequential tests has the geometric distribution

$$\{P(0)\}^{(s-1)}\{1 - P(0)\}, \qquad s = 1, 2, \ldots.$$

Thus on average there are $\{1 - P(0)\}^{-1}$ sequential tests in a single run of a decision interval scheme of which just one terminates on the upper boundary. If $N(0)^u$, $N(0)^l$ are the average sample numbers of sequential tests terminating on the upper and lower boundary respectively, the ARL of the decision interval scheme is

$$
\begin{aligned}
L(0) &= N(0)^u + \left\{ \frac{1}{1 - P(0)} - 1 \right\} N(0)^l \\
&= \frac{1}{1 - P(0)} \{(1 - P(0))N(0)^u + P(0)N(0)^l\} \\
&= \frac{N(0)}{1 - P(0)}.
\end{aligned}
$$

Now the ARL is the expectation of the distribution of run length, and it is very useful to have a formula for it. However, further information about the run length distribution can easily be obtained. Let $p(n, z) =$ probability that a test starting at z has run length n, then by following an argument similar to that leading to (8.18) we have

$$p(n, z) = p(n - 1, 0)F(k - z) + \int_0^h p(n - 1, y)f(y + k - z)\,dy.$$

$$(8.17)$$

Denote the moment generating function of the run length distribution by $\phi(z, t)$

$$\phi(z, t) = \sum_{1}^{\infty} p(n, z)e^{nt}$$

then from (8.17) we have

$$e^{-t}\phi(z, t) = 1 - F(h + k - z) + \phi(0, t)F(k - z)$$
$$+ \int_{0}^{h} \phi(y, t)f(y + k - z)\,dy. \tag{8.18}$$

By successively differentiating (8.18) and putting $t = 0$ we can obtain integral equations for the moments of the run length distribution. Ewan and Kemp (1960) also obtained an approximation for the variance of the run length distribution,

$$V(n) \simeq L^2(0) + V(N)/\{1 - P(0)\} \tag{8.19}$$

where $V(N)$ is the variance of the sample number of single sequential test, and the approximation is valid when $P(0)$ is close to unity. The authors also conjectured that a close approximation to the run length distribution is

$$p(n, 0) \simeq \frac{1}{L(0)} \exp\left\{-\frac{(n - 1)}{L(0)}\right\}. \tag{8.20}$$

Throughout this theory, we have assumed that the observations x are continuous, but the methods used can be followed through in the discrete case also. Ewan and Kemp (1960) gave values of the ARL for the case when the observations have a Poisson distribution, as well as for the normal distribution case.

8.4.2 Johnson's approximate approach

Johnson (1961) gave an approximate approach for a CuSum chart with a V-mask, which arrives at some remarkably simple answers.

We first reverse a CuSum chart, and look at it as if it were proceeding backwards. Figure 8.1 shows approximately how Fig. 7.6 would be reversed. The method is now to regard the outer arms of the V-mask as boundaries of a test of three simple hypotheses using the sequential probability ratio test (Wetherill and Glazebrook 1986).

Suppose we have three hypotheses, that observations are independently and normally distributed with distributions as follows:

$$H_{-1}: N(-\delta\sigma, \sigma^2); \qquad H_0: N(0, \sigma^2); \qquad H_1: N(\delta\sigma, \sigma^2).$$

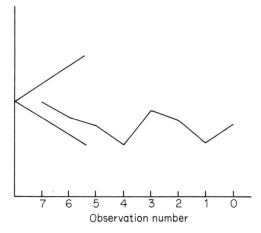

Figure 8.1 Johnson's approach to V-mask theory.

Suppose, further, that we want a probability $(1 - 2\alpha_0)$ of accepting H_0 if it is true, and a probability $(1 - \alpha_1)$ of accepting H_1 or H_{-1} if they are true; then the boundaries for the sequential probability ratio test of these hypotheses are as illustrated in Fig. 8.2.

The outer boundaries are

$$\sum_{i=1}^{n} x_i = \left[\frac{1}{\delta} \log_e\{(1 - \alpha_1)/\alpha_0\} + \tfrac{1}{2}\delta n\right]\sigma \qquad (8.21)$$

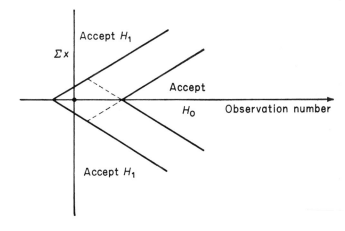

Figure 8.2 Sequential tests of three hypotheses.

and

$$\sum_{i=1}^{n} x_i = -\left[\frac{1}{\delta}\log_e\{(1 - \alpha_1)/\alpha_0\} + \tfrac{1}{2}\delta n\right]\sigma \qquad (8.22)$$

Now the outer boundaries of the V-mask in Fig 7.5, using the current point as origin, are

$$\sum x = 2\sigma(h + nf) \qquad (8.23)$$

and

$$\sum x = -2\sigma(h + nf) \qquad (8.24)$$

where 2σ is the scale factor of the CuSum chart and where $H = h\sigma$, and $F = f\sigma$; see Chapter 7. It follows that if we identify (8.21) with (8.23) and (8.22) with (8.24), we shall have a V-mask in which, approximately, the probability of a path crossing an outer boundary is $2\alpha_0$, when the process is in control. By identifying these pairs of equations we obtain

$$f = \delta/4 \qquad (8.25)$$
$$h = \log_e\{(1 - \alpha_1)/\alpha_0\}/2\sigma \qquad (8.26)$$

Unfortunately α_1 in this last equation is difficult to interpret, since there is no 'accept H_0' boundary on Fig. 7.5. However, since α_1 is usually small, we have

$$h \simeq -\log_e(\alpha_0)/2\sigma \qquad (8.27)$$

These results can be used in the following way. First decide on the least change in the mean which it is desired to detect with reasonable certainty; let the standardized value, standardized by σ, be δ. We must now decide on the greatest tolerable probability, $2\alpha_0$, of false indications of lack of control; values near 0.002 are traditional for this in control chart work. Use of (8.25) and (8.27) now give θ and h corresponding to this pair of (δ, α_0). The properties of the selected (h, θ) can be checked from tabulated ARL curves, and modified if they are not satisfactory.

Johnson points out that this theory throws some further light on CuSum charts. Since CuSum charts are like a two-sided sequential probability ratio test (SPRT) without a middle boundary, and there is no decision to 'accept H_0', a path which would have been terminated on an SPRT could go on and cross one of the decision boundaries. Therefore paths which cross the decision boundaries a long way from the vertex should be regarded with suspicion.

8.4.3 Markov chain approach

Brook and Evans (1972) used the Markov chain approach described in section 8.3 to obtain a very good approximation to the ARL of a one-sided decision interval scheme. The idea is simply to approximate the normal distribution by a set of discrete (equidistant) values. In this way we get a finite set of states, and the calculations proceed as described earlier.

Let there be t states, E_0 to E_t, with the last being the absorbing state, corresponding to an action signal. If the width of the grouping interval is ω, then action corresponds to a score greater than $(t - \frac{1}{2})\omega$, so that

$$H = (t - \tfrac{1}{2})\omega, \qquad \omega = 2H/(2t - 1).$$

Let the distribution of the observations Z be normal with mean γ and variance one. Then the decision interval scheme accumulates values of $(Z - K)$ where K is the reference value. We can therefore write $X = Z - K$, so that X is normal with mean $\mu = \gamma - K$, and unit variance. The distribution of X is then discretized by calculating the standard normal distribution at the $(2t - 1)$ points.

$$(a - \mu), (a - \mu) + \omega, (a - \mu) + 2\omega, \ldots, (a - \mu) + (2t - 2)\omega = H - \mu$$

where $a = -(H - \omega)$. The lowest of these values is the distance from E_{t-1} to E_0, and the highest is the distance from E_0 to E_H.

The transition matrix can now be written in the form

	E_0	E_1	$\ldots$	E_t
E_0	⋮	⋮		⋮
E_1	⋮	⋮		⋮
⋮	⋮	⋮		⋮
E_t	⋮	⋮		⋮

and the last row and column correspond to the absorbing state, as before.

Brook and Evans report that reasonable results were obtained for $t = 5$, and that $t = 10$ gave three significant figure accuracy.

As a modification, it is suggested that the calculation be performed at several t values and that the approximation

$$\text{ARL} = A + B/t + C/t^2$$

be fitted and then used to extrapolate to large values of t.

This Markov chain method is an excellent way of examining the ARL for cumulative sum charts.

8.4.4 Proof of equation (8.12)

Figure 8.3 shows a decision interval scheme, and once a decision boundary is crossed, the chart automatically restarts at zero. It can easily be shown that if, say, the upper decision boundary is crossed, plotting on the lower chart will have terminated at the 'in control' boundary; see Exercise 8B.4. Therefore this automatic resetting of the scheme has no effect on the plotting.

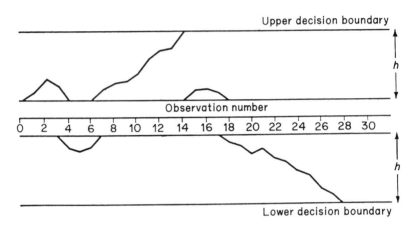

Figure 8.3 Series of two-sided decision interval schemes.

Let S_u, S_l and S_t be the run lengths of the upper, lower and two-sided decision interval schemes respectively, and let L_u, L_l and L_t be the corresponding ARLs for an in control process. Then clearly

$$S_y = \min(S_u, S_l)$$

and

$$L_l = E(S_l) = E(S_t) + E(S_l - S_t)$$
$$= L_u + E\{S_l - S_t | S_l > S_t\}\Pr(S_l > S_t),$$

since $S_l - S_t \geq 0$. Since the lower scheme restarts from the zero boundary when the upper scheme terminates, and by independence, we have

$$E\{S_l - S_t | S_l > S_t\} = L_l.$$

Therefore we obtain

$$L_l = L_t + L_l \Pr(S_l > S_t)$$
$$L_t = L_l[1 - \Pr(S_l > S_t)] = L_l \Pr(S_t = S_l).$$

Similarly we obtain

$$L_t = L_u \Pr(S_t = S_u).$$

Now we have

$$\Pr(S_t = S_u) + \Pr(S_t = S_l) = 1$$

so that

$$\frac{L_t}{L_u} + \frac{L_t}{L_l} = 1$$

or

$$\frac{1}{L_t} = \frac{1}{L_u} + \frac{1}{L_l}.$$

This proof is due to Rowlands (personal communication).

8.4.5 Sensitivity to departures from assumptions

Before employing CuSums too widely, it is important to have some appreciation of the effect of deviations from the various assumptions.

Firstly, a value of σ has to be assumed, and it is quite clear that the effect of departures from the assumed value on the ARL can be dramatic; see comments on this in De Bruyn (1968, pp.44, 45). Overestimation of σ increases the ARL, and underestimation reduces it. Great care must be taken over the choice of σ.

Bissell (1969) studied the effect of skewness of the underlying distribution, and provided a nomogram to assess the effect on the ARL. His general conclusion is intuitively clear from the way in which CuSum cumulations arise. At the RQL, most of the distribution contributes to the cumulations, and the effect of skewness is very small, but the position is different at the AQL. For positive skewness, the proportion (and mean) of observations contributing to cumulations will increase, while at the same time the proportion (and mean) of observations detracting from cumulations will decrease. The result is that positive skewness can seriously reduce the ARL at the AQL. By similar reasoning, negative skewness increases the ARL at the AQL.

The effect of serial correlation between observations has been studied by Goldsmith and Whitfield (1961) using simulation, and by Johnson and Bagshaw (1974) and Bagshaw and Johnson (1975) by theoretical means. Tables 8.7 and 8.8 were obtained by Rowlands (1976). These tables illustrate the general conclusions obtained. They are derived for a first order autocorrelated model, given by equation (3.6). The conclusions are as follows:

(1) Positive autocorrelation reduces the ARL, and negative autocorrelation increases it.
(2) The effect of autocorrelation is slight at the RQL, but quite dramatic at the AQL.

Table 8.7 Run length distribution for a one-sided CuSum scheme. Data from a first order autocorrelated process. ($h = 2$, $\sigma = 1$, $\mu - K = 1$)

n	$\rho = 0.8$	$\rho = 0.6$	$\rho = 0.2$	$\rho = 0.0$	$\rho = -0.2$	$\rho = -0.6$	$\rho = -0.8$
1	0.1587	0.1587	0.1587	0.1587	0.1587	0.1587	0.1587
2	0.3413	0.3431	0.3560	0.3665	0.3794	0.4139	0.4398
3	0.1478	0.1726	0.2215	0.2451	0.2682	0.3125	0.3315
4	0.0825	0.1011	0.1217	0.1241	0.1211	0.0967	0.0685
5	0.0552	0.0660	0.0659	0.0579	0.0466	0.0158	0.0028
6	0.0406	0.0453	0.0353	0.0263	0.0169	0.0022	0.0001
7	0.0314	0.0320	0.0190	0.0118	0.0060	0.0003	
8	0.0251	0.0229	0.0123	0.0053	0.0021		
9	0.0204	0.0164	0.0055	0.0024	0.0007		
10	0.0167	0.0118	0.0030	0.0011	0.0003		
11	0.0138	0.0085	0.0016	0.0005	0.0001		
12	0.0114	0.0061	0.0009	0.0002			
13	0.0095	0.0044	0.0005	0.0001			
14	0.0078	0.0031	0.0002				
15	0.0065	0.0023	0.0001				
ARL	4.18	3.45	2.90	2.74	2.61	2.40	2.32

Table 8.8 ARL of a one-sided CuSum scheme. Data with mean on target, but with first order autocorrelated process ($h = 2$, $\sigma = 1$)

ρ	ARL	Standard deviation	Mode	Lower quartile	Median	Upper quartile
0.8	88	88	3	25	60	122
0.6	79	77	3	22	54	107
0.4	101	99	4	29	70	138
0.2	151	149	5	43	105	207
0.0	258	256	5	74	179	355
−0.2	458	457	5	131	317	633
−0.4	665	664	4	191	460	920
−0.6	715	714	2	205	495	990
−0.8	952	952	1	274	659	1319

(*Note*: The run length distribution is not unimodal when $\rho = -0.8$; besides the mode at $n = 1$ there are lesser modes at $n = 4, 6, 8, 10$ and 12.)

Johnson and Bagshaw (1974) say: 'Our primary conclusion is that the CuSum test is not robust with respect to departures from independence. The use of CuSum tests is now widespread, and the presence of serial correlation common so that attention should be drawn to the seriousness of this lack of robustness.'

8.5 CHARTS FOR CONTROL OF PROCESS SPREAD

The theory for obtaining properties of charts for control of process spread follows the methods described above for control of process average level, but much less work has been done in this area. A comparison of range, standard deviation and CuSum charts is given by Tuprah and Ncube (1987). Some of their results are given in Tables 8.9 and 8.10. The schemes are designed for $\sigma = 1$ and the ARLs at set values of σ are given. These results demonstrate that CuSums do not gain so much over Shewhart charts in comparison with charts for control of process average level. They also show that CuSum charts for standard deviation are more sensitive to small changes of process spread than CuSum charts for range.

Table 8.9 ARL values for Shewhart control charts with warning lines

Group size	5		10		15		20	
	R-chart	S-chart	R-chart	S-chart	R-chart	S-chart	R-chart	S-chart
UWL	3.97	1.5829	4.577	1.3984	4.984	1.3213	5.1060	1.278
UAL	5.00	1.9702	5.530	1.6463	5.800	1.518	5.9920	1.443
σ								
1.0	200.00	200.00	200.00	200.00	200.00	200.00	200.00	200.00
1.1	63.40	60.00	50.00	41.70	43.80	32.40	39.90	26.50
1.2	27.20	25.10	18.40	14.40	14.90	10.00	12.80	7.60
1.3	14.40	13.20	9.00	6.90	7.00	4.70	5.90	3.60
1.4	8.90	8.20	5.30	4.10	4.10	2.90	3.50	2.20
1.5	6.20	5.70	3.70	2.80	2.80	2.10	2.40	1.70
1.6	4.60	4.30	2.80	2.30	2.20	1.70	1.90	1.40
1.7	3.60	3.40	2.20	1.90	1.80	1.40	1.60	1.20
1.8	3.00	2.80	1.90	1.60	1.50	1.30	1.40	1.10
1.9	2.60	2.40	1.70	1.40	1.40	1.20	1.20	1.10
2.0	2.30	2.20	1.50	1.30	1.30	1.10	1.20	1.00

UWL is the Shewhart upper warning line, and UAL is the Shewhart upper action line.

Table 8.10 ARL values for CuSum procedures

Group size	5		10		15		20	
	R-chart	S-chart	R-chart	S-chart	R-chart	S-chart	R-chart	S-chart
H	3.20	2.66	3.50	2.45	4.20	2.20	4.80	1.60
K	2.80	1.48	2.86	1.56	2.90	2.00	3.08	2.50
σ								
1.0	200.00	200.00	200.00	200.00	200.00	200.00	200.00	200.00
1.1	46.00	42.50	40.10	38.20	35.50	32.00	30.30	25.00
1.2	21.20	16.70	15.60	12.20	10.40	8.00	8.00	5.50
1.3	10.10	9.50	9.00	7.40	6.80	5.00	4.40	3.80
1.4	5.20	4.00	3.20	2.20	2.00	1.25	1.20	1.10
1.5	2.50	2.00	1.80	1.50	1.20	1.12	1.10	1.05
1.6	1.80	1.50	1.20	1.10	1.08	1.02	1.00	1.00
1.7	1.20	1.00	1.00	1.00	1.00	1.00	1.00	1.00
1.8	1.00	1.00	1.00	1.00	1.00	1.00	1.00	1.00
1.9	1.00	1.00	1.00	1.00	1.00	1.00	1.00	1.00
2.0	1.00	1.00	1.00	1.00	1.00	1.00	1.00	1.00

EXERCISES 8B

1. Refer back to the details in Ewan and Kemp (1960) and show how to evaluate the ARL for a CuSum scheme on variances of normally distributed data.

2. Study how to set about a thorough investigation into the effects of deviations from assumptions, such as non-normality and serial correlation upon the run length distribution of a decision interval scheme.

3. All our treatment of CuSum schemes has assumed that observations are taken in groups of n at equally spaced intervals. Set out a model for examining an optimum choice of group size and sampling interval. (You may be guided by similar work referred to in earlier chapters.)

4. For the two-sided decision interval scheme discussed in section 7.1.7, let the two reference values be $\pm k$. Show that if plotting on one chart ends at a decision boundary, plotting on the other must have ended at the 'in control' boundary. (See Kemp (1981), p.151.)

5. Set out the Markov chain model for deriving the ARL of a Shewhart chart with action lines at $\pm 3\sigma/\sqrt{n}$, and warning lines at $\pm 2\sigma/\sqrt{n}$. Action is to be signalled if one point is beyond the action line or two out of three points in the same warning region.

6. One rule which has been proposed for Shewhart charts is to take action if one point is over the action lines, or else if there are seven successive increasing or decreasing points. Set out a simulation study to compare the effects of this rule with action lines only.

9

The design of control charts from specification limits

9.1 SINGLE SPECIFICATION LIMITS

9.1.1 Single specification limits – objectives

We frequently find industrial processes where there are single specification limits, such as the following:

(1) The tensile strength of a test piece of polymer laminate should be greater than a given limit.
(2) The percentage purity of a chemical must be greater than 99.5%
(3) The amount of a specific impurity in a chemical product should be less than 20 parts per million.
(4) The average weight of filled packets must be greater than a given limit.

The objective of statistical process control in cases such as these just given may be simply to keep the process well clear of the given limit. We may not need to attempt statistical control of the process in the sense we have discussed earlier. However, we should be clear before using the methods given below that this is what we want. There can be an advantage in attempting statistical control by Shewhart or CuSum charts, even where there is only one specification limit, or where there is high capability. The methods of this chapter apply particularly where the process capability is large, and we can afford to look at specification limits.

In the first part of this chapter we shall assume a single upper specification limit, such as case (3) above, and describe how to set up plans for this. The design of plans for a single lower specification limit are similar. We shall let the specification limit be the zero of the scale, and measure distances from it, as in Fig. 9.1.

The methods given here are fairly sensitive to the assumption of Normality, and if this is in doubt, rather greater margins need to be left. A Normality check should always be carried out when using these methods.

We shall assume that the process produces observations which are independently and identically distributed with a variance σ^2, and we shall assume that an estimate of σ is available; see the next section for a discussion about this.

The procedures given below all use control charts, rather than cumulative sum charts. Cumulative sum charts can also be designed, using nomograms such as those given in section 7.4; see also Woodward and Goldsmith (1964). However, control charts have a great popularity in practice because of the simplicity of operation.

Finally, the examples given above show that there are two types of requirement. In many situations the requirement is that each individual measurement, or each item produced if it is separate items, are within the specification. Secondly, there are situations where it is satisfactory to have the process average within specification.

9.1.2 What is σ?

The question as to what the relevant σ is turns out to be a deeper question than we might think. In a typical situation there may be several separate components of variation:

(1) Local random variation, reflecting the fact that it is very rarely possible to produce items or material with exactly the same weight, tensile strength, percentage of water, etc., continuously.
(2) Measurement and sampling error, which is often more substantial than it is thought to be. Many laboratory tests and measurements are thought to be precise, but in fact have an error variance.
(3) Variations in the mean of the process. Industries with more complex processes often show autocorrelated or other variations in the mean; see section 3.3.3.
(4) Inter-laboratory error. Sometimes it is crucial that a customer's measurement of the percentage of an impurity, etc., is within specification. This variation can be estimated only by carrying out actual tests in a designed experiment. Again, this source of variation is often much greater than it is thought to be.

All of these components of variation can be estimated, but only by an appropriately designed experiment. Clearly, if we have one-at-a-time data it will be impossible to separate some of these components of variation. In the next section we discuss the choice between these components for scaling our charts.

9.1.3 Discussion

The easiest way to discuss this is to take some specific examples. In a practical case it would be important to look at some data before deciding.

(1) Suppose we have discrete items such as packets or bags, which are filled, and the quantity to control is weight. Here the relevant σ is likely to reflect the natural distribution of filled weights resulting from the apparatus. Obviously, the objective is that *all* filled weights satisfy a specification.

(2) Suppose we have antifreeze, tested for ppm of water. We assume that the measurement error is small, but the mean of the process varies in a general autocorrelated manner. The objective is that no measurement shall be out of specification. Here the relevant σ is the one reflecting the variation of the observations over time, and not the *local* variation, which may be smaller.

(3) Suppose the important requirement for antifreeze is that it must be tested in a *customer's* laboratory and found to be within specification. Here the appropriate variation is the inter-laboratory variation.

What is really required is for a variety of real situations to be studied and modelled, and these models would include different components of variation. The treatment given below is simplified, but satisfactory for many applications. A deeper study of this problem has not been attempted.

Warning: Before proceeding, it should be noted that the methods given in this chapter are particularly sensitive to non-Normality.

9.2 SINGLE SPECIFICATION LIMITS: CHART FOR MEANS

9.2.1 Design requirements

The type of method we shall be using is as follows. Suppose we have a single specification limit; then we take groups of n observations at regular intervals, and plot the means, as in Fig. 9.1. Then we have a simple rule to decide when to take action, such as when a sample mean goes beyond the action boundary in Fig. 9.1. The ARL curve for this type of procedure has the shape shown in Fig. 9.2, but the ARL curves will be different for different group sizes n and different distances $k_A \sigma$

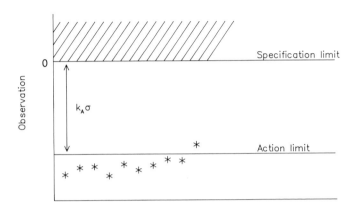

Figure 9.1 A procedure for a single specification limit.

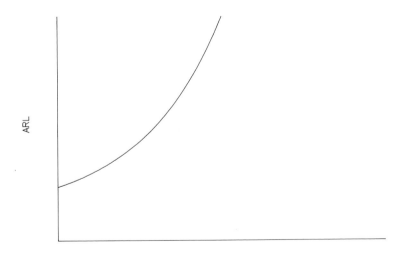

Figure 9.2 ARL curve for single specification limit procedure.

of the action boundary from the specification limit. We need some way of choosing one particular scheme, and therefore one particular ARL curve from the set of all possible.

Ideally, we would like a very steep ARL curve, but this cannot be achieved without a very large group size, n. We have to take risks in order to achieve a practicable procedure. We have to accept a low risk of false alarms, and also a risk of not detecting a real change for a long time. The problem of design is how to set these risks, and we approach this using the ARL concept.

We suppose that we have rather narrow-minded producers and consumers, who put requirements on what they want. The producer is only interested in ensuring that when his process average level and process spread are such that if there is only a small probability p_a of the distribution beyond the specification limits, then the ARL is at least L_a. From Normal tables we can equate this probability p_a to a distance $Z_{p_a}\sigma$ of the mean from the specification limit, so that $p = 1 - \phi(Z_p)$, where $\phi(Z)$ is the standard normal integral.

For example, suppose a producer decides that if only 0.001 is beyond the specification limit, the ARL must be at least 500. For a probability 0.001 beyond specification, the process mean must be 3.0902σ from the specification limit.

		Notation
	Probability beyond spec. = 0.001	p_a
Producer's risk point	Process mean = 3.0902σ	$Z_{p_a}\sigma$
	ARL = 500	L_a

Similarly, we suppose a narrow-minded consumer who insists that if the probability beyond specification is $p_{r'}$ then the ARL must be no more than L_r. Again, we can give an equivalent position for the process mean which gives a probability p_r beyond the specification limit.

For example, if the probability beyond specification is 0.01, the consumer may set $L_r = 5$. We then have

		Notation
	Probability beyond spec. = 0.01	p_r
Consumer's risk point	Process mean = 2.3263σ	$Z_{p_r}\sigma$
	$L_r = 5$	L_r

The distances Z_{p_a} and Z_{p_r} are not used in the approximate solution method given next, but are required for the more exact method and for the theory.

9.2.2 Single specification limit: action limit for $\bar{x}$ only. (Approximate solution)

Suppose that observations are taken in groups of n at a time, and that a single action limit is placed at a distance $k_A \sigma$ from the specification limit. Later in the chapter (section 9.2.5) a more efficient procedure is introduced, which uses a warning limit as well. However, there are many industrial situations in which the introduction of a warning limit as well as an action limit and a specificiation limit causes too much complication, so that the method below is used. The approximate method and nomogram given in this subsection is based on work by Wilrich (1970) and uses the theory given in section 9.2.4.

METHOD SUMMARY 9.1

Single specification limit. Position of action limit

Step 1 Determine a producers risk point (p_a, L_a) and consumers risk point (p_r, L_r) as outlined in section 9.2.1.

Step 2 Draw lines on the nomogram joining p_a to L_a and p_r to L_r. The intersection gives the values of the sample size n and the distance k_A for the action limit, on the appropriate scales.

Step 2' (Alternative) Given either a producers risk point or a consumers risk point and a sample size, the nomogram Fig. 9.3 can be used to plot the ARL curve.

Example 9.1

For the problem set in section 9.2.1 we have $p_a = 0.001$, $L_a = 500$, $p_r = 0.01$, $L_r = 5$. By following through Steps 1 and 2 above we get $n = 7$, $k_A = 2.02$. This might seem a large group size, and if so, we might go back and revise our requirements in order to lower it.

This method might also be used as an approximation for a one-sided running average chart, with one-at-a-time data. The theory in section 9.2.4 is based on independence, which is clearly not true if running averages are used. However, exact calculations for a one-sided running average chart have not yet been evaluated.

9.2.3 Single specification limit: action limit $\bar{x}$ only

The purpose of this subsection is to give a more accurate algorithm for finding the sample size and the position of the action limit for the problem studied in section 9.2.1. The theory is given in section 9.2.4.

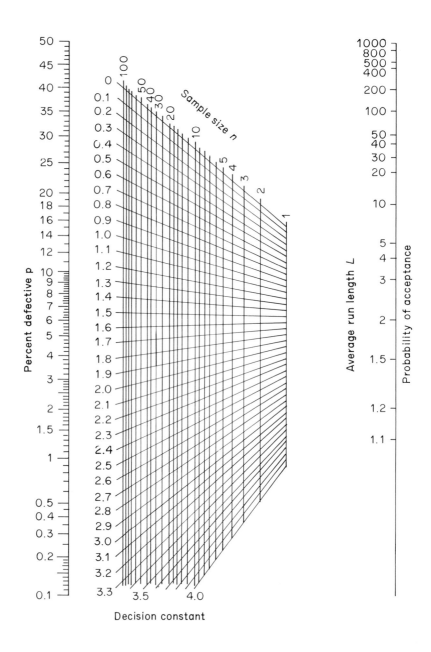

Figure 9.3 Nomogram for single specification limit, action line only.

METHOD SUMMARY 9.2

Single specification limit. Position of action limit (More accurate method)

Step 1   Decide on a producers risk point (p_a, L_a), and obtain the equivalent process mean value $Z_{p_a}\sigma$; see section 9.2.1.

Step 2   Decide on a consumers risk point (p_r, L_r), and obtain the equivalent process mean value, $Z_{p_r}\sigma$.

Step 3   Find the Normal variates corresponding to

$$q_a = 1/L_a \quad \text{and} \quad q_r = 1/L_r.$$

Let these be Z_{q_a} and Z_{q_r} respectively.

Step 4   Use a group size n as the lowest integer greater than

$$n = (Z_{q_a} - Z_{q_r})^2 / (Z_{p_a} - Z_{p_r})^2.$$

Step 5   Put the action limit at $k_A\sigma$, where

$$k_A = Z_{p_a} - Z_{q_a}/\sqrt{n}. \tag{9.1}$$

Step 6   Plot running means of n (or group means of n) on the chart. Search for a special cause when one point is above the action limit.

Notes

(1)   Step 4 may well result in a value of n which is too large. In this case a compromise will have to be reached on the design requirements. Either L_a must be reduced, or L_r increased, or both.

(2)   If observations are sampled in groups of n at a time, and we plot running averages of k means of these groups, the corresponding formula in Step 5 is

$$k_A = Z_{p_a} - Z_{q_a}/\sqrt{(kn)}.$$

(3)   The ARLs are calculated on a basis of independent sampling, rather than running averages. They are likely to underestimate the true ARL by about one-third.

Example 9.2

For the example in section 9.2.1, we have

Producers risk point: $p_a = 0.001$ Mean $= 3.0902\sigma$ $L_a = 500$
Consumers risk point: $p_r = 0.01$ Mean $= 2.3263\sigma$ $L_r = 5$

then we have

$$q_a = 0.002 \quad Z_{q_a} = 2.8782$$
$$q_r = 0.20 \quad Z_{q_r} = 0.8416$$

leading to $n = 7.11$ or $n = 8$, and $k_A = 2.07$.

9.2.4* Single specification limit: action limit for $\bar{x}$ only (Derivation)

Suppose that observations are taken in groups of n at a time and that an action limit is placed at a distance $k_A\sigma$ from the specification limit. Let the mean of the observations be $\mu\sigma$, then the probability of being beyond the limits is $p(\mu, k_A, n)$ where

$$p(\mu, k_A, n) = 1 - \Phi\{(\mu - k_A)\sqrt{n}\} = \Phi\{(k_A - \mu)\sqrt{n}\} \quad (9.2)$$

The distribution of run length until a point is beyond the action limit is geometric:

$$\Pr(r) = (1 - p)^{r-1}p$$

where $p = p(\mu, k_A, n)$, so that the expectation and variance of the run length are

$$E(R) = 1/p$$
$$V(R) = (1 - p)/p^2$$

In order to satisfy the design requirements we require an ARL of L_a when $\mu = Z_a$, and an ARL of L_r when $\mu = Z_{p_r}$. If we put

$$q_a = 1/L_a \quad \text{and} \quad q_r = 1/L_r \quad (9.3)$$

then we must satisfy

$$p(\mu, k_A, n) = q$$

for (μ, q) set at $(Z_{p_a}\sigma, q_a)$ and $(Z_{p_r}\sigma, q_r)$ (see Fig. 9.4), which leads to

$$Z_{q_a} = (Z_{p_a} - k_A)\sqrt{n} \quad (9.4)$$

and

$$Z_{q_r} = (Z_{p_r} - k_A)\sqrt{n} \quad (9.5)$$

or

$$n = (Z_{q_a} - Z_{q_r})^2/(Z_{p_a} - Z_{p_r})^2 \quad (9.6)$$

and

$$k_A = Z_{p_a} - Z_{q_a}/\sqrt{n} \quad (9.7)$$

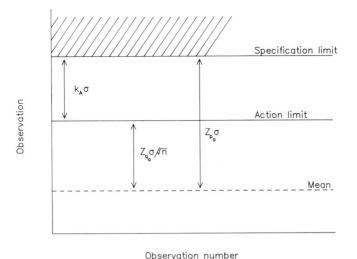

Figure 9.4 Action limit for a specification limit.

Owing to discreteness it will not be possible to solve these exactly. It turns out better to satisfy (9.4) rather than (9.5) for defining k_A. Once an n and k_A are chosen, the exact ARL for the plan is given by (9.2).

Typically, when this method is used in practice, a value of n will emerge that is too large. The engineer will then have to modify his requirements, by changing the ARLs required, or by increasing the sampling frequency.

9.2.5 Single specification limit: one-sided $\bar{X}$ chart

If we have data sampled in groups of n at a time, a one-sided $\bar{X}$ chart can be used. In an ordinary $\bar{X}$ chart, the distance between the warning and action boundaries is

$$(3.09 - 1.96)\sigma/\sqrt{n} = 1.13\sigma/\sqrt{n}.$$

For reasons which will be clear later, we preserve this distance. The crucial question is how far to put the action boundary from the specification limit. We denote this distance $k_B\sigma$ (see Fig. 9.5) and we wish to choose k_B and the group size n to satisfy design requirements. Basically, the method used in the previous section can be repeated.

The one-sided chart is used in the usual way – one point outside the action limit or two successive points outside the warning limits gives a signal to take action on the process.

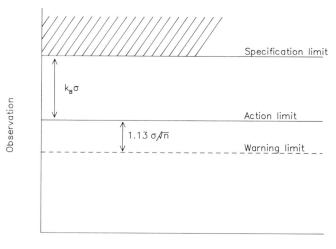

Figure 9.5 One-sided $\bar{X}$ chart.

METHOD SUMMARY 9.3

Single specification limit. One-sided $\bar{X}$-chart (More accurate method)

Step 1 Decide on a producers risk point (p_a, L_a) and obtain the equivalent process mean value $Z_{p_a}\sigma$; see section 9.2.1.

Step 2 Decide on a consumers risk point (p_r, L_r) and obtain the equivalent process mean value, $Z_{p_r}\sigma$.

Step 3 From Table 9.1 or Fig. 9.6 read off the standardized Z_{L_r} and Z_{L_r} corresponding to L_a and L_r.

Step 4 Use a group size n, where n is the lowest integer greater than

$$n = (Z_{L_a} - Z_{L_r})^2/(Z_{p_a} - Z_{p_r})^2.$$

Step 5 Put the action limit at $k_B\sigma$ where

$$k_B = Z_{p_a} - Z_{L_a}/\sqrt{n}$$

Note

Step 4 may frequently result in a group size which is unacceptably large, and then we shall have to compromise on the design requirements.

Table 9.1 ARL values for one-sided $\bar{X}$ chart

Mean	ARL	Mean	ARL	Mean	ARL
0	1.67	2.88	295.5	3.21	1014.8
0.1	1.76	2.90	317.4	3.22	1055.2
0.2	1.86	2.92	341.0	3.23	1097.3
0.3	1.99	2.94	366.6	3.24	1141.2
0.4	2.13	2.96	394.4	3.25	1187.0
0.5	2.29	2.98	424.3	3.26	1234.7
0.6	2.49	3.00	456.8	3.27	1284.4
0.7	2.71	3.01	474.0	3.28	1336.3
0.8	2.99	3.02	492.0	3.29	1390.3
0.9	3.31	3.03	510.6	3.30	1446.7
1.0	3.71	3.04	530.0	3.31	1505.5
1.1	4.19	3.05	550.2	3.32	1566.8
1.2	4.78	3.06	571.3	3.33	1630.7
1.3	5.52	3.07	593.2	3.34	1697.4
1.4	6.44	3.08	616.0	3.35	1766.9
1.5	7.60	3.09	639.7	3.36	1839.5
1.6	9.08	3.10	664.5	3.37	1915.2
1.7	11.00	3.11	690.2	3.38	1994.1
1.8	13.49	3.12	717.0	3.39	2076.4
1.9	16.77	3.13	745.0	3.40	2162.4
2.0	21.15	3.14	774.1	3.42	2345.6
2.70	158.5	3.15	804.4	3.44	2545.1
2.75	187.7	3.16	835.9	3.46	2762.5
2.80	223.0	3.17	868.8	3.48	2999.2
2.82	239.1	3.18	903.1	3.50	3257.3
2.84	265.6	3.19	938.8	3.55	4008.8
2.86	275.2	3.20	976.0	3.60	4942.2

Example 9.3

For the example in section 9.2.1 we have

$$L_a = 500 \quad Z_a = 3.025$$
$$L_r = 5 \quad\ \ Z_r = 1.22$$

leading to $n = 5.58$ or $n = 6$ and $k_B = 1.86$.

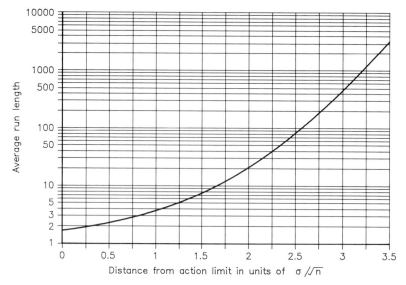

Figure 9.6 ARL curve for one-sided $\bar{X}$ chart.

9.2.6* Single specification limit. Derivation of one-sided $\bar{X}$ chart

The method here is very similar to that in previous sections. First we establish a relationship between the process mean μ and the ARL, and then we determine the sample size n, and the constant k_B as before.

Let us denote

p_0 = probability of a point below the warning limit
p_1 = probability of a point between the action and warning limit
p_2 = probability of a point above the action limit
L_0 = ARL of a process started by a point below the warning limit
L_1 = ARL of a process started by a point between the action
    and warning limits.

Then we have

$$L_0 = 1 + p_0 L_0 + p_1 L_1$$

$$L_1 = 1 + p_0 L_0.$$

This leads to

$$L_0 = (1 + p_1)/(1 - p_0 - p_1 p_0) \tag{9.8}$$

This formula assumes that we take at least one observation.

For the system we have defined, with a process mean of $(\mu\sigma/\sqrt{n})$ above the action limit,

$$p_0 = 1 - \phi(-\mu - 1.13) \tag{9.9}$$

$$p_1 = \phi(-\mu + 1.13) - \phi(-\mu) \tag{9.10}$$

A plot of the ARL for the one-sided $\bar{X}$ chart is shown in Fig. 9.6, and some values are given in Table 9.1. The figure and table are plotted in terms of the variable μ, which is the distance of the mean from the action limit, in standard error units. We can therefore read off the distances, Z_a and Z_r corresponding to ARL values of L_a and L_r respectively. Thus we have

$$(Z_{p_a} - k_B)\sqrt{n} = Z_a$$

$$(Z_{p_r} - k_B)\sqrt{n} = Z_r$$

leading to

$$n = (Z_a - Z_r)^2/(Z_{p_a} - Z_{p_r})^2 \tag{9.11}$$

and

$$k_B = Z_{p_a} - Z_a/\sqrt{n}. \tag{9.12}$$

Again, a convenient way of using this method would be by a nomogram but a suitable chart is not yet available.

9.2.7 Single specification limit. Chart for maximum values

Wilrich (1970) also gave a maximum value chart for use in the single specification limit case. An action line is drawn such that action is taken when the maximum value crosses the line. The theory is similar to that given previously. Clearly, this method is very sensitive to the presence of outliers, but may nevertheless be useful in the correct circumstances. We refer to the source paper for details.

9.3 DOUBLE SPECIFICATION LIMITS: HIGH-CAPABILITY PROCESSES

At this point we introduce a discussion about the use of control charts for high-capability processes. We suppose that we have specification limits, U and L, such that any measurement outside these represents a defective. The estimates of between- and within-group variance will be assumed to have been made, and the correct value for chart plotting, $\hat{\sigma}_e$, obtained. The discussion in this section applies only when $U - L$ is rather greater than $6\hat{\sigma}_e$. In this situation it is not necessary to control the process average level as closely as in the ordinary Shewhart chart. Again, the point made in section 9.1.1 should be considered, whether we ought to insist on statistical control anyway. However, there are situations when it is appropriate to allow a greater variation of the process, but keep it well within the specification limits.

It is necessary to go into this topic in some detail, as industrial manuals are extant in which an unsatisfactory approach is put forward, notwithstanding objections raised by Hill (1956). We first describe this (unsatisfactory) method, and the objections to it.

Let the specification limits be U and L as shown in Fig. 9.7. If the mean of the process is at B, then only 0.1% of the items will have measurements above U, and we may consider the upper specification to be met. Therefore, B and C are regarded as limiting positions for the process mean level. Following the usual method for Shewhart charts, evidence that the process mean is above B is shown by a group average above A, where $A - B$ is $3.09\sigma/\sqrt{n}$. (Some people use a distance $1.96\sigma/\sqrt{n}$.) The lower limit follows similarly, and the modified control

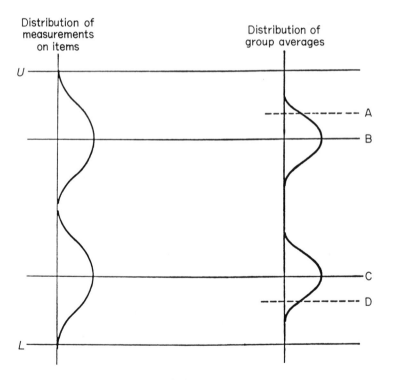

Figure 9.7 Standard deviation of modified control limits.

limits are A and D. If the specified tolerance $U - L$ is only 6.18σ wide, the lines B and C are identical, and the modified limits reduce to the ordinary action for Shewhart charts (but without warning limits).

The main fallacy in this argument is that the original action limits for Shewhart charts are based on the concept of statistical control, whereas with modified control limits, the process mean is allowed to wander, and we no longer have control. Thus in the Shewhart control chart, a point near (but inside) the action limits is taken as evidence that the process is still in control, and the true mean is less than the observed mean. With modified control charts we have no basis for assuming that the true mean is at all less than the observed mean. Therefore by using the modified limits of Fig. 9.7, the process mean would be allowed to rise above B without any action being deemed necessary, and a considerable proportion of non-conforming product could be produced.

It is somewhat surprising that the modified limits are placed outside the limiting positions for the process mean. By doing so we arrive at the paradox that by *increasing the group size*, n, the modified limits would be placed *further away from the tolerances*!!

Further objection to the theory outlined above is that it depends heaviliy on Normality. The Shewhart $\bar{X}$ chart is a technique for controlling a mean, and no assumptions are made about the tolerance satisfied by individual items. The above theory in contrast depends rather heavily on tail area probabilities of the Normal distribution, and so is sensitive to the Normality assumption.

Hill (1956) pointed out that many authors have recognized the objections to the standard approach to modified limits, and stressed the need for extra caution. Hill suggested that the modified limits should be placed so that if the process mean reached the positions B or C in Fig. 9.7, there is only a 5% probability of *not* taking action. This leads to placing the modified limits at a position $1.645\sigma/\sqrt{n}$ *inside* B and C. The width of these modified limits is therefore

$$(U - L) - 2(3.09 + 1.645/\sqrt{n})\sigma.$$

If these limits are narrower than ordinary limits, that is less than $6.18\sigma/\sqrt{n}$, then the best we can do is to use the ordinary limits.

Therefore we use ordinary limits whenever

$$(U + L)/\sigma < (6.18 + 9.47/\sqrt{n}).$$

The procedure is therefore as follows. Use action limits only, and place them

$$(3.09 + 1.645/\sqrt{n})\sigma$$

inside the specification limits U and L. Take action to search for an

Table 9.2 Values for modified control charts

n	$3.09 + 1.645/\sqrt{n}$
2	4.25
3	4.04
4	3.91
5	3.83
6	3.76
7	3.71
8	3.67
9	3.64
10	3.61

assignable cause of variation whenever any point is outside these new limits.

An alternative approach to this problem has been proposed in a draft British Standard of 1989. However, the method given in the next section seems to be preferable.

9.4 DOUBLE SPECIFICATION LIMITS: AN ALTERNATIVE APPROACH

The problem studied in section 9.3 has been looked at by several authors, including Freund (1957) and Duncan (1974); see also Montgomery (1985). These authors use an action boundary only, with the distance from the specification limits set to achieve a specified probability of taking action for a fixed n and given mean.

A better approach seems to be to use action and warning limits at each of the specification limits, designed in the manner set out in section 9.2.5. The chart suggested is shown in Fig. 9.8. Although this chart looks like a standard $\bar{X}$ chart, the difference is that the boundaries are positioned by their distance from the specification limits, and the distance between the warning limits is more than $2 \times 1.96\sigma/\sqrt{n}$.

The chart is drawn up with action limits at a distance $C\sigma$ from the specification limits. The distance between the warning and action limits is kept to $1.13\sigma/\sqrt{n}$, the distance in a standard $\bar{X}$ chart.

The chart is used in the usual way; an action signal is given whenever there are two successive points between the action and warning limits, or one point over the action limits. As statistical control in its usual sense is *not* being applied, and the process is allowed to wander in the central region, the use of warning limits is especially worthwhile.

If process capability is high, then the limits can be designed using the

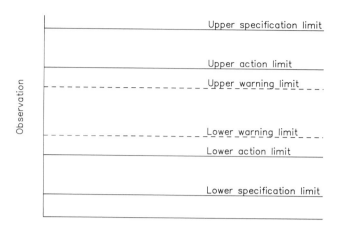

Figure 9.8 Control chart for high-capability processes.

method of section 9.2.5 at each end. However, if process capability is not quite so high the ARL at one boundary is affected by the presence of the other.

The ARL formula for a chart such as that given in Fig. 9.8 was derived in section 5.6.2, leading to

$$L_0 = (1 + p_1 + p_2 + p_1p_2)/(1 - p_0 - p_0p_1 - p_0p_2 - p_1p_2 - p_0p_1p_2)$$
(9.13)

where

p_0 = probability of a point in the central region
p_1 = probability of a point between the upper action and warning limits
p_2 = probability of a point between the lower action and warning limits.

If we have symmetry, with the starting mean at the centre of the central region, then $p_1 = p_2$, and

$$L_0 = (1 + p_1)/(1 - p_0 - p_1 - p_0p_1)$$
(9.14)

There is a simple relationship between the ARL of the two-sided scheme and the ARLs of one-sided scheme given in (9.14). Let the ARLs of the one-sided upper and lower schemes, run separately by L_u and L_1, then it can be shown that

$$\frac{1}{L} = \frac{1}{L_u} = \frac{1}{L_1}$$
(9.15)

This result also follows from a general result by De Bruyn (1968). Clearly, if either L_u or L_l are large, the ARL function for the one-sided scheme is a good approximation in the two-sided case.

A satisfactory method of designing the boundaries shown in Fig. 9.8 is therefore as follows:

(1) Decide on producers' and consumers' risk points for each specification limit.
(2) If the process mean for the two producers' risk points are more than 6σ apart, and do not overlap, then it is satisfactory to use the single limit method at each end.
(3) If condition (2) is not satisfied, then we should settle on a common producers risk point. The single limit method can now be used, with the ARL at the producers risk point equal to *double* that desired.

Clearly, when the two producers' risk points get closer, even the ARLs at the consumers' risk points will be affected by the presence of the other limit, and it will be necessary to use formula (9.15).

EXERCISES 9A

1. Derive action limit only schemes for the following sets of parameters.

p_a	0.001	0.001	0.002	0.01	0.02	0.01	0.01
L_a	400	300	500	500	500	500	300

p_r	0.01	0.01	0.01	0.05	0.05	0.05	0.05
L_r	7	10	5	5	5	3	5

2. Derive one-sided $\bar{X}$ chart schemes for the sets of parameters given in Question 1.

EXERCISES 9B

1. Design a set of simulation experiments to assess the effect of non-normality on the methods given in this chapter.

2. Derive the ARL curve of the maximum value chart, as follows.

Assume that variables are independently and normally distributed with mean μ and variance σ^2, and that observations are taken in groups of n. The action line is to be put at a distance $k_c\sigma$ from the specification limit. Show that

ARL = 1/Pr{at least one sample value beyond action line}

and obtain an expression for the required probability (see Wilrich 1970).

10

Control of discrete data processes

10.1 INTRODUCTION

10.1.1 Types of discrete data chart

We have considered how to operate Shewhart control charts and CuSum charts on continuous data, and now we turn to discrete data. We consider two types of data, *attribute data* and *countable data*, which we described in section 2.1, and the following examples illustrate these types of data.

Example 10.1
In the production of chips of an engineering plastic, 2-kg samples are taken from the production and examined for 'longs'. 'Longs' are unusual shapes, and if there are too many the product does not meet its specification. Fifty such samples of chips were taken at regular intervals, and the number of samples not meeting specification noted. (Note that although the following data represent a high proportion of defective samples, this can occur in two situations. Firstly, the process may be out of control. Secondly, the specifications can be artificially tightened for testing purposes, so as to give a greater chance of detecting changes in the process.) The numbers of defective samples are as follows:

12	11	18	11	10	16	9	11	14	15
11	9	10	13	12	8	12	13	10	12
13	16	12	18	16	10	16	10	12	14

Each result in Example 10.1 represents the number of samples out of 50 which are defective; this is *attribute* data.

Example 10.2

At a later stage in the process referred to in Example 10.1, the process had been brought under control. Instead of merely recording whether each sample was in or out of specification, counts were recorded for the numbers of 'longs' in pairs of samples (i.e. 4 kg of material). The numbers were as follows:

11	8	13	11	13	17	25	23	11	16
9	15	10	16	12	8	9	15	4	12
12	12	15	17	14	17	12	12	7	16

Each result in Example 10.2 represents the number of events of a given type, 'longs', which occur in a set amount of material. This is *countable* data.

In Example 10.1 the results can only be one of the integers 0 to 50, and we might expect the binomial distribution to apply. In Example 10.2 the result can be any positive integer, and might conceivably be quite large; we might expect the Poisson distribution to apply. The Poisson distribution might also be expected to apply if for example we record the number of reportable accidents in a week. The Poisson distribution applies to events distributed randomly in space or time.

Observed results can be recorded and charted in one of two ways:

> *Total* number of observations
> Number of observations *per item* or *per unit interval*.

In Example 10.1 the results quoted are totals, whereas per sample we would get

$$12/50 = 0.24, \quad 11/50 = 0.22, \quad 18/50 = 0.36, \text{ etc.}$$

Similarly, the results given in Example 10.2 are totals for 4 kg of material, whereas the results per kilogram would be one quarter of those shown.

It is possible to make control charts based on each of these methods of recording results, so we have four possibilities:

	Total	Per item/unit
Attribute data	*np* charts	*p* charts
Countable data	*c* charts	*u* charts

These charts are described below.

When the size of the sample is always the same each time the test is carried out then either type of chart can be used; one is a constant multiple of the other. In this case it is usually preferable to use a control chart for total number (c or np), as it avoids one step in the calculations. If the sample size varies at all then the chart must control observations per item, or per unit of sample size (u or p charts).

Since charts of this kind need to be revised as quality improves, and part of this revision may involve an adjustment in sampling size and frequency it may be that in practice we are nearly always dealing in the long run with a situation of varying sample size, so that for ease of comparison the proportional chart (u or p) may be preferable even though it is not essential. Nevertheless, we describe first how to set up charts for total count, and then how to adapt them.

10.1.2 Samples – how and when to take them

Discrete data charts need larger samples than charts based on continuous measurements, and this is especially true for attribute charts. However, the taking of an observation is frequently so much easier and quicker for discrete data charts that they are very frequently used.

BS 5701 has some good practical advice on sampling. It suggests that if the likelihood of producing a defective is high, then it is better to sample after each stage of production. If defectives appear rather rarely, several stages of production can be inspected together.

Two popular methods of sampling are 'random sampling' and 'last-off sampling'. Random sampling is preferred, and is much less likely to miss vital changes in product quality. Last-off sampling is much easier to administrate, and can be used with care.

BS 5701 suggests that sample sizes should be such that on average between 1 and 3 defectives occur in each sample but this is not always practicable or desirable in every situation. In setting the frequency of sampling it is necessary to bear two factors in mind:

(1) There should be very little chance of defective quality developing and disappearing between samples.
(2) Sampling costs should be considered alongside the cost of defective quality when this develops immediately after a sample.

BS 5701 suggests that initially, the sample size and frequency be set so that about 5% of output is inspected. (It indicates that reasons may occur for wide departure from this rule.)

10.1.3 Important assumptions

In most accounts of discrete data charts it is usual to assume that attribute data has a binomial distribution, and that countable data has a

Poisson distribution. These distributions will arise if both the following are true:

(1) All occurrences of the counted event or attribute are independent.
(2) When the process is on target the *average* rate (or average probability) of occurrence of an event is *constant*.

However, an essential step is to check whether or not the binomial or Poisson models are valid; see below. This leads to a rather different approach to charting to that usually recommended for these types of data.

(a) *Poisson variables*
If we are satisfied that the Poisson distribution applies in a situation such as that set out in Example 10.2, then we can construct charts similar to the Shewhart charts of Chapter 5 very easily. There are two ways of proceeding:

(1) Use the exact theory of the Poisson distribution to set action limits at the outer 0.001 probability levels, and warning limits at the outer 0.025 probability levels. The calculation is made easier by using the following relationship between the Poisson and χ^2 distributions.

$$P = \sum_0^x e^{-\mu} \frac{\mu^r}{r!} = \Pr\{\chi^2 > 2\mu | \text{d.f.} = 2(x + 1)\} \qquad (10.1)$$

Therefore, for example, if we want $P \geq 0.999$ then we must have

$$\mu \leq \tfrac{1}{2}\chi^2_{0.999} \ (\text{d.f.} = 2(x + 1))$$

(2) The Poisson distribution tends to normality for large μ, so that an approximation is to use the normal distribution with expectation μ and variance μ. This particular approximation is widely used in SPC, but in fact is not particularly good unless μ is quite large. Other normal approximations could be used, but no others have found favour in SPC circles as yet.

(b) *Binomial variables*
For the binomial distribution, we can proceed in similar ways:

(1) Use exact theory based on summation of binomial probabilities. This is very rarely done, as many SPC applications are designed without the aid of computers. Clearly, it would be very easy to write an algorithm which calculated 'exact' limits for situations where the binomial distribution applies.
(2) Use the Poisson approximation to the binomial distribution.

$$\sum_0^x \binom{n}{r} p^r (1 - p)^{n-r} \simeq \sum_0^x e^{-np} \frac{(np)^r}{r!} \qquad (10.2)$$

This is a very common method, and is used later in this chapter.

(3) Use the normal approximation to the binomial distribution, so that we have expectation (np) and variance $np(1 - p)$. This approximation is not particularly good even for moderate n, and its popular use in SPC leads sometimes to action limits outside the range of the binomial variable, such as negative.

(c) *Discussion*

It is very important to test the validity of the binomial or Poisson distribution assumptions because of the likely presence of between-group variation. For example, in the binomial case it is almost inconceivable that p is held absolutely constant in an industrial process. The extra variation in p will inflate the observed variance of the data. It is therefore important to carry out the *dispersion test*, given in the next section, to check the distributional fit.

If the dispersion test is significant, and the binomial or Poisson models do not apply, then our next route is to see if the data is nevertheless approximately normal, though with an inflated variance over the theoretical models.

If neither binomial or Poisson nor the normal distribution give a good enough fit to the data, special methods will have to be constructed.

At this point we should emphasize again that 'inflated' variances should not be just calmly accepted, and charts drawn with widened limits. In every case a close examination of the data and process should be made to see if the inflated variances are due to causes which can be removed.

10.1.4 The dispersion test

The dispersion test is a very good general test for the binomial or Poisson distribution. The procedure is simply to calculate the ratio

$$D = \frac{\text{observed variance} \times (\text{no. of observations} - 1)}{\text{theoretical variance}} \qquad (10.3)$$

and refer this to tables of the χ^2 distribution on a two-sided test. The theoretical variances are

$$\text{Binomial: } np(1 - p)$$
$$\text{Poisson: } \mu$$

where p and μ will have to be estimated from the data. The relevant χ^2 distribution is for degrees of freedom = (number of observations) − 1,   (10.4)

and χ^2 tables are given in the Appendix tables.

Example 10.3
For 10.1 we obtain

$$\bar{x} = 12.47 \quad s^2 = 7.15 \quad s = 2.67$$

An estimate of p is therefore $\hat{p} = 12.47/50 = 0.249$.
The ratio (10.3) is therefore

$$D = 7.15 \times 29/50 \times 0.249 \times 0.751 = 22.18$$

on 29 d.f. This is not significant, and there is no reason to suspect the assumptions made in the binomial distribution are violated.

Example 10.4
For 10.2 we have

$$\bar{x} = 13.07 \quad s^2 = 19.237 \quad s = 4.39$$

An estimate of μ is $\hat{\mu} = \bar{x} = 13.07$, so that the ratio D is

$$D = 19.237 \times 29/13.07 = 42.68$$

on 29 d.f. This is just beyond the upper 5% point, so that we might be a bit doubtful about the validity of the Poisson distribution in Example 10.2. We would usually require D to reach the $2\frac{1}{2}\%$ points at either end of the range to be regarded as significant. In a practical case we would look back to see if some of the results, such as the two large ones, 23 and 25, were due to some special cause.

In the notes given below, we shall use Examples 10.1 and 10.2 as illustrations, disregarding the results of this dispersion test. This will enable us to explore the difference between the methods. By the dispersion test, both data sets are consistent with their theoretical distributions.

When we do the dispersion test, we are testing agreement of the observed and theoretical variances. It is therefore of interest to calculate the ratio

$$V = \frac{\text{observed variance}}{\text{theoretical variance}} \tag{10.5}$$

If this ratio is not in the range 0.8 to 1.25, then we ought to look rather carefully at the data set to try to understand the cause of this. The ratio V is more readily interpreted than the ratio D, which is simply a scaled version.

For Example 10.2 above, the ratio V is

$$V = 19.237/13.07 = 1.47$$

so that the observed variance is nearly 50% more than the theoretical figure. This is certainly cause for investigation, even though the significance is doubtful.

10.2 SHEWHART CHARTS FOR COUNTABLE DATA (c AND u)

10.2.1 Which method?

The first step is to calculate the mean and variance of the data, estimate μ, and to carry out the dispersion test. We usually use $\hat{\mu} = \bar{x}$, but if sample sizes are not equal, then we use

$$\hat{\mu} = \text{(total count)}/\text{(total sample size)} = \bar{c}.$$

An estimate of the sample variance when there are different sample sizes is obtained by calculating the sample variances for groups of data of each sample size, and then combine them using formula (3.10). We shall denote the sample variance s_c^2.

If the Poisson distribution fits, then for small values of $\hat{\mu}$ we can use the 'exact' method outlined in section 10.1.3, and tables are provided below. For larger values of $\hat{\mu}$ it is necessary to use the normal approximation.

If the Poisson distribution does not fit, then we should check whether the normal distribution fits, using the observed variance, rather than the theoretical variance. We also need to check that $\hat{\mu} > 3\hat{\sigma}$, or a negative lower action limit will result.

This is set out in Fig. 10.1, and we see that if for some reason the normal distribution does not fit then special methods will need to be created.

If this situation arises, the first step is to uncover the reason for the non-Normality. Sometimes, for example, non-Normality is due to the mixing of several populations, and these can be separated. If the non-Normality is inherent in the data, a transformation to normality can be used.

Methods A, B and C below assume that the sample size (2 kg of chips in Example 10.1) is constant.

10.2.2 Method A: Shewhart chart construction for small values of $\bar{c}$ (Poisson distribution)

If c or np are small the Normal approximation method of constructing charts is inaccurate, and the method set out in Method Summary 10.1

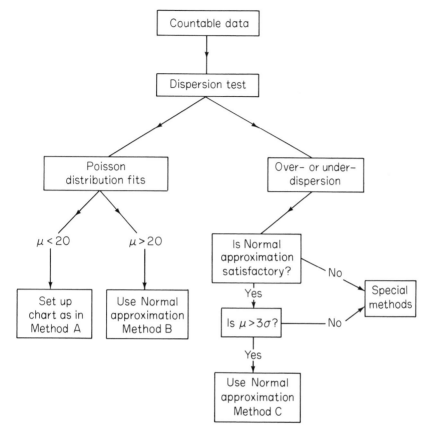

Figure 10.1 Which chart for countable data?

should be used. An alternative is to use moving-average charts, and this may be preferred in some circumstances. The method is based on the *Poisson* distribution, but it can also be used (as an approximation) for *Binomial* variables.

METHOD SUMMARY 10.1

Shewhart chart for countable data (small values of $\bar{c}$)

Step 1 Estimate the mean $\bar{c}$ and variance of the data, and carry out the dispersion test of section 10.1.4. Proceed only if the result is not significant.

Step 2 Look up Table 10.1(a) for $\bar{c}$ in the '$\bar{c}$ interval' line. The corresponding 'value' beneath is the limit.

Table 10.1 Control limits for countable and attribute data

10.1(a)
Upper action limits

$\hat{\mu}$ or $n\hat{p}$	0	0.001	0.045	0.191	0.429	0.739	1.11	1.52	1.97	2.45	2.96
action limit		1	2	3	4	5	6	7	8	9	10

$\hat{\mu}$ or $n\hat{p}$	2.96	3.49	4.04	4.61	5.20	5.80	6.40	7.03	7.66	8.30	8.96
action limit		11	12	13	14	15	16	17	18	19	20

$\hat{\mu}$ or $n\hat{p}$	8.96	9.64	10.31	10.99	11.66	12.34	13.08	13.75	14.45	15.17	15.87
action limit		21	22	23	24	25	26	27	28	29	30

$\hat{\mu}$ or $n\hat{p}$	15.87	17.33	18.06	19.52
action limit	31	32	33	34

10.1(b)
Upper warning limits

$\hat{\mu}$ or $n\hat{p}$	0	0.025	0.242	0.619	1.09	1.62	2.20	2.81	3.45	4.12	4.80
warning limit		1	2	3	4	5	6	7	8	9	10

$\hat{\mu}$ or $n\hat{p}$	4.80	5.49	6.20	6.92	7.65	8.40	9.15	9.91	10.67	11.44	12.22
warning limit		11	12	13	14	15	16	17	18	19	20

$\hat{\mu}$ or $n\hat{p}$	12.22	13.01	13.80	14.60	15.39	16.18	16.99	17.81	18.62	19.43	20.24
warning limit		21	22	23	24	25	26	27	28	29	30

10.1(c)
Lower warning limits

$\hat\mu$ or $n\hat p$ warning limit	3.69	5.57	7.22	8.77	10.24	11.67	13.06	14.42	15.76	17.08	18.39
	0	1	2	3	4	5	6	7	8	9	

$\hat\mu$ or $n\hat p$ warning limit	18.39	19.68	20.96	22.23	23.49
	10	11	12	13	

10.1(d)
Lower action limits

$\hat\mu$ or $n\hat p$ action limit	6.91	9.23	11.23	13.06	14.79	16.45	18.06	19.63	21.16
	0	1	2	3	4	5	6	7	

Note: In each row the upper line is $\hat\mu$ (usually the average $\bar c$). The limits corresponding to the intervals in the upper line are the integers in the lower line.

Steps 3–5 Repeat the procedure of Step 2 for the upper warning limit, the lower warning and action limits, using Table 10.1(b), (c), (d) respectively.

There are several points to note about this procedure:

(1) For marginal cases, round them up for upper limits and down for lower limits. Thus 0.191 corresponds to an upper action limit of 4.
(2) For values of $\bar{c}$ beyond the table revert to the normal approximation method.
(3) For binomial variables with $p \leq 0.1$, replace $\bar{c}$ by $n\bar{p}$.

Example 10.5

As an example of Method A we use the data of Example 10.2, and in Example 10.4 we established that $\bar{c} = 13.07$. On following through the steps of Method Summary 10.1 we get

Upper action limit	= 26	Lower warning limit	= 6
Upper warning limit	= 22	Lower action limit	= 3

10.2.3 Method B: Shewhart chart construction for large values of $\bar{c}$ (Poisson distribution)

This method is based on the normal approximation to the Poisson distribution, and is set out in Method Summary 10.2.

METHOD SUMMARY 10.2

Shewhart chart for countable data (large values of $\bar{c}$)

Step 1 Carry out Step 1 of Method A (section 10.2.2).
Step 2 Scale the chart so that the vertical axis extends between about $\bar{c} \pm 4\sqrt{\bar{c}}$. Mark in $\bar{c}$ on the chart.
Step 3 Calculate the action limits and mark them on the chart.

$$\text{Action limits: } \bar{c} \pm 3.09\sqrt{\bar{c}} \qquad \text{(probability)}$$
$$\text{or: } \bar{c} \pm 3\sqrt{\bar{c}} \qquad \text{(popular)}$$

(If the lower limit is negative you should use Method A).
Step 4 Calculate and mark on the warning limits.

$$\text{Warning limits: } \bar{c} \pm 1.96\sqrt{\bar{c}} \qquad \text{(probability)}$$
$$\text{or: } \bar{c} \pm 2\sqrt{\bar{c}} \qquad \text{(popular)}$$

Step 5 Plot the initial data counts on the chart if this is appropriate. If an assignable cause of variation is found for any extreme group omit it from the calculations and revise the chart accordingly.

Example 10.6

Although Example 10.2 data does not fall within the rules for using Method Summary 10.2 (Method B) we shall continue this example, in order to show the differences between the boundaries. We obtain, using probability limits.

Upper action limit	$\bar{c} + 3.09\sqrt{\bar{c}}$	$= 24.24$
Upper warning limit	$\bar{c} + 1.96\sqrt{\bar{c}}$	$= 20.15$
Lower warning limit	$\bar{c} - 1.96\sqrt{\bar{c}}$	$= 5.98$
Lower action limit	$\bar{c} - 3.09\sqrt{\bar{c}}$	$= 1.90$

The limits and data are shown in Fig. 10.2.

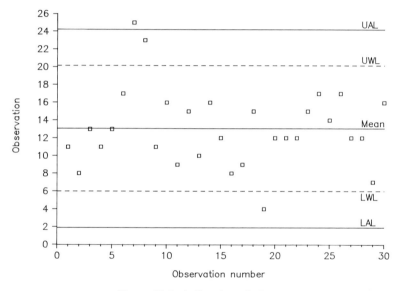

Figure 10.2 A Shewhart $\bar{c}$ chart.

If the data of Example 10.2 was being used to set up charts, then an examination of point seven would be made to see if a special cause was present. If so, this point would be omitted and the limits recalculated.

10.2.4 Method C: Shewhart chart construction for countable data with large value of $\bar{c}$ when the Poisson distribution does not apply

If the dispersion test has shown that the dispersion of the data is either too large or too small to use the Poisson distribution as a model it may first be worth investigating why this is so. If a cause cannot be found, or is not removable, Shewhart charts may still be set up using the Normal approximation, provided this is a reasonable approximation.

METHOD SUMMARY 10.3

Shewhart chart for countable data (over or under dispersion)

Step 1 Use a Normal probability plot (section 2.9) to check that the approximation is reasonable.

Step 2 Calculate the average $\bar{c}$ and s_c as described in section 10.2.1.

Step 3 Scale the chart so that the vertical axis extends between $\bar{c} \pm 4s_c$.

Step 4 Put action limits on the chart at

$$\bar{c} \pm 3.09s_c \quad \text{(probability)}$$
$$\text{or } \bar{c} \pm 3s_c \quad \text{(popular)}$$

If the lower limit is negative it is advisable to consult a statistician for guidance.

Step 5 Put warning limits at

$$\bar{c} \pm 1.96s_c \quad \text{(probability)}$$
$$\text{or } \bar{c} \pm 2s_c \quad \text{(popular)}$$

If the lower warning limit is negative this is definitely *not* an appropriate chart. Consider using a moving-average chart to solve this problem. Otherwise consult a statistician.

Step 6 Plot the data, and recalculate limits if any extreme point has an assignable cause of variation.

Example 10.7

We continue using Example 10.2 for illustration even though Method A is appropriate. The limits are as follows:

$$\text{Upper action limit } \bar{c} + 3.09s_c = 26.64$$
$$\text{Upper warning limit } \bar{c} + 1.96s_c = 21.67$$
$$\text{Lower warning limit } \bar{c} - 1.96s_c = 4.46$$
$$\text{Lower action limit } \bar{c} - 3.09s_c = \text{(no value)}$$

10.2.5 Shewhart *u* charts

Countable data might arise from observing the number of special features in a given amount of material, as in Example 10.1, or from counting the number of defects on a sample of items. We shall call the amount of material, or number of items, the sample size. In Methods A, B and C we assumed a constant sample size, but in practice the sample size often varies. It is then best to use a *u chart*, in which results are presented per unit amount of material or per item. In section 10.1 we indicated that there might be other reasons for preferring a *u* chart.

The construction of a *u* chart is simple. A chart for *total count* based on the average sample size is constructed using the Methods A, B or C as appropriate. All action and warning limits are then scaled down to present the results on a per unit basis. Thus if the average sample size is t and the average count is $\bar{c}$, the Normal approximation method gives action lines for total counts at $\bar{c} \pm 3\sqrt{\bar{c}}$, so that action limits for a *u* chart are at

$$(\bar{c} \pm 3\sqrt{\bar{c}})/t = \bar{u} \pm 3\sqrt{(\bar{u}/t)}$$

where $\bar{u} = \bar{c}/t$; see Fig. 10.3.

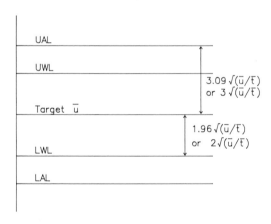

Figure 10.3 A Shewhart $\bar{u}$ chart when $\bar{c}$ is large and the Poisson distribution is appropriate.

Provided the sample size does not vary by more than 25%, only one set of limits can be used. When there is greater variation in the sample size it is necessary to recalculate the limits for each sample size. This results in a chart such as in Fig. 10.4.

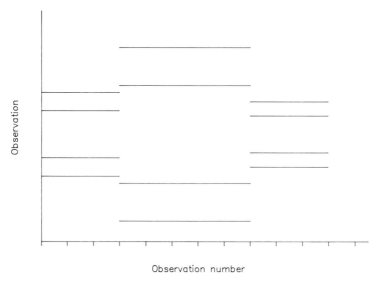

Figure 10.4 A $\bar{u}$ chart with varying sample size.

10.2.6 Moving-average charts for c or u

If the average rate of occurrence of defects or other events is low the sampling interval may contain very few such events. It may then be appropriate or even essential to use a moving-average chart for c (or equivalently for u) so that sample intervals are effectively added together. The steps below are appropriate for moving averages of k sample points at a time.

METHOD SUMMARY 10.4

Moving-average charts for countable data (k steps)

Step 1 Estimate $\bar{c}$ for a single sampling interval as before (section 10.2.2) and test whether the Poisson distribution is appropriate.

Step 2 Choose the appropriate method of setting up a Shewhart chart (see Fig. 10.1) for data with a mean of $k\bar{c}$.

Step 3 Calculate action limits only (warning limits are *not* used in moving-average charts) using the method selected in Step 2, and a mean count of $k\bar{c}$.

Step 4 Divide these limits by k to obtain the action limit for a moving-average c chart. If required, divide again by $\bar{i}$ to obtain limits for a u chart.

10.3 SHEWHART CHARTS FOR ATTRIBUTE DATA (np AND p)

10.3.1 Estimation

The methods here are very similar to those given in section 10.2.1 for countable data, and the reasoning will not be repeated. The only difference is that 'exact' methods based on actual calculations with the binomial distribution are not usually recommended. When $n\hat{p}$ is small, and the dispersion test is not significant, the Poisson approximation is usually satisfactory, so that Method A of section 10.2.2 can be used.

An overall estimate of p is obtained by using

$$\hat{p} = (\text{total no. of defects})/(\text{total sample size}),$$

omitting any group of data for which a special cause is known. The dispersion test is carried out as in section 10.1.4, and the flow chart for choosing the appropriate chart is shown in Fig. 10.5; see also section 10.1.3. We shall denote the standard deviation of the observed counts by s_c.

10.3.2 Shewhart chart construction for np or p, for data from a binomial distribution with small values of $n\hat{p}$

Using the value of $\bar{c} = n\hat{p}$ go through the steps set out in section 10.2.2. This will give a chart for monitoring the actual count (np) of non-conforming items in equal-sized samples. If a chart for monitoring the proportion p is preferred – as it often will be, see section 10.1 – then all action and warning limits are divided by the sample size n.

If samples are of somewhat different sizes, use the average sample size $\bar{n}$ as the divisor. However, this is reasonable only if sample size varies by about 25% either way of $\bar{n}$, otherwise limits must be calculated separately for the different sample sizes.

Strictly speaking the method of section 10.2.2 is for Poisson data only, but the approximation is reasonable provided $\hat{p}$ is small (≤ 0.1). If you have data for which this is *not* true you can use the method of section 10.3.3 if $n\hat{p} \geq 10$, but otherwise special methods may need constructing.

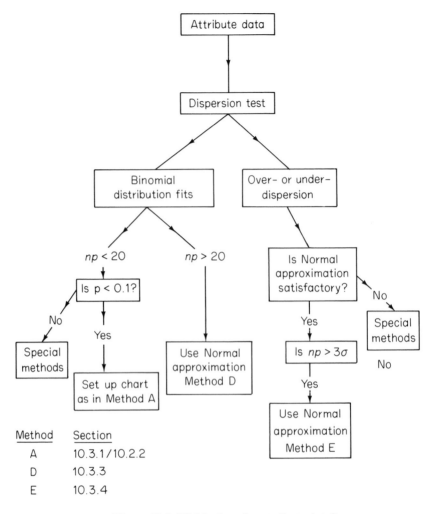

Figure 10.5 Which chart for attribute data?

Example 10.8
For Example 10.1 data we have $\hat{p} = 0.2493$, $n = 50$, so that $np = 12.47$. Method A is appropriate, and gives the following boundaries:

Upper action limit	= 26	Lower warning limit	= 5
Upper warning limit	= 21	Lower action limit	= 2

To construct a p chart these values are divided by 50.

10.3.3 Method D: Shewhart chart construction for Binomial data when $n\hat{p}$ is large

This method uses the normal approximation to the binomial distribution, and it is summarized in Method Summary 10.5.

METHOD SUMMARY 10.5

np charts using the normal approximation to the binomial distribution

Step 1 Calculate $\hat{p}$ as in section 10.3.1 and check that the binomial distribution is appropriate, and that $n\hat{p} \geq 10$ and preferably $n\hat{p} \geq 20$.

Step 2 Scale the chart so that the vertical axis extends

$$p \text{ chart} \quad \text{between } \hat{p} \pm 4\sqrt{(\hat{p}/n)}$$
$$np \text{ chart} \quad \text{between } n\hat{p} \pm 4\sqrt{(n\hat{p})}.$$

Step 3 Set the action limits as follows:

	Probability	*Popular*
p chart	$\hat{p} \pm 3.09\sqrt{\{\hat{p}(1 - \hat{p})/n\}}$	$\hat{p} \pm 3\sqrt{\{\hat{p}(1 - \hat{p})/n\}}$
np chart	$n\hat{p} \pm 3.09\sqrt{\{n\hat{p}(1 - p)\}}$	$n\hat{p} \pm 3\sqrt{\{n\hat{p}(1 - \hat{p})\}}.$

If the lower limit is negative use the method of section 10.3.2 to set up the chart.

Step 4 Set warning limits as follows:

	Probability	*Popular*
p chart	$\hat{p} \pm 1.96\sqrt{\{\hat{p}(1 - \hat{p})/n\}}$	$\hat{p} \pm 2\sqrt{\{\hat{p}(1 - \hat{p})/n\}}$
np chart	$n\hat{p} \pm 1.96\sqrt{\{n\hat{p}(1 - \hat{p})\}}$	$n\hat{p} \pm 2\sqrt{\{n\hat{p}(1 - \hat{p})\}}$

Example 10.9

We continue using Example 10.1 data for illustration even though Method A is appropriate. The limits are as follows:

Upper action limit	21.92	0.438
Upper warning limit	18.46	0.369
Lower warning limit	6.47	0.129
Lower action limit	3.01	0.060

The limits and data are plotted in Figs. 10.6 and 10.7.

It is clear from the calculations done on Examples 10.1 and 10.2 that the normal approximation method can be substantially in error at small values of $n\hat{p}$.

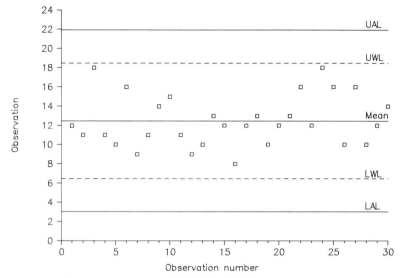

Figure 10.6 An *np* chart for the data of Example 10.1.

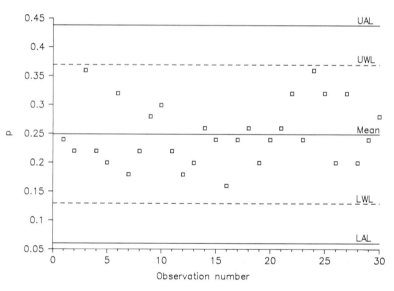

Figure 10.7 A *p* chart for the data of Example 10.1.

10.3.4 Method E: Shewhart chart construction for attribute data when $n\hat{p}$ is large and the binomial distribution is not appropriate

Over-dispersion can often occur in what we might expect to be binomially distributed data. This is generally due to the fact that the true proportion defective varies from batch to batch or from day to day. Underdispersion is seldom seen for such data, but may occasionally occur. In either case it may be well worth the effort of investigating the reason for such under- or overdispersion, as this may lead to ways of reducing the overall proportion of non-conforming items being produced.

Shewhart charts are set up as in Method Summary 10.6, using the Normal approximation.

METHOD SUMMARY 10.6

np charts using a direct normal approximation

Step 1 Use a Normal probability plot (section 2.9) to check that the proposed approximation is reasonable.

Step 2 Calculate $\hat{p}$ and s_c as in section 10.3.1.

Step 3 The scale of the vertical axis should cover the range

p chart	$\hat{p} \pm 4s_c/n$
np chart	$n\hat{p} \pm 4s_c.$

Step 4 Action limits are calculated:

	Probability	*Popular*
p chart	$\hat{p} \pm 3.09s_c/n$	$\hat{p} \pm 3s_c/n$
np chart	$n\hat{p} \pm 3.09s_c$	$n\hat{p} \pm 3s_c$

If the lower limit is negative this may not be an appropriate way to set up the chart.

Step 5 Warning limits are set:

	Probability	*Popular*
p chart	$p \pm 1.96s_c/n$	$\hat{p} / 2s_c/n$
np chart	$n\hat{p} \pm 1.96s_c$	$n\hat{p} \pm 2s_c$

If the lower limit is negative this is not the right way to set up a Shewhart chart. Consult a statistician.

10.3.5 Moving-total and moving-average proportion charts for p

As with the c chart it may be that a single sample contains so few non-conforming items that it is not possible to set up a satisfactory Shewhart chart for individual samples. Again, using a moving-total or moving-average effectively increases the sample size. The disadvantage is that a sudden large increase in the proportion defective may be averaged out, and so not detected immediately.

METHOD SUMMARY 10.7

Moving-average p or np charts

Step 1 Choose the (average) size n of individual samples, and k, the number of samples in the moving total or moving average.

Step 2 Obtain suitable data from the process, calculate $\bar{c}$ and s_c, for individual samples of size n, and hence calculate $\hat{p}$ and V (equation (10.5)).

Step 3 Use this if $V \neq 1$.

If $kn\hat{p} \geq 3\sqrt{k}s_c$, then set action limits for charts thus:

	Probability	Popular
Moving total	$kn\hat{p} \pm 3.09s_c\sqrt{k}$	$kn\hat{p} \pm 3s_c\sqrt{k}$
Moving average proportion	$\hat{p} \pm 3.09s_c/n\sqrt{k}$	$\hat{p} \pm 3s_c/n\sqrt{k}$

Step 4 Use this if $V \simeq 1$.

(a) If $kn\hat{p} < 20$ *and* if $\hat{p} \leq 0.1$
Use Table 10.1 with $\bar{c} = kn\hat{p}$, to set action limits for a moving-total chart. Divide these by kn to give limits for a moving-average proportion.

(b) If $kn\hat{p} > 10$, with no restriction on $\hat{p}$ action lines are set:

	Probability	Popular
Moving total	$kn\hat{p} \pm 3.09\sqrt{\{kn\hat{p}(1 - \hat{p})\}}$	$kn\hat{p} \pm 3\sqrt{\{kn\hat{p}(1 - \hat{p})\}}$
Moving average proportion	$\hat{p} \pm 3.09\sqrt{\left\{\dfrac{n\hat{p}(1 - \hat{p})}{kn}\right\}}$	$\hat{p} \pm 3\sqrt{\left\{\dfrac{n\hat{p}(1 - \hat{p})}{kn}\right\}}$

10.4 CuSum CHARTS FOR COUNTABLE DATA: GENERAL POINTS

10.4.1 Introduction

The International Standard on CuSum charts listed in section 13.5 contains a detailed discussion of the application of CuSums to countable or attributable data, and it contains much practical advice. Sections 10.4–10.6 of this book follow that standard closely.

However, it applies *only* to situations where the assumptions underlying the Poisson distribution are valid, namely

(1) constant size of observation interval;
(2) independence of events;

(3) constant average rate of occurrence of events.

It is important to use the dispersion test to check whether these assumptions are reasonable. This can be considered as the equivalent of testing for additional components of variation for continuous measurements, as discussed in Chapter 3.

If it is found that the ratio V lies outside the range 0.8 to 1.25 this should be investigated. If the causes of extra variation are not found, or they are found but cannot yet be eliminated, the method of section 10.7 should be used to set up CuSum charts.

Scaling
The general convention used is that the distance between samples on the horizontal scale represents $2\sigma_e$ units on the vertical scale. In the context of countable or attribute data, this leads to using the following theoretical values for σ_e:

Countable data	Poisson distribution	$\hat{\sigma}_e = \sqrt{\bar{c}}$
Attribute data	Binomial distribution	$\hat{\sigma}_e \sqrt{[n\hat{p}(1 - \hat{p})]}$

where $\bar{c}$ is the estimated mean of the Poisson distribution, and $\hat{p}$ is the estimated proportion with the attribute, for attribute data. Note that when $\bar{c}$ (or $n\hat{p}$) is less than 1 special rules apply (see Step 5 of section 10.5.2).

10.4.2 Form of mask

The distributions arising with countable and attribute data are usually skew, so that a symmetrical mask as used in Chapter 7 is not appropriate. In any case, for countable and attribute data it is nearly always increases in the mean which are critical. For these reasons, a one-sided mask is suggested as shown in Fig. 10.8, so that only increases in the mean are detected. The parameters of the mask are H, the decision interval, and F the slope per unit. The other parameter often quoted is the reference value $K = C_T + F$, where C_T is the target value.

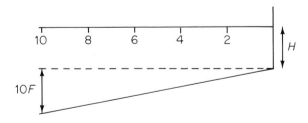

Figure 10.8 Mask for countable and attribute data.

10.4.3 Decision rules

The International Standard referred to gives two sets of parameters for CuSum schemes – one set, the C1 schemes, when the ARL is about 1000 when the process is on target and the other set, the C2 schemes, when the ARL is about 200 for a process on target. A very large number of schemes could be constructed, but those tabulated by the International Standard should be satisfactory for most purposes. If the rates of occurrence of countable or attribute data is very large, the Normal approximation can be used, so that we revert to the methods of section 7.2, and specific rules are given below.

For both countable and attribute data detailed tables are needed for implementation, and it is impracticable to give more than a limited number of sets of parameters. For this reason, interpolation may be required in the schemes given below. As the manner of using the table of parameters is more complicated than for CuSums with continuous variables, we discuss this first, and then list the detailed steps involved in running a scheme. In each case there is the possibility of using a CuSum plot, or a decision interval scheme.

10.5 CuSum CHARTS FOR COUNTABLE DATA

10.5.1 Use of tables

Obtain the process average $\bar{c}$, in a similar way to that described in section 10.2.1. Any group for which there is an identifiable cause of variation should be omitted. Check that $V = s_e^2/\bar{c} \simeq 1$.

In order to select a CuSum scheme we need to choose a target value for the process average number of defects or counts, C_T. This will usually be the process average $\bar{c}$, but it may be some other value that we expect to be able to achieve; for example, certain preferred values of C_T are given in Table 10.2 and one of these might be used if it is close to $\bar{c}$.

Table 10.2 CuSum parameters for countable data

Event rate at AQL C_T	CuSum parameters for C1 schemes		CuSum parameters for C2 schemes	
	H	K	H	K
0.1	1.5	0.75	2	0.25
0.125	2.5	0.5	2.5	0.25
0.16	3.0	0.5	2	0.5
0.2	3.5	0.5	2.5	0.5
0.25	4.0	0.5	3	0.5

Table 10.2 (*cont.*)

Event rate at AQL C_T	CuSum parameters for C1 schemes		CuSum parameters for C2 schemes	
	H	K	H	K
0.32	3.0	1.0	4	0.5
0.4	2.5	1.5	3	1
0.5	3	1.5	2	1.5
0.64	*3.5 or 4	1.5	2	2.0
0.8	5	1.5	3.5	1.5
1.0	5	2	5	1.5
1.25	4	3	5	2
1.6	5	3	4	3
2.0	*7 or 8	3	5	3
2.5	7	4	5	4
3.2	7	5	5	5
4.0	8	6	6	6
5.0	9	7	7	7
6.4	9	9	9	8
8.0	9	11	9	10
10.0	11	13	11	12
10	11	13	11	12
15	16	18	11	18
20	20	23	14	23
25	24	28	17	28

Table 10.2 shows two sets of CuSum schemes, C1 and C2, appropriate to a range of values of C_T. The procedure for choosing a set of parameters, H and K, is given in Method Summary 10.8.

METHOD SUMMARY 10.8

CuSum charts for countable data: Choosing parameters

Step 1 Choose C_T, and decide upon C1 or C2 schemes.

Step 2a For C_T in the range (0.1 to 10.0), choose a line of the table close to the observed value $\bar{c}$. It should be satisfactory to use the C_T value listed in the table, rather than $\bar{c}$. Record H and K.

Step 2b For C_T in the range 10–25 use linear interpolation between the lines of the table, rounding both H and K in the same way to integers (i.e. both rounded up or both rounded down). It may be better to choose a value of C_T to make calculations easier, such as an integer value, or a C_T listed in the table.

Step 2c For C_T greater than 25 use CuSum schemes for Normally distributed variables with target C_T and $\sigma_e = \sqrt{C_T}$. It should be noted that CuSum schemes for Poisson variables designed in this way have ARLs about 40% lower at target than those for Normally distributed data.

10.5.2 Operating a CuSum scheme for countable data

The method of operation is set out in Method Summary 10.9, and an example chart is shown in Fig. 10.9.

METHOD SUMMARY 10.9

Operating a CuSum scheme for countable data

Step 1 The set-up phase is very similar to that set out in section 5.1.3. When this is completed we shall usually have available at least 20 groups of n observations each, with records of the numbers of counts or defects, $c_1, c_2, \ldots, c_{20}$.

Step 2 Calculate the process average

$$\bar{c} = (\Sigma c_i)/(\text{No. of groups}).$$

Any group for which an assignable cause of variation is identified should be omitted from the calculation.

Step 3 Settle on a set of parameters C_T, H and K as outlined in section 10.5.1.

Step 4 Decide on whether to use a CuSum plot or a decision interval scheme.

Step 5 Scale the plots so that one unit on the horizontal scale represents $2\sqrt{C_T}$ units on the vertical scale, provided $C_T > 1$. If $C_T < 1$, mark the *horizontal* scale in intervals of the quantity

greatest integer in $1/C_T$

and then mark the vertical scale in intervals of the same length as the horizontal scale, but mark them successive *even* integers from zero, 0, 2, 4, ...

Note

The scaling in Step 5 arises because with very low C_T, a large number of samples are taken to obtain (on average) one count. The suggested scaling for $C_T < 1$ is more appropriate for this situation.

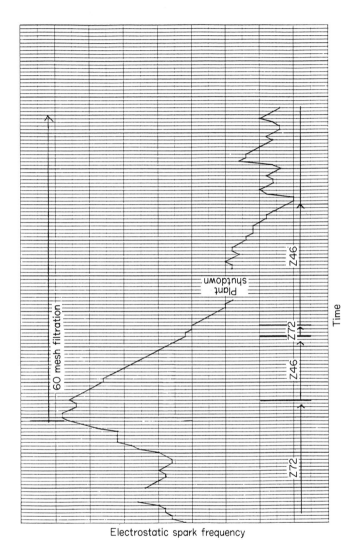

Figure 10.9 A CuSum plot of countable data.

The problem giving rise to Fig. 10.9 was actually electrostatic sparking, which interrupted the process and caused deterioration in the product. The chief changes in the plot seem to be due to coincidental changes in filtration, and due to operations done during a plant shut-down. In fact product grade changes (Z72, Z46, etc.) might also be responsible.

The ability of CuSum plots to pinpoint the time when a change occurred is very helpful, but doesn't entirely remove the ambiguity when several changes to the process are made close together in time.

10.6 CuSum CHARTS FOR ATTRIBUTE DATA

The situation here is very similar to the case for countable data outlined in section 10.5. We assume that we take groups of n observations at a time, and record the numbers r_1, r_2, ..., r_{20} of defectives or the numbers with the attribute in question. The next step is to calculate

$$p_i = r_i/n \quad \text{and} \quad \bar{p} = (\Sigma r_i)/\{n \times (\text{no. of groups})\}.$$

The difficulty with attribute data is that there are two parameters, n and p, for the data as compared with one, the mean, for countable data. Because of this, the construction of comprehensive tables would be impracticable. Fortunately, two approximations deal with a majority of situations.

Case 1 $\bar{p} < 0.1$. In this situation, the CuSum schemes for countable data may be used, with $\bar{c} = n\bar{p}$. This will cover the majority of practical applications.

Case 2 $n\bar{p} > 20$. In this situation CuSum schemes based on the Normal approximation may be used. Values of h and f are chosen from Table 7.5 as for a Normally distributed variable, and used as follows:

$$H = h\sqrt{\{n\bar{p}(1 - \bar{p})\}}$$
$$K = n\bar{p} + f\sqrt{\{n\bar{p}(1 - \bar{p})\}}$$

and H and K are rounded to the nearest integers.
Case 3 *other values of n and p*. Here a special table is necessary, and reference should be made to the International Standard.

10.7 CuSum PLOTS FOR COUNTABLE OR ATTRIBUTE DATA WHEN THE POISSON OR BINOMIAL DISTRIBUTION DOES NOT APPLY

All methods given in section 10.4–6 are sensitive to the assumptions given in section 10.4.1. But it may often be the case that one or more of these assumptions is invalid. In particular, the likelihood of an event or of a defective item may not be constant over the long term. Indeed, in many cases it can be argued that if the process were genuinely in control the defective rate can often be controlled so as to be negligible. While this is a desirable goal to aim for we do require realistic control charts to operate on the way.

If calculation of the ratio

$$V = \frac{s_c^2}{\bar{c}} \text{ or } \frac{s_c^2}{n\hat{p}(1 - \hat{p})}$$

gives a value that is appreciably different from 1 the causes should first be investigated. If it is not currently possible to identify and/or remove the cause of under- or overdispersion, then a CuSum chart can be set up as follows, *provided* that $\bar{c}$ is at least $1\frac{1}{2}$ times as great as s_c, and preferably appreciably larger than this.

METHOD SUMMARY 10.10

CuSum charts for countable and attribute data when Poisson or binomial distribution does not apply

Step 1 Calculate $\bar{c}$ and s_c. Check that $\bar{c} > 1\frac{1}{2}s_c$.

Step 2 Set up a one-sided or two-sided CuSum plot or decision interval scheme with

$$T = \bar{c}$$
$$H = hs_c$$
$$F = fs_c$$
$$K = T + F$$

where the parameters h and f are obtained from Table 7.5, depending on the approximate ARL properties required.

Step 3 To obtain a CuSum chart for u or for p divide each of the parameters T, H, F and K by $\bar{t}$ or by n as appropriate.

10.8 COMPARISON OF SHEWHART AND CuSum SCHEMES

The gain in ARL is not so great with countable or attribute data as with continuous data. However, there is some gain, and the visual interpretation of CuSum charts etc., also give the CuSum schemes advantages. Alternatively a moving-total or moving-average chart may be more straightforward to operate and could have similar ARL properties to a CuSum scheme if k is chosen appropriately.

EXERCISES 10.A

1. For the situation described in Example 10.2 it has been decided that in future $\frac{1}{2}$-kg samples will be taken, but that the chart should be set up to record longs per kilogram. Set up the chart.

2. Carry out a study of the accuracy of the Normal approximation method for the Poisson distribution, using a range of values of $\bar{c}$.

3. Set up CuSum charts from the data given in Examples 10.1 and 10.2.

EXERCISE 10.B

1. A property of the Poisson distribution is the equality

$$\Pr(X \leq x | \text{mean} = \mu) = \Pr(\chi^2 > 2\mu | 2(x + 1) \text{ d.f.}).$$

Use this to check the validity of Table 10.1.

11

Sampling inspection

11.1 INTRODUCTION

11.1.1 Where inspection?

In any industrial process there are three points at which we can attempt to control the outgoing quality, as pictured diagrammatically in Fig. 11.1.

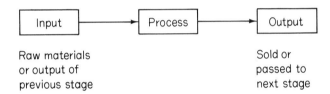

Raw materials
or output of
previous stage

Sold or
passed to
next stage

Figure 11.1 Sites for sampling inspection.

The methods we have been considering are all attempts to control the output from a process, by observing it, and by taking control actions on it. The other points at which some control can be exercised are to inspect the input and output; see Fig. 11.1.

Input. We can inspect the input to ensure that it is of sufficiently high quality. It is clearly a waste of money to process material which is of substandard quality at the input stage.

Output. We can inspect the output to attempt to filter out the non-conforming material, or in order to grade it for sale.

Attempts to filter out non-conforming quality at the output stage are costly, and not very effective. Wherever possible, input inspection should be avoided by making special agreements with the supplier so that he installs appropriate SPC methods, and so that data are obtained from his output inspection. Frequently, however, needless losses are incurred by failing to carry out adequate incoming inspection. Satisfactory agreements with suppliers are not always possible.

The following examples illustrate some uses of sampling inspection:

Example 11.1
Child-proof screw caps are delivered packed in large cartons. A number of these are taken out and tested on a standard bottle before deciding whether the carton is to be used or rejected. Each cap can be classified as conforming or non-conforming to a given specification.

Example 11.2
At certain factory bags of pellets of catalyst are submitted to incoming inspection. Typically, three variables are measured: crushing strength, amount of activity and pore size. The crushing strength and activity levels must meet given specifications, and the pore size distribution must be satisfactory; or the bag is rejected.

Example 11.3
In the manufacture of a pharmaceutical product, there is a small percentage of byproduct in the final production material after going through a purification process. The percentage byproduct is measured by a chromatographic analysis. The percentage of byproduct must be kept within limits for the product to be released.

In the first two examples, the inspection is fairly cheap compared with the costs involved in Example 11.3. The examples also illustrate both *incoming* and *outgoing* inspection.

In this chapter we give a brief overview of sampling inspection, and discuss sampling inspection by attributes. For more information consult Schilling (1982) or Wetherill (1977); for theory of sampling inspection by attriutes see Hald (1976).

Before proceeding, we need some terminology. A *batch* or *lot* is a collection of produced items, or an amount of produced material, which is passing through an inspection station as a unit. These are usually packaged or bagged together. As a result of inspection, we *sentence* the batch, which means that we accept it or reject it, or perhaps accept it or sell it at a reduced price, etc. For the most part, we consider inspection by attributes (see below) of batches of items. Usually, each batch is sentenced on the basis of a *sample* of items.

11.1.2 Sampling inspection or 100% inspection

In industry it is sometimes necessary to defend inspection by samples against 100% inspection, and to explain why sample procedures are reliable. Clearly there are some situations in which 100% inspection is desired rather than sampling inspection, but such situations are infrequent. The reasons why sample methods are preferred are as follows:

(1) We never require absolutely accurate information about a batch or quantity of goods to be sentenced. Thus in Example 11.1 it would be sufficient to estimate the percentage of non-conforming types in the batch to within $\frac{1}{2}$% or so. Complete inspection in Example 11.1 would be an unnecesary waste of time and labour. For the purpose of sentencing the batch, an estimate of the fraction non-conforming is quite sufficient.

(2) A point allied to (1) is that under the usual assumptions, the standard error of an estimate reduces as the number of observations increases, approximately as the reciprocal of the square root of the number of observations. Therefore in order to halve the standard error we must take four times as many observations. Beyond a certain point it is either impractical or not worth while achieving greater accuracy.

(3) Even if the entire batch is inspected in Example 11.1 say, we still do not have an absolute accurate estimate of the fraction non-conforming *unless inspection is perfect*. In industrial situations inspection is very rarely perfect and Hill (1962) quotes a probability of 0.9 as being 'not unreasonable' for the probability of recognising defects by visual inspection. Some experiments have indicated that if inspectors are faced with batches for 100% inspection, then the inspection tends to be less accurate than if sample methods are used.

(4) In some cases, such as in Example 11.3, inspection by laboratory analysis is very costly and 100% inspection is obviously ruled out. Another case of this is *destructive testing*, as in testing of artillery shells.

One situation where 100% inspection is appropriate is when it can be arranged cheaply by some automatic device. More usually sample methods will be appropriate.

When sample methods are employed we shall usually make the assumption that sampling is *random*. Thus in Example 11.1 a sample should be taken in such a way that every item in the batch is equally likely to be taken. In practice this assumption is rarely satisfied and this has to be taken into account when drawing up a plan.

Sometimes it is possible to stratify the items to be sentenced, and use this to draw up a more efficient sample procedure. For example, in the transport of bottled goods in cartons, the bottles next to the face of the carton are more likely to be damaged than those in the interior. In this case it would be better to define two strata, one being those bottles next to a face of the carton, and the other stratum being the remainder. A procedure which sampled these strata separately would be more efficient than a straight random sample. To the authors' knowledge very little use has been made of this kind of device.

11.1.3 Flow chart for acceptance inspection

In any realistic assessment of alternative sampling inspection plans, the mechanics of the actual situation into which a sampling plan fits must be considered in some detail. In many papers we find that important – even drastic – assumptions are made, both implicity and explicitly, as to the manner in which a plan works. In this section we do not attempt to give a complete catalogue of inspection situations, but we aim to give sufficient to form a basis.

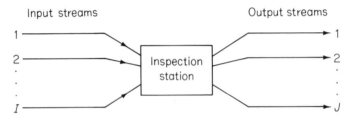

Figure 11.2 An inspection situation.

Consider the following situation. Batches of approximately N items reach an inspection station through one of I streams. For a consumer, these streams might be different production lines; it is possible that the most common case is $I = 1$. The quality of batches in the streams may or may not be correlated with the quality of other neighbouring batches in the same stream or in other streams. It is also possible that these input streams may have different states; for example, a production process may be either in control or out of control. It seems obvious that when several states exist in the input streams, the inspection plan should be specially designed to deal with this.

At the inspection station a sample of items is selected from some or all of the batches and the samples are inspected. Each batch is then sentenced, and placed in one of the J output streams.

If there are only two output streams, these are usually referred to as the *accepted* and the *rejected* batches. (A better term for rejected batches might be 'not accepted'.) For final inspection by a producer, the accepted batches are those passes on for sale to customers. There are many possibilities for the rejected lots, and some of these are set out in Fig. 11.3, some of which is taken from Hald (1960). However, this diagram is really appropriate when items are simply classified as effective or defective. More frequently there might be different types of non-conformity, and different action taken on each type.

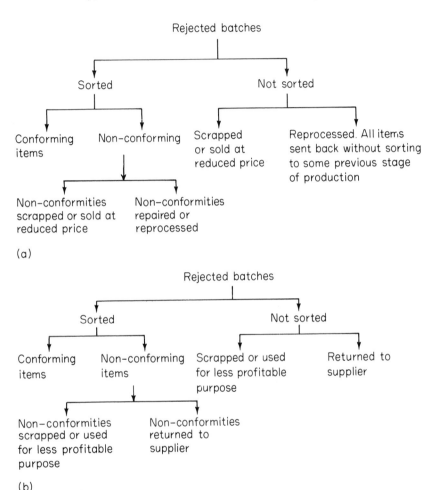

(a)

(b)

Figure 11.3 Some possible courses of action on rejected batches: (a) final inspection by a producer; (b) inspection by a consumer.

In some applications of inspection plans there may be more than two output streams. For example, there may be two grades of accepted batches, for different uses, or for sale at different prices. Similarly, there could be two grades of rejected batches. However, such plans would often be considered unduly complicated, and liable to lead to gross errors on the part of the inspector. Here we consider two output streams and call them accepted and rejected batches.

Another point with regard to the flow chart, Fig. 11.2, is to specify which parts of this chart work at a given rate, and which parts can work at varying rates. For final inspection by a producer, the input streams are fixed, but for inspection by a consumer, the quantity usually fixed is the number of accepted batches passed. In addition to either of these possibilities, the labour and resources available at the inspection station will usually be fixed, and variable only in a long-term sense.

The purpose for which inspection is being applied also needs to be considered in some detail. For a producer, some possible aims are:

(1) to satisfy some requirement for a National or International Standard;
(2) to grade batches for sale;
(3) to prevent non-conforming batches being passed on to customers;
(4) to provide information from which a quality control plan can be operated.

The aims for a consumer might be:

(5) to confirm that the quality of goods supplied is up to standard;
(6) to prevent non-conforming batches being passed on to a production process,
(7) to grade batches for different uses;
(8) to encourage the producer to provide the quality desired (Hill 1960). This purpose can only be achieved if the consumer uses a substantial part of the supplier's output.

It is probable that in many situations in which sampling inspection plans are applied, the aims are not easy to define precisely.

We can see throughout this discussion that inspection by a producer is in general very different from that by a consumer.

An extended discussion of some case studies of quality control practices arising in industry is given by Chiu and Wetherill (1975).

11.2 CLASSIFICATION OF INSPECTION PLANS

Any system of classifying inspection plans is unsatisfactory in that borderline categories exist. Nevertheless it will be found useful to have some classification system. We shall first list different inspection situations and then give alternative sampling plans.

11.2.1 Inspection situations

(a) *Batch inspection or continuous product inspection*
Batch inspection occurs when we have items presented in bags or cartons, as in Example 11.1, and it is desired to pass sentence on each bag of items together, and not on each individual item. If on the other hand we have continuous powder or a production line of continuously produced small items such as chips of plastic and items are *not* treated in batches for sentencing, then we have continuous product inspection. The essential distinction is whether items are batched for inspection purposes or not; often with a continuous production process, items are batched for inspection purposes. With batch inspection there is no need for any order in the batches presented, although sometimes there is an order, and this information can be used; see below. Example 11.4 illustrates one of the earliest types of continuous sampling plans (CSP); batch inspection plans are illustrated later in this section.

Example 11.4 Dodge plan
At the outset inspect every item until i successive conforming items are found. Then inspect every nth item until a non-conforming item is found, at which point 100% inspection is restored.

(b) *Rectifying inspection or acceptance inspection*
If, say, batches of items are presented for sentencing, and the possible decisions are, say, accepted or rejected, or accept or sell at a reduced price, etc., we have acceptance inspection. Rectifying inspection occurs when one of the possible decisions is to sort out the non-conforming items from a batch and adjust or rectify them, or else replace them. That is, with rectifying inspection, the proportion of defective items may be changed.

(c) *Inspection by attributes or inspection by variables*
Inspection by attributes occurs when items are classified simply as conforming or non-conforming, or when mechanical parts are checked by go–no-go gauges. The opposite of this is inspection by variables when the result of inspection is a measurement of length, crushing strength, weight, the purity of a chemical, etc. An intermediate classification between these is when items are graded. There is frequently a choice between inspection by attributes or by variables, and also a choice of the number of such characteristics inspected. The choice between these depends on the cost of inspection, the type of labour employed, and also on the assumptions which can be made about the probability distribution of the measured quantities. Recently, Baillie

(1989) has introduced some multivariate plans which are mixed attributes and variables plans.

11.2.2 Alternative sampling plans

We shall be mainly concerned here with batch inspection plans. Example 11.4 illustrates a continuous production inspection plan. An intermediate situation occurs when items are batched in order from a production process.

It is then possible to operate *serial sampling plans* or *deferred sentencing sampling plans*, in which the sentence on a batch depends not only on the results on the batch itself, but also on results from preceding or following batches. The plans described below all treat each batch independently; the effect of operating such plans as serial sampling plans would be to modify the sentencing rules depending on the results of inspection on neighbouring batches. As an example, a possible rule would be to inspect n items from each batch, and to accept if either there were no non-conforming items in the current batch, or one non-conforming item and no non-conforming items in the previous k batches.

(a) *Single sampling plan*

Suppose we have batches of items presented, and items are to be classified merely as conforming or non-conforming to a set standard. A single sampling plan consists of selecting a fixed random sample of n items from each batch for inspection, and then sentencing each batch depending upon the results. If the sentence is to be either accept or reject the batch, then each batch is accepted if the number of non-conforming items r found in the n items is less than or equal to *the acceptance number*, c. We summarize as follows:

Single sampling plan:

$$
\left.
\begin{array}{ll}
(1) & \text{select } n \text{ items,} \\
(2) & \text{accept batch if number of non-conforming items} \leq c, \\
(3) & \text{reject batch if number of non-conforming items} > c + 1
\end{array}
\right\} \quad (11.1)
$$

For inspection by variables we have a corresponding sentencing rule. There is no need for the restriction to two terminal decisions and we could have, for example, accept, reject, or sell at a reduced price.

Example 11.5

For batch inspection, one possible sampling plan might be to use a single sampling plan with $n = 30$, $c = 2$. That is, if there are two or fewer non-conforming items in the sample, the batch is accepted.

(b) *Double sampling plan*

In this plan a first sample of n_1 items is drawn, as a result of which we may either accept the batch, reject it, or else take a further sample of n_2 items. If the second sample is taken, a decision to accept or reject the batch is taken upon the combined results.

Example 11.6

A double sampling plan for use instead of the plan in Example 11.5 might be as follows. Select 12 items from the batch and

(1)   accept the batch if there are no non-conforming items,
(2)   reject the batch if there are 3 or more non-conforming items,
(3)   select another sample of 24 items if there are 1 or 2 non-conforming items.

When the second sample is drawn, we count the number of non-conforming items in the combined sample of 36 items and

(4)   accept the batch if number of non-conforming items ≤ 2
(5)   reject the batch if number of non-comforming items > 3.

A natural extension of double sampling plans is to have multiple sampling plans, with many stages. It is difficult to see how double or multiple sampling plans would be used when there are more than two terminal decisions, unless more than one attribute (or variable) is measured and a much more complex sentencing rule introduced.

(c) *Sequential sampling plan*

A further extension of the multiple sampling idea is the full sequential sampling plan. In this plan, items are drawn from each batch one by one, and after each item a decision is taken as to whether to accept the batch, reject the batch, or sample another item. A simple method of designing sequential sampling plans was discovered by Professors G. A. Barnard and A. Wald during the 1939–45 war. An essential point is that the sample size is not fixed in advance, but it depends on the way the results turn out.

Sequential sampling plans can save a substantial amount of inspection effort, although the overall gain in efficiency is often not great unless inspection is expensive, as is the case in Example 11.3, concerning chromatographic analysis. Another characteristic of plans where sequential sampling can give great gains in efficiency is when the incoming quality is very variable. Here, Example 11.2 provides just such a situation, as the pellets being examined may come from different producers and be of variable quality.

The theory of sequential sampling plans is discussed by Wetherill and Glazebrook (1986) and will not be discussed further in this text.

11.2.3 Discussion

We have described many different types of inspection situations and inspection plans, and a number of questions arise. What are the relative merits of different types of plan? How should the sample sizes and acceptance numbers be chosen, and upon what principles? In attempting to answer these questions we should consider carefully the aims for which the inspection plan was instituted. There are several different schemes for selecting sampling plans, appropriate to different situations. Before describing some alternative sampling schemes, we outline some properties of sampling plans.

11.3 SOME PROPERTIES OF SAMPLING PLANS

11.3.1 The OC-curve

This section is concerned with inspection situations in which the items are classified as either conforming or non-conforming, and where the items are presented in batches. One of the most important properties of a sampling plan is the operating characteristic curve.

Suppose batches of quality θ are presented (so that θ is the proportion which is non-conforming) and the single sample plan (11.1) of section 11.2.2 is used. That is, n items are selected at random from each batch, and a batch is accepted if c or fewer non-conforming items are found in it.

Then if the batch is large it follows that the probability that a batch of quality θ will be accepted is given by the binomial distribution and is

$$P(\theta) = \sum_{r=0}^{c} \binom{n}{r} \theta^r (1 - \theta)^{n-r} \qquad (11.2)$$

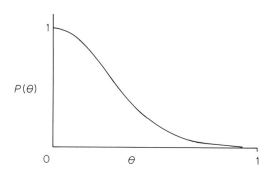

Figure 11.4 The OC-curve.

This function is illustrated in Fig. 11.4. Clearly, when $\theta = 0$, all batches are accepted and $P(\theta) = 1$. As θ increases $P(\theta)$ decreases, until it is zero at $\theta = 1$ (it will be negligible long before $\theta = 1$). This curve, shown in Fig. 11.4 is called the *operating characteristic curve*, or *OC-curve*.

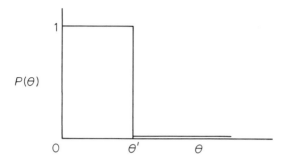

Figure 11.5 An ideal OC-curve.

For any given sampling plan, the OC-curve can be calculated, and compared with what we think the OC-curve should be like. Ideally, we might wish to have an OC for which all batches with $\theta < \theta'$ were accepted, and all others rejected. This would be

$$P(\theta) = \begin{cases} 1 & \theta < \theta' \\ 0 & \theta > \theta' \end{cases}$$

and is shown in Fig. 11.5. This OC-curve is impossible to achieve without almost 100% inspection. An alternative specification would be to set

$$P(\theta) = \begin{cases} 1 & \theta < \theta' \\ & \theta' < \theta'' \\ 0 & \theta > \theta'' \end{cases}$$

leaving the region (θ', θ'') in which we do not mind what happens. This is shown in Fig. 11.6.

Unfortunately, even this alternative formulation cannot be achieved without almost 100% sampling. A formulation which can be achieved is as follows. We specify a good quality, θ_1, at which we require the sampling plan to accept batches with a probability greater than $(1 - \alpha)$.

$$\text{Pr(accept batches of quality } \theta_1) \geq 1 - \alpha \qquad (11.3)$$

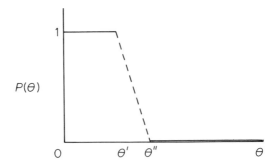

Figure 11.6 An alternative form of ideal OC curve.

We call this the *producers' risk point*, and it represents the risk of the producer having good-quality product rejected.

We also specify a poor quality, θ_2, at which we require the sampling plan to reject batches with a probability greater than $(1 - \beta)$. Alternatively we write

$$\text{Pr(accept batches of quality } \theta_2) \leq \beta \qquad (11.4)$$

We call this the *consumers' risk point*. The risk of a consumer accepting quality poorer than θ_2 is set to be at most β. By specifying the producers' and consumers' risk points (Fig.11.7) we are setting two points on the OC-curve. These concepts suppose rather narrow-minded producers and consumers, but even so, they help to fix what is required of a sampling plan. No real producer or consumer could define his requirements quite so narrowly.

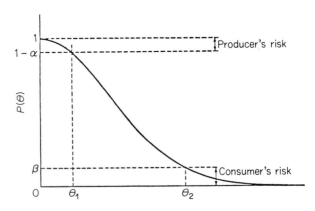

Figure 11.7 Producer's and consumer's risks.

As an example, suppose that in a certain process batches of product are subject to acceptance inspection. We may set $\theta = 0.5\%$ as conforming product, which we want accepted 98% of the time:

Pr(accept batches with 0.5% non-conforming items) = 0.98.

Similarly we may set $\theta = 3\%$ as non-conforming product, which we want rejected 95% of the time:

Pr(reject batches with 3% non-conforming items) = 0.95.

The indifference quality
Finally, one quantity sometimes used in sampling inspection is the *indifference quality*. It is the quality of batches which, when submitted for inspection, is accepted only 50% of the time. It is denoted $\theta_{0.50}$.

Pr(accept batches of quality $\theta_{0.50}$) = 0.50.

An approximate rule which may be useful for any single sampling plan is given by

$$\theta_{0.50} = (c + \tfrac{2}{3})/n \tag{11.5}$$

For a derivation of this see Wetherill and Kollerström (1979); see also Exercise 11.B.1.

11.3.2 The average run length

This concept was introduced in Chapters 7–9 when we dealt with Shewhart and CuSum charts; it has found widespread application in industry.

Suppose we have continuous production inspection (of single items), or else batch inspection of an ordered sequence of batches, then the run length is defined as the number of batches (or items) sampled until one is rejected. The distribution of run length for any sampling plan is positively skew with a very long tail. Often we do not consider the whole run length distribution, but limit consideration to the *average run length* or ARL.

Suppose that we have batch inspection using a plan which accepts each batch independently of others with an OC-curve $P(\theta)$. Then the probability that a run length of r batches is observed is

$$\{P(\theta)\}^{r-1}\{1 - P(\theta)\}, \qquad r = 1, 2, \ldots \tag{11.6}$$

and the ARL is $1/\{1 - P(\theta)\}$. In this situation, therefore, the OC-curve and the ARL function are exactly equivalent. However, it can be argued (particularly in some situations) that the ARL is more directly meaningful. The ARL tells us how much of a given quality is accepted on average, before some action is taken.

In some sampling plans, the plans are altered according to the process average as determined from sampling. For such plans the ARL and OC-curve may not be directly equivalent, and the ARL appears to be the more meaningful concept. Another situation when the ARL should be used is when we have plans which are being used for process control, for the ARL shows how frequently corrective action is initiated. In other cases it may be helpful to use both the ARL and the OC-curve concepts. Many of the published tables for sampling inspection, such as British Standard tables, emphasize the OC-curve concept.

Finally, we note that it is sometimes useful to distinguish between the average *sample* run length (ASRL), which is the average of the number of sampling points, and the average *article* run length (AARL), which is the average of the number of items sampled or observations taken.

11.3.3 The process curve

The long run distribution of the quality of batches of items arriving at the inspection station is called the process curve. Now in practice, batch quality may vary in some way similar to the patterns of variation shown in section 3.2, and contain periodic effects, etc., but this is usually ignored in batch inspection, partly on the grounds that it is very difficult in practice to obtain information on the process. With continuing production inspection, there is no meaning to the process curve without either arbitrarily batching it, or else bringing in the stochastic element. A typical process curve is shown as the full line curve in Fig. 11.8.

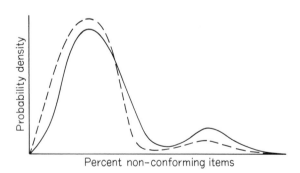

Figure 11.8 Typical process curve for percentage non-conforming.

The act of sampling and sentencing batches of material filters out the bad quality to some extent, and produces a more satisfactory distribution such as the dotted curve in Fig. 11.8.

For various practical reasons, data on the process curve is often very difficult to get. However, some vague knowledge is required in order to design a sampling inspection plan. We need to know roughly how likely it is that batches of any given quality will occur, in order to decide how much protection we need at various levels.

11.3.4* Mood's theorem

An important result which throws some light on the importance of the process curve was derived by Mood (1943). He showed that when the probability of a defective is constant, there is no correlation between the quality of batches accepted and rejected by a sampling scheme. One conclusion which we can draw from this result is that there is no point in sampling when the batch quality is stable (except, maybe, to reject the entire production). Sampling makes sense only with variable quality. We therefore need to take care about schemes worked out on a basis of stable production. The proof follows, for those interested in it.

Consider a single sample plan for fraction non-conforming, from batches of size N. Any given batch quality can be represented by a point on the batch line in Fig. 11.9, and any sample result is represented by a point on the sample line. Consider a batch of qualilty represented by the point P, then the probability that the sample result is given by Q is

$$\Pr(Q|P) = \frac{\text{no. of paths } OP \text{ via } Q}{\text{total no. of paths } OP} = \binom{n}{b}\binom{N-n}{B-b} \Big/ \binom{N}{B}$$

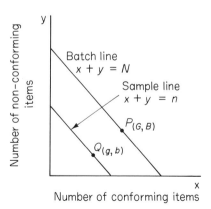

Figure 11.9 Illustration of Mood's theorem.

Now suppose that the process curve is binomial:

$$\binom{N}{B} p^B q^G$$

corresponding to stable production at a probability p of a defective. Then the total probability of obtaining a batch and sample represented by P and Q respectively is

$$\binom{N}{B} p^B q^G \binom{n}{b}\binom{N-n}{B-b} \Big/ \binom{N}{B} = \binom{n}{b} p^b q^g \binom{N-n}{B-b} p^{B-b} q^{G-g}.$$

This last statement shows that the sample result (g, b) is *statistically independent* of the quality of the remainder of the batch $(G - g, B - b)$. In particular, b is statistically independent of $(B - b)$.

Mood actually found that the correlation between b and $B - b$ is zero for a binomial process curve, and negative and positive for leptokurtic (sharp peaked) and platykurtic (flat topped) process curves respectively.

What Mood's result shows is that if the production process is such that there is a constant probability of obtaining a non-conforming item, and if a sample is drawn, then the distributions of quality in the sample and in the remainder of the batch are independent. Therefore batches selected because of poor quality in the sample will not tend to be worse than accepted batches.

11.4 METHODS OF CHOOSING SAMPLING PLANS FOR ATTRIBUTES

11.4.1 The producer's and consumer's risk point method

In this book we shall use the term sampling system to refer to a set of principles used to determine sampling plans, resulting in a collection or table of individual sampling plans indexed ready for use. There are various sampling systems available, each appropriate in certain circumstances, and we discuss the underlying principles of some of these below.

Suppose that we have large batches of items presented for acceptance inspection, where the items are classified as conforming or non-conforming, then the sampling plan (11.1) has two parameters to be fixed, the sample size n and the acceptance number c; clearly we need two equations to determine these quantities. One way of obtaining two equations is to pick two points on the OC-curve, and determine n and c so that the OC-curve of our plan goes through (or very near to) these points. Following our discussion in section 11.3.1 one convenient pair of points to choose is the producers' risk point (11.3) and the consumers' risk point (11.4); these points are shown on Fig. 11.7. In this section we follow through an approximate method of determining a sampling plan in this way. Clearly, since the binomial distribution applies, we have discreteness problems, and it will not usually be possible to satisfy any pair of inequalities exactly. A range of possible sample sizes results; see below. The steps are set out below and the first two involve the choice of the producer's and consumer's risk points. We settle on good quality such that we want the risk of rejection to be small, e.g. with material at only 1% non-conforming we may want the risk of rejection to be less than 3%. We also settle on poor quality such as 5% non-conforming, and require the risk of acceptance to be small, say 2%. This means that for our example we have $(\theta_1 = 1\%, \alpha = 3\%; \theta_2 = 5\%, \beta = 2\%)$. The appropriate values for particular applications can be judged with experience.

The theory of the method is discussed in section 11.4.2, but it is based on firstly using the Poisson distribution as an approximation to the binomial, and secondly, using a known relation between Poisson probabilities and the χ^2 distribution.

METHOD SUMMARY 11.1

Producer's and consumer's risk method of determining attribute sampling plans

Step 1 Determine the producers' risk point θ_1 and producers' risk α.

Step 2 Determine the consumers' risk point θ_2 and consumers' risk β.

Step 3 Look up Table 11.1 to find the smallest value of c satisfying $r(c) < \theta_2/\theta_1$.

Step 4 Look up the χ^2 tables, Table 11.2, and calculate the interval

$$\frac{\chi^2_{1-\beta}}{2\theta_2} < n < \frac{\chi^2_\alpha}{2\theta_1}$$

where the χ^2 values are looked up for $2(c + 1)$ degrees of freedom. (*Note*: this inequality must be true *in the order stated*, and not in the reverse direction.)

Step 5 Any n in the interval given in Step 4 solves the problem. If there is no integral value of n in the interval, increase c by 1 and repeat Step 4. A convenient choice for n is the smallest value.

Step 6 The sampling is given by n, c so determined.

Table 11.1 Values of $r(c)$ for the producer's and consumer's risk point method

| (a) $\alpha = 0.100$ | | | | | (b) $\alpha = 0.050$ | | | |
| $1 - \beta$ | | | | | $1 - \beta$ | | | |
c	0.900	0.950	0.975	0.990	c	0.900	0.950	0.975	0.990
0	21.85	28.43	35.01	43.71	0	44.89	58.40	71.92	89.78
1	7.31	8.92	10.48	12.48	1	10.95	13.35	15.68	18.68
2	4.83	5.71	6.56	7.63	2	6.51	7.70	8.84	10.28
3	3.83	4.44	5.02	5.76	3	4.89	5.67	6.42	7.35
4	3.29	3.76	4.21	4.77	4	4.06	4.65	5.20	5.89
5	2.94	3.34	3.70	4.16	5	3.55	4.02	4.47	5.02
6	2.70	3.04	3.35	3.74	6	3.21	3.60	3.98	4.44
7	2.53	2.82	3.10	3.44	7	2.96	3.30	3.62	4.02
8	2.39	2.66	2.90	3.20	8	2.77	3.07	3.36	3.71
9	2.28	2.52	2.75	3.02	9	2.62	2.89	3.15	3.46
10	2.19	2.42	2.62	2.87	10	2.50	2.75	2.98	3.27
11	2.12	2.33	2.51	2.74	11	2.40	2.63	2.84	3.10
12	2.06	2.25	2.42	2.64	12	2.31	2.53	2.73	2.97
13	2.00	2.18	2.35	2.55	13	2.24	2.44	2.63	2.85
14	1.95	2.12	2.28	2.47	14	2.18	2.37	2.54	2.75
15	1.91	2.07	2.22	2.40	15	2.12	2.30	2.47	2.66
16	1.87	2.03	2.17	2.34	16	2.07	2.24	2.40	2.59
17	1.84	1.99	2.12	2.29	17	2.03	2.19	2.34	2.52
18	1.81	1.95	2.08	2.24	18	1.99	2.15	2.29	2.46
19	1.78	1.92	2.04	2.19	19	1.95	2.10	2.24	2.40
20	1.76	1.89	2.01	2.15	20	1.92	2.07	2.20	2.35

| (c) $\alpha = 0.025$ | | | | | (d) $\alpha = 0.010$ | | | |
| $1 - \beta$ | | | | | $1 - \beta$ | | | |
c	0.900	0.950	0.975	0.990	c	0.900	0.950	0.975	0.990
0	90.95	118.33	145.70	181.89	0	229.10	298.07	367.04	458.21
1	16.06	19.59	23.00	27.41	1	26.18	31.93	37.51	44.69
2	8.60	10.18	11.68	13.59	2	12.21	14.44	16.57	19.28
3	6.13	7.11	8.04	9.22	3	8.12	9.42	10.65	12.20
4	4.92	5.64	6.31	7.15	4	6.25	7.16	8.01	9.07
5	4.21	4.77	5.30	5.95	5	5.20	5.89	6.54	7.34
6	3.74	4.21	4.64	5.18	6	4.52	5.08	5.60	6.25
7	3.41	3.81	4.18	4.63	7	4.05	4.52	4.96	5.51
8	3.16	3.51	3.83	4.23	8	3.70	4.12	4.49	4.96
9	2.96	3.28	3.56	3.92	9	3.44	3.80	4.14	4.55
10	2.81	3.09	3.35	3.67	10	3.23	3.56	3.85	4.22
11	2.68	2.69	3.17	3.47	11	3.06	3.35	3.63	3.96

| (c) $\alpha = 0.025$ | | | | (d) $\alpha = 0.010$ | | | | |
| | $1 - \beta$ | | | | | $1 - \beta$ | | |
c	0.900	0.950	0.975	0.990	c	0.900	0.950	0.975	0.990
12	2.57	2.81	3.03	3.30	12	2.92	3.19	3.44	3.74
13	2.48	2.70	2.90	3.15	13	2.80	3.05	3.28	3.56
14	2.40	2.61	2.80	3.03	14	2.69	2.93	3.14	3.40
15	2.33	2.53	2.71	2.92	15	2.60	2.82	3.02	3.27
16	2.27	2.45	2.62	2.83	16	2.52	2.73	2.29	3.15
17	2.21	2.39	2.55	2.74	17	2.45	2.65	2.83	3.05
18	2.16	2.33	2.49	2.67	18	2.39	2.58	2.75	2.96
19	2.12	2.28	2.43	2.61	19	2.34	2.52	2.68	2.87
20	2.08	2.24	2.38	2.55	20	2.29	2.46	2.61	2.80

Table 11.2 Percentage points of the χ^2 distribution

| Degrees of freedom | Probability in percent | | | | | |
	99.0	95.0	10.0	5.0	1.0	0.1
1	0.03157	0.00393	2.71	3.84	6.63	20.83
2	0.0201	0.103	4.61	5.99	9.21	13.81
3	0.115	0.352	6.25	7.81	11.34	16.27
4	0.297	0.711	7.78	9.49	13.28	18.47
5	0.554	1.15	9.24	11.07	15.09	20.52
6	0.872	1.64	10.64	12.59	16.81	22.46
7	1.24	2.17	12.02	14.07	18.48	24.32
8	1.65	2.73	13.36	15.51	20.09	26.12
9	2.09	3.33	14.68	16.92	21.67	27.88
10	2.56	3.94	15.99	18.31	23.21	29.59
11	3.05	4.57	17.28	19.68	24.73	31.26
12	3.57	5.23	18.55	21.03	26.22	32.91
14	4.66	6.57	21.06	23.68	29.14	36.12
16	5.81	7.96	23.54	26.30	32.00	39.25
18	7.01	9.39	25.99	28.87	34.81	42.31
20	8.26	10.85	28.41	31.41	37.57	45.31
22	9.54	12.34	30.81	33.92	40.29	48.27
24	10.86	13.85	33.20	36.42	42.98	51.18
26	12.20	15.38	35.56	38.89	45.64	54.05
28	13.56	16.93	37.92	41.34	48.28	56.89
30	14.95	18.49	40.26	43.77	50.89	59.70

For d.f. > 30, treat $\sqrt{(2\chi^2)}$ as approximately Normally distributed with mean $\{2 \times (\text{d.f.}) - 1\}$ and unit standard deviation.
The entry for 99.0 per cent, d.f. = 1 is 0.000157.

Example 11.7

Suppose we choose

Producer's risk point $\theta_1 = 0.01$ Producer's risk 0.05

Consumer's risk point $\theta_2 = 0.04$ Consumer's risk 0.05

then we have $\theta_2/\theta_1 = 4$, and so

Step 3   Use $c = 6$ since $r(6) = 3.60 < 4$.

Step 4 $\chi^2_{0.05}$ for $2(c + 1) = 14$ d.f. is 6.57

             $\chi^2_{0.95}$ for $2(c + 1) = 14$ d.f. is 23.68

             $\chi^2_{1-\beta}/2\theta_2 = 23.68/0.08 = 296.0$

             $\chi^2_{\alpha}/2\theta_1 = 6.57/0.02 = 328.5$

Step 5   Any n in the interval $296 \leq n \leq 328$ will be satisfactory. Suggest $n = 300$.

Step 6   The sampling plan is $n = 300$, $c = 6$.

This sampling plan will give a risk of less than 5% of rejecting batches with 1% conforming items, and a 5% chance of accepting batches with 4% non-conforming items.

We notice that the producer's and consumer's risk points specified in Example 11.7 have led to an extremely large sample size. If this were a practical case, we would seek to modify the risk points and try again, etc., until we arrived at a sampling plan which was felt to be 'reasonable'. This type of iterative process can be defended on the grounds that one is trying to balance the cost of sampling against the costs of wrong decisions. For any batch of quality θ, the probability that it will be accepted is given by the OC-curve. Thus by looking at the OC-curve, we can see the probability that poor quality will be accepted and good quality rejected. The probabilities of these wrong decisions can be reduced – but only by increasing the sample size and so increasing sampling costs. The essential point about the balancing of costs referred to here is that it is not formalized. The final decision on a sampling plan is made subjectively, by someone with a detailed knowledge of the set-up.

A number of tables of sampling plans have been constructed based upon principles rather similar to the above. Peach (1947) listed sampling plans for which the producer's and consumer's risks were both set at 0.05. Horsnell (1954) tabulated plans for producer's risks of 0.01 or 0.05 and consumer's risks of 0.01, 0.05 or 0.10.

The most comprehensive set of tables of this kind is provided by Hald and Kousgaard (1967). Essentially they give tables of

$$\sum_{n=0}^{c} \binom{n}{r} \theta^r (1 - \theta)^{n-r} = P$$

for c in steps 1 from 0 to 100, 15 values of P, and values of $0 < \theta < 0.50$. Simple illustrations are given of the use of these tables to obtain a single sampling plan with set producer's and consumer's risks.

Two main criticisms can be levelled at the producer's and consumer's risks method of determining sampling plans. The first is that, except in very small batch sizes, the resulting plans are independent of the batch size. Since the costs of wrong decisions increase with batch size, it is obvious that the probabilities of error (α, β) should reduce with increasing batch size.

The second criticism is that it is in general rather difficult to choose the parameters (θ_1, α; θ_2, β). If we are dealing with an endless sequence of batches, the OC-curve points could be expressed as ARLs which might have more meaning, but the choice has to be made in consultation with production staff and others who do not appreciate the full depth of the concepts involved.

It is important to realize that the OC-curve does *not* give the proportion of batches of any given quality among accepted batches, since it is necessary to use the process curve to obtain this quantity. The probability distribution of θ among accepted batches is clearly the result of the effect of sampling, given by the OC-curve, on the input quality, which is represented by the process curve. The effect of a sampling plan is to change the distribution of batch quality from the (input) process curve to a similar distribution but with some of the defective quality filtered out. When using an OC-curve sampling scheme we have to keep this in mind. Figure 11.10 illustrates the effect of a sampling plan.

11.4.2 Theory behind the method given in section 11.4.1

The crux of the problem is to find the smallest values of (n, c) satisfying (11.3) and (11.4). Owing to the discreteness of the binomial distribution it may not be possible to satisfy them exactly, and we can restate them as

$$\sum_{0}^{c} \binom{n}{r} \theta_1^r (1 - \theta_1)^{n-r} \geq 1 - \alpha \qquad (11.7)$$

$$\sum_{0}^{c} \binom{n}{r} \theta_2^r (1 - \theta_2)^{n-r} \leq \beta. \qquad (11.8)$$

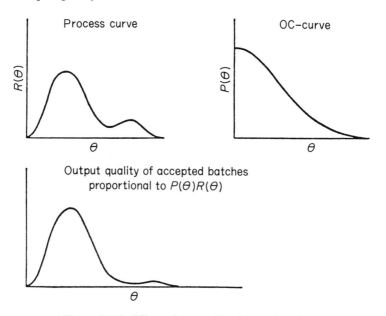

Figure 11.10 Effect of a sampling inspection plan.

We need to find a pair of values (n, c) satisfying these inequalities, and an approximate solution can be obtained as follows. (See Hald (1967) for a further discussion of the method given here, together with approximate solutions etc.).

First we replace the binomial terms by Poisson terms for the same means, to obtain

$$\sum_0^c e^{-n\theta_1}(n\theta_1)^r/r! \geq 1 - \alpha \tag{11.9}$$

$$\sum_0^c e^{-n\theta_2}(n\theta_2)^r/r! \geq \beta \tag{11.10}$$

Now the cumulative Poisson distribution can be related to the cumulative χ^2 distribution since we can show by integration by parts that

$$\frac{1}{c!}\int_m^\infty t^c e^{-t}\, dt = \sum_0^c e^{-m}m^r/r! \tag{11.11}$$

and hence that

$$\sum_0^c e^{-m}m^r/r! = \Pr\{\chi^2 > 2m \,|\, 2(c + 1) \text{ d.f.}\} \tag{11.12}$$

since the integral on the left-hand side of (11.11) is the probability that

χ^2 is greater than $2m$, for a χ^2 distribution having $2(c + 1)$ degrees of freedom. Inequalities (11.7) and (11.8) are therefore equivalent to

$$\Pr\{\chi^2 > 2n\theta_1 | 2(c + 1) \text{ d.f.}\} \geq 1 - \alpha$$
$$\Pr\{\chi^2 > 2n\theta_2 | 2(c + 1) \text{ d.f.}\} \leq \beta.$$

If we denote the 100α-percentile of the χ^2 distribution with $2(c + 1)$ degrees of freedom by χ^2_α, then these inequalities are

$$2n\theta_1 \leq \chi^2_\alpha \tag{11.13}$$
$$2n\theta_2 \geq \chi^2_{1-\beta}. \tag{11.14}$$

If we now put

$$r(c) = \chi^2_{1-\beta}/\chi^2_\alpha$$

then c is the smallest value satisfying

$$r(c - 1) > \theta_2/\theta_1 > r(c).$$

We can solve (11.13) and (11.14) for n to get

$$\chi^2_{1-\beta}/2\theta_2 \leq n \leq \chi^2_\alpha/2\theta_1 \tag{11.15}$$

with the χ^2s having $2(c + 1)$ degrees of freedom. Any n in the interval (11.15) will solve the problem, and we can choose which inequality (11.13) or (11.14) is nearer to being satisfied as an equality, by choice of n nearer to one or other limit. If (11.15) does not contain an integral value of n, we must increase c and obtain a new interval.

In this way a sampling plan approximately satisfying the original requirements is easily obtained, and tables of $r(c)$ and of χ^2 percentage points are given in the Appendix tables. Once an (n, c) is determined, an approximate OC-curve can be plotted using standard χ^2 percentage points and equation (11.12).

11.4.3 A simple semi-economic scheme (ASSES)

Wetherill and Chiu (1974) have followed up some theoretical work by proposing a very simple but highly efficient scheme.

A theoretical investigation of sampling plans, based on an economic approach of minimizing costs, shows that an important parameter is the *break-even quality*, p_0. This is the quality such that it is equally costly to accept or reject the batch. Further theoretical investigations have shown that an optimum sampling plan should have

$$c \cong np_0$$

or to a better approximation

$$c \cong np_0 - \tfrac{2}{3}. \tag{11.16}$$

This can be used to determine a sampling plan, and the theory of the method is given in the next section. The underlying idea is to fix two points on the OC-curve, one of them being the producer's risk at the process averge $\bar{p}$, and the other being the indifference quality, defined in section 11.3.1, which we put equal to p_0 from (11.16). A crucial step in the method is to determine p_0 by economic criteria.

METHOD SUMMARY 11.2

A simple semi-economic scheme

Step 1 Determine the break-even quality, p_0, and the process average, $\bar{p}$.

Step 2 Choose the producer's risk, α, at the process average, $\bar{p}$.

Step 3 Look up Table 11.3 to find the smallest value of c such that the table entry is greater than or equal to $\bar{p}/p_0$.

Step 4 Use the formula

$$n = (c + \tfrac{2}{3})/p_0.$$

Table 11.3 Values for ASSES

c	$\alpha = 0.005$	0.01	0.025	0.05
0	0.0072	0.0145	0.0365	0.0740
1	0.0617	0.0885	0.1443	0.2117
2	0.1263	0.1631	0.2314	0.3058
3	0.1831	0.2242	0.2968	0.3721
4	0.2308	0.2738	0.3476	0.4218
5	0.2711	0.3149	0.3883	0.4608
6	0.3055	0.3494	0.4220	0.4926
7	0.3352	0.3789	0.4503	0.5191
8	0.3613	0.4046	0.4747	0.5416
9	0.3844	0.4271	0.4960	0.5611
10	0.4051	0.4472	0.5147	0.5782
11	0.4236	0.4652	0.5314	0.5934
12	0.4405	0.4814	0.5464	0.6070

Example 11.7

Suppose we have $\alpha = 0.025$, $p_0 = 0.05$, $\bar{p} = 0.02$, then we find $\bar{p}/p_0 = 0.40$, $c = 6$. Hence $n = 134$.

This sampling scheme is very easy to apply, and does have the virtue of making the indifference quality approximately equal to the break-even quality.

11.4.4 Dodge and Romig's schemes

Dodge and Romig (1929, 1959) pioneered sampling inspection from about 1920 onwards, and they proposed two different schemes, both assuming that rectifying inspection is involved. That is, they assume that rejected batches are 100% sorted, and all non-conforming items replaced or rectified.

One approach was through a quantity they defined as the lot tolerance percent defective (LTPD), which is 'some chosen limiting value of per cent defective in a lot', respresenting what the consumer regards as borderline quality. The tables always used LTPD with a consumer's risk of 0.10, so that the LTPD is effectively the quality corresponding to a consumer's risk of 0.10. However, the LTPD only gives us one restriction, and two are required to determine a single sample plan. For the second restriction, Dodge and Romig minimized the average amount of inspection at the process average and subject to the LTPD, values of (n, c) were chosen to minimize the average amount of inspection at the process average quality, θ.

The other approach Dodge and Romig used involved a quantity defined as the average outgoing quality limit, AOQL. To obtain this we notice that if on average I items per batch are rectified, an average of $N - I$ remain unrectified. The average outgoing quality is therefore

$$AOQ = (N - I)\theta/N.$$

It is readily seen that the AOQ has a graph roughly as shown in Fig. 11.11 and passes through a maximum with respect to θ, and there is an

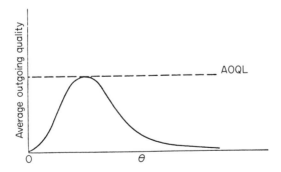

Figure 11.11 The average outgoing quality limit.

upper limit to the average outgoing percent defective called the AOQL.

In the second approach, Dodge and Romig produce sampling plans having set values of the AOQL, which also minimize the average amount of inspection at the process average. If all rejected batches are 100% inspected and an average quality guarantee is satisfactory, the AOQL approach may be a good scheme to use.

Some criticisms of Dodge and Romig's methods are given by Hill (1962). In particular he criticizes the AOQL concept as being very sensitive to imperfect inspection, as there then may be no upper limit to the AOQ.

11.4.5 Defence sampling plans

A series of developments starting in World War II has resulted in an International Standard. As this is used a great deal, a separate chapter is devoted to it (Chapter 13).

EXERCISES 11.A

1. Work out attribute sampling schemes for the data in Table 11.4.

Table 11.4 Parameter settings for sampling schemes

θ_1	α	θ_2	β	n	c
0.01	5%	0.04	5%		
0.01	5%	0.05	5%		
0.01	5%	0.06	5%		
0.01	5%	0.04	10%		
0.01	5%	0.05	10%		
0.01	5%	0.06	10%		

2. Use ASSES for the parameters given in Table 11.5.

Table 11.5 Parameter settings for sampling schemes

$\bar{p}$	α	p_0	n	c
0.01	5%	0.025		
0.015	5%	0.025		

EXERCISES 11.B

1. Check the indifference quality level formula (11.5) by finding the values of m for which

$$\sum_0^c e^{-m} m^r / r! = 0.50$$

   for $c = 0, 1, 2, 3$. A simple iteration scheme can be used starting with the values

$$m = c + \tfrac{2}{3}.$$

2. Check the derivation of Table 11.3 (section 11.4.3) as follows. We require

$$\sum_0^c e^{-m_1} m_1^r / r! = 1 - \alpha \qquad \text{for } m_1 = n\bar{p}_0$$

   and

$$\sum_0^c e^{-m_0} m_0^r / r! = 0.50 \qquad \text{for } m_0 = np_0.$$

   Use (11.12) to relate these to χ^2 variables, and hence find the values for the ratio

$$\bar{p}/p_0 = m_1/m_0.$$

3. The Poisson summation approximates the binomial,

$$P = \sum_0^c \binom{n}{r} p^r (1 - p)^{n-r} \simeq \sum_0^c e^{-m} m^r / r!$$

   for $r = np$. Given that for $c = 0$, $m = 0.0513$ gives $P = 0.95$ and that for $c = 1$, $m = 0.355$ also gives $P = 0.95$, carry out calculations to check the Poisson approximation to the binomial distribution, for small values of n.

4. Use the Markov chain methods of Chapter 8 to investigate the ARL properties of the following sampling plan:

   (1) inspect 10 items at random and classify as conforming or non-conforming
   (2) accept if there are no non-conforming items in the current batch
   (3) accept if there is one non-conforming item in the current batch and none in the previous three batches,
   (4) otherwise reject.

Define the following states:

State 1: no non-conforming items in the current batch
State 2: one non-conforming item in the current batch and none in the previous batch
State 3: one non-conforming item in the current batch and none in the previous two batches
State 4: current batch accepted
State 5: current batch rejected.

Define the run length as the number of batches to a rejection, and assume that all items have a constant probability p of being defective.

5. Show that for a single sample rectifying inspection plan with sample size n and batch size N the AOQL is approximately

$$AOQL = \left[\sum_0^c e^{-(N-n)p} \frac{\{(N-n)p\}^r}{r!} \right] \left[\frac{N-n}{N} \right] p.$$

Calculate and plot the AOQL for a simple plan.

6. (a) Show that when an attributes acceptance inspection scheme is run with a zero acceptance number ($c = 0$), then the OC-curve is convex throughout.

(b) A modification for zero acceptance plans suggested by Dodge (1955), is as follows:
Accept the batch if no non-conforming items are found.
Reject the batch if two or more non-conforming items are found.
For one non-conforming item, accept the batch only if the previous i batches are free of non-conforming items.
Evaluate the OC-curve for these plans for $i = 1, 3, 5$. (These are called chain sampling plans.)

12

Inspection by variables

12.1 INTRODUCTION

In the previous chapter we concentrated on sampling inspection by attributes, when inspected items are simply classified as conforming or non-conforming. When our quality characteristic is a continuous variable, we may be able to operate an 'inspection by variables' plan. We shall assume that the underlying distribution of the quality characteristic is Normal and that there is a range of the quality characteristic from L to U, in which the quality is acceptable (one-sided limits being special cases of this). The way inspection by variables operates is that the sentencing of a batch depends on the observed $\bar{x}$ and s of the sample, and not on the number of non-conforming items. Consider the following example.

Example 12.1
The following data are measurements of crushing strength of 16 catalyst pellets, which are subject to incoming inspection. The specification is that the strengths of pellets should be between 90 and 140 kg. On the basis of this sample, it is desired to accept or reject the batch.

120.6	108.1	99.8	115.6	118.2	107.3
126.6	102.1	101.4	91.2	106.8	101.2
106.1	103.1	97.0	114.0		

It can be shown that this data is consistent with the distribution of quality measurements for the whole batch being Normal, with mean $\hat{\mu} = \bar{x} = 107.4$ and standard deviation $\hat{\sigma} = s = 9.39$.

This distribution is shown in Fig. 12.1, and it is readily checked that 3.2% of the distribution lies below the lower limit and the percentage above the upper limit is negligible. If the total percentage non-conforming is regarded as too high, then we reject the batch. This gives a general idea of how inspection by variables plans were originally developed. The theory below approaches the topic by an analogous but more appropriate method.

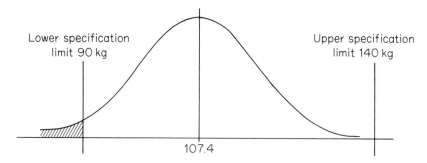

Figure 12.1 Inspection by variables – using data from Example 12.1.

There are some advantages and disadvantages of inspection by variables plans. The chief advantage is that because we are using information more efficiently, the sample size necessary can be reduced considerably. There is also much greater information about the process than if simply a conforming/non-conforming classification is used.

The disadvantages of inspection by variables plans are as follows:

(1) Firstly, they depend rather heavily on Normality.
(2) Most of the available reference material concerns itself with one measured quality characteristic at a time, as multivariate methods have only recently been developed.
(3) The taking of measurements usually requires a higher technical level for the inspection staff.
(4) We could easily get a batch rejected, because of an excessive *predicted* proportion non-conforming, based on Normality, without there being an actual defective in the observed sample, and Example 12.1 illustrates this.

The key advantage of inspection by variables plans is that much more accurate information on batch quality is available from much smaller sample sizes so that, with appropriate safeguards, variables plans are well worth considering, and should be used more frequently than they are.

In the discussion below we deal with four cases, which lead to increasing complexity of the plans:

(1) single specification limit, σ known
(2) single specification limit, σ unknown
(3) double specification limit, σ known
(4) double specification limit, σ unknown.

An International Standard for inspection by variables exists, ISO 3951 (corresponding to BS 6002), and this is based on very similar principles to the standard for attributes inspection. They are both described in Chapter 13.

The sections below do not follow the International Standards method and instead the approach is to choose two points on the OC-curve, and find a plan which fits. All methods in effect reject batches when the estimated fraction non-conforming is too large, but for single specification limits, a direct estimation of the fraction non-conforming can be avoided; see below.

For a single specification limit, non-conforming material is defined as material with values above a limit U (or below a limit L). There is therefore a simple relationship between the (theoretical) mean and standard deviation of the material and the fraction non-conforming, p. With this in mind, producer's and consumer's risk points (p_1, α), (p_2, β) can be defined as in section 11.3.1.

A simple decision rule is to reject batches when the sample mean is too large (for an upper limit) or too small (for a lower limit). The problem is then to find the sample size and acceptance limit for the mean which give us (approximately) the risks we require. The derivation is given in section 12.2.2, but the method is given in section 12.2.1.

The relationship between the fraction non-conforming and the parameters (μ, σ) of the normal distribution are slightly more complicated in the double limits situation, but similar principles apply. We have to distinguish in the double limits case between satisfying a restriction on the overall fraction non-conforming, and satisfying separate restrictions on the fraction non-conforming at each end. The double limits case is dealt with in section 12.5.

For some theoretical work relevant to the material in this chapter see Bravo (1980; 1981), Wetherill and Kollerström (1979), and Baillie (1987; 1988).

12.2 SINGLE SPECIFICATION LIMIT, σ KNOWN

12.2.1 Statement of the method

Following the discussion given in the previous chapter, we shall adopt a producer's and consumer's risk approach to designing a sampling plan and we shall discuss only the design of single sampling plans. It is clear from section 12.1 that, for a single upper specification limit U, an appropriate decision rule is to accept if the sample mean $\bar{x}$ satisfies

$$\bar{x} + k_\sigma \sigma \leq U \quad \text{for some constant } k_\sigma. \tag{12.1}$$

We shall denote the sample size for a σ-known plan by n_σ. For a single lower specification limit we accept if

$$\bar{x} - k_\sigma \sigma \geq L. \tag{12.2}$$

With this formulation, we wish to choose our parameters (k_σ, n_σ) to satisfy two requirements:

Producer's risk If the fraction non-conforming is p_1, we wish to accept the batch with a probability $(1 - \alpha)$, where p_1 and α are small.

Consumer's risk If the fraction non-conforming is $p_2 > p_1$, we wish to accept the batch with a probability no more than β, where β is small.

As we noted in the previous chapter, the constants (p_1, α) (p_2, β) can be rather difficult to choose, and often some iterative procedure is adopted. Once the engineer sees the consequences of choosing a particular set $(p_1, \alpha; p_2, \beta)$, in terms of sample size, he may wish to modify his choices.

A solution to this problem of choosing (n_σ, k_σ) to satisfy $(p_1, \alpha; p_2, \beta)$ is set out in Method Summary 12.1, and the derivation is given in section 12.2.2. The nomogram is from Wilrich (1970).

METHOD SUMMARY 12.1

Inspection by variables, single specification limit, σ known

Step 1 Choose a quality level p_1 at which the probability of acceptance is required to be $(1 - \alpha)$ and a quality level p_2 at which the probability of acceptance is required to be β (p_1 is smaller than p_2 and $(1 - \alpha)$ is greater than β).

Step 2 Use the nonogram in Fig. 12.2 to find the point of intersection of the lines joining p_1 with $(1 - \alpha)$ and p_2 with β.

Step 3 Read off the value of k on the appropriate scale.

Step 4 Read off the sample size n_σ on the appropriate scale.

Step 5 Accept the batch if either

$$\bar{x} - k_\sigma \sigma \geq L \quad \text{for a lower specification limit}$$

or

$$\bar{x} + k_\sigma \sigma \leq U \quad \text{for an upper specification limit.}$$
$$\text{Otherwise reject the batch.}$$

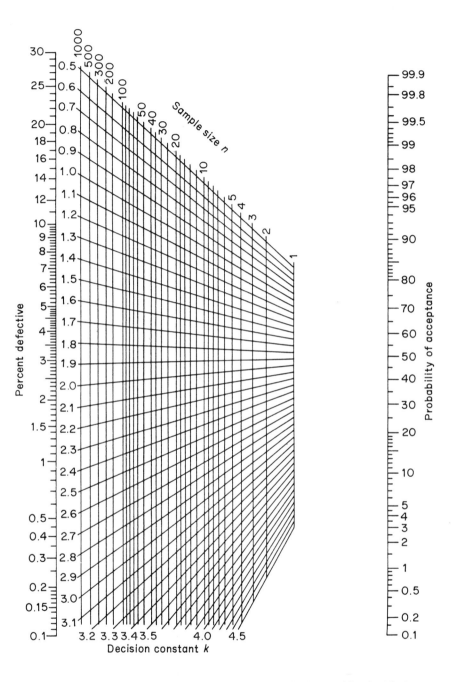

Figure 12.2 Nomogram for inspection by variables, single specification limits, σ unknown.

Example 12.2

If ($p_1 = 0.01$, $1 - \alpha = 0.99$) and ($p_2 = 0.07$, $\beta = 0.05$) then we obtain $n_\sigma = 22$, $k_\sigma = 1.82$. The method of using the nomogram is shown in Fig. 12.3.

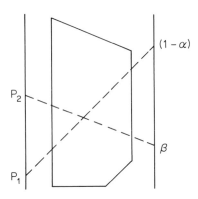

Figure 12.3 Use of nomogram for σ known and for σ unknown.

12.2.2* Derivation of method for single specifaction limit, σ known

Let us suppose that our measurements are normally distributed with unknown mean μ and known variance σ^2. Suppose also that there is a single specification limit U, and that we take a single sample of size n_σ, resulting in a mean $\bar{x}$. The fraction non-conforming in the batch is then

$$p = \int_U^\infty \frac{1}{\sqrt{(2\pi)}\sigma} \exp\left(-\frac{(x - \mu)^2}{2\sigma^2}\right) dx = 1 - \Phi((U - \mu)/\sigma) = \Phi(-v)$$

where $v = (U - \mu)/\sigma$. Another way of stating this is that for the fraction non-conforming to be p, the mean μ must be at

$$\mu = U - v\sigma. \tag{12.3}$$

Now the decision rule is to accept if

$$\bar{x} + k_\sigma\sigma < U$$

and if the probability of this is P we have

$$P = \Pr(\bar{x} + k_\sigma\sigma < U)$$

$$= \Pr\{z < (U - \mu - k_\sigma\sigma)\sqrt{n_\sigma}/\sigma\}$$

where z has a standard normal distribution. Therefore

$$P = \Phi(w) \tag{12.4}$$

where $w = \sqrt{(n_\sigma)}(U - \mu - k_\sigma\sigma)/\sigma$. Another way of stating this is that for the sample mean to be accepted with probability P the mean μ must be at

$$\mu = U - k_\sigma\sigma - w\sigma/\sqrt{n_\sigma} \tag{12.5}$$

where w is given by (12.4). By equating (12.3) and (12.5) we obtain

$$v = k_\sigma + w/\sqrt{n_\sigma}.$$

This equation must hold for the two points (p_1, P_1) and (p_2, P_2). By solving these two equations for n_σ and k_σ we obtain

$$n_\sigma = \left(\frac{w_1 - w_2}{v_1 - v_2}\right)^2 \quad \text{and} \quad k_\sigma = \left(\frac{v_1 w_2 - v_2 w_1}{w_2 - w_1}\right) \tag{12.6}$$

where

$$v_i = -\Phi^{-1}(p_i) \quad \text{and} \quad w_i = \Phi^{-1}(P_i). \tag{12.7}$$

In practice n_σ will have to be rounded up to the nearest integer, and this will mean that the OC-curve will pass approximately through the producer's and consumer's risk points. Once n_σ and k_σ are set, the actual OC-curve is given by (12.4), where μ has to be related to p by (12.3).

12.3 SINGLE SPECIFICATION LIMIT, σ UNKNOWN

12.3.1 Statement of the method

The approach here is very similar to that used in section 12.2.1 for the σ-known case, but using an estimated value of σ. The underlying theory is rather more complicated, and this is set out in section 12.3.2. The sample size is denoted n_s, and the decision rules are given in Step 5 of Method Summary 12.2. The nomogram given in Fig. 12.4 is from Wilrich (1970).

METHOD SUMMARY 12.2

Inspection by variables, single specification limit, σ unknown

Step 1 Choose a quality level p_1 at which the probability of acceptance is required to be $1 - \alpha$ and a quality level p_2 at which the probability of acceptance is required to be β (p_1 is smaller than p_2 and $1 - \alpha$ is greater than β.)

Step 2 Use the nomogram of Fig. 12.4 to find the point of intersection of the lines joining p_1 with $1 - \alpha$ and p_2 with β.

Step 3 Read off the value of k on the appropriate scale.

Step 4 Read off the sample size n_s on the appropriate scale. (This generally gives a higher sample size than for σ known, and this allows for the uncertainty of our knowledge of the standard deviation.)

Step 5 Accept the batch if either

$$\bar{x} - k_s s \geq L \qquad \text{for a lower specification limit}$$

or

$$\bar{x} + k_s s \leq U \qquad \text{for an upper specification limit.}$$

Otherwise reject the batch.

Example 12.3
If $(p_1 = 0.01,\ P_1 = 0.99)$, and $(p_2 = 0.07,\ P_2 = 0.05)$, then we obtain $n_s = 60,\ k_s = 1.83$.

12.3.2* Derivation of method for single specification limit, σ unknown

The assumptions here are similar to those in section 12.2.2 except that σ is unknown. Again we will assume a single upper specification limit U, and the decision rule is to accept if

$$\bar{x} + k_s s \leq U. \tag{12.8}$$

The probability of acceptance is

$$P = \Pr(\bar{x} \leq U - k_s s) = \Pr\{(Z + \delta)/(Y/f)^{1/2} \leq -\sqrt{n_s} k_s\} \tag{12.9}$$

where

$$Z = \sqrt{n_s}(\bar{x} - \mu)/\sigma \text{ is standard normal}$$

$$Y = fs^2/\sigma^2 \text{ is a } \chi^2 \text{ random variable}$$
$$\text{with } f \text{ degrees of freedom}$$

$$\delta = \sqrt{n_s}(\mu - U)/\sigma = \sqrt{n_s}\Phi^{-1}(p)$$

where $\Phi(x)$ is the standard Normal distribution and

$$f = (n_s - 1).$$

Equation (12.9) can be rewritten

$$P = \Pr(T_f \geq \sqrt{nk}|\delta) \tag{12.10}$$

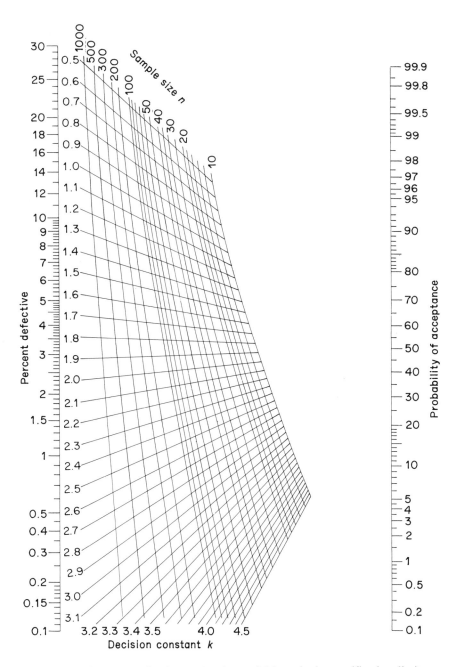

Figure 12.4 Nomogram for inspection by variables, single specification limit, σ unknown.

where T_f represents a non-central t random variable with f degrees of freedom and non-centrality parameter δ. This distribution is complicated to work with, but an approximation developed by Hamaker (1979), see also Wetherill and Kollerström (1979), enables us to obtain a solution.

If σ were known a batch would be accepted if, based on a sample of size n_σ, we get $\bar{x} \leq U - k_\sigma \sigma$ for some constant k_σ. The σ-known and σ-unknown cases will have practically the same OC-curve if n_s and k_s are adjusted such that $\bar{x} + k_s s$ has the same mean and variance as $\bar{x} + k_\sigma \sigma$ with sample size n_σ. By equating the mean and variance of $\bar{x} + k_s s$ respectively with the mean and variance of $\bar{x} + k_\sigma \sigma$ we get, approximately,

$$k_s = \sqrt{\{(3n_s - 3)(3n_s - 4)\}} k_\sigma \qquad (12.11)$$

and

$$n_s = \{1 + 3n_s k_\sigma^2/(6n_s - 8)\} n_\sigma. \qquad (12.12)$$

A method given by Enkawa (1980), starts with

$$n_s = (1 + k_\sigma^2/2) n_\sigma$$

and iterates. Equations (12.11) and (12.12) show how the parameters n_s and k_s of the plan for unknown variance must change from the σ-known plan in order to get approximately the same OC-curve. We see that the sample size has to be increased by a factor in excess of $(1 + k_\sigma^2/2)$.

Flesselles (1985) has shown that a direct solution of (12.11) and (12.12) is given by

$$n_s = n_\sigma + (u + \sqrt{(u^2 + 24v)})/12 \qquad (12.13)$$

where

$$u = 3n_\sigma(k_\sigma^2 - 2) + 8$$

and

$$v = 3n_\sigma^2 k_\sigma^2$$

and then

$$k_s = k_\sigma \sqrt{\{(3n_s - 3)/(3n_s - 4)\}}. \qquad (12.14)$$

Using Hamaker's approximation we can now easily calculate the probability of acceptance as follows:

$$P = P(\bar{x} + k_s s \leq U | n_s, \mu, \sigma) \simeq P(\bar{x} + k_\sigma \sigma \leq U | n_\sigma) = \Phi(\theta) \qquad (12.15)$$

where

$$\theta = \frac{U - \mu - k_s \sigma \sqrt{\{(3n_s - 4)/(3n_s - 3)\}}}{\sigma[(1 + 3n_s k_s^2/(6n_s - 8))/n_s]^{1/2}}$$

If the fraction non-conforming is p the probability of acceptance is written

$$p = \Phi(\theta_p),$$

where

$$\theta_p = [Z_p - k_s \sqrt{\{(3n_s - 4)/(3n_s - 3)\}}]/\{(1 + 3n_s k_s^2/(6n_s - 8))/n_s\}^{1/2}$$

and where Z_p is defined by the relation

$$\Phi(Z_p) = 1 - p.$$

12.4 ESTIMATION OF FRACTION NON-CONFORMING, SINGLE SPECIFICATION LIMIT

12.4.1 Statement of the method, σ known

In sections 12.2 and 12.3 the decision rule used to sentence the batch depends on the value of the sample mean, as in (12.1). An alternative is to use the sample data to estimate the fraction non-conforming in the batch, and then sentence the batch on the basis of the estimated fraction non-conforming.

If the measurements are normally distributed $N(\mu, \sigma)$ with a single upper specification limit U, the fraction non-conforming is the area under the normal curve to the right of U,

$$p_u = \Phi((\mu - U)/\sigma)$$

Since μ is unknown, we can use the sample mean $\bar{x}$ as an estimate of μ, and we might think of using

$$\Phi((\bar{x} - U)/\sigma)$$

to estimate the fraction non-conforming. This is not the best estimate, and it turns out better to use

$$\hat{p}_u = \Phi\left(\frac{(\bar{x} - U)}{\sigma} \sqrt{\left(\frac{n}{(n-1)}\right)}\right) \qquad (12.16)$$

where $\Phi(x)$ is looked up in standard normal tables, and similarly

$$\hat{p}_L = \Phi\left(\frac{(L - \bar{x})}{\sigma} \sqrt{\left(\frac{n}{(n-1)}\right)}\right) \qquad (12.17)$$

for a single lower limit. These estimates are 'uniformly minimum variance unbaised estimates', and the derivation is given by Lieberman and Resnikoff (1955).

For a single upper specification limit, we could accept provided

$$\hat{p}_u \le p^* \tag{12.18}$$

for some chosen p^*. Now if we denote by Z_p the normal deviate corresponding to p,

$$p = \Phi(-Z_p)$$

then (12.18) is equivalent to

$$\left(\frac{(\bar{x} - U)}{\sigma}\right)\sqrt{\left(\frac{n}{(n-1)}\right)} \le -Z_{p^*}$$

or

$$\bar{x} + \left(Z_{p^*}\sqrt{\left(\frac{(n-1)}{n}\right)}\right)\sigma \le U. \tag{12.19}$$

In order for this procedure to be identical to (12.1) we must have

$$k_\sigma = Z_{p^*}\sqrt{\left(\frac{(n-1)}{n}\right)}. \tag{12.20}$$

Similarly, for a single lower specification limit we obtain

$$\bar{x} - \left(Z_{p^*}\sqrt{\left(\frac{(n-1)}{n}\right)}\right)\sigma \ge L. \tag{12.21}$$

This results in the following method summaries. An advantage of this approach is that the procedure involves a direct estimation of the fraction non-conforming, which is a meaningful quantity.

METHOD SUMMARY 12.3

Inspection by variables, single specification limit, σ known. Fraction non-conforming method

Step 1 Determine n_σ and k_σ using Method Summary 12.1. Also determine p^* as the tail area normal probability corresponding to

$$Z_{p^*} = k_\sigma\sqrt{[n/(n-1)]}.$$

Step 2 Calculate

$$\hat{p}_U = \Phi\left(\frac{(\bar{x} - U)}{\sigma}\sqrt{\left(\frac{n}{(n-1)}\right)}\right)$$

for an upper specification limit

and

$$\hat{p}_L = \Phi\left(\frac{(L - \bar{x})}{\sigma}\sqrt{\left(\frac{n}{(n-1)}\right)}\right)$$

for a lower specification limit

by using standard normal tables of $\Phi(x)$.

Step 3 Accept the batch if

$$\hat{p}_U \leq p^* \quad \text{or} \quad \hat{p}_L \leq p^*$$

respectively.

12.4.2* Derivation of the estimate, σ known

The derivation (Lieberman and Resnikoff, 1955) is a straightforward application of the Rao–Blackwell lemma. We are given a sample mean $\bar{x}$ based on n observations, and we assume a single upper specification limit U. We let y be dependent on the first observation, defining

$$y = \begin{cases} 0 \text{ if } x_1 \leq U \\ 1 \text{ otherwise.} \end{cases} \tag{12.22}$$

Then a crude estimate of the fraction non-conforming is y, and this is clearly unbiased. Since $\bar{x}$ is the sufficient statistic, the uniformly minimum variance unbiased estimate is given by

$$\hat{p} = E(y|\bar{x}) \tag{12.23}$$

by the Rao–Blackwell lemma. Now it is easily shown that the joint distribution of (y, x) is

$$g(y, x) = \frac{n}{2\pi\sigma\sqrt{(n-1)}}\exp\left\{-\frac{n}{2\sigma^2}\left((\bar{x} - \mu)^2 + \frac{(y - \bar{x})^2}{(n-1)}\right)\right\}.$$

Therefore the conditional distribution of y given $\bar{x}$ is

$$h(y|\bar{x}) = \frac{1}{\sqrt{(2\pi)}\sigma}\exp\left\{-\frac{n(y - \bar{x})^2}{2\sigma^2(n-1)}\right\}\sqrt{\left(\frac{n}{(n-1)}\right)}. \tag{12.24}$$

By using this we see that (12.23) becomes

$$\hat{p} = \int_X^\infty \frac{1}{\sqrt{(2\pi)}}\exp\left(-\frac{t^2}{2}\right)dt$$

where

$$X = \left(\frac{U - \bar{x}}{\sigma}\right)\sqrt{\left(\frac{n}{(n-1)}\right)}.$$

This establishes the method given in Method Summary 12.3.

12.4.3 Statement of the method, σ unknown

This method follows using methods similar to the other cases. Unfortunately the mathematics involved is complex, and an extra approximation is necessary: see the derivation in the next section.

METHOD SUMMARY 12.4

Inspection by variables, single specification limit, σ unknown. Fraction non-conforming method

Step 1 Determine n_s and k_s using Method Summary 12.2. Also determine p^* as the tail area normal probability corresponding to

$$Z_{p^*} = k_s \sqrt{(n_s/(n_s - 1))}.$$

Step 2 Calculate $Q_s = (U - \bar{x})/s$, or $Q_s = (\bar{x} - L)/s$ for an upper or lower specification limit respectively.

Step 3 Calculate

$$\hat{p} = 1 - \Phi(\lambda_s Q_s)$$

where $\lambda_s = \sqrt{\{(2n_s - 1)/(2n_s - Q_s^2)\}}$ and accept the batch if $\hat{p} < p^*$.

12.4.4* Derivation of the estimate, σ unknown

The derivation of the estimate for the σ-unknown case follows the same principles as for the σ-known case of section 12.4.2. We again use the Rao-Blackwell lemma, and obtain a minimum variance unbiased estimate of $\hat{p}$, by taking expectations of an estimate based on the first observation y, (12.22). The sufficient statistics are now

$$\bar{x} = \sum x_i/n, \qquad s^2 = \sum(x_i - \bar{x})^2/(n - 1)$$

$$\hat{p} = E(y|\bar{x}, s^2). \tag{12.25}$$

In order to do this calculation we need the joint distribution of $(y, \bar{x}, s^2)$, and then the conditional distribution $h(y|\bar{x}, s^2)$. The details are given in Lieberman and Resnikoff (1955), but the conditional distribution is

$$g(z) = \frac{\Gamma(n - 2)}{\{\Gamma(n - 2)/2\}^2} z^{[(n/2)-1]-1}(1 - z)^{[(n/2)-1]-1}, \qquad 0 \le z \le 1 \tag{12.26}$$

where $z = \frac{1}{2} + (\bar{x} - y)\sqrt{n}/2s(n - 1)$. This is a symmetrical beta distribution with both parameters $\{(n/2) - 1\}$, which we denote $\beta((n/2) - 1)$. The estimator is therefore

$$\hat{p} = \int_0^{\max\{0,(1/2)-(U-\bar{x})\sqrt{n/2s(n-1)}\}} d\beta\left(\frac{n}{2} - 1\right) \qquad (12.27)$$

for a single upper specification limit, and

$$\hat{p} = \int_0^{\max\{0,(1/2)-(\bar{x}-L)\sqrt{n/2s(n-1)}\}} d\beta\left(\frac{n}{2} - 1\right) \qquad (12.28)$$

for a single lower specification limit.

The approximation stated in Method Summary 12.4 was given by Wilrich and Hennings (1987) based on the work of Stange (1961).

12.5 DOUBLE SPECIFICATION LIMIT, σ KNOWN

12.5.1 Double specification limits: discussion

The design of sampling plans for double specification limits is rather more complicated than we might expect. The chief problem is that under certain combinations of (μ, σ), we can get non-conforming product at both ends of the range. This in turn means that we cannot simply combine two single specification limit plans, unless U and L are sufficiently far apart in terms of σ. It also means, and this is a deeper point, that there is a limiting value of σ such that whatever μ, the quality is at best equal to that desired, and considerably worse for other values of μ and larger values of σ. Thus there is a limiting value of σ such that batches can be rejected, whatever the value of the process mean.

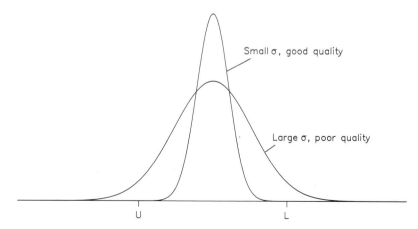

Figure 12.5 Double specification limits.

Another important question concerns the decision rule to be used. It is clear that the key quantity is the total fraction non-conforming,

$$\hat{p} = \hat{p}_U + \hat{p}_L \tag{12.29}$$

and a decision rule can be formed on this basis, so that we accept provided $\bar{p} < p^*$, say. With this decision rule, the OC-curve depends not just on the true value of p, the fraction non-conforming, but also on the particular values of μ and σ.

A straightforward application of the rule (12.29), using (12.16) and (12.17), leads to boundaries in the $(\bar{x}, \sigma)$ plane as in Fig. 12.6. The acceptance region is to the left of the boundary shown.

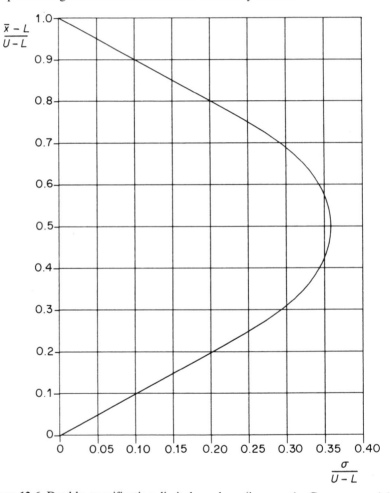

Figure 12.6 Double specification limit boundary (incorrect). Crown copyright. Reproduced by permission of the Controller of HMSO.

It can be shown that the OC-curve for this type of plan is as given in Fig. 12.7, and the OC-curve is not a curve, but a very broad band. This is clearly unsatisfactory, and is a feature of most published plans up until 1988. This was studied by Bravo (1984) who proposed a couple of possible revisions, and Baillie (1988) advised of specific revisions to published plans.

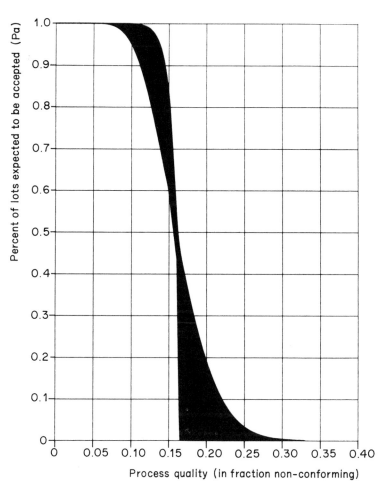

Figure 12.7 Band of OC-curves for decision rule (12.29). Crown copyright. Reproduced by permission of the Controller of HMSO.

The correct procedure is to use decision rule (12.29) *coupled with* a limit on the value of σ. If it is desired to have plans with an AQL p_1, then if

$$(U - L)/2\sigma > Z_{p_1/2}$$

then the batch quality is worse than the AQL anyway, even if the process mean is centred between U and L. The boundaries such as Fig. 12.6 should therefore be terminated at the maximum process standard deviation

$$\sigma_M = (U - L)/2Z_{p_1/2}. \tag{12.30}$$

Some typical boundaries are shown in Fig. 12.8, and this results in much tighter bands of OC-curves, see Fig. 12.9. The acceptance region is to

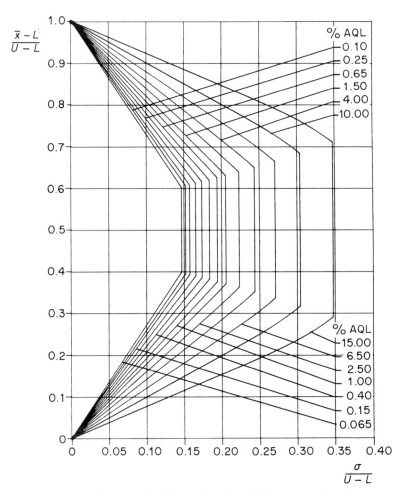

Figure 12.8 Boundaries for double specification limits (correct). Crown copyright. Reproduced by permission of the Controller of HMSO.

the left of the boundaries; for further details, see Baillie (1988). Charts like Fig. 12.8, with accompanying tables, are being issued in the second edition of ISO 3951.

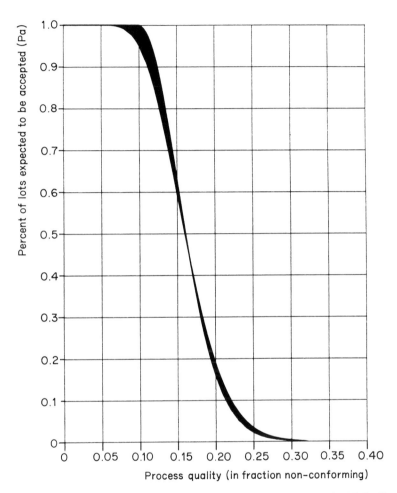

Figure 12.9 Band of OC curves for a typical boundary from Fig. 12.8. Crown copyright. Reproduced by permission of the Controller of HMSO.

12.5.2 Statement of the method

The method given here is based on the work of Bravo (1980, 1981, 1984), Baillie (1988), Duncan (1974), and Schilling (1982).

METHOD SUMMARY 12.5

Inspection by variables, double specification limit, σ known

Step 1 Choose a quality level p_1 at which the probability of acceptance is required to be $1 - \alpha$, and a quality level p_2 at which the probability of acceptance is required to be β (p_1 is smaller than p_2 and $1 - \alpha$ is greater than β).

Step 2 Check that

$$\sigma \leq \sigma_M = (U - L)/2Z_{p_1/2}$$

and reject the batch outright if this is not satisfied.

Step 3 Determine n_σ and k_σ using Method Summary 12.1. Also determine p^* as the tail area normal probability corresponding to

$$Z_{p^*} = k_\sigma \sqrt{[n_\sigma/(n_\sigma - 1)]}.$$

Step 4 Calculate $Z_{p_0} = (U - L)/2\sigma$, and find the value p_0 from normal tables. If

$p_0 \leq p_1/4$ use two separate single specification limit plans

$p_0 \geq p_1$ reject the batch without sampling.

Otherwise, proceed to Step 5.

Step 5 Use the decision rule to accept if $\hat{p} < p^*$, where

$$\hat{p} = \hat{p}_U + \hat{p}_L$$

and $\hat{p}_U$ and $\hat{p}_L$ are given by (12.16) and (12.17).

12.5.3 Derivation

The reasoning behind the method is given in section 12.5.1. It is readily seen that the estimate of the combined fraction non-conforming is

$$\hat{p} = \hat{p}_U + \hat{p}_L$$

where $\hat{p}_U$ and $\hat{p}_L$ are derived in section 12.4.

When σ is very small, the existence of, say the lower limit L, is irrelevant to determining the boundary in Fig. 12.8 for the upper specification limit. Therefore the boundaries in Fig. 12.8 must tend to (12.1) and (12.2) at small values of σ.

Finally, we restate the argument showing that the boundaries of Fig. 12.6 leading to the OC-curve of Fig. 12.7, and are wrong. For any given σ, there are limits for the mean,

$$\bar{x}_L < \bar{x} < \bar{x}_U$$

such that batches are accepted for values of $\bar{x}$ between them. The OC-curve is therefore

$$P(\mu, \sigma) = \Phi\{\sqrt{n}(\bar{x}_U - \mu)/\sigma\} - \Phi\{\sqrt{n}(\bar{x}_L - \mu)/\sigma\}$$

Now for values of σ close to the apex of the curve in Fig. 12.6, the limits $(\bar{x}_L, \bar{x}_U)$ are very close together, and eventually identical. For any such value of σ, the probability of acceptance is small or zero. Therefore the OC-curve has the general shape shown in Fig. 12.7; for further details see Baillie (1988).

12.6 DOUBLE SPECIFICATION LIMIT, σ UNKNOWN

The general outline of sampling by variables for double specification limits and σ unknown is rather similar to the discussion in section 12.5 for σ known and the derivation is similar to that discussed in section 12.4.4, based on the work of Lieberman and Resnikoff (1955). Method Summary 12.6 depends on an approximation given by Wilrich and Hennings (1987).

METHOD SUMMARY 12.6

Inspection by variables, double specification limit, σ unknown

Step 1 Choose a quality level p_1 at which the probability of acceptance is required to be $1 - \alpha$ and a quality level $p_2(> p_1)$ at which the probability of acceptance is required to be β.

Step 2 Apply Method Summary 12.4 to both the upper and lower specification limits separately to obtain $\hat{p}_U$ and $\hat{p}_L$ respectively. (The n_s and k_s are identical.)

Step 3 Accept the batch if

$$\hat{p}_U + \hat{p}_L = \hat{p} < \hat{p}^*.$$

12.7 MULTIVARIATE SAMPLING PLANS

There are many situations where the conformity of a product depends simultaneously on several variables, and it is unsatisfactory to deal with these variables separately. For example, when considering the accuracy of firing a missile at a target, at least two dimensions must be studied simultaneously. Baillie (1987) has studied the multivariate case extensively for both the situations when the variables are independent and dependent. The dependent case is complicated, and needs special computer software to run it, and will not be discussed further here. In contrast, the multivariate independent case is very simple, and can be dealt with by reference to previous Method Summaries.

Let there be k variables, and denote the estimate for the fraction non-conforming in the jth variable by $\hat{p}_j$, where this estimate is obtained as in Method Summaries 12.5 or 12.6 for σ known and unknown respectively. Then for independence, the estimate of the overall fraction non-conforming is

$$\hat{p}_0 = 1 - \prod_{i=1}^{k}(1 - \hat{p}_j). \tag{12.31}$$

The decision rule is to accept the batch if $\hat{p}_0 < p^*$, for some chosen p^*.

Baillie (1987) shows that the bands of OC-curves for this type of plan are narrow, particularly for σ unknown, except for high AQL values in small sample sizes, and is independent of k. Therefore a plan is designed as for one variable only, but it is then used using the estimate (12.31).

EXERCISES 12A

1. Obtain σ-known and σ-unknown sampling plans for the sets of parameters shown in Table 12.1.

Table 12.1 Parameter settings for sampling schemes

p_1	α	p_2	β
0.01	5%	0.04	5%
0.01	5%	0.03	5%
0.01	2%	0.04	5%
0.01	5%	0.04	2%
0.02	5%	0.03	5%

13

Standard sampling systems

13.1 INTRODUCTION

A series of sampling systems have been developed during and since World War II for use in military contracts, and are now established as British, American and International Standards. They are all based on similar principles.

The first step was that a table was drawn up which in effect fixes the relationship between batch size and sample size to be one of three or five purely arbitrary functions. The sample sizes were made to increase with batch size in a manner thought to be reasonable.

Next the concept of acceptable quality level (AQL) was introduced, but the actual definition of this differs in the different schemes. The Statistical Research Group tables (Freeman *et al.*, 1948) fixed the AQL as the quality for which the probability of acceptance was 0.95. Unfortunately this has some undesirable consequences: since the sample size is already fixed, this automatically determines the sampling plan, and some rather large consumers' risks result. Other sampling systems, such as the US Army Service Forces tables (1944), MIL-STD-105 (A, B, C, D), and the British DEF-131 (Hill, 1962), have let the probability of acceptance at the AQL vary in a rather unsystematic way, so as to share the risks between producer and consumer more equitably. The most satisfactory definition of AQL is the one used in the current International Standard, (ISO 2859), that it is the maximum percentage defective which can be considered satisfactory as a process average. That is, the AQL is a property required of the product. The variation of the probability of acceptance at AQL is considerable, ranging from 0.80 for the lowest sample sizes to 0.99 for the largest.

Finally, all of the defence sampling tables use *switching rules*. The idea is that watch is kept on the inspection results, and according to certain rules, a much stricter form of inspection called 'tightened' inspection is introduced if necessary. The introduction of tightened inspection produces a wholesale change of the OC-curve along the lines shown in Fig. 13.1. This puts considerable pressure on the producer, since even goods of AQL quality would be rejected much more frequently. *It should be clear that a major part of the quality assurance given by the schemes lies in the use of this switching rule pressure tactic.* A producer is forced to send goods of AQL quality or better, to have them accepted at a satisfactory rate, and to avoid tightened inspection.

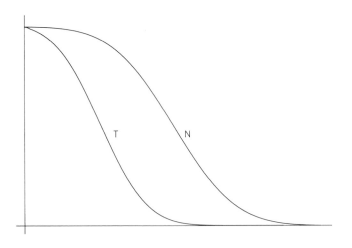

Fraction defective

Figure 13.1 OC-curves for normal (N) and tightened (T) inspection.

The switching rules currently in use are as follows.

(1) *Normal to tightened inspection:* When 2 out of 5 successive batches are rejected.
(2) *Tightened to normal inspection:* When 5 consecutive batches are accepted at tightened inspection.

It should be clear that the effect of the above rules is quite stringent, since it is rather more difficult to satisfy tightened inspection than normal. There are also switches to 'reduced' inspection, applicable when quality is very good. The rules used for switching have varied. Ideally, a watch should be kept on the process average, such as by a CuSum chart, but this was criticized as being too complicated.

A good description of a modern scheme, together with some tables, is readily accessible in the paper by Hill (1962), to which readers are referred for further details. A complete description of the schemes, together with tables for use is given in the International Standard ISO 2859 (see BS 6000 and 6001). The description of the procedures below is based on the International Standards; for a list of Standards and their equivalents see Appendix C.

There are two main criticisms of this approach. One obvious point is the arbitrariness of the batch-sample size relationship. There is no theoretical backing of any of the relationships used although they are 'reasonable'. A rather more important criticism, however, is that the switching rules pressure tactic is not always practicable. There may not be an indefinite sequence of batches, and the consumer may not be in a position to exert much pressure on the producer. (A government department is usually in a different position.) However, in places where switching rules can be used, the defence sampling systems method pays off well.

Double, multiple and sequential sampling plans are available in the international standards listed in Appendix C. In this chapter we only consider single sampling plans.

13.2 STATEMENT OF METHOD FOR INSPECTION BY ATTRIBUTES

The statement given below is a brief summary, and reference should be made to the appropriate standard for further details.

METHOD SUMMARY 13.1

Inspection by attributes using ISO 2859 (BS 6001)

Step 1 Choose a sample size code letter appropriate to your batch size, using Table 13.1. (General inspection level II is usually used.)

Step 2 Choose normal, tightened and reduced sampling plans using Tables 13.2–4.

Step 3 Operate the plans, starting with normal inspection, using the switching rules.

Example 13.1
If we have batch size = 2000, General inspection level II, then the Code letter is K. For an AQL of 1% the sample size is 125 and the acceptance numbers are:

$$\text{normal inspection,} \quad c = 3$$
$$\text{tightened inspection,} \quad c = 2.$$

The reduced inspection plan is $n = 50$, $c = 1$.

Table 13.1 Sample size code letters
Extracts from British Standards are reproduced with the permission of BSI.

Lot or batch size	Special inspection levels				General instpection levels		
	S-1	S-2	S-3	S-4	I	II	III
2–8	A	A	A	A	A	A	B
9–15	A	A	A	A	A	B	C
16–25	A	A	B	B	B	C	D
26–50	A	B	B	C	C	D	E
51–90	B	B	C	C	C	E	F
91–150	B	B	C	D	D	F	G
151–280	B	C	D	E	E	G	H
281–500	B	C	D	E	F	H	J
501–1 200	C	C	E	F	G	J	K
1 201–3 200	C	D	E	G	H	K	L
3 201–10 000	C	D	F	G	J	L	M
10 001–35 000	C	D	F	H	K	M	N
35 001–150 000	D	E	G	J	L	N	P
150 001–500 000	D	E	G	J	M	P	Q
500 001 and over	D	E	H	K	N	Q	R

A good description of the inspection levels and how to choose them is given in the appropriate standard. The tables allow for 'defects per unit' as well as percent defective, so the AQL values extend as shown.

13.3 INSPECTION BY VARIABLES (ISO 3951)

The method here is very similar to that described in the previous section for attribute inspection. There are two approaches:

   s method: for use when σ is estimated;
   σ method: for use when σ is considered known.

In each case methods are given for single or double specification limits. The notation used here is as given in Chapter 12. The plans given here are broadly equivalent to attributes plans with the same AQL, so an approximate comparison of sample sizes is easily achieved. In the tables below, only the s method is given, and for other tables see the full Standard. The double specification limits case used a chart in which $(\bar{x}, s)$ or $(\bar{x}, \sigma)$ are plotted; only one such chart is given here, and again for more details see the full Standard.

Table 13.2 Single sampling plans for normal inspection (master table). Extracts from the British Standards are reproduced with the permission of BSI.

Acceptable quality levels (normal inspection). Each AQL column shows the acceptance number (Ac) and rejection number (Re). ↓ = use first sampling plan below arrow. ↑ = use first sampling plan above arrow.

Sample size code letter	Sample size	0.010	0.015	0.025	0.040	0.065	0.10	0.15	0.25	0.40	0.65	1.0	1.5	2.5	4.0	6.5	10	15	25	40	65	100	150	250	400	650	1000
		Ac Re	Ac Re	Ac Re	Ac Re	Ac Re	Ac Re	Ac Re	Ac Re	Ac Re	Ac Re	Ac Re	Ac Re	Ac Re	Ac Re	Ac Re	Ac Re	Ac Re	Ac Re	Ac Re	Ac Re	Ac Re	Ac Re	Ac Re	Ac Re	Ac Re	Ac Re
A	2	↓	↓	↓	↓	↓	↓	↓	↓	↓	↓	↓	↓	↓	↓	↓	↓	0 1	1 2	2 3	3 4	5 6	7 8	10 11	14 15	21 22	30 31
B	3	↓	↓	↓	↓	↓	↓	↓	↓	↓	↓	↓	↓	↓	↓	↓	0 1	1 2	2 3	3 4	5 6	7 8	10 11	14 15	21 22	30 31	44 45
C	5	↓	↓	↓	↓	↓	↓	↓	↓	↓	↓	↓	↓	↓	↓	0 1	1 2	2 3	3 4	5 6	7 8	10 11	14 15	21 22	30 31	44 45	↑
D	8	↓	↓	↓	↓	↓	↓	↓	↓	↓	↓	↓	↓	↓	0 1	1 2	2 3	3 4	5 6	7 8	10 11	14 15	21 22	30 31	44 45	↑	↑
E	13	↓	↓	↓	↓	↓	↓	↓	↓	↓	↓	↓	↓	0 1	1 2	2 3	3 4	5 6	7 8	10 11	14 15	21 22	30 31	44 45	↑	↑	↑
F	20	↓	↓	↓	↓	↓	↓	↓	↓	↓	↓	↓	0 1	1 2	2 3	3 4	5 6	7 8	10 11	14 15	21 22	30 31	44 45	↑	↑	↑	↑
G	32	↓	↓	↓	↓	↓	↓	↓	↓	↓	↓	0 1	1 2	2 3	3 4	5 6	7 8	10 11	14 15	21 22	30 31	44 45	↑	↑	↑	↑	↑
H	50	↓	↓	↓	↓	↓	↓	↓	↓	↓	0 1	1 2	2 3	3 4	5 6	7 8	10 11	14 15	21 22	30 31	44 45	↑	↑	↑	↑	↑	↑
J	80	↓	↓	↓	↓	↓	↓	↓	↓	0 1	1 2	2 3	3 4	5 6	7 8	10 11	14 15	21 22	30 31	44 45	↑	↑	↑	↑	↑	↑	↑
K	125	↓	↓	↓	↓	↓	↓	↓	0 1	1 2	2 3	3 4	5 6	7 8	10 11	14 15	21 22	30 31	44 45	↑	↑	↑	↑	↑	↑	↑	↑
L	200	↓	↓	↓	↓	↓	↓	0 1	1 2	2 3	3 4	5 6	7 8	10 11	14 15	21 22	30 31	44 45	↑	↑	↑	↑	↑	↑	↑	↑	↑
M	315	↓	↓	↓	↓	↓	0 1	1 2	2 3	3 4	5 6	7 8	10 11	14 15	21 22	30 31	44 45	↑	↑	↑	↑	↑	↑	↑	↑	↑	↑
N	500	↓	↓	↓	↓	0 1	1 2	2 3	3 4	5 6	7 8	10 11	14 15	21 22	30 31	44 45	↑	↑	↑	↑	↑	↑	↑	↑	↑	↑	↑
P	800	↓	↓	↓	0 1	1 2	2 3	3 4	5 6	7 8	10 11	14 15	21 22	30 31	44 45	↑	↑	↑	↑	↑	↑	↑	↑	↑	↑	↑	↑
Q′	1250	↓	↓	0 1	1 2	2 3	3 4	5 6	7 8	10 11	14 15	21 22	30 31	44 45	↑	↑	↑	↑	↑	↑	↑	↑	↑	↑	↑	↑	↑
R	2000	↓	0 1	1 2	2 3	3 4	5 6	7 8	10 11	14 15	21 22	30 31	44 45	↑	↑	↑	↑	↑	↑	↑	↑	↑	↑	↑	↑	↑	↑

⇩ = use first sampling plan below arrow. If sample size equals, or exceeds, lot or batch size, do 100 percent inspection.

⇧ = use first sampling plan above arrow.

Ac = acceptance number.

Re = rejection number.

Table 13.3 Single sampling plans for tightened inspection (master table). Extracts from the British Standards are reproduced with the permission of BSI.

Acceptable quality levels (tightened inspection). Each cell gives the pair Ac Re (acceptance number, rejection number). ↓ = use first sampling plan below the arrow; ↑ = use first sampling plan above the arrow.

Sample size code letter	Sample size	0.010	0.015	0.025	0.040	0.065	0.10	0.15	0.25	0.40	0.65	1.0	1.5	2.5	4.0	6.5	10	15	25	40	65	100	150	250	400	650	1000
A	2	↓	↓	↓	↓	↓	↓	↓	↓	↓	↓	↓	↓	↓	↓	↓	↓	↓	0 1	1 2	2 3	3 4	5 6	8 9	12 13	18 19	27 28
B	3	↓	↓	↓	↓	↓	↓	↓	↓	↓	↓	↓	↓	↓	↓	↓	↓	0 1	1 2	2 3	3 4	5 6	8 9	12 13	18 19	27 28	41 42
C	5	↓	↓	↓	↓	↓	↓	↓	↓	↓	↓	↓	↓	↓	↓	↓	0 1	1 2	2 3	3 4	5 6	8 9	12 13	18 19	27 28	41 42	↑
D	8	↓	↓	↓	↓	↓	↓	↓	↓	↓	↓	↓	↓	↓	↓	0 1	1 2	2 3	3 4	5 6	8 9	12 13	18 19	27 28	41 42	↑	↑
E	13	↓	↓	↓	↓	↓	↓	↓	↓	↓	↓	↓	↓	↓	0 1	1 2	2 3	3 4	5 6	8 9	12 13	18 19	27 28	41 42	↑	↑	↑
F	20	↓	↓	↓	↓	↓	↓	↓	↓	↓	↓	↓	↓	0 1	1 2	2 3	3 4	5 6	8 9	12 13	18 19	27 28	41 42	↑	↑	↑	↑
G	32	↓	↓	↓	↓	↓	↓	↓	↓	↓	↓	↓	0 1	1 2	2 3	3 4	5 6	8 9	12 13	18 19	27 28	41 42	↑	↑	↑	↑	↑
H	50	↓	↓	↓	↓	↓	↓	↓	↓	↓	↓	0 1	1 2	2 3	3 4	5 6	8 9	12 13	18 19	27 28	41 42	↑	↑	↑	↑	↑	↑
J	80	↓	↓	↓	↓	↓	↓	↓	↓	↓	0 1	1 2	2 3	3 4	5 6	8 9	12 13	18 19	27 28	41 42	↑	↑	↑	↑	↑	↑	↑
K	125	↓	↓	↓	↓	↓	↓	↓	↓	0 1	1 2	2 3	3 4	5 6	8 9	12 13	18 19	27 28	41 42	↑	↑	↑	↑	↑	↑	↑	↑
L	200	↓	↓	↓	↓	↓	↓	↓	0 1	1 2	2 3	3 4	5 6	8 9	12 13	18 19	27 28	41 42	↑	↑	↑	↑	↑	↑	↑	↑	↑
M	315	↓	↓	↓	↓	↓	↓	0 1	1 2	2 3	3 4	5 6	8 9	12 13	18 19	27 28	41 42	↑	↑	↑	↑	↑	↑	↑	↑	↑	↑
N	500	↓	↓	↓	↓	↓	0 1	1 2	2 3	3 4	5 6	8 9	12 13	18 19	27 28	41 42	↑	↑	↑	↑	↑	↑	↑	↑	↑	↑	↑
P	800	↓	↓	↓	↓	0 1	1 2	2 3	3 4	5 6	8 9	12 13	18 19	27 28	41 42	↑	↑	↑	↑	↑	↑	↑	↑	↑	↑	↑	↑
Q'	1250	↓	↓	↓	0 1	1 2	2 3	3 4	5 6	8 9	12 13	18 19	27 28	41 42	↑	↑	↑	↑	↑	↑	↑	↑	↑	↑	↑	↑	↑
R	2000	↓	↓	0 1	1 2	2 3	3 4	5 6	8 9	12 13	18 19	27 28	41 42	↑	↑	↑	↑	↑	↑	↑	↑	↑	↑	↑	↑	↑	↑
S	3150	↓	0 1	1 2	2 3	3 4	5 6	8 9	12 13	18 19	27 28	41 42	↑	↑	↑	↑	↑	↑	↑	↑	↑	↑	↑	↑	↑	↑	↑

Table 13.4 Single sampling plans for reduced inspection (master table). Extracts from the British Standards are reproduced with the permission of BSI.

Sample size code letter	Sample size	Acceptable quality levels (reduced inspection)†																									
		0.010	0.015	0.025	0.040	0.065	0.10	0.15	0.25	0.40	0.65	1.0	1.5	2.5	4.0	6.5	10	15	25	40	65	100	150	250	400	650	1000
		Ac Re	Ac Re	Ac Re	Ac Re	Ac Re	Ac Re	Ac Re	Ac Re	Ac Re	Ac Re	Ac Re	Ac Re	Ac Re	Ac Re	Ac Re	Ac Re	Ac Re	Ac Re	Ac Re	Ac Re	Ac Re	Ac Re	Ac Re	Ac Re	Ac Re	Ac Re
A	2	↓	↓	↓	↓	↓	↓	↓	↓	↓	↓	↓	↓	↓	↓	0 1	↓	↓	1 2	2 3	3 4	5 6	7 8	10 11	14 15	21 22	30 31
B	2	↓	↓	↓	↓	↓	↓	↓	↓	↓	↓	↓	↓	↓	0 1	↑	↓	0 2	1 3	2 4	3 5	5 6	7 8	10 11	14 15	21 22	30 31
C	2	↓	↓	↓	↓	↓	↓	↓	↓	↓	↓	↓	↓	0 1	↑	↓	0 2	1 3	1 4	2 5	3 6	5 8	7 10	10 13	14 17	21 24	↑
D	3	↓	↓	↓	↓	↓	↓	↓	↓	↓	↓	↓	0 1	↑	↓	0 2	1 3	1 4	2 5	3 6	5 8	7 10	10 13	14 17	21 24	↑	↑
E	5	↓	↓	↓	↓	↓	↓	↓	↓	↓	↓	0 1	↑	↓	0 2	1 3	1 4	2 5	3 6	5 8	7 10	10 13	14 17	21 24	↑	↑	↑
F	8	↓	↓	↓	↓	↓	↓	↓	↓	↓	0 1	↑	↓	0 2	1 3	1 4	2 5	3 6	5 8	7 10	10 13	↑	↑	↑	↑	↑	↑
G	13	↓	↓	↓	↓	↓	↓	↓	↓	0 1	↑	↓	0 2	1 3	1 4	2 5	3 6	5 8	7 10	10 13	↑	↑	↑	↑	↑	↑	↑
H	20	↓	↓	↓	↓	↓	↓	↓	0 1	↑	↓	0 2	1 3	1 4	2 5	3 6	5 8	7 10	10 13	↑	↑	↑	↑	↑	↑	↑	↑
J	32	↓	↓	↓	↓	↓	↓	0 1	↑	↓	0 2	1 3	1 4	2 5	3 6	5 8	7 10	10 13	↑	↑	↑	↑	↑	↑	↑	↑	↑
K	50	↓	↓	↓	↓	↓	0 1	↑	↓	0 2	1 3	1 4	2 5	3 6	5 8	7 10	10 13	↑	↑	↑	↑	↑	↑	↑	↑	↑	↑
L	80	↓	↓	↓	↓	0 1	↑	↓	0 2	1 3	1 4	2 5	3 6	5 8	7 10	10 13	↑	↑	↑	↑	↑	↑	↑	↑	↑	↑	↑
M	125	↓	↓	↓	0 1	↑	↓	0 2	1 3	1 4	2 5	3 6	5 8	7 10	10 13	↑	↑	↑	↑	↑	↑	↑	↑	↑	↑	↑	↑
N	200	↓	↓	0 1	↑	↓	0 2	1 3	1 4	2 5	3 6	5 8	7 10	10 13	↑	↑	↑	↑	↑	↑	↑	↑	↑	↑	↑	↑	↑
P	315	↓	0 1	↑	↓	0 2	1 3	1 4	2 5	3 6	5 8	7 10	10 13	↑	↑	↑	↑	↑	↑	↑	↑	↑	↑	↑	↑	↑	↑
Q	500	0 1	↑	↓	0 2	1 3	1 4	2 5	3 6	5 8	7 10	10 13	↑	↑	↑	↑	↑	↑	↑	↑	↑	↑	↑	↑	↑	↑	↑
R	800	↑	↑	0 2	1 3	1 4	2 5	3 6	5 8	7 10	10 13	↑	↑	↑	↑	↑	↑	↑	↑	↑	↑	↑	↑	↑	↑	↑	↑

↓ = use first sampling plan below arrow. If sample size equals or exceeds lot or batch size, do 100 percent inspection.

↑ = use first sampling plan above arrow.

Ac = acceptance number.

Re = rejection number.

† = if the acceptance number has been exceeded, but the rejection number has not been reached, accept the lot, but reinstate normal inspection.

METHOD SUMMARY 13.2

Inspection by variables, *s* method (ISO 3951)

Step 1 Choose a sample size code letter using Table 13.5. (General inspection level II is usually used.)

Step 2 Determine the sample sizes and acceptability constants k_s for normal tightened and reduced inspection using Tables 13.6–13.8.

Step 3 For a single upper specification limit U, accept the batch if $Q_U \geq k_s$, where

$$Q_U = (U - \bar{x})/s.$$

For a single lower specification limit L accept the batch if $Q_L \geq k_s$, where

$$Q_L = (\bar{x} - L)/s.$$

For double specification limits plot $(\bar{x}, s)$ in a specially prepared chart (see for example Fig. 12.8).

Note It is essential to check the data for normality and for outliers.

Example 13.2

As an illustration we continue the problem given in Example 13.1, with a batch size of 2000 and an AQL of 1%. For General inspection level II, the appropriate code letter is K. From Tables 13.6–13.8 we have

normal inspection	$n = 50$	$k_s = 1.93$
tightened inspection	$n = 50$	$k_s = 2.08$
reduced inspection	$n = 20$	$k_s = 1.69$.

The saving in sample size over attribute inspection is seen to be very considerable. The σ-known plans give an even greater saving, with a sample size of 17 for normal inspection. Provided the assumptions hold, the variables and attributes plans give almost the same OC-curve.

13.4 INTERNATIONAL STANDARDS FOR PROCESS AND QUALITY CONTROL

A lot of work has been done in recent years in providing National and International Standards for the application of statistical methods to industry. The standards cover a wide area, including terminology, sampling materials, data analysis, acceptance sampling and statistical process control. Students who propose to apply statistical methods to industry should have some knowledge of these standards, and an abbreviated list appears in Appendix C.

Table 13.5 Sample size code letters for inspection by variables. Extracts from the British Standards are reproduced with the permission of BSI.

Lot size	special inspection levels		General inspection levels		
	S-3	S-4	I	II	III
2–8	↓	↓	↓	↓	C
9–15				B	D
16–25			B	C	E
26–50		↓	C	D	E
51–90		B	D	E	G
91–150	↓	C	E	F	H
151–280	B	D	F	G	I
281–500	C	E	G	H/I*	J
501–1 200	D	F	H	J	K
1 201–3 200	E	G	I	K	L
3 201–10 000	F	H	J	L	M
10 001–35 000	G	I	K	M	N
35 001–150 000	H	J	L	N	P
150 001–500 000	I	K	M	P	↑
500 001 and over	J	L	N	↑	↑

* Use H for lot size 281–400 and I for lot size 401–500

Notes (1) The code letters and inspection levels in this standard correspond to those given in BS 6001; they are not indentical with those given in MIL STD 414.

(2) Symbol

There is no suitable sampling plan in this area; use the first sampling plan below or above the arrow. This refers to both the sample size and acceptability constant k_s (or k_σ).

Table 13.6 Single sampling plans for normal inspection (master table): 's' method. Extracts from the British Standards are reproduced with the permission of BSI.

Sample size code letter	Sample size	Acceptable quality levels (normal inspection)										
		0.10	0.15	0.25	0.40	0.65	1.00	1.50	2.50	4.00	6.50	10.00
		k_s	k_s	k_s	k_s	k_s	k_s	k_s	k_s	k_s	k_s	k_s
B	3	↓	↓	↓	↓	↓	↓	↓	1.12	0.958	0.765	0.566
C	4	↓	↓	↓	↓	↓	1.45	1.34	1.17	1.01	0.814	0.617
D	5	↓	↓	↓	↓	1.65	1.53	1.40	1.24	1.07	0.874	0.675
E	7	↓	↓	2.00	1.88	1.75	1.62	1.50	1.33	1.15	0.955	0.755
F	10	↓	2.24	2.11	1.98	1.84	1.72	1.58	1.41	1.23	1.03	0.828
G	15	2.42	2.32	2.20	2.06	1.91	1.79	1.65	1.47	1.30	1.09	0.886
H	20	2.47	2.36	2.24	2.11	1.96	1.82	1.69	1.51	1.33	1.12	0.917
I	25	2.50	2.40	2.26	2.14	1.98	1.85	1.72	1.53	1.35	1.14	0.936
J	35	2.54	2.45	2.31	2.18	2.03	1.89	1.76	1.57	1.39	1.18	0.969
K	50	2.60	2.50	2.35	2.22	2.08	1.93	1.80	1.61	1.42	1.21	1.00
L	75	2.66	2.55	2.41	2.27	2.12	1.98	1.84	1.65	1.46	1.24	↑1.03
M	100	2.69	2.58	2.43	2.29	2.14	2.00	1.86	1.67	1.48	↑1.26	1.05
N	150	2.73	2.61	2.47	2.33	2.18	2.03	1.89	1.70	↑1.51	1.29	1.07
P	200	2.73	2.62	2.47	2.33	2.18	2.04	1.89	↑1.70	1.51	1.29	1.07

Notes (1) All AQL values are in percent defective.
  (2) The code letters and inspection levels in this standard correspond to those given in BS 6001; they are not identical with those given in MIL STD 414.
  (3) Symbols

↓ There is no suitable sampling plan in this area; use the first sampling plan below the arrow. This refers to both the sample size and acceptability constant k_s (or k_σ).

↑ The plan given in this area gives a high degree of security but at the expense of a large sample. At the discretion of the responsible authority the next plan above the arrow may be used.

⌐ The heavy lines indicate the boundary of the equivalent attribute sampling plans in BS 6001.

Table 13.7 Single sampling plans for tightened inspection (master table): 's' method. Extracts from the British Standards are reproduced with the permission of BSI.

Sample size code letter	Sample size	Acceptable quality levels (tightened inspection)										
		0.10 k_s	0.15 k_s	0.25 k_s	0.40 k_s	0.65 k_s	1.00 k_s	1.50 k_s	2.50 k_s	4.00 k_s	6.50 k_s	10.00 k_s
B	3	↓	↓	↓	↓	↓	↓	↓	↓	1.12	0.958	0.765
C	4	↓	↓	↓	↓	↓	↓	1.45	1.34	1.17	1.01	0.814
D	5	↓	↓	↓	↓	↓	1.65	1.53	1.40	1.24	1.07	0.874
E	7	↓	↓	↓	2.00	1.88	1.75	1.62	1.50	1.33	1.15	0.955
F	10	↓	↓	2.24	2.11	1.98	1.84	1.72	1.58	1.41	1.23	1.03
G	15	2.53	2.42	2.32	2.20	2.06	1.91	1.79	1.65	1.47	1.30	1.09
H	20	2.58	2.47	2.36	2.24	2.11	1.96	1.82	1.69	1.51	1.33	1.12
I	25	2.61	2.50	2.40	2.26	2.14	1.98	1.85	1.72	1.53	1.35	1.14
J	35	2.65	2.54	2.45	2.31	2.18	2.03	1.89	1.76	1.57	1.39	1.18
K	50	2.71	2.60	2.50	2.35	2.22	2.08	1.93	1.80	1.61	1.42	1.21
L	75	2.77	2.66	2.55	2.41	2.27	2.12	1.98	1.84	1.65	1.46	1.24
M	100	2.80	2.69	2.58	2.43	2.29	2.14	2.00	1.86	1.67	1.48	1.26
N	150	2.84	2.73	2.61	2.47	2.33	2.18	2.03	1.89	1.70	1.51	1.29
P	200	2.85	2.73	2.62	2.47	2.33	2.18	2.04	1.89	1.70	1.51	1.29

Notes (1) All AQL values are in percent defective.
(2) The code letters and inspection levels in this standard correspond to those given in BS 6001; they are not identical with those given in MIL STD 414.
(3) Symbols

↓ There is no suitable sampling plan in this area; use the first sampling plan below the arrow. This refers to both the sample size and acceptability constant k_s (or k_σ).

⇧ The plan given in this area gives a high degree of security but at the expense of a large sample. At the discretion of the responsible authority the next plan above the arrow may be used.

⌐ The heavy lines indicate the boundary of the equivalent attribute sampling plans in BS 6001.

Table 13.8 Single sampling plans for reduced inspection (master table): s method. Extracts from the British Standards are reproduced with the permission of BSI.

Sample size code letter	Sample size	Acceptable quality levels										
		0.10	0.15	0.25	0.40	0.65	1.00	1.50	2.50	4.00	6.50	10.00
		k_s	k_s	k_s	k_s	k_s	k_s	k_s	k_s	k_s	k_s	k_s
B	3							1.12	0.958	0.765	0.566	0.341
C	3							1.12	0.958	0.765	0.566	0.341
D	3							1.12	0.958	0.765	0.566	0.341
E	3							1.12	0.958	0.765	0.566	0.341
F	4					1.45	1.34	1.17	1.01	0.814	0.617	0.393
G	5				1.65	1.53	1.40	1.24	1.07	0.874	0.675	0.455
H	7		2.00	1.88	1.75	1.62	1.50	1.33	1.15	0.955	0.755	0.536
I	10	2.24	2.11	1.98	1.84	1.72	1.58	1.41	1.23	1.03	0.828	0.611
J	15	2.32	2.20	2.06	1.91	1.79	1.65	1.47	1.30	1.09	0.886	0.664
K	20	2.36	2.24	2.11	1.96	1.82	1.69	1.51	1.33	1.12	0.917	0.695
L	25	2.40	2.26	2.14	1.98	1.85	1.72	1.53	1.35	1.14	0.936	0.712
M	35	2.45	2.31	2.18	2.03	1.89	1.76	1.57	1.39	1.18	0.969	0.745
N	50	2.50	2.35	2.22	2.08	1.93	1.80	1.61	1.42	1.21	1.00	0.774
P	75	2.55	2.41	2.27	2.12	1.98	1.84	1.65	1.46	1.24	1.03	0.804

Notes (1) All AQL values are in percent defective.
(2) The code letters and inspection levels in this standard correspond to those given in BS 6001; they are not identical with those given in MIL STD 414.
(3) Symbols

There is no suitable sampling plan in this area; use the first sampling plan below the arrow. This refers to both the sample size and acceptability constant k_s (or k_σ).

The plan given in this area gives a high degree of security but at the expense of a large sample. At the discretion of the responsible authority the next plan above the arrow may be used.

The heavy lines indicate the boundary of the equivalent attribute sampling plans in BS 6001.

14*

Adaptive sampling plans

14.1 BASIC DESCRIPTION AND AIMS

In section 11.2.1 we drew a distinction between batch inspection and continuous production inspection, and we explained that the latter deals with the inspection of either truly continuous material such as nylon thread, or else of conveyorized production of separate items such as chocolate bars. The material of Chapters 11–13 relate to batch inspection. However, a special set of inspection plans, usually known as continuous (or adaptive) sampling plans (CSP), has been introduced for use in continuous production inspection.

The earliest CSP, introduced by Dodge (1943), has already been described in Example 11.4, and this plan is referred to as CSP-1. In CSP-1 there are two levels of inspection, 100% inspection and an inspection rate of $1/n$, and there is a simple rule to determine when to change between these levels. Variations on this basic plan are either to use a more complex rule for changing inspection levels, or else to introduce more levels.

One possible approach to continuous production inspection is to group the product artificially in batches. It is frequently necessary to group the material for transit purposes; these groups could be used as batches for inspection. However, any artificial batching may have unfortunate results. Firstly, the operation of artificially batched sampling plans can lead to the possibility of rejecting items not yet produced. Secondly, when inspection involves disassembly, or is time-consuming, many practical difficulties arise, such as storage problems. Nevertheless, artificial batching of continuous output is used as a method of reducing the problems of designing inspection plans to that described in Chapter 11. In the present chapter we discuss sampling plans suitable when artificial batching is not appropriate.

A producer operating a continuous sampling plan such as CSP-1 may have any or all of three different aims in view:

(1) *Product screening*. The aim of this case has been emphasized

throughout Chapter 11. The product is to be sorted, usually into two grades, an acceptable grade and one which needs to be rejected or rectified.

(2) *Process trouble shooting*. This was discussed in Chapters 5–10. Typically, the assumption is that product quality is occasionally disturbed by 'assignable causes of variation', which can be traced and eliminated.

(3) *Adaptive control*. Here the inspection results are to be used to indicate the precise amount of any adjustment needed to the process in order to keep quality up to standard.

The original work by Dodge (1943), and much work since, such as Dodge and Torrey (1951a), Lieberman and Solomon (1955), has emphasized product screening although process trouble shooting is also in view. The term adaptive control was used by Box and Jenkins (1962, 1963), but some earlier work by Girshick and Rubin (1952), Bishop (1957, 1960) and a large literature on control theory is relevant. Savage (1959) designed a plan specifically for trouble shooting. General reviews of the literature are given by Bowker (1956), Chiu and Wetherill (1973), Duncan (1974, Chapter 17), Liberman (1965), and Phillips (1969).

14.2 CSP-1 AND THE AOQL CRITERION

It is convenient here to restate the CSP-1 sampling plan.

CSP-1 Inspect every item until i successive items are found free of defects, and then inspect at a rate of one in every nth item. When a defective item is found, revert to 100% inspection, and continue until i successive items are found free of defects.

Dodge required the sampling at a rate 1 in n to be carried out by stratified random selection so as to ensure an unbiased sample. In practice inspectors are likely to select approximately every nth item, but it is wise to vary this interval a little.

The way that the CSP-1 and similar plans operate is to vary the inspection rate as quality varies. Clearly, a theoretical model is required to give a guide on how the inspection rate varies with p, for various choices of n and i.

In most theoretical treatments of CSP-1 the following three assumptions are made.

Assumption 1 All defectives found during inspection are rectified or replaced by good items.

Assumption 2 Inspection is perfect, i.e. mistakes in identifying defectives are never made.

Assumption 3 Theoretical calculations are made on the assumption that the process is producing defectives with probability p, and that the probability that any item is defective is independent of the quality of other items.

Assumption 1 is often realistic, but if it is not, account of this can be taken in the theory. Assumption 2 is unrealistic and we shall have to discuss this later. Assumption 3 is effectively that the process is in a steady state and provided that we realize the implications, it is realistic enough to proceed with some simple theory.

In the next section we show that on these three assumptions, the average fraction of production inspected is

$$F(p) = 1/\{1 + (n - 1)q^i\} \tag{14.1}$$

where $q = 1 - p$. On Assumption 1, the average outgoing proportion defective is therefore

$$\text{Outgoing proportion defective} = p \left\{ 1 - \frac{1}{\{1 + (n - 1)q^i\}} \right\}$$

$$= \frac{p(n - 1)q^i}{\{1 + (n - 1)q^i\}}. \tag{14.2}$$

It should be stressed that this formula assumes a constant p; if p has, say, a cyclic variation, quite a different result will hold.

Now (14.2) has approximately the shape shown in Fig. 14.1. For low p, the outgoing proportion defective is low. For high p, the average

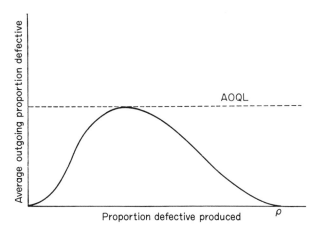

Figure 14.1 Operation of CSP-1.

fraction of production inspection is high, and again the outgoing proportion defective is low. For intermediate values of p, there is a maximum value to the average outgoing proportion defective for a given n and i, and this is defined as the average outgoing quality limit, AOQL.

The AOQL is the maximum of (14.2), and by differentiation we find that this is at a value $p = p_1$, where

$$(i + 1)p_1 - 1 = (n - 1)(1 - p_1)^{i+1} \tag{14.3}$$

and by inserting this we find that the AOQL is

$$\text{AOQL} = (n - 1)(1 - p_1)^{i+1}/i \tag{14.4}$$

which can be regarded as a function of n and i.

Figure 14.2 shows approximately how the AOQL is related to n and i. Dodge suggested that a producer be asked to specify an AOQL, so that this sets a relationship between n and i. The final choice of n and i was to be made on practical considerations such as the work load on inspectors, and it may be best to have an i no greater than a small multiple of the number of units on the production line at any time.

This method of designing a CSP-1 has certainly been used a great deal since Dodge suggested it. However, let us reflect on how artificial is the concept of the AOQL:

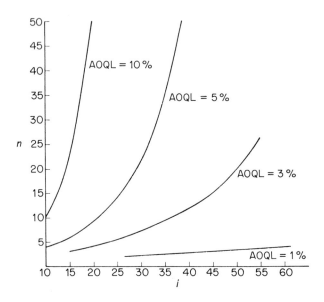

Figure 14.2 Relation between AOQL, n and i.

(1) The AOQL is an upper limit to the proportion defective only in a long-run average sense. In the short run, a sudden deterioration of quality could lead to a large number of defectives being passed before a defective was found on inspection. This should clearly be borne in mind when choosing n; see section 14.4.

(2) We have made Assumption 3, that the process is in control. If the process has varying quality, with changes exactly in phase with changes in the inspection level, the AOQL no longer applies.

(3) The quality, p, of the uninspected production process at which the AOQL is obtained may be known to occur only very rarely.

(4) We have made Assumption 2. If defective items are only recognized with a probability of, say 0.90 or 0.95, Fig. 14.1 does not apply, and instead we have Fig. 14.3. This situation is therefore likely to make nonsense of the whole AOQL concept. Hill (1962) has stressed that the AOQL concept is particularly sensitive to the assumption that inspection is perfect.

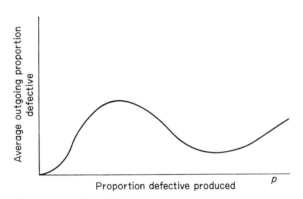

Figure 14.3 The CSP-1 when inspection is not perfect.

Notwithstanding these criticisms, it should be emphasized that the CSP-1 has been successfully designed and used in the way Dodge suggested, although there is clearly a need for other design criteria.

14.3 THEORY OF CSP-1

In this section we derive the theory of CSP-1 on the three assumptions stated in the previous section.

The first step is to break up the run of inspected items at every defective. Dodge calls these short sequences 'terminal defect sequences', and the following are examples; O stands for a good item and X for a defective (Table 14.1).

Table 14.1

Sequence	Probability	Length
X	p	1
0 X	pq	2
0 0 X	pq^2	3
. . .	. . .	. . .
0 0 . . . 0 X	pq^i	$(i + 1)$
. . .	. . .	. . .

Once a defective has been observed, 100% inspection is started and continued until a sequence of i good items is observed. Before this occurs, a series of terminal defect sequences may occur of length less than or equal to i. The probability of a terminal defect sequence of length less than or equal to i is

$$\sum_{r=0}^{i-1} pq^r = 1 - q^i = P, \quad \text{say.} \tag{14.5}$$

The number of terminal defective sequences in a run of 100% inspection has a geometric distribution $(1 - P)P^r$, $r = 0, 1, 2, \ldots$; the average number of such sequences is therefore

$$E(l) = \sum r(1 - P)P^r = P/(1 - P) = (1 - q^i)/q^i. \tag{14.6}$$

Now the average length of a terminal defect sequence of length less than or equal to i is

$$T = \frac{1}{(1 - q^i)} \sum_{r=0}^{i-1} (r + 1)pq^r = \frac{1 - q^i(1 + pi)}{p(1 - q^i)}. \tag{14.7}$$

The average length of a run of 100% inspection is therefore

$$TE(l) + i = (1 - q^i)/pq^i. \tag{14.8}$$

The number of periodic samples taken in between runs of 100% inspection has the geometric distribution pq^{r-1}, $r = 1, 2, \ldots$. The average number of items passed in such an interval is therefore

$$n\sum rpq^{r-1} = n/p. \tag{14.9}$$

The average number of items produced between the start of successive runs of 100% inspection is therefore

$$(1 - q^i)/pq^i + n/p$$

while the amount inspection in such an interval is

$$(1 - q^i)/pq^i + 1/p.$$

The average fraction inspected is therefore

$$F = \frac{(1 - q^i)/pq^i + 1/p}{(1 - q^i)/pq^i + n/p} = \frac{1}{1 + (n - 1)q^i}. \qquad (14.10)$$

This is the formula quoted in (14.1), from which (14.2)–(14.4) follow.

When interpreting this result, reference should be made to the criticisms listed at the end of the previous section.

14.4 THE AEDL CRITERION

In section 14.2 we remarked that if there was a sudden deterioration of quality, a number of defective items could be passed by the CSP-1 before 100% inspection was instituted. Hillier (1964) proposed another measure, the average extra defectives limit (AEDL), the purpose of which is to put a limit on the average number of defectives passed upon such a deterioration of quality. The AEDL criterion can be used along with the AOQL to select a particular CSP-1.

Suppose a process is producing defectives with probability p_0, and suddenly it changes to producing defectives with probability $p_1 > p_0$. Let D be the number of uninspected defectives among the next L items after this deterioration of quality. Then for an AOQL of θ, the average extra number of defectives passed above the limit prescribed by the AOQL is

$$\{E(D) - \theta L\}$$

and this will be a function of p_0, p_1, and L. The AEDL, written D_L, is defined as

$$D_L = \max_{p_0, p_1, L} \{E(D) - \theta L\}. \qquad (14.11)$$

For the CSP-1, Hillier shows that (14.11) achieves its maximum for $p_0 = 0$, $p_1 = 1$, and $L = L^*$, where

$$L^* = \log\left\{(1 - n) \log\left\{\frac{n-1}{n}\right\}\middle/\theta\right\}\middle/\log\left\{\frac{n-1}{n}\right\}. \qquad (14.12)$$

Hillier shows that the AEDL for CSP-1 is then

$$D_L = (n - 1)\left\{1 - \left\{\frac{n - 1}{n}\right\}^{L^*}\right\} - \theta L^* \qquad \text{if } L^* > 0$$

$$= 0 \qquad \text{if } L^* \leq 0. \quad (14.13)$$

In a particular case there may be reason to use a value of L other than (14.12), for example, if items are packaged in batches of a given size. This draws attention to the fact that the AEDL is a number of defectives calculated over a somewhat arbitrary length of production.

The other criticisms of the AOQL criterion made at the end of section 14.2 will be found to apply also to the AEDL. In particular the values $p_0 = 0$ and $p_1 = 1$ at which the AEDL is calculated are both rather unlikely values for the proportion defective. However, the use of the AEDL together with the AOQL would seem to be a better method of choosing a particular CSP-1 than the use of the AOQL alone, and Hillier gives a simple example. The AEDL provides a method of choosing n, by using (14.13).

Hillier suggests that this method of choosing a CSP-1 can be improved further if account is taken of the probability distribution of D for given values of L. It would then be possible to make the probability that D is less than a given number to be greater than a specified value. See Hillier (1964) for details of this method. Unfortunately there is very little published information on the probability distribution of D; see Hillier (1961, 1964).

14.5 DECISION-THEORY APPROACH TO CSP-1

Anscombe (1958) gives a critique of the AOQL approach to choosing a CSP-1, and discusses an approach based on costs. He points out that the AOQL concept is very artificial, and would not usually correspond to what a user required of a continuous sampling plan. The problem is basically an economic one of balancing inspection costs against the costs of passing defective items. The usual objection to an economic approach is that the cost data may be difficult to obtain. However, Anscombe says: 'What is important is that we realise what the problem really is, and solve that problem as well as we can, instead of inventing a substitute problem that can be solved exactly but is irrelevant.' If the cost of passing defectives is known only roughly, then an approximate solution to the problem will be satisfactory, provided we are solving the real problem.

Admittedly, there are other aims in inspection besides the strict economic aim of limiting the amount of bad material passed, but this aim is likely to be the over-riding one. The approach adopted by

Anscombe requires very little economic information, but this small amount is vital.

We shall again make the three assumptions listed in section 14.2. Let the cost of inspection be k cost units, where the unit of costs is the excess cost of passing a defective item above the cost of rectifying it or replacing it during inspection. The cost of 100% inspection is therefore k per item produced, and the cost of passing production without inspection is p per item produced. By this model therefore, it would be best to carry out 100% inspection if $k < p$, and best not to inspect at all if $k > p$. In practice the proportion defective, p, varies, and a sampling plan is operated.

If we operate a CSP-1, the cost of this plan per item produced is

$$C = \text{(cost of inspection)} + \text{(cost of passing defective items)}$$

$$= k \times \text{(fraction inspected)} + p \times \text{(fraction not inspected)}$$

or

$$C = Fk + (1 - F)p \qquad (14.14)$$

where F is given by (14.1). As indicated above, the best possible action if we knew p is

$$\text{for } p < k, \quad C = p \qquad (F = 0 \text{ in } (14.14))$$

and

$$\text{for } p > k, \quad C = k \qquad (F = 1 \text{ in } (14.14)).$$

The excess cost ΔC over the best possible action is therefore

$$\Delta C = \begin{cases} (k - p)F & p < k \\ (p - k)(1 - F) & p > k \end{cases} \qquad (14.15)$$

Anscombe now simplifies the problem by inserting an arbitrary rule which appears to be near optimum. Since the best possible action changes from no inspection to 100% inspection at $p = k$, it is reasonable to choose $F = \frac{1}{2}$ when $p = k$. By inserting this rule into (14.1) we obtain

$$(n - 1)(1 - k)^i = 1 \qquad (14.16)$$

which can be used to calculate i for a given n and k. If k is given, there remains only one parameter of the CSP-1, namely n, which we wish to optimize.

The next step is to find the average value of ΔC over the process curve for p, assuming that p varies slowly enough for (14.2) to remain valid. Anscombe introduced a further approximation here, by using a uniform distribution for p in the range $(0, 2k)$. (If the variation of p does not span the point $p = k$, the optimum will be either no inspection or 100% inspection. Furthermore it turns out that for a wide range of distributions the value of $E(\Delta C)$ obtained is not very different from that obtained under the uniform distribution.) By numerical integration, Anscombe now checks that the empirical formula

$$E(\Delta C) = 0.3k/\sqrt{n} \qquad (14.17)$$

holds very well.

In order to be able to determine an optimum for n we must introduce one further factor in the costs. Equation (14.17) will give an approximation to the long-run costs of a CSP-1 at a stable value of p. When p changes, a further cost arises, called a transition cost. This is the cost of the extra defectives passed after a sudden deterioration of quality, and before the CSP-1 changes to 100% inspection. If p changes suddenly from a very small value to a very large value, at a random point in an inspection interval, then on average slightly less than $n/2$ defectives will be passed. Anscombe showed that $n/2$ is a good approximation to the average transition cost under more general conditions.

If sudden deteriorations of quality occur on average once in every M items produced, the average transition costs are $n/2M$ per item produced.

The total cost of operating the CSP-1 is therefore approximately

$$\frac{0.3k}{\sqrt{n}} + \frac{n}{2M} \qquad (14.18)$$

and by differentiating we find that the optimum choice of n is

$$n = (0.3kM)^{3/2}. \qquad (14.19)$$

In obtaining this result we have used the rule $f = \frac{1}{2}$ at $p = k$, the uniform distribution as an approximation to the process curve, the empirical approximation (14.17), and the approximations to the transition costs. Further investigation shows that none of these approximations have much effect on the solution. The important quantities are M, the average interval between sudden deteriorations of quality, and

$$k = \frac{\text{cost of inspecting an item}}{\text{excess cost of passing a defective}}.$$

It is interesting that in the methods suggested earlier in this chapter for choosing a CSP-1, neither k nor M were mentioned, and these are the quantities upon which an optimum solution strongly depends.

14.6 MODIFICATIONS TO CSP-1

Over the years various modifications have been suggested to CSP-1. Dodge and Torrey (1951a) suggested the following two plans:

CSP-2 Proceed as in CSP-1 except that, once partial inspection is instituted, 100% inspection is only introduced when two defectives occur spaced less than *m* items apart.

This plan is less likely to revert to 100% inspection because of isolated defectives than is the CSP-1, and the number of abrupt changes of inspection level will also be reduced. However, there is a higher risk of accepting short runs of poor quality, and so CSP-3 is suggested.

CSP-3 Proceed as in CSP-2 except that when a defective is found, the next four items are inspected.

The theory of these two plans follows a similar pattern to the theory given in section 14.3 for CSP-1, although in each case it is more complicated.

Another line of development attempts to devise plans which guarantee an AOQL without assuming statistical control of the process. The starting point of these investigations is a paper by Lieberman (1953), who examined the AOQL of the CSP-1 without the assumption of control. It is not difficult to see that this is attained by a process which produces good items throughout periods of 100% inspection, and defectives throughout periods of partial inspection. Periods of 100% inspection are therefore exactly i items long, and the average number of items produced between the start of such periods is $(n + i)$. One defective item will be inspected, and consequently replaced by a good item. The average fraction defective remaining after inspection is therefore $(n - 1)/(n + i)$, which can be considerably greater than (14.2). For a formal proof of this formula, see Derman *et al.* (1959). When interpreting this result, however, it is important to take note of the pathological nature of the production process model which produces it.

Derman *et al.* (1959) present two variants of CSP-1 which have improved properties when control is not assumed.

CSP-4 Proceed as in CSP-1 except that partial inspection is carried out by separating production into segments of size n, and taking one item at random from each segment. When a defective is found, the remaining $n - 1$ items in the segment are eliminated from the production process, and 100% inspection started with the first item of the following segment.

The idea of CSP-4 is that there is a reluctance to pass a segment of production in which a defective is found. Items eliminated from the production process might be sorted and the good items used as a stock for replacing defectives found in inspection. A more realistic plan would be to allow the good items from this 'eliminated' segment to be passed, and so we have CSP-5.

CSP-5 Proceed as in CSP-4 except that all items in a segment in which a defective is found are sorted.

The modifications given in CSP-4 and CSP-5 result in a more complicated set-up when control is not assumed. The production process model giving the AOQL is no longer the trivial one described earlier for CSP-1. The theory is not simple, and we refer readers to the source paper. In practice, Derman *et al.* (1959) suggest that CSP-4 and CSP-5 plans should be chosen using the CSP-1 formula derived under the assumption of control.

Another important type of plan is the multilevel plan, discussed by Lieberman and Solomon (1954), and we shall designate this MLP-1.

MLP-1 Proceed as in CSP-1 except as follows. If in partial inspection i successive items are found free of defects, reduce the inspection rate from $1/n$ to $1/n^2$. In this way, several inspection levels can be used. When a defective is found, revert to 100% inspection.

Usually MLP-1 will be used with between two and six levels. Lieberman and Solomon (1954) obtained the AOQL for two levels and for an infinite number of levels, and gave a method of interpolation for other levels. Clearly, a whole range of different types of multilevel plan is possible, but no systematic study of the possibilities seems to have been undertaken.

In nearly all of the work an AOQL approach is adopted, and the AEDL criterion has only been applied to CSP-1. Anscombe's decision-theory approach, described in section 14.5, has not been extended to cover other plans. That is, with very few exceptions, Dodge's original formulation of the continuous inspection problem has not been questioned.

Read and Beattie (1961) give a plan of the same general type as CSP-1, but modified to fit their practical conditions. The inspection rate on line is held constant, and the product is artificially batched. Depending on the results of inspection, some batches are set aside for 100% inspection later. This plan forms a link between the Dodge type continuous inspection plans, and batch inspection plans discussed earlier.

A collection of continuous sampling plans, indexed for use as a United States Army military standard, is available as MIL-STD-1235 (ORD). This standard is currently being revised, and for a description and discussion of the revision principles see Banzhaf and Bruger (1970), Duncan (1974), and Grant and Leavenworth (1972).

14.7 PROCESS TROUBLE SHOOTING

So far we have been concentrating mostly on the product screening aspect of continuous inspection. Girshick and Rubin (1952), in an important paper, gave a Bayes approach to process trouble shooting, and we briefly describe their theory below.

The production process is assumed to be either in a good state (state 1), or a bad state, (state 2). After every item produced there is a probability g that the process will move from state 1 to 2, but once in state 2, the process remains in that state until it is brought to repair. Girshick and Rubin derive an optimum rule for deciding when to put the process in repair. If the process is put into repair when it is in state 1, it is said to be in state 3, and if it is put into repair from state 2, it is said to be in state 4. When the process is put into states 3 or 4, it remains there for n_j time units, $j = 3, 4$, where one time unit is the time for one item to be produced. Two cases are considered:

(1) 100% inspection is operated and the problem is merely to find the optimum rule for deciding when to put the process in repair.
(2) Sampling inspection can be used, so that the optimum rule must also specify when items are to be inspected.

These two cases are discussed separately below.

The quality of each item produced is represented by a variable x, and the probability density function of x is taken to be $f_j(x)$, $j = 1, 2$, for states 1 or 2 respectively. The value of an item of quality x is $V(x)$, and the cost per unit time of the repair states is c_j, $j = 3, 4$. The model is now precisely defined, and we have to find the decision rules which maximize income per unit time. This model is sufficiently general and realistic to be used as a means of comparing various continuous inspection procedures, but no such comparisons have yet been made.

When the production process is in use, the vital question is to decide whether it is in state 1 or state 2. Clearly, the optimum decision rule will depend on the posterior probability that the next item will be produced in state 1. For case (1) above and when the kth item has just been inspected this probability is

$$q_k = \frac{(1 - g)q_{k-1}f_1(x_k)}{q_{k-1}f_1(x_k) + (1 - q_{k-1})f_2 x_k)} \qquad (14.20)$$

where $q_0 = 1 - g$. (The denominator is the probability that x_k is observed, and the numerator is the probability that x_k is produced in state 1, and that the process remains in state 1 for the $(k + 1)$th item.)

Girshick and Rubin showed that the optimum rule is to put the process in repair whenever $q_k \leq q^*$. This is equivalent to putting the process in repair whenever $Z_k \geq a^*$, where

$$Z_k = y_k(1 + Z_{k-1}), \qquad Z_0 = 0, \qquad (14.21)$$

and

$$y_k = f_2(x_k)/\{1 - g)f_1(x_k)\}. \qquad (14.22)$$

The parameter a^* has to be chosen to maximize income per unit time, and this involves solving an integral equation.

When sampling inspection can be used, the argument and result are very similar. The optimum rule is again defined in terms of Z_k, where y_k is given by (14.21) if the kth item is inspected and by

$$y_k = (1 - g)^{-1} \qquad (14.23)$$

if the kth item is not inspected. Girshick and Rubin show that the optimum rule is to inspect items whenever

$$b^* \leq Z_k < a^*,$$

to put the process in repair when $Z_k \geq a^*$, and to pass production without inspection whenever $Z_k < b^*$. Again the constants b^* and a^* have to be chosen to maximize income per unit time, and this involves solving integral equations.

In both cases the integral equations are very difficult to solve, and detailed calculations do not appear to have been carried out.

14.8 ADAPTIVE CONTROL

There is now a very large literature on control theory, and this text would be incomplete without a brief introduction to it. Those interested in pursuing the topic further should read the general accounts by Barnard (1959), Lieberman (1965), White (1965), Box and Jenkins (1962, 1976), and Pandit and Wu (1983) and the references contained in these. The following account is largely based on Box and Jenkins (1962).

Suppose a process is sampled at equal time intervals, and that provided no adjustments are made to the process the observation at the jth sample point is

$$z_j = \theta_j + u_j,$$

where u_j are the errors which are normally and independently distributed with a variance σ_u^2 and θ_j follows some stochastic process.

Adjustments can be made to the process at each sample point, and the aim of these adjustments is to keep θ_j at a target value, which we may without loss of generality take to be zero. If the total adjustment applied at the jth sample point is X_j, the observation made is the apparent deviation from the target value, which is

$$e_j = z_j - X_j = \theta_j - X_j + u_j = \varepsilon_j + u_j,$$

where ε_j is the actual deviation from the target value.

Suppose adjustments have been made on some basis or other, and that we have data $X_1, X_2, X_3, \ldots, X_j$, and $e_1, e_2, e_3, \ldots, e_j$, then our problem is to determine the increment x_{j+1} to apply to the adjustment at the $(j + 1)$th sample point, so that the total adjustment is then

$$X_{j+1} = X_j + x_{j+1}.$$

We are assuming, of course, that adjustments can be applied at every sample point without extra cost.

Let the loss caused by an actual deviation from target of ε_j be proportional to ε_j^2; then we must determine x_{j+1} to be a linear function of $e_j, e_{j-1}, \ldots$, which means that we must determine x_{j+1},

$$x_{j+1} = \hat{\theta}_{j+1} - \hat{\theta}_j = \sum_{r=0}^{\infty} w_r e_{j-r} \qquad (14.24)$$

where the w_rs are chosen so that $\hat{\theta}_{j+1}$ is the minimum mean square error estimate of θ_{j+1}. In fact the central problem as stated here is seen to be equivalent to the problem of predicting the coming value of θ_{j+1}. The problem can therefore be restated as the problem of determining weights μ_r so that

$$\theta_{j+1} = \sum_{r=0}^{\infty} \mu_r z_{j-r} \qquad (14.25)$$

is the minimum mean square error predictor of θ_{j+1}. (Again, a linear function is assumed for simplicity.) This implies, of course, a relationship between the w_rs and the μ_rs.

So far we have said nothing about the stochastic process to be assumed for θ_j, and it would be unrealistic to assume that it was stationary. Suppose that θ_j can be separated into two components,

$$\theta_j = m_j + \phi_j,$$

where m_j is a sequence of known means, and where ϕ_j is a first-order autoregressive process,

$$\phi_{j+1} = \rho \phi_j + \eta_j$$

where the η_j are independently and normally distributed with a variance σ_η^2. In a practical case the m_j would not be known, but we first obtain the optimum weights assuming them to be known.

A further simplification is introduced by assuming the weights μ_r to be zero for $r \geq h$, for some specified h. With these assumptions the covariance matrix of $z'_j = (z_j, z_{j-1}, \ldots, z_{j-h+1})$ is

$$
T = \begin{bmatrix}
\rho \sigma_\theta^2 + \sigma_u^2 & \rho^2 \sigma_\theta^2 & \rho^3 \sigma_\theta^2 & \cdots \\
\rho^2 \sigma_\theta^2 & \rho \sigma_\theta^2 + \sigma_u^2 & \rho^2 \sigma_\theta^2 & \cdots \\
\vdots & \vdots & &
\end{bmatrix}
$$

where $\sigma_\theta^2 = \sigma_\eta^2/(1 - \rho^2)$.

Box and Jenkins (1962) show that the weights μ_j which give the minimum mean square error predictor are

$$
\boldsymbol{\mu} = T^{-1} \rho \tag{14.26}
$$

where $\boldsymbol{\mu}' = (\mu_0, \mu_1, \ldots, \mu_{h-1})$ and $\boldsymbol{\rho}' = (\rho, \rho^2, \ldots, \rho^h)$, and where we use the estimate

$$
\theta_{j+1} = m_{j+1} + \sum_{r=0}^{h} \mu_r (z_{j-r} - m_{j-r}). \tag{14.27}
$$

Now if the m_j are not known, we shall have to use the estimate (14.25), and there will be a bias. However, if the m_j follows a polynomial of degree k, constraints can be imposed on the weights μ_r so that the bias is zero. The optimum weights can now be found subject to these constraints, but the result is rather complicated to state, and we refer the reader to Box and Jenkins (1962). The authors evaluate the optimum constrained predictors for some simple cases, and show that they are such that a good approximation to the optimum change x_{j+1} is

$$
x_{j+1} = \gamma_{-1} \Delta e_j + \gamma_0 e_j + \gamma_1 \sum_{r=0}^{\infty} e_{j-r} \tag{14.28}
$$

or a simple generalization of it. Box and Jenkins then examine the stochastic process for which an adjustment of the type (14.28) would be optimum, and they consider methods of estimating the parameters of this process from data. All this theory therefore leads to the following empirical approach; a process model is fitted to past data, so determining a set of parameters $\gamma_{-1}, \gamma_0, \gamma_1, \ldots$, and then an adjustment of the type (14.28) is used, inserting the fitted parameters. An interesting paper by Hunter (1986) shows the value of the exponentially weighted moving average in this context.

The discussion in Box and Jenkins (1962) is more general than the discussion given above, but the authors state that some of the more general results are unlikely to be used because of their complexity. In a subsequent paper, Box and Jenkins (1963) again consider the above problem, but with the introduction of a cost for being off target and a cost for making a change; the optimum plan then involves making adjustments to the process less frequently.

Further developments would be of interest. For example, it may be desirable to vary the inspection rate depending upon the results. Another point which does not seem to be adequately cleared up is the relationship of the methods suggested in this section to adaptive control by CuSum methods, and some remarks by Barnard in the discussion of Box and Jenkins (1962) relate to this. Barnard suggests that CuSum methods may be preferred because of simplicity in cases where computers are not available to do the calculations, but that in certain circumstances, CuSum methods may be slightly better anyway.

14.9 USE OF CuSum TECHNIQUES

A general question is opened up by the closing remarks of the last section, relating to the possibility of basing continuous sampling plans on CuSum techniques. One such plan is given by Beattie (1968) in an important paper dealing with patrol inspection, when an inspector is asked to cover a large area of a factory taking small samples.

One plan proposed by Beattie (1962, 1968) is as follows. The inspector makes periodic inspections and on each occasion he selects n items, finding d_i defectives, $i = 1, 2, \ldots$ A CuSum is now plotted for $\Sigma(d_i - k)$, where k is some reference value, as shown in Fig. 14.4. The stream of product is accepted while plotting is on the lower chart. When

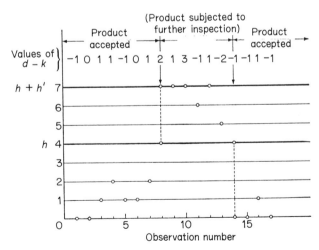

Figure 14.4 A two-stage semi-continuous plan (a combination of CuSum charts).

the plot on the lower chart reaches the decision interval, the product is rejected, and plotting is started on the upper chart. Plotting on the upper chart continues until the decision interval is reached, when the stream of product is again accepted, and plotting on the lower chart restarted.

The rejected product is separated into lots, and a single sample plan applied to each lot. The plan therefore operates in rather a similar way to the CSP-1. In general only periodic samples of size n are taken, but periods of acceptance sampling of lots are required, when quality deteriorates.

Clearly, when acceptance sampling is being operated, a double or sequential sampling plan can be used instead of a single sampling plan.

For theoretical purposes let us suppose that production is artificially separated into lots, and that m such lots pass in between inspection periods by the patrol inspector. In calculating ARLs, we shall use this lot size as a unit.

The CuSum chart just described is similar to that described in section 7.1.7. Let z be the score on the lower chart and $L(z, p)$ be the ARL for a starting score of z, where p is the proportion defective. Then by following the discrete analogue of (8.15) we have

$$L(z, p) = 1 + L(0, p)\sum_{x=0}^{k-z}f(x) + \sum_{x=1}^{h-1}L(x)f(y + k - z) \quad (14.29)$$

where

$$f(x) = \binom{n}{x} p^x(1 - p)^{n-x}$$

which is the probability that x defectives are found in the first sample of size n. Equation (14.29) can be solved to obtain $L(0,p)$. Similarly we can obtain the ARL $L'(0, p)$ of the upper chart. The probability P, that lot inspection is not used, is then seen to be

$$P_1(p) = L(0, p)/\{L(0, p) + L'(0, p)\}. \quad (14.30)$$

If the lot inspection plan leads to acceptance with a probability $P_2(p)$, the total probability of acceptance is

$$P_a(p) = P_1(p) + \{1 - P_1(p)\}P_2(p). \quad (14.31)$$

If the sample size for the lot inspection plan is n', the average sample number per lot inspected is

$$\text{ASN} = n/m + n'(1 - P_1). \quad (14.32)$$

Expressions (14.31) and (14.32) are functions of n, n', h, h', k, p, and the acceptance number for the lot inspection plan. In choosing a particular plan Beattie suggests using OC-curve considerations, together with consideration of the average sample number (ASN) at the expected quality level. However, there are clearly other schemes for choosing a particular plan, and this aspect does not appear to have been thoroughly investigated.

For further work on this type of use of CuSum charts see Beattie (1968), Prairie and Zimmer (1970), and Rai (1971); the last two of these references relate to inspection by variables.

14.10 SKIP-LOT SAMPLING PLANS

This chapter would not be complete without a brief mention of an important type of sampling plan introduced by Dodge (1956), see also Perry (1973).

The idea is to use a combination of CSP-1 and a reference sampling plan. At the outset, the reference sampling plan is used on every batch. When i successive batches are accepted under normal inspection, we move to skip-lot inspection, in which only every nth batch is inspected. As soon as a batch is rejected normal inspection of every batch is resumed. The important feature of this plan is that it is self-adaptive, in varying the inspection load according to submitted quality. In this respect skip-lot plans are a competitor of defence sampling schemes, and for a comparison see Lenz and Wilrich (1978), and Lenz and Rendtel (1984).

EXERCISES 14B

1. Discuss how CuSum charts might be used for the continuous sampling problems mentioned in section 14.1.

2. Check the derivation of (14.3) and (14.4) from (14.2).

3. Examine how the properties of CSP-1 (section 14.2) are altered when inspection is imperfect, and find the conditions under which there is a true maximum to the average outgoing quality.

4. Examine numerically the relationship (14.16) for $k = 0.05$.

5. Show that an approximation to (14.16) is
$$ki \simeq \log_e n.$$

6. Make the three assumptions listed in section 14.2, and find the formulae equivalent to (14.1) and (14.2) for CSP-2 and CSP-3, when $k = i$. See Bowker (1956).

7. Find q_k in terms of Z_k and g; see section 14.7.

8. In the theory of section 14.7, the quality x of each item is assumed to be observed exactly. What happens if the quality of each item is observed with error?

15

Some further topics

15.1 COMPUTING

15.1.1 General points

In the early stages of learning SPC it is quite crucial that there be a hands-on pencil-and-paper approach. This is necessary in order that the topics be properly learned, to ensure that those studying gain the confidence necessary to apply the methods themselves, and in order to get the feel of data. In practice computer packages are often required for serious applications. One reason for this, for example, is that it is usually necessary to create a database of results to enable staff to pinpoint more easily the source of quality problems. A second reason is that the computational speed of a computer and its ability to generate graphics quickly allow several SPC methods to be carried out simultaneously and transparently to the user. For example, simultaneous diagnostic checks for Normality, Shewhart chart and CuSum analysis, carried out automatically by computer, would be of great benefit, yet would be tortuous if attempted by hand.

It should be noted that the sort of computer packages we refer to will most frequently be used by people who are not trained statisticians, who are not always clear about the appropriate techniques to use, and who are not aware of pitfalls. This implies certain general requirements of a good SPC package.

There are two situations in which SPC can be carried out and which are fundamentally different. In turn, these situations require quite different computer solutions.

One situation is where SPC is being used to monitor a process and give control action signals in 'real time'. Real time can have many meanings depending on the industry and process in question but is likely to apply where adjustments to the process must be carried out on a time-scale from seconds, up to about 10 minutes. Here the SPC implementation on computers must automatically warn of out of control situations by visual and audible alarms. The SPC procedures are thus assessing process measurements as they are received via the instrument –computer interface. The need for real-time response poses further problems where there are many critical process variables to be controlled. Here an operator will require a computer screen or output device which continuously provides a current status report of all variables. In addition, the ability to request more detailed information on a specified variable is important. This information includes a control chart of recent data and perhaps an up-to-date assessment of capability.

An SPC package designed for this function will either be a bespoke system which performs only that SPC methodology chosen by an SPC manager, for example $\bar{X}$, σ charts, or be a general SPC package which provides a wide range of options from which the preferred options have been selected and fixed by a responsible manager.

Any SPC implementation which is not operated in real time, as described above, is not actually being used from process *control* in the literal sense. SPC is frequently used for retrospective analysis of process data, though this could involve data only 15 minutes old or up to many hours. The use of this methodology by production managers to assess process performance over weeks or months is also a perfectly legitimate application of SPC. In fact this form of SPC application is most likely in process industries where knowing how to identify what has caused a problem and then responding with a control action can be very complex.

A computer system for this form of SPC will operate with a data storage (management information) system. Examination of data will require the system user to request an appropriate period of production data and then SPC analysis will be initiated. Thus, in contrast to real-time applications, here SPC analysis is only instigated *on demand* and not automatically observation by observation. The purpose of SPC use by supervisors, foremen or quality engineers is likely to be to view longer-term trends in process performance and its capability which will stimulate process investigation studies.

To carry out thorough analysis of process data a wide range of SPC and statistical tools will be required. The useful SPC system will therefore allow access to a suite of modules for distribution checking, analysis of variation, time-series analysis, multiple regression etc. To make full use of such facilities the SPC system should have an easy interface to the plant information system. Information data bases typically installed as part of process control computer systems often allow little facility to examine data collected. They operate as data sinks. Computerized SPC can give these data a raison d'être!

15.1.2 Requirements for SPC packages

Following the above discussion, we suggest the following requirements for a good SPC package.

User interface. This needs to be very user friendly, and have adequate on-line help and guidance. An interface was designed at the University of Kent, UK, in connection with a multiple regression package, and a survey analysis program for the developing countries (Wetherill et al. 1985a, 1985b, 1986), although developments in computing would facilitate improvements.

Data structures. A considerable amount of research went into the design of the data structures for the survey analysis program referred to above. Similarly, the data structures and database for process control need to be carefully worked out, especially in the process industries where vast amounts of data on many variables accumulate rapidly.

Validation of data input. A considerable amount of work has been done on data quality control in the survey analysis context. This work was started in Statistics Canada and the US Bureau of the Census and the work can be accessed through Wetherill et al (1985b), and Wetherill and Gerson (1987). The methods can be applied whenever there is an multivariate dataset in which relationships between the variables can be used for editing. In the survey analysis context, imputation is often used, and this would not normally be used in process control, but unusual records can be flagged for action.

Expert system checking and guidance. The regression program referred to above contains built-in diagnostic checks for normality, outliers, multicollinearity, etc., the results of these checks being simple messages. A similar approach needs to be adopted for SPC to include checks for distribution, including normality, checks for long-term and short-term variation, autocorrelation, cyclic behaviour, etc. These checks should be transparent, and any messages simple. In addition, there should be built-in guidance using a rule-based expert system to lead people to the correct choice of scheme. An approach similar to that used in Williams (1988) for experimental design, could be used. A simple guidance system for sampling inspection is discussed in Wetherill and Curram (1984).

Other points. It needs to be recognized that the SPC techniques themselves are only part of the story. An expert system is really required to assist in the problem of identification, problem analysis, and process capability stages.

15.1.3 Outline of an SPC system

A brief outline of a basic SPC system is as follows:

(1) *Data acquisition and data editing.* There should be adequate facilities to acquire data in various ways, including from automatic data collection devices. Simple editing and data transformation methods should be provided. Means of sampling from large data sets are also required.

(2) *Exploratory data analysis.* The process capability analysis phase involves use of a range of EDA techniques, including CuSums. For the less experienced, some expert system features would be invaluable here including automated methods of picking out outliers, turning points, and underlying relationships.

(3) *Distribution and model fitting.* The package should be able to identify the appropriate model, check for normality, etc., and check for long-term and short-term variation and autocorrelation. The process capability can then be established. Where there is long-term variation, there needs to be a dialogue with the customer about this. It should not be simply 'assumed'.

(4) *Choice of SPC techniques.* At this stage the package should have an expert system section, using knowledge already gained, to help guide customers towards appropriate techniques and away from inappropriate ones.

(5) *Charting.* Charting methods should cope with variable numbers of observations in groups, one-at-a-time data, and they should incorporate automatic reassessment of process capability. Most process industry applications have many variables, and the package should be capable of monitoring many variables in parallel, each on several charts.

(6) *Reporting facility.* A report generating facility is required.

This is a basic system. In a moderate-sized industry, database handling problems frequently occur. Also, it has been clear at various stages of this book that the use of SPC is closely connected with the design of experiments, analysis of variance, regression, multivariate analysis and other statistical techniques. The package therefore needs smooth linking to suitable packages for these techniques. It is now possible to write software which is simple to use, and yet which does include validity checks, expert guidance, etc. Unfortunately, few existing packages come anywhere near this standard. In many cases it is even difficult to get them to produce the correct charts.

15.2 ECONOMIC APPROACHES TO THE DESIGN OF CHARTS AND SAMPLING PLANS

It is clearly recognized that the design of SPC charts and sampling plans is basically an economic problem, of balancing the costs of inspection effort against the costs of producing defective material. A great deal of research has been carried out into models and methods for designing charts and sampling plans from an economic viewpoint, mostly using a Bayesian approach. This field is omitted from the present text for several reasons:

(1) A large part of the financial gain is obtained by applying the procedures as given. The extra benefit from applying economically optimum plans is often much smaller.
(2) The economic design of the procedures usually requires the assessment of costs such as the cost of passing on defective material to customers, which can be very difficult to estimate.
(3) The present volume is already large enough, and the extra material is highly mathematical.

The work on economic approaches makes very interesting reading, and could be of value in the future, coupled with expert system approaches, and adequate algorithms to calculate and solve the equations and formulae. Those interested should consult Chiu and Wetherill (1973), Wetherill and Chiu (1975), Chiu (1973) and Collani (1989).

15.3 SOME FURTHER CHARTING METHODS

15.3.1 Double CuSums

Davies and Goldsmith (1972) introduce what they call 'Double CuSums', for the situation where the element size varies. For example, suppose that the planned production of some factory is constant for the next few months, then an ordinary CuSum chart can be used to check the differences of actual production from a target level. However, with seasonally dependent products, the planned production would vary. This can be allowed for in a CuSum chart by letting the interval on the x-axis vary.

Another example for Double CuSums is when the production of a commodity is subject to 'breaks', but that the production rate varies due to fluctuations in demand. A Double CuSum can be used to check for differences in the rate of the breaks.

As a further example, suppose we have routine sampling inspection of discrete items, but that a multiple sampling plan is used because inspection is expensive. For long-term monitoring of the fraction non-conforming a CuSum can be used, but the numbers of items sampled at each time point varies.

The Double CuSum procedure is extremely simple. The x axis unit is allowed to vary to allow for the different numbers of units sampled, different planned production rates, etc.

Let the x axis units be x_i and the observations y_i, and let T be the target value for the observations for unit x. The double CuSum plots

$$\sum(y_i - Tx_i) \quad \text{against} \quad \sum x_i.$$

The x's are usually measured without error, but the variance of the observations will usually depend on x_i. The most common situation is given by

$$V(y_i) = x_i \sigma^2.$$

For scaling, it is necessary to pick on a typical x_i, and scale the chart accordingly. For further information on double CuSums see Davies and Goldsmith (1972) or Bissell (1973).

15.3.2 Regression control charts

For the most part we have assumed that any process being controlled is basically stationary, apart from isolated out of control conditions. In practice this is sometimes not the case. For example, if a catalyst ages and has to be renewed, or if a tool wears and has to be replaced, then there will be a continuous trend in the results.

One way of dealing with this is to estimate the regression, and put the action and warning lines either side of this, as in Figure 15.1. Another way of handling the problem is to take out the regression, or other fitted model, and plot the residuals. In this case it is also necessary to keep a plot of the actual means, since a series of small changes, modelled by a regression, could easily take the means beyond specification limits. In theory, complex models, including cycles and auto-correlated behaviour, can be handled the same way, but checks on the fitted model also need to be carried out. Models fitted by robust techniques appear to be most suited to such applications.

15.3.3 Difference control charts

Sometimes the results of tests vary from time to time, either due to environmental conditions, or due to the need to reset a testing apparatus each time. Grubbs (1946) suggested using the 'difference control chart' for such situations.

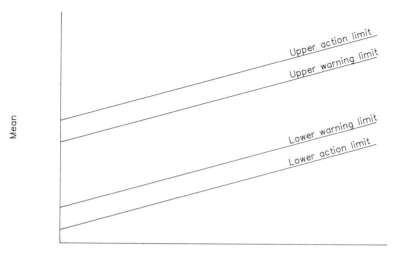

Figure 15.1 A regression control chart.

The method is simply to keep some material to use as a 'standard'. Tests are then performed by sampling m units from the standard, and n units from current production. A control chart is then based on the difference between the standard and current sample means.

If the sample means are $\bar{x}_s$ and $\bar{x}_c$ for the standard and current results, with individual variances σ_s^2 and σ_c^2 respectively, then the quantity plotted is $(\bar{x}_s - \bar{x}_c)$, which has a variance

$$V(\bar{x}_s - \bar{x}_c) = (\sigma_s^2/m + \sigma_c^2/n),$$

and this is used in the construction of charts.

When the difference control chart is used, the range or standard deviation chart is kept using current results only, as usual.

15.3.4 Confidence interval charts

As an alternative to ordinary control charts, a chart can be plotted with each sample mean, and its associated 95% or 99.8% confidence interval. The chart is regarded as giving an out of control signal whenever the confidence intervals cross specification limits.

One advantage of these charts is that they give an accurate picture of our knowledge about a process mean. The width of the confidence interval is also of interest in showing how precise our knowledge of the process mean is.

15.4 MULTIVARIATE METHODS

15.4.1 Hotelling's T^2 methods

It frequently occurs that material is judged on several variables simultaneously, such as tensile strength in different directions, thickness, etc., and clearly these variables are likely to be related.

Suppose we observe a vector variable x, with a mean vector μ and covariance matrix Σ. Then Jackson and Morris (1957), Jackson (1959) and Jackson and Mudhalkar (1979) suggested using a plot of Hotelling's T^2 values, where

$$T^2 = n(\mu_0 - \bar{x})'\Sigma^{-1}(\mu_0 - \bar{x})$$

and where μ_0 is the target mean vector. Murphy (1987) shows clearly why such a plot is better than keeping parallel individual value plots. When the mean is on target T^2 has a χ^2 distribution on p degrees of freedom, where p is the number of dimensions, so that an out of control signal is given when $T^2 > K$, for some K.

The difficulty with the T^2 plot is that it gives no indication of which variable or variables are causing the problem. Jackson (1980) suggested keeping principal component plots and individual value plots as well, but this collection of plots can be very difficult to interpret. A better method is given by Murphy (1987), who suggests an approach based on discrimination, in which the variables are partitioned into a subset thought to be causing the problem, and then calculating the difference between the T^2 statistics based on full and subset variables.

A key difficulty with these suggestions is that of using such plots in the plant control room or on the shop floor, but some developments of these methods may be easier to use and interpret. It should be noted that all T^2 methods will be sensitive to the assumed value of the covariance matrix.

15.4.2 CuSum methods

Woodall and Ncube (1985) suggested keeping p independent CuSums, and simply taking action as soon as the first action signal occurred. With this structure, the run length is the minimum of p separate run lengths. The authors discuss the derivation of the ARL curve, and give some results for two variables.

Healy (1987) shows that CuSums are simply sequential likelihood ratio procedures, and by using this derivation, CuSums are easily extended to the multivariate case. However, this approach gets back to one of the difficulties of T^2, of finding out which of the variables is causing the trouble.

It seems clear that further work needs to be done on multivariate charting methods. In the process industries the key multivariate problem is not that of charting, but of relating the product variables to the many process variables, and hence instituting some control.

Appendix A

Statistical tables

Table 1 Cumulative distribution function of the standard normal distribution
(a) For x in 0.1 intervals

x	P	x	P	x	P
0.0	0.5000	1.3	0.9032	2.6	0.9953
0.1	0.5398	1.4	0.9192	2.7	0.9965
0.2	0.5793	1.5	0.9332	2.8	0.9974
0.3	0.6179	1.6	0.9452	2.9	0.9981
0.4	0.6554	1.7	0.9554	3.0	0.9987
0.5	0.6915	1.8	0.9641	3.1	0.9990
0.6	0.7257	1.9	0.9713	3.2	0.9993
0.7	0.7580	2.0	0.9772	3.3	0.9995
0.8	0.7881	2.1	0.9821	3.4	0.99966
0.9	0.8159	2.2	0.9861	3.5	0.99977
1.0	0.8413	2.3	0.9893	3.6	0.99984
1.1	0.8643	2.4	0.9918	3.7	0.99989
1.2	0.8849	2.5	0.9938	3.8	0.99993

(b) For x in 0.01 intervals

x	P	x	P	x	P
1.60	0.9452	1.87	0.9693	2.14	0.9838
1.61	0.9463	1.88	0.9699	2.15	0.9842
1.62	0.9474	1.89	0.9706	2.16	0.9846
1.63	0.9484	1.90	0.9713	2.17	0.9850
1.64	0.9495	1.91	0.9719	2.18	0.9854
1.65	0.9505	1.92	0.9726	2.19	0.9857
1.66	0.9515	1.93	0.9732	2.20	0.9861
1.67	0.9525	1.94	0.9738	2.21	0.9865
1.68	0.9535	1.95	0.9744	2.22	0.9868
1.69	0.0545	1.96	0.9750	2.23	0.9871
1.70	0.9554	1.97	0.9756	2.24	0.9875
1.71	0.9564	1.98	0.9761	2.25	0.9878
1.72	0.9573	1.99	0.9767	2.26	0.9881
1.73	0.9582	2.00	0.9772	2.27	0.9884
1.74	0.9591	2.01	0.9778	2.28	0.9887
1.75	0.9599	2.02	0.9783	2.29	0.9890
1.76	0.9608	2.03	0.9788	2.30	0.9893
1.77	0.9616	2.04	0.9793	2.31	0.9896
1.78	0.9625	2.05	0.9798	2.32	0.9898
1.79	0.9633	2.06	0.9803	2.33	0.9901
1.80	0.9641	2.07	0.9808	2.34	0.9904
1.81	0.9649	2.08	0.9812	2.35	0.9906
1.82	0.9656	2.09	0.9817	2.36	0.9909
1.83	0.9664	2.10	0.9821	2.37	0.9911
1.84	0.9671	2.11	0.9826	2.38	0.9913
1.85	0.9678	2.12	0.9830	2.39	0.9916
1.86	0.9686	2.13	0.9834	2.40	0.9918

The function tabulated is

$$\Pr(X > x) = \int_x^\infty \frac{1}{\sqrt{(2\pi)}} e^{-(1/2)x^2} \, dx = P/100$$

Table 2 Percentiles of the standard normal distribution

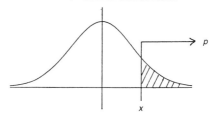

P	x	P	x	P	x
50	0	10	1.2816	2	2.0537
40	0.2533	6	1.5548	1	2.3263
30	0.5244	5	1.6449	0.5	2.5758
20	0.8416	3	1.8808	0.1	3.0902
15	1.0364	2.5	1.9600	0.05	3.2905

This table gives one-sided percentage points,

$$P/100 = \int_x^\infty \frac{1}{\sqrt{(2\pi)}} e^{-(1/2)x^2} \, dx.$$

The two-sided percentage appropriate to any x is $2P$.

Table 3 Percentage points of the *t*-distribution

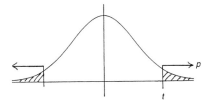

Degrees of freedom (*v*)	Probability in per cent 20	10	5	2	1	0.1
1	3.08	6.31	12.71	31.82	63.66	636.62
2	1.89	2.92	4.30	6.96	9.92	31.60
3	1.64	2.35	3.18	4.54	5.84	12.92
4	1.53	2.13	2.78	3.75	4.60	8.61
5	1.48	2.01	2.57	3.36	4.03	6.87
6	1.44	1.94	2.45	3.14	3.71	5.96
7	1.42	1.89	2.36	3.00	3.50	5.41
8	1.40	1.86	2.31	2.90	3.36	5.04
9	1.38	1.83	2.26	2.82	3.25	4.78
10	1.37	1.81	2.23	2.76	3.17	4.59
11	1.36	1.80	2.20	2.72	3.11	4.44
12	1.36	1.78	2.18	2.68	3.05	4.32
13	1.35	1.77	2.16	2.65	3.01	4.22
14	1.34	1.76	2.14	2.62	2.98	4.14
15	1.34	1.75	2.13	2.60	2.95	4.07
20	1.32	1.72	2.09	2.53	2.85	3.85
25	1.32	1.71	2.06	2.48	2.79	3.72
30	1.31	1.70	2.04	2.46	2.75	3.65
40	1.30	1.68	2.02	2.42	2.70	3.55
60	1.30	1.67	2.00	2.39	2.66	3.46
120	1.29	1.66	1.98	2.36	2.62	3.37
∞	1.28	1.64	1.96	2.33	2.58	3.29

This table gives two-sided percentage points,

$$P/100 = 2\int_t^\infty f(x|v)\,dx$$

where $f(x|v)$ is the p.d.f. of the *t*-distribution.

For one-sided percentage points the percentages shown should be halved.

Table 4 Percentage points of the χ^2 distribution

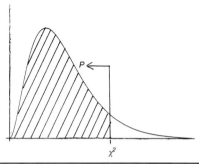

Degrees of freedom (v)	Probability in per cent					
	1	5	90	95	99	100
1	0.03157	0.00393	2.71	3.84	6.63	20.83
2	0.0201	0.103	4.61	5.99	9.21	13.81
3	0.115	0.352	6.25	7.81	11.34	16.27
4	0.297	0.711	7.78	9.49	13.28	18.47
5	0.554	1.15	9.24	11.07	15.09	20.52
6	0.872	1.64	10.64	12.59	16.81	22.46
7	1.24	2.17	12.02	14.07	18.48	24.32
8	1.65	2.73	13.36	15.51	20.09	26.12
9	2.09	3.33	14.68	16.92	21.67	27.88
10	2.56	3.94	15.99	18.31	23.21	29.59
11	3.05	4.57	17.28	19.68	24.73	31.26
12	3.57	5.23	18.55	21.03	26.22	32.91
14	4.66	6.57	21.06	23.68	29.14	36.12
16	5.81	7.96	23.54	26.30	32.00	39.25
18	7.01	9.39	25.99	28.87	34.81	42.31
20	8.26	10.85	28.41	31.41	37.57	45.31
22	9.54	12.34	30.81	33.92	40.29	48.27
24	10.86	13.85	33.20	36.42	42.98	51.18
26	12.20	15.38	35.56	38.89	45.64	54.05
28	13.56	16.93	37.92	41.34	48.28	56.89
30	14.95	18.49	40.26	43.77	50.89	59.70

The table gives the percentage points χ^2, where

$$P/100 = \int_0^{\chi^2} g(y|v)\,dy$$

where $g(y|v)$ is the probability density function of the χ^2 distribution.

For $v > 30$, $\sqrt{(2\chi^2)}$ is approximately normally distributed with mean $(2v - 1)$ and unit variance.

Table 5 Percentage points of the F-distribution

(a) 95% points

v_2	Degrees of freedom of numerator (v_1)									
	1	2	3	4	5	6	8	12	24	∞
1	161.4	199.5	215.7	224.6	230.2	234.0	238.9	243.9	249.0	254.3
2	18.51	19.00	19.16	19.25	19.30	19.33	19.37	19.41	19.45	19.50
3	10.13	9.55	9.28	9.12	9.01	8.94	8.85	8.74	8.64	8.53
4	7.71	6.94	6.59	6.39	6.26	6.16	6.04	5.91	5.77	5.63
5	6.61	5.79	5.41	5.19	5.05	4.95	4.82	4.68	4.53	4.36
6	5.99	5.14	4.76	4.53	4.39	4.28	4.15	4.00	3.84	3.67
7	5.59	4.74	4.35	4.12	3.97	3.87	3.73	3.57	3.41	3.23
8	5.32	4.46	4.07	3.84	3.69	3.58	3.44	3.28	3.12	2.93
9	5.12	4.26	3.86	3.63	3.48	3.37	3.23	3.07	2.90	2.71
10	4.96	4.10	3.71	3.48	3.33	3.22	3.07	2.91	2.74	2.54
11	4.84	3.98	3.59	3.36	3.20	3.09	2.95	2.79	2.61	2.40
12	4.75	3.89	3.49	3.26	3.11	3.00	2.85	2.69	2.51	2.30
14	4.60	3.74	3.34	3.11	2.96	2.85	2.70	2.53	2.35	2.13
16	4.49	3.63	3.24	3.01	2.85	2.74	2.59	2.42	2.24	2.01
18	4.41	3.55	3.16	2.93	2.77	2.66	2.51	2.34	2.15	1.92
20	4.35	3.49	3.10	2.87	2.71	2.60	2.45	2.28	2.08	1.84
25	4.24	3.39	2.99	2.76	2.60	2.49	2.34	2.16	1.96	1.71
30	4.17	3.32	2.92	2.69	2.53	2.42	2.27	2.09	1.89	1.62
40	4.08	3.23	2.84	2.61	2.45	2.34	2.18	2.00	1.79	1.51
60	4.00	3.15	2.76	2.53	2.37	2.25	2.10	1.92	1.70	1.39
∞	3.84	3.00	2.60	2.37	2.21	2.10	1.94	1.75	1.52	1.00

Degrees of freedom of denominator (v_2)

(b) 97.5% points

v_2 \ v_1	1	2	3	4	5	6	8	12	24	∞
1	648	800	864	900	922	937	957	977	997	1018
2	38.5	39.0	39.2	39.2	39.3	39.3	39.4	39.4	39.5	39.5
3	17.4	16.0	15.4	15.1	14.9	14.7	14.5	14.3	14.1	13.9
4	12.2	10.6	9.98	9.60	9.36	9.20	8.98	8.75	8.51	8.26
5	10.0	8.43	7.76	7.39	7.15	6.98	6.76	6.52	6.28	6.02
6	8.81	7.26	6.60	6.23	5.99	5.82	5.60	5.37	5.12	4.85
7	8.07	6.54	5.89	5.52	5.29	5.12	4.90	4.67	4.42	4.14
8	7.57	6.06	5.42	5.05	4.82	4.65	4.43	4.20	3.95	3.67
9	7.21	5.71	5.08	4.72	4.48	4.32	4.10	3.87	3.61	3.33
10	6.94	5.46	4.83	4.47	4.24	4.07	3.85	3.62	3.37	3.08
11	6.72	5.26	4.63	4.28	4.04	3.88	3.66	3.43	3.17	2.88
12	6.55	5.10	4.47	4.12	3.89	3.73	3.51	3.28	3.02	2.72
14	6.30	4.86	4.24	3.89	3.66	3.50	3.29	3.05	2.79	2.49
16	6.12	4.69	4.08	3.73	3.50	3.34	3.12	2.89	2.63	2.32
18	5.98	4.56	3.95	3.61	3.38	3.22	3.01	2.77	2.50	2.19
20	5.87	4.46	3.86	3.51	3.29	3.13	2.91	2.68	2.41	2.09
25	5.69	4.29	3.69	3.35	3.13	2.97	2.75	2.51	2.24	1.91
30	5.57	4.18	3.59	3.25	3.03	2.87	2.65	2.41	2.14	1.79
40	5.42	4.05	3.46	3.13	2.90	2.74	2.53	2.29	2.01	1.64
60	5.29	3.93	3.34	3.01	2.79	2.63	2.41	2.17	1.88	1.48
∞	5.02	3.69	3.12	2.79	2.57	2.41	2.19	1.94	1.64	1.00

Degrees of freedom of numerator (v_1)

Degrees of freedom of denominator (v_2)

(c) 99% points

Degrees of freedom of denominator (v_2)	Degrees of freedom of numerator (v_1)									
	1	2	3	4	5	6	8	12	24	∞
1	4052	4999	5403	5625	5764	5859	5981	6106	6235	6366
2	98.50	99.00	99.17	99.25	99.30	99.33	99.37	99.42	99.46	99.50
3	34.12	30.82	29.46	28.71	28.24	27.91	27.49	27.05	26.60	26.13
4	21.20	18.00	16.69	15.98	15.52	15.21	14.80	14.37	13.93	13.46
5	16.26	13.27	12.06	11.39	10.97	10.67	10.29	9.89	9.47	9.02
6	13.74	10.92	9.78	9.15	8.75	8.47	8.10	7.72	7.31	6.88
7	12.25	9.55	8.45	7.85	7.46	7.19	6.84	6.47	6.07	5.65
8	11.26	8.65	7.59	7.01	6.63	6.37	6.03	5.67	5.28	4.86
9	10.56	8.02	6.99	6.42	6.06	5.80	5.47	5.11	4.73	4.31
10	10.04	7.56	6.55	5.99	5.64	5.39	5.06	4.71	4.33	3.91
11	9.65	7.21	6.22	5.67	5.32	5.07	4.74	4.40	4.02	3.60
12	9.33	6.93	5.95	5.41	5.06	4.82	4.50	4.16	3.78	3.36
14	8.86	6.51	5.56	5.04	4.69	4.46	4.14	3.80	3.43	3.00
16	8.53	6.23	5.29	4.77	4.44	4.20	3.89	3.55	3.18	2.75
18	8.29	6.01	5.09	4.58	4.25	4.01	3.71	3.37	3.00	2.57
20	8.10	5.85	4.94	4.43	4.10	3.87	3.56	3.23	2.86	2.42
25	7.77	5.57	4.68	4.18	3.86	3.63	3.32	2.99	2.62	2.17
30	7.56	5.39	4.51	4.02	3.70	3.47	3.17	2.84	2.47	2.01
40	7.31	5.18	4.31	3.83	3.51	3.29	2.99	2.66	2.29	1.80
60	7.08	4.98	4.13	3.65	3.34	3.12	2.82	2.50	2.12	1.60
∞	6.63	4.60	3.78	3.32	3.02	2.80	2.51	2.18	1.79	1.00

The table gives for various degrees of freedom, v_1, v_2, the values of F such that

$$P = 100 \int_0^F h(z|v_1, v_2)\, dz$$

where $h(z|v_1, v_2)$ is the probability density function of the F-ratio.

Table 6 Conversion of range to standard deviation

n	d_n	n	d_n	n	d_n	n	d_n
2	1.128	6	2.534	10	3.078	14	3.407
3	1.683	7	2.704	11	3.173	15	3.472
4	2.059	8	2.847	12	3.258	16	3.532
5	2.326	9	2.970	13	3.336	17	3.588

An estimate of σ of a normal population can be obtained by dividing the range of a sample size n, or the average range of a set of samples of the same size n, by d_n.

Table 7 Percentage points of the distribution of the relative range (range/σ)

Sample size	0.1	1.0	2.5	5.0	90	95.0	97.5	99.0	99.9
2	0.00	0.02	0.04	0.09	2.33	2.77	3.17	3.64	4.65
3	0.06	0.19	0.30	0.43	2.90	3.31	3.68	4.12	5.06
4	0.20	0.43	0.59	0.76	3.24	3.63	3.98	4.40	5.31
5	0.37	0.66	0.85	1.03	3.48	3.86	4.20	4.60	5.48
6	0.54	0.87	1.06	1.25	3.66	4.03	4.36	4.76	5.62
7	0.69	1.05	1.25	1.44	3.81	4.17	4.49	4.88	5.73
8	0.83	1.20	1.41	1.60	3.93	4.29	4.61	4.99	5.82
9	0.96	1.34	1.55	1.74	4.04	4.39	4.70	5.08	5.90
10	1.08	1.47	1.67	1.86	4.13	4.47	4.79	5.16	5.97
11	1.20	1.58	1.78	1.97	4.21	4.55	4.86	5.23	6.04
12	1.30	1.68	1.88	2.07	4.28	4.62	4.92	5.29	6.09

Table 8 Table of values sampled from a Normal distribution with mean zero and standard deviation one

−0.73	−2.09	0.31	0.25	−0.92	−0.09	2.71	−0.14
−0.17	−0.15	0.36	−2.19	−0.76	0.47	−1.44	−0.40
0.40	−0.03	−1.50	−0.54	−0.29	−1.07	−0.41	0.14
1.19	−0.18	0.56	−0.08	−1.66	0.23	0.87	0.62
0.85	0.06	−0.08	−2.36	−1.42	1.30	0.08	−0.36
1.18	1.23	0.76	−0.48	−1.88	0.12	0.58	0.20
−0.29	0.46	−0.24	−0.54	−1.49	0.92	0.61	−2.14
1.43	0.12	1.26	0.60	0.42	0.67	−1.34	0.03
1.34	−0.85	1.26	−0.19	0.41	−0.14	0.32	1.19
0.75	0.21	−1.04	0.61	0.20	0.25	1.01	1.13
−1.07	−0.50	0.05	0.05	−1.60	−1.72	0.21	2.15
0.53	2.73	0.76	−0.33	1.73	−0.10	−1.07	−0.57
−1.52	0.36	−1.20	−1.33	−0.71	−1.73	−1.22	1.04
−0.45	0.73	−0.07	1.50	0.84	1.76	−1.83	−0.60
−0.87	0.86	2.03	−0.37	0.23	−2.30	0.20	−0.37
−1.51	−1.70	0.81	−1.67	−1.75	0.35	0.19	−0.86
1.01	0.12	−1.35	0.74	−1.84	−0.18	0.82	1.74
−0.02	0.01	−0.18	−0.02	0.68	0.34	0.43	−0.59
0.71	0.39	0.38	−0.86	−0.26	−1.93	0.53	0.96
0.29	0.67	1.08	1.53	0.06	−1.20	−0.16	−2.14
1.82	2.23	−1.07	−1.32	−1.01	0.34	0.59	−0.32
0.54	0.72	0.96	1.44	−1.06	−0.34	−0.24	1.61
−0.16	−1.25	0.16	1.32	−1.27	−0.34	1.83	2.26
1.52	0.00	−1.32	−1.13	0.36	0.14	−1.59	−0.30
−0.16	0.21	−0.33	−0.93	−1.24	−0.58	1.09	−0.82
−0.76	0.36	0.59	0.95	1.19	−0.46	1.37	0.06
−0.07	1.00	2.20	0.66	−0.39	−0.87	−1.05	0.83
−0.34	0.95	−0.48	−0.33	0.80	0.45	−0.13	−0.39
1.41	−0.23	−0.52	−1.30	−0.71	0.41	0.78	−1.76
1.13	0.38	0.22	0.07	−0.90	0.36	−0.67	0.72
1.20	−1.21	0.24	−0.59	1.38	−0.83	−0.44	0.07
−0.63	1.60	0.53	0.77	0.65	−0.13	0.42	−1.13
3.98	0.13	−1.21	0.89	−0.58	−0.64	−0.61	−0.10
−0.28	−1.10	−0.78	−0.42	1.10	−1.03	1.28	−0.24
−0.21	0.37	0.32	1.06	1.69	0.84	0.88	1.34
−2.12	−0.61	1.88	0.98	0.39	1.03	−1.50	−1.82
−0.53	0.28	0.67	0.08	−1.26	−0.39	0.76	−0.53
−1.60	−0.91	−0.91	0.38	0.06	−0.29	−1.46	0.42
−0.71	−0.41	0.24	0.11	−0.37	0.79	−0.46	−0.05
0.91	0.57	−0.70	−0.22	−0.26	−0.76	−1.53	−0.01
1.14	0.12	−1.46	0.64	0.44	0.91	−0.23	1.69
0.22	−0.96	0.60	−0.80	−0.73	2.65	−0.44	−0.81
−0.06	0.24	−1.41	1.10	0.24	−0.22	0.06	−3.38

Table 8 (*cont.*)

0.49	1.38	−0.52	−0.82	0.20	−0.91	1.02	−0.47
−0.99	0.09	0.22	0.72	1.51	1.64	−1.34	−0.17
0.60	0.23	−0.07	−0.49	−1.19	0.72	−0.15	−0.48
−0.47	−0.63	0.56	0.13	−0.40	0.22	−0.17	1.36
−1.00	0.07	−1.26	0.59	0.31	−1.68	−0.63	1.00
0.95	1.85	0.32	−0.29	−0.77	−0.55	−0.56	−1.44
1.00	−0.49	−0.25	0.57	−0.73	0.77	−0.07	1.73
0.49	0.25	−0.55	0.09	0.96	−0.17	−0.09	1.79
−0.65	−2.09	0.50	0.84	−1.09	0.80	0.16	−0.03
−1.51	−0.79	−0.91	0.75	0.21	−0.87	1.80	1.86
1.41	−0.99	−0.12	0.66	0.75	−0.21	0.29	−1.62
−1.34	0.57	−1.61	−0.27	−0.78	0.10	0.93	−0.58
−0.54	−1.61	0.13	0.40	−0.95	−1.59	−1.19	−0.82
−2.35	−1.32	0.84	−0.23	−0.47	0.22	−0.66	0.24
0.84	−0.20	0.00	−0.14	−1.16	0.28	−1.05	0.60
2.29	−1.44	0.05	−0.45	−0.71	−0.47	0.51	0.65
−0.60	1.27	0.58	−0.01	0.67	−0.92	0.90	1.64

Table 9 List of working tables and nomograms in text

Appendix B

Data sets for sampling experiment

SAMPLING EXPERIMENT

DATASET NUMBER I 1   NAME _____

Sample no.	DATA				Mean	SD	Range
1	133	125	134	126	129.5	4.7	9
2	145	127	127	137	134.0	8.7	18
3	126	137	133	127	130.8	5.2	11
4	132	140	138	139	137.3	3.6	8
5	129	117	124	138	127.0	8.8	21
6	126	134	139	123	130.5	7.3	16
7	128	137	124	134	130.8	5.9	13
8	136	123	127	127	128.3	5.5	13
9	123	131	131	139	131.0	6.5	16
10	125	128	132	135	130.0	4.4	10
11	137	125	130	138	132.5	6.1	13
12	121	128	132	138	129.8	7.1	17
13	133	131	125	130	129.8	3.4	8
14	131	130	124	121	126,5	4.8	10
15	129	118	132	123	125.5	6.2	14
16	129	128	120	134	127.8	5.8	14
17	125	130	127	129	127.8	2.2	5
18	134	126	121	135	129.0	6.7	14
19	128	123	127	136	128.5	5.4	13
20	130	117	123	131	125.3	6.6	14
21	132	126	133	135	131.5	3.9	9
22	124	125	137	135	130.3	6.7	13
23	129	139	124	139	132.8	7.5	15
24	119	124	123	126	123.0	2.9	7
25	132	117	127	125	125.3	6.2	15
26	133	136	130	137	134.0	3.2	7
27	130	126	127	130	128.3	2.1	4

Sample no.	DATA				Mean	SD	Range
28	128	140	131	125	131.0	6.5	15
29	116	124	124	132	124.0	6.5	16
30	136	127	143	133	134.8	6.7	16

SEED = 6238

SAMPLING EXPERIMENT

DATASET NUMBER I 2　　　　　NAME _____

Sample no.	DATA				Mean	SD	Range
1	133	127	134	127	130.3	3.8	7
2	129	131	129	133	130.5	1.9	4
3	141	135	122	130	132.0	8.0	19
4	134	136	133	143	136.5	4.5	10
5	131	127	132	138	132.0	4.5	11
6	117	133	134	134	129.5	8.3	17
7	128	129	117	130	126.0	6.1	13
8	134	130	121	117	125.5	7.9	17
9	133	129	131	131	131.0	1.6	4
10	129	141	127	123	130.0	7.7	18
11	135	122	131	124	128.0	6.1	13
12	122	133	130	129	128.5	4.7	11
13	133	128	136	132	132.3	3.3	8
14	128	131	134	134	131.8	2.9	6
15	132	130	145	127	133.5	7.9	18
16	142	122	133	135	133.0	8.3	20
17	133	122	125	133	128.3	5.6	11
18	133	130	120	135	129.5	6.7	15
19	128	124	137	121	127.5	7.0	16
20	131	115	128	120	123.5	7.3	16
21	133	132	132	135	133.0	1.4	3
22	132	132	127	125	129.0	3.6	7
23	139	132	134	132	134.3	3.3	7
24	118	128	133	135	128.5	7.6	17
25	141	130	118	131	130.0	9.4	23
26	128	139	132	134	133.3	4.6	11
27	131	124	135	129	129.8	4.6	11
28	129	124	125	122	125.0	2.9	7
29	116	132	126	125	124.8	6.6	16
30	129	134	135	142	135.0	5.4	13

SEED = 4205

SAMPLING EXPERIMENT

DATASET NUMBER I 3   NAME _____

Sample no.	DATA				Mean	SD	Range
1	131	134	127	128	130.0	3.2	7
2	126	128	130	121	126.3	3.9	9
3	134	128	138	124	131.0	6.2	14
4	129	138	123	125	128.8	6.7	15
5	137	131	128	121	129.3	6.7	16
6	128	130	129	129	129.0	0.8	2
7	118	126	118	128	122.5	5.3	10
8	132	133	135	135	133.8	1.5	3
9	133	131	133	126	130.8	3.3	7
10	139	122	133	135	132.3	7.3	17
11	141	129	129	124	130.8	7.2	17
12	132	128	133	137	132.5	3.7	9
13	140	141	126	141	137.0	7.3	15
14	129	136	135	142	135.5	5.3	13
15	132	140	125	127	131.0	6.7	15
16	122	125	132	132	127.8	5.1	10
17	136	131	126	133	131.5	4.2	10
18	122	135	132	133	130.5	5.8	13
19	136	126	124	137	130.8	6.7	13
20	131	121	130	126	127.0	4.5	10
21	121	133	128	127	127.3	4.9	12
22	113	140	138	117	127.0	14.0	27
23	128	133	132	129	130.5	2.4	5
24	119	125.	134	138	129.0	8.6	19
25	122	131	130	123	126.5	4.7	9
26	126	147	138	135	136.5	8.7	21
27	133	134	123	127	129.3	5.2	11
28	132	124	128	130	128.5	3.4	8
29	138	127	132	133	132.5	4.5	11
30	138	129	131	135	133.3	4.0	9

SEED = 9441

SAMPLING EXPERIMENT

DATASET NUMBER I 4   NAME _____

Sample no.	DATA				Mean	SD	Range
1	129	138	137	128	133.0	5.2	10
2	127	125	133	126	127.8	3.6	8
3	127	130	133	125	128.8	3.5	8
4	123	125	126	127	125.3	1.7	4
5	131	127	132	135	131.3	3.3	8
6	126	115	127	128	124.0	6.1	13
7	133	125	120	134	128.0	6.7	14
8	134	130	130	127	130.3	2.9	7
9	123	128	122	133	126.5	5.1	11
10	127	137	131	137	133.0	4.9	10
11	143	133	118	139	133.3	11.0	25
12	131	132	135	118	129.0	7.5	17
13	134	122	131	138	131.3	6.8	16
14	138	127	124	126	128.8	6.3	14
15	123	132	129	145	132.3	9.3	22
16	131	131	142	139	135.8	5.6	11
17	129	137	130	127	130.8	4.3	10
18	129	138	134	138	134.8	4.3	9
19	132	139	120	138	132.3	8.7	19
20	127	125	128	131	127.8	2.5	6
21	133	129	128	137	131.8	4.1	9
22	131	129	131	137	132.0	3.5	8
23	134	130	125	141	132.5	6.8	16
24	125	136	128	122	127.8	6.0	14
25	133	140	126	135	133.5	5.8	14
26	126	141	144	125	134.0	9.9	19
27	129	126	129	125	127.3	2.1	4
28	119	137	121	130	126.8	8.3	18
29	136	142	132	132	135.5	4.7	10
30	126	131	135	128	130.0	3.9	9

SEED = 1866

SAMPLING EXPERIMENT

DATASET NUMBER I 5   NAME _____

Sample no.	DATA				Mean	SD	Range
1	129	136	129	138	133.0	4.7	9
2	138	132	137	144	137.8	4.9	12
3	130	136	133	132	132.8	2.5	6
4	126	129	122	132	127.3	4.3	10
5	135	118	139	132	131.0	9.1	21
6	132	127	133	129	130.3	2.8	6
7	130	118	142	128	129.5	9.8	24
8	142	131	138	121	133.0	9.2	21
9	129	129	128	132	129.5	1.7	4
10	143	116	126	117	125.5	12.5	27
11	128	128	124	125	126.3	2.1	4
12	128	132	128	138	131.5	4.7	10
13	137	121	123	126	126.8	7.1	16
14	124	129	130	130	128.3	2.9	6
15	123	134	124	123	126.0	5.4	11
16	130	133	137	136	134.0	3.2	7
17	139	130	124	130	130.8	6.2	15
18	126	130	126	130	128.0	2.3	4
19	139	125	133	130	131.8	5.9	14
20	126	128	123	138	128.8	6.5	15
21	135	143	136	120	133.5	9.7	23
22	131	123	120	134	127.0	6.6	14
23	125	123	138	132	129.5	6.9	15
24	120	136	129	127	128.0	6.6	16
25	135	128	139	132	133.5	4.7	11
26	136	117	137	137	131.8	9.8	20
27	124	118	134	127	125.8	6.7	16
28	125	124	133	125	126.8	4.2	9
29	126	123	127	140	129.0	7.5	17
30	134	135	135	128	133.0	3.4	7

SEED = 1607

SAMPLING EXPERIMENT

DATASET NUMBER A 1   NAME _____

Sample no.	DATA				Mean
1	130	133	123	136	130.5
2	121	127	139	126	128.3
3	129	130	122	128	127.3
4	141	116	124	132	128.3
5	136	126	138	124	131.0
6	123	133	126	122	126.0
7	125	127	141	124	129.3
8	132	131	128	130	130.3
9	120	131	125	126	125.5
10	139	139	119	127	131.0
11	147	131	126	138	135.5
12	129	137	135	135	134.0
13	130	133	133	130	131.5
14	128	141	132	133	133.5
15	133	134	141	123	132.8
16	130	126	134	136	131.5
17	136	125	132	136	132.3
18	131	133	118	141	130.8
19	135	131	121	137	131.0
20	130	127	138	130	131.3
21	127	140	137	131	133.8
22	131	142	127	128	132.0
23	129	123	139	136	131.8
24	132	129	135	127	130.8
25	130	130	126	132	129.5
26	135	136	135	131	134.3
27	144	134	130	123	132.8
28	135	141	147	129	138.0
29	138	139	129	133	134.8
30	146	132	138	139	138.8
31	139	129	136	136	135.0
32	137	132	142	139	137.5
33	134	126	133	135	132.0
34	136	126	140	119	130.3
35	129	121	130	133	128.3
36	135	132	136	133	134.0
37	134	136	128	136	133.5
38	123	139	120	136	129.5
39	139	136	133	140	137.0
40	135	119	134	131	129.8

Sample no.	DATA				Mean
41	134	140	138	127	134.8
42	135	130	132	121	129.5
43	128	137	132	135	133.0
44	140	138	133	133	136.0
45	128	134	133	139	133.5
46	132	130	141	129	133.0
47	143	129	128	127	131.8
48	138	134	135	133	135.0
49	142	140	127	134	135.8
50	137	125	136	128	131.5

SAMPLING EXPERIMENT

DATASET NUMBER A 2   NAME _____

Sample no.	DATA				Mean
1	127	134	134	133	132.0
2	117	136	125	142	130.0
3	121	131	131	127	127.5
4	123	123	139	127	128.0
5	135	126	127	125	128.3
6	140	138	123	128	132.3
7	131	126	127	134	129.5
8	124	131	131	135	130.3
9	125	128	123	127	125.8
10	132	132	131	128	130.8
11	136	136	129	127	132.0
12	135	131	137	130	133.3
13	141	127	124	131	130.8
14	131	128	121	144	131.0
15	148	126	128	128	132.5
16	133	128	127	138	131.5
17	128	136	133	134	132.8
18	124	136	145	135	135.0
19	122	141	131	138	133.0
20	134	124	122	122	125.5
21	133	134	132	125	131.0
22	129	132	124	136	130.3
23	133	130	141	133	134.3
24	127	129	135	132	130.8
25	121	130	137	130	129.5
26	125	129	129	126	127.3

Sample no.	DATA				Mean
27	132	144	128	138	135.5
28	135	135	125	138	133.3
29	130	145	132	127	133.5
30	139	133	133	126	132.8
31	138	129	128	110	126.3
32	144	131	138	138	137.8
33	142	141	122	132	134.3
34	139	129	137	125	132.5
35	134	132	127	127	130.0
36	133	135	143	147	139.5
37	137	133	137	130	134.3
38	134	125	136	130	131.3
39	141	141	135	135	138.0
40	144	131	128	125	132.0
41	134	132	142	139	136.8
42	132	134	140	127	133.3
43	130	126	134	143	133.3
44	131	130	127	124	128.0
45	133	132	125	131	130.3
46	138	123	137	124	130.5
47	132	132	137	134	133.8
48	131	137	136	127	132.8
49	145	129	132	131	134.3
50	128	130	140	135	133.3

SAMPLING EXPERIMENT

DATASET NUMBER A 3   NAME _____

Sample no.	DATA				Mean
1	128	125	135	124	128.0
2	138	125	139	126	132.0
3	134	121	120	129	126.0
4	120	147	138	122	131.8
5	125	130	136	126	129.3
6	129	136	132	127	131.0
7	124	141	143	129	134.3
8	128	122	119	133	125.5
9	136	127	132	131	131.5
10	124	122	129	129	126.0
11	142	122	151	130	136.3
12	133	126	122	130	127.8

Sample no.	DATA				Mean
13	135	131	132	131	132.3
14	139	134	134	142	137.3
15	143	141	135	141	140.0
16	139	137	139	138	138.3
17	138	129	140	140	136.8
18	143	140	127	139	137.3
19	137	140	142	134	138.3
20	124	134	127	130	128.8
21	127	130	131	137	131.3
22	134	122	135	143	133.5
23	139	123	127	127	129.0
24	125	131	137	131	131.0
25	125	147	130	130	133.0
26	146	130	125	138	134.8
27	134	143	144	136	139.3
28	145	140	138	134	139.3
29	138	140	120	133	132.8
30	127	130	126	135	129.5
31	129	140	135	146	137.5
32	133	131	121	128	128.3
33	132	133	135	143	135.8
34	130	141	141	134	136.5
35	133	139	136	137	136.3
36	133	124	131	127	128.8
37	130	133	133	136	133.0
38	134	145	130	127	134.0
39	128	137	123	126	128.5
40	138	131	133	134	134.0
41	131	131	129	132	130.8
42	136	126	130	134	131.5
43	137	132	135	131	133.8
44	134	124	125	125	127.0
45	126	133	127	132	129.5
46	126	137	136	132	132.8
47	126	139	140	140	136.3
48	131	136	136	137	135.0
49	125	120	129	133	126.8
50	122	138	122	135	129.3

SAMPLING EXPERIMENT

DATASET NUMBER A 4   NAME _____

Sample no.	DATA				Mean
1	130	128	133	129	130.0
2	141	132	129	124	131.5
3	118	140	130	134	130.5
4	136	137	141	131	136.3
5	135	128	129	137	132.3
6	129	136	130	129	131.0
7	121	128	130	138	129.3
8	130	130	124	136	130.0
9	125	123	130	124	125.5
10	131	119	129	128	126.8
11	134	134	131	129	132.0
12	130	130	124	132	129.0
13	134	132	133	149	137.0
14	134	135	127	139	133.8
15	132	132	122	127	128.3
16	129	135	140	137	135.3
17	126	127	133	132	129.5
18	126	134	126	138	131.0
19	133	121	133	130	129.3
20	129	131	134	130	131.0
21	136	139	134	144	138.3
22	132	132	139	132	133.8
23	139	135	132	125	132.8
24	126	132	117	135	127.5
25	135	138	137	129	134.8
26	129	142	136	131	134.5
27	134	127	135	137	133.3
28	137	142	128	132	134.8
29	147	121	132	131	132.8
30	136	126	134	134	132.5
31	130	137	128	132	131.8
32	137	130	140	138	136.3
33	134	142	116	133	131.3
34	134	123	126	130	128.3
35	131	128	133	134	131.5
36	129	134	128	122	128.3
37	138	135	129	131	133.3
38	128	142	138	121	132.3
39	133	126	139	130	132.0
40	136	112	125	126	124.8

Sample no.	DATA				Mean
41	133	143	140	121	134.3
42	137	131	140	132	135.0
43	129	130	132	134	131.3
44	136	132	139	141	137.0
45	128	137	143	132	135.0
46	125	137	127	137	131.5
47	138	128	139	129	133.5
48	131	130	145	137	135.8
49	130	138	135	135	134.5
50	127	135	136	139	134.3

SAMPLING EXPERIMENT

DATASET NUMBER A 5   NAME _____

Sample no.	DATA				Mean
1	129	127	132	118	126.5
2	130	133	117	132	128.0
3	136	134	123	142	133.8
4	133	130	125	136	131.0
5	133	139	121	133	131.5
6	129	121	123	122	123.8
7	116	136	132	130	128.5
8	125	130	133	128	129.0
9	131	133	132	128	131.0
10	127	121	132	127	126.8
11	133	140	139	134	136.5
12	134	134	141	133	135.5
13	120	149	134	133	134.0
14	130	127	132	146	133.8
15	141	129	128	132	132.5
16	130	134	128	132	131.0
17	133	143	148	130	138.5
18	131	136	134	133	133.5
19	131	125	127	129	128.0
20	136	140	134	140	137.5
21	143	136	123	130	133.0
22	131	122	133	138	131.0
23	127	140	126	137	132.5
24	143	133	144	135	138.8
25	130	137	137	133	134.3
26	128	133	138	134	133.3

Sample no.	DATA				Mean
27	132	141	145	127	136.3
28	137	139	132	118	131.5
29	134	144	137	136	137.8
30	133	134	132	136	133.8
31	131	131	125	128	128.8
32	132	137	136	133	134.5
33	141	133	137	132	135.8
34	139	135	130	128	133.0
35	144	130	133	135	135.5
36	134	145	116	131	131.5
37	131	131	128	120	127.5
38	132	131	139	131	133.3
39	132	142	135	133	135.5
40	138	135	134	128	133.8
41	135	126	130	141	133.0
42	135	129	132	131	131.8
43	128	135	129	133	131.3
44	130	133	137	134	133.5
45	130	127	133	136	131.5
46	136	133	124	139	133.0
47	149	133	135	135	138.0
48	140	124	136	136	134.0
49	129	131	137	139	134.0
50	138	135	133	128	133.5

SAMPLING EXPERIMENT

DATASET NUMBER B 1   NAME _____

Sample no.	DATA				Mean
1	131	119	119	118	121.8
2	122	128	126	139	128.8
3	130	130	127	120	126.8
4	126	117	139	123	126.3
5	128	130	132	125	128.8
6	128	131	125	133	129.3
7	139	123	129	133	131.0
8	130	130	128	126	128.5
9	135	126	124	124	127.3
10	131	122	129	128	127.5
11	123	135	129	110	124.3
12	128	118	122	130	124.5

Sample no.	DATA				Mean
13	124	129	117	122	123.0
14	123	113	118	116	117.5
15	121	127	125	119	123.0
16	130	136	124	127	129.3
17	127	115	122	122	121.5
18	123	111	127	126	121.8
19	124	135	132	122	128.3
20	122	130	119	126	124.3
21	124	127	119	127	124.3
22	126	124	125	130	126.3
23	120	119	129	129	124.3
24	135	117	126	124	125.5
25	127	116	122	130	123.8
26	132	124	136	125	129.3
27	129	123	121	131	126.0
28	118	120	139	137	128.5
29	127	130	120	130	126.8
30	127	126	118	132	125.8
31	125	113	125	123	121.5
32	127	124	117	115	120.8
33	121	116	134	125	124.0
34	131	116	125	118	122.5
35	133	126	111	132	125.5
36	125	117	137	116	123.8
37	130	124	124	122	125.0
38	126	124	118	120	122.0
39	124	119	116	122	120.3
40	119	121	127	124	122.8
41	127	125	124	127	125.8
42	122	122	120	125	122.3
43	116	125	127	137	126.3
44	128	123	121	123	123.8
45	116	113	123	121	118.3
46	131	119	122	132	126.0
47	120	125	121	126	123.0
48	124	119	118	116	119.3
49	117	121	125	122	121.3
50	118	110	117	121	116.5

SAMPLING EXPERIMENT

DATASET NUMBER B 2   NAME _____

Sample no.	DATA				Mean
1	127	137	144	121	132.3
2	141	135	139	135	137.5
3	124	120	136	119	124.8
4	129	125	146	135	133.8
5	136	132	133	124	131.3
6	125	137	131	122	128.8
7	120	133	128	124	126.3
8	137	123	125	131	129.0
9	126	123	122	126	124.3
10	127	123	119	127	124.0
11	123	122	127	121	123.3
12	114	125	123	131	123.3
13	110	117	120	118	116.3
14	116	132	128	126	125.5
15	133	126	121	113	123.3
16	134	121	134	136	131.3
17	117	133	125	124	124.8
18	132	116	112	122	120.5
19	127	134	122	137	130.0
20	122	122	130	136	127.5
21	128	128	114	128	124.5
22	116	124	124	123	121.8
23	122	115	133	119	122.3
24	132	125	118	112	121.8
25	117	122	121	125	121.3
26	123	119	124	118	121.0
27	121	114	122	123	120.0
28	130	115	128	130	125.8
29	130	132	114	112	122.0
30	129	131	119	119	124.5
31	129	127	120	118	123.5
32	122	116	121	122	120.3
33	126	123	127	123	124.8
34	118	122	121	121	120.5
35	108	131	127	121	121.8
36	121	110	124	123	119.5
37	129	123	124	118	123.5
38	122	133	128	129	128.0
39	123	127	130	137	129.3
40	125	113	130	122	122.5

Sample no.	DATA				Mean
41	137	128	126	117	127.0
42	128	131	126	126	127.8
43	128	133	119	122	125.5
44	122	121	120	121	121.0
45	120	127	116	125	122.0
46	125	126	127	117	123.8
47	117	123	124	124	122.0
48	127	120	133	118	124.5
49	117	122	126	127	123.0
50	130	120	119	127	124.0

SAMPLING EXPERIMENT

DATASET NUMBER B 3   NAME _____

Sample no.	DATA				Mean
1	133	130	124	130	129.3
2	126	139	132	136	133.3
3	134	129	143	117	130.8
4	139	129	120	127	128.8
5	140	137	130	118	131.3
6	132	124	133	134	130.8
7	126	127	128	123	126.0
8	128	130	134	136	132.0
9	122	134	129	124	127.3
10	131	118	123	128	125.0
11	126	128	120	128	125.5
12	120	118	122	123	120.8
13	120	131	119	121	122.8
14	128	123	117	139	126.8
15	129	121	123	129	125.5
16	126	124	116	124	122.5
17	121	124	116	132	123.3
18	125	126	129	127	126.8
19	114	127	134	126	125.3
20	124	131	130	120	126.3
21	124	132	127	119	125.5
22	134	133	132	135	133.5
23	130	123	132	119	126.0
24	127	122	118	129	124.0
25	111	108	121	133	118.3
26	120	125	126	128	124.8
27	125	119	121	126	122.8

Sample no.	DATA				Mean
28	135	125	128	127	128.8
29	129	130	113	120	123.0
30	131	120	122	130	125.8
31	128	133	116	127	126.0
32	124	116	125	138	125.8
33	125	121	124	135	126.3
34	133	138	120	124	128.8
35	122	126	126	120	123.5
36	123	123	123	130	124.8
37	123	125	128	127	125.8
38	128	125	142	118	128.3
39	121	122	127	122	123.0
40	115	119	121	119	118.5
41	119	128	115	126	122.0
42	113	121	118	122	118.5
43	123	130	119	124	124.0
44	118	126	116	125	121.3
45	120	119	125	122	121.5
46	119	118	120	119	119.0
47	114	132	116	128	122.5
48	127	125	115	116	120.8
49	127	118	133	129	126.8
50	124	114	123	117	119.5

SAMPLING EXPERIMENT

DATASET NUMBER B 4   NAME _____

Sample no.	DATA				Mean
1	130	125	128	127	127.5
2	128	124	133	132	129.3
3	124	132	128	129	128.3
4	114	131	132	137	128.5
5	128	137	133	124	130.5
6	129	140	123	136	132.0
7	117	122	126	131	124.0
8	129	123	137	118	126.8
9	116	118	129	125	122.0
10	116	120	125	122	120.8
11	128	128	132	137	131.3
12	124	122	118	124	122.0
13	127	117	113	117	118.5

Sample no.	DATA				Mean
14	128	126	130	129	128.3
15	120	123	122	122	121.8
16	122	123	128	130	125.8
17	123	126	113	132	123.5
18	125	114	129	128	124.0
19	121	119	128	128	124.0
20	121	123	120	121	121.3
21	129	127	125	111	123.0
22	120	124	130	122	124.0
23	117	131	125	130	125.8
24	135	131	121	130	129.3
25	130	126	122	118	124.0
26	124	119	125	127	123.8
27	117	133	132	129	127.8
28	120	120	127	121	122.0
29	113	124	130	131	124.5
30	117	121	125	130	123.3
31	114	124	125	122	121.3
32	123	129	128	131	127.8
33	120	128	132	129	127.3
34	130	138	134	115	129.3
35	109	125	128	125	121.8
36	124	133	123	120	125.0
37	122	124	123	124	123.3
38	123	113	120	123	119.8
39	131	138	119	114	125.5
40	129	117	131	135	128.0
41	125	128	133	110	124.0
42	127	117	120	132	124.0
43	113	126	116	114	117.3
44	127	124	122	116	122.3
45	120	129	116	119	121.0
46	126	118	119	128	122.8
47	122	123	122	113	120.0
48	131	132	119	130	128.0
49	138	130	126	118	128.0
50	117	134	124	122	124.3

SAMPLING EXPERIMENT

DATASET NUMBER B 5   NAME _____

Sample no.	DATA				Mean
1	129	125	134	134	130.5
2	123	128	130	123	126.0
3	137	129	140	126	133.0
4	135	125	120	122	125.5
5	124	138	134	132	132.0
6	139	129	118	135	130.3
7	125	125	129	122	125.3
8	138	124	133	124	129.8
9	128	114	117	115	118.5
10	115	125	124	124	122.0
11	123	127	122	120	123.0
12	133	129	125	129	129.0
13	116	117	133	117	120.8
14	137	122	124	124	126.8
15	121	123	120	132	124.0
16	127	121	125	128	125.3
17	121	115	128	117	120.3
18	118	115	122	129	121.0
19	125	122	121	131	124.8
20	127	120	117	130	123.5
21	124	124	135	120	125.8
22	107	125	131	123	121.5
23	124	118	137	125	126.0
24	121	127	129	137	128.5
25	123	130	125	123	125.3
26	127	123	124	119	123.3
27	119	125	128	131	125.8
28	125	137	129	122	128.3
29	123	129	130	122	126.0
30	123	129	133	136	130.3
31	121	129	122	129	125.3
32	133	126	130	121	127.5
33	135	125	118	127	126.3
34	122	126	120	122	122.5
35	132	129	122	116	124.8
36	110	133	120	118	120.3
37	123	117	132	132	126.0
38	120	127	129	125	125.3
39	129	130	127	121	126.8
40	131	118	129	122	125.0

Sample no.	DATA				Mean
41	132	120	126	114	123.0
42	119	118	129	130	124.0
43	120	119	129	129	124.3
44	130	126	127	139	130.5
45	121	127	116	131	123.8
46	118	124	128	127	124.3
47	133	126	118	124	125.3
48	120	124	127	130	125.3
49	128	122	130	126	126.5
50	130	133	124	123	127.5

SAMPLING EXPERIMENT

DATASET NUMBER C 1   NAME _____

Sample no.	DATA				Mean
1	127	136	134	123	130.0
2	125	134	121	132	128.0
3	124	131	128	124	126.8
4	130	130	129	129	129.5
5	137	136	125	128	131.5
6	133	137	139	119	132.0
7	141	136	133	136	136.5
8	129	142	136	136	135.8
9	128	120	121	111	120.0
10	117	130	119	110	119.0
11	129	121	125	123	124.5
12	117	125	127	138	126.8
13	119	122	125	121	121.8
14	131	132	121	122	126.5
15	121	122	116	119	119.5
16	128	121	120	133	125.5
17	117	127	127	122	123.3
18	124	127	121	129	125.3
19	116	115	130	129	122.5
20	120	122	120	118	120.0
21	124	124	127	118	123.3
22	116	128	126	122	123.0
23	125	123	122	132	125.5
24	123	124	125	136	127.0
25	118	121	131	115	121.3
26	125	118	118	122	120.8

Sample no.	DATA				Mean
27	128	119	123	122	123.0
28	117	111	127	119	118.5
29	130	124	127	112	123.3
30	115	127	122	118	120.5
31	126	113	118	128	121.3
32	129	133	119	117	124.5
33	133	122	116	105	119.0
34	126	127	125	118	124.0
35	112	126	118	126	120.5
36	122	116	118	125	120.3
37	114	110	116	117	114.3
38	130	122	122	122	124.0
39	118	124	112	121	118.8
40	117	125	123	130	123.8
41	116	121	113	125	118.8
42	126	119	108	116	117.3
43	118	123	118	119	119.5
44	121	128	123	119	122.8
45	117	105	130	114	116.5
46	110	123	126	122	120.3
47	122	123	121	122	122.0
48	127	128	119	115	122.3
49	124	129	119	122	123.5
50	114	124	117	128	120.8

SAMPLING EXPERIMENT

DATASET NUMBER C 2   NAME _____

Sample no.	DATA				Mean
1	132	123	130	127	128.0
2	135	125	122	126	127.0
3	130	135	129	120	128.5
4	132	136	105	126	124.8
5	128	128	126	124	126.5
6	123	121	133	121	124.5
7	116	130	128	134	127.0
8	125	134	120	135	128.5
9	125	110	119	118	118.0
10	110	119	120	129	119.5
11	127	131	125	129	128.0
12	123	124	108	134	122.3

Sample no.	DATA				Mean
13	119	125	117	120	120.3
14	118	120	110	119	116.8
15	122	124	117	116	119.8
16	113	114	118	123	117.0
17	122	128	122	115	121.8
18	132	116	123	120	122.8
19	126	124	114	118	120.5
20	119	121	126	123	122.3
21	127	127	123	119	124.0
22	114	107	127	119	116.8
23	122	128	124	119	123.3
24	123	116	120	119	119.5
25	128	117	123	122	122.5
26	123	112	124	139	124.5
27	117	118	118	119	118.0
28	135	125	122	118	125.0
29	127	119	111	116	118.3
30	114	125	124	124	121.8
31	118	123	114	115	117.5
32	126	111	123	122	120.5
33	115	128	122	122	121.8
34	118	117	133	123	122.8
35	120	133	116	124	123.3
36	113	126	106	123	117.0
37	132	119	135	123	127.3
38	126	122	123	115	121.5
39	123	122	125	121	122.8
40	121	129	121	110	120.3
41	124	118	114	121	119.3
42	132	122	124	127	126.3
43	125	123	122	118	122.0
44	122	115	127	133	124.3
45	119	123	119	122	120.8
46	102	122	117	124	116.3
47	121	124	116	125	121.5
48	118	116	118	113	116.3
49	121	117	121	120	119.8
50	127	120	113	112	118.0

SAMPLING EXPERIMENT

DATASET NUMBER C 3   NAME _____

Sample no.	DATA				Mean
1	128	127	130	127	128.0
2	123	130	129	129	127.8
3	130	129	132	134	131.3
4	129	116	132	131	127.0
5	129	131	140	130	132.5
6	130	123	128	129	127.5
7	133	129	136	123	130.3
8	139	127	136	128	132.5
9	125	114	118	113	117.5
10	117	121	112	129	119.8
11	131	124	123	121	124.8
12	123	116	127	124	122.5
13	121	118	122	115	119.0
14	125	116	126	118	121.3
15	115	121	125	127	122.0
16	123	120	126	109	119.5
17	119	114	120	125	119.5
18	108	126	139	111	121.0
19	122	102	109	131	116.0
20	125	122	121	117	121.3
21	121	119	123	123	121.5
22	123	119	116	122	120.0
23	114	118	132	132	124.0
24	120	126	123	126	123.8
25	128	122	117	122	122.3
26	124	121	124	121	122.5
27	122	125	125	126	124.5
28	129	123	128	123	125.8
29	124	130	122	111	121.8
30	112	122	122	124	120.0
31	133	119	111	111	118.5
32	128	129	117	126	125.0
33	113	131	124	116	121.0
34	113	121	125	125	121.0
35	109	122	124	124	119.8
36	120	115	123	115	118.3
37	115	120	116	120	117.8
38	132	121	119	128	125.0
39	123	117	114	118	118.0
40	118	117	127	121	120.8
41	126	122	125	114	121.8

Sample no.	DATA				Mean
42	118	120	114	130	120.5
43	117	115	123	125	120.0
44	119	130	113	118	120.0
45	130	122	112	125	122.3
46	131	116	118	117	120.5
47	121	125	124	100	117.5
48	126	118	128	121	123.3
49	128	122	125	119	123.5
50	130	123	119	125	124.3

SAMPLING EXPERIMENT

DATASET NUMBER C 4   NAME _____

Sample no.	DATA				Mean
1	128	126	126	135	128.8
2	138	134	124	135	132.8
3	142	136	121	134	133.3
4	126	128	128	125	126.8
5	129	131	129	123	128.0
6	135	122	133	130	130.0
7	138	119	139	126	130.5
8	129	135	138	127	132.3
9	129	116	115	117	119.3
10	113	127	127	122	122.3
11	121	136	128	124	127.3
12	105	125	126	134	122.5
13	115	120	128	131	123.5
14	117	124	113	120	118.5
15	114	131	119	117	120.3
16	128	116	122	125	122.8
17	115	127	118	122	120.5
18	125	118	116	121	120.0
19	120	118	129	125	123.0
20	123	119	120	112	118.5
21	120	113	114	105	113.0
22	125	114	119	126	121.0
23	122	113	123	111	117.3
24	115	128	116	122	120.3
25	121	119	110	127	119.3
26	109	118	120	120	116.8
27	120	127	120	132	124.8

Sample no.	DATA				Mean
28	121	132	108	119	120.0
29	123	113	116	118	117.5
30	116	124	116	123	119.8
31	132	126	125	125	127.0
32	124	114	136	119	123.3
33	126	119	124	125	123.5
34	125	124	114	110	118.3
35	127	121	122	114	121.0
36	114	118	115	106	113.3
37	124	130	127	129	127.5
38	122	124	132	120	124.5
39	117	114	114	114	114.8
40	124	121	115	123	120.8
41	118	110	127	135	122.5
42	127	119	118	115	119.8
43	114	121	123	118	119.0
44	119	124	113	124	120.0
45	121	128	119	123	122.8
46	122	126	122	124	123.5
47	125	127	124	116	123.0
48	124	116	128	115	120.8
49	124	112	129	114	119.8
50	123	121	128	127	124.8

SAMPLING EXPERIMENT

DATASET NUMBER C 5   NAME _____

Sample no.	DATA				Mean
1	132	118	134	131	128.8
2	127	115	139	137	129.5
3	132	127	132	139	132.5
4	133	129	138	127	131.8
5	129	129	136	131	131.3
6	127	129	128	144	132.0
7	138	139	124	130	132.8
8	130	133	131	127	130.3
9	118	119	111	110	114.5
10	120	121	131	126	124.5
11	130	114	126	117	121.8
12	120	116	113	129	119.5
13	122	114	127	116	119.8

Sample no.	DATA				Mean
14	122	117	126	122	121.8
15	119	119	119	113	117.5
16	116	121	124	125	121.5
17	117	118	135	111	120.3
18	130	114	123	111	119.5
19	127	117	122	117	120.8
20	121	120	113	113	116.8
21	116	136	121	125	124.5
22	124	120	113	115	118.0
23	135	110	131	119	123.8
24	108	121	128	118	118.8
25	122	121	126	120	122.3
26	132	121	130	117	125.0
27	111	108	123	135	119.3
28	122	121	120	111	118.5
29	122	127	127	115	122.8
30	121	130	119	127	124.3
31	118	122	120	113	118.3
32	131	116	113	115	118.8
33	121	120	118	118	119.3
34	113	124	125	122	121.0
35	131	115	115	122	120.8
36	115	125	115	117	118.0
37	127	124	109	117	119.3
38	123	112	129	120	121.0
39	112	124	119	119	118.5
40	125	119	116	128	122.0
41	115	121	119	122	119.3
42	126	124	115	130	123.8
43	123	117	113	125	119.5
44	120	123	120	116	119.8
45	117	117	124	132	122.5
46	120	119	121	127	121.8
47	120	120	128	123	122.8
48	132	115	130	119	124.0
49	111	118	110	113	113.0
50	131	123	119	121	123.5

SAMPLING EXPERIMENT

DATASET NUMBER D 1   NAME _____

Sample no.	DATA				Mean
1	133	131	123	120	126.8
2	134	128	133	131	131.5
3	128	140	133	128	132.3
4	131	120	134	132	129.3
5	121	139	129	133	130.5
6	132	128	128	129	129.3
7	129	128	134	128	129.8
8	132	135	133	127	131.8
9	126	129	131	123	127.3
10	131	129	129	123	128.0
11	132	123	130	138	130.8
12	139	136	136	126	134.3
13	135	139	119	126	129.8
14	135	137	128	119	129.8
15	133	123	130	135	130.3
16	133	133	135	133	133.5
17	133	136	130	120	129.8
18	115	131	135	127	127.0
19	137	127	131	133	132.0
20	134	135	132	133	133.5
21	135	141	126	133	133.8
22	127	125	125	123	125.0
23	143	131	133	126	133.3
24	134	136	128	134	133.0
25	130	142	139	126	134.3
26	119	130	135	132	129.0
27	129	139	127	119	128.5
28	126	136	133	137	133.0
29	120	137	129	137	130.8
30	125	129	126	125	126.3
31	128	133	132	130	130.8
32	128	125	130	140	130.8
33	129	127	127	134	129.3
34	139	134	120	127	130.0
35	125	122	126	133	126.5
36	126	116	127	134	125.8
37	139	146	136	129	137.5
38	130	136	125	127	129.5
39	124	128	131	138	130.3
40	136	133	126	129	131.0

Sample no.	DATA				Mean
41	134	140	126	141	135.3
42	125	136	126	141	132.0
43	131	121	129	127	127.0
44	129	138	140	123	132.5
45	134	142	128	139	135.8
46	129	133	136	137	133.8
47	133	137	119	133	130.5
48	136	122	135	128	130.3
49	134	126	150	130	135.0
50	135	132	133	130	132.5

SAMPLING EXPERIMENT

DATASET NUMBER D 2   NAME _____

Sample no.	DATA				Mean
1	128	121	135	138	130.5
2	138	138	128	115	129.8
3	132	125	127	132	129.0
4	135	123	129	131	129.5
5	129	127	128	128	128.0
6	139	119	127	125	127.5
7	121	128	121	130	125.0
8	127	127	135	139	132.0
9	133	129	129	131	130.5
10	123	143	130	122	129.5
11	138	135	140	135	137.0
12	126	137	131	131	131.3
13	134	146	135	134	137.3
14	126	129	123	131	127.3
15	127	133	133	126	129.8
16	144	137	139	131	137.8
17	138	148	129	123	134.5
18	136	129	134	140	134.8
19	133	133	134	134	133.5
20	126	134	128	128	129.0
21	145	125	135	127	133.0
22	139	136	118	128	130.3
23	140	138	128	133	134.8
24	132	135	123	126	129.0
25	135	136	127	127	131.3
26	132	128	134	134	132.0

Sample no.	DATA				Mean
27	125	136	130	141	133.0
28	140	133	128	129	132.5
29	122	128	132	124	126.5
30	131	133	131	128	130.8
31	132	124	143	132	132.8
32	138	138	127	134	134.3
33	129	123	129	127	127.0
34	140	137	141	136	138.5
35	130	123	126	128	126.8
36	123	125	136	144	132.0
37	136	137	137	132	135.5
38	134	123	129	151	134.3
39	129	128	141	137	133.8
40	123	125	136	135	129.8
41	135	143	139	127	136.0
42	145	128	125	138	134.0
43	126	137	118	135	129.0
44	126	130	134	125	128.8
45	126	131	119	128	126.0
46	126	124	127	133	127.5
47	134	131	135	129	132.3
48	131	126	134	137	132.0
49	132	129	126	137	131.0
50	124	120	143	130	129.3

SAMPLING EXPERIMENT

DATASET NUMBER D 3   NAME _____

Sample no.	DATA				Mean
1	129	126	135	147	134.3
2	132	128	131	124	128.8
3	135	127	122	130	128.5
4	131	140	119	128	129.5
5	135	140	129	133	134.3
6	125	147	138	132	135.5
7	122	128	125	117	123.0
8	131	134	127	141	133.3
9	130	124	124	125	125.8
10	131	140	129	128	132.0
11	128	123	131	133	128.8
12	126	143	139	127	133.8
13	135	143	135	126	134.8

Sample no.	DATA				Mean
14	129	124	141	131	131.3
15	142	124	139	136	135.3
16	132	133	132	127	131.0
17	129	135	134	127	131.3
18	136	127	134	142	134.8
19	137	131	132	131	132.8
20	133	137	124	135	132.3
21	132	124	123	134	128.3
22	127	137	140	135	134.8
23	138	127	134	131	132.5
24	136	128	129	139	133.0
25	133	127	137	137	133.5
26	131	141	127	133	133.0
27	126	125	145	133	132.3
28	140	132	133	128	133.3
29	120	126	135	134	128.8
30	130	130	131	133	131.0
31	142	140	135	133	137.5
32	130	138	134	150	138.0
33	133	121	142	119	128.8
34	133	135	121	124	128.3
35	133	128	126	145	133.0
36	133	127	136	135	132.8
37	142	133	131	127	133.3
38	130	128	139	131	132.0
39	133	140	126	137	134.0
40	130	128	132	129	129.8
41	136	135	137	135	135.8
42	127	126	148	136	134.3
43	143	128	125	133	132.3
44	139	135	137	138	137.3
45	136	140	130	120	131.5
46	126	139	129	133	131.8
47	137	133	134	139	135.8
48	121	130	135	124	127.5
49	123	137	133	136	132.3
50	125	133	139	139	134.0

SAMPLING EXPERIMENT

DATASET NUMBER D 4   NAME _____

Sample no.	DATA				Mean
1	129	134	135	132	132.5
2	132	124	124	135	128.8
3	124	140	126	130	130.0
4	126	133	131	129	129.8
5	134	121	128	136	129.8
6	139	128	135	123	131.3
7	118	130	126	131	126.3
8	126	128	129	136	129.8
9	133	127	117	137	128.5
10	128	123	133	142	131.5
11	130	123	128	133	128.5
12	140	135	141	139	138.8
13	121	118	130	137	126.5
14	142	134	144	140	140.0
15	126	127	124	121	124.5
16	142	144	124	130	135.0
17	130	137	138	135	135.0
18	130	132	129	124	128.8
19	131	134	130	127	130.5
20	133	138	132	122	131.3
21	130	130	131	127	129.5
22	126	134	133	138	132.8
23	132	134	129	133	132.0
24	130	130	130	134	131.0
25	135	127	137	127	131.5
26	129	120	124	125	124.5
27	135	134	148	138	138.8
28	134	138	129	127	132.0
29	137	154	133	128	138.0
30	126	144	127	143	135.0
31	132	135	121	136	131.0
32	134	131	129	136	132.5
33	123	132	122	133	127.5
34	125	139	138	132	133.5
35	129	132	124	141	131.5
36	130	131	126	134	130.3
37	124	129	139	132	131.0
38	133	135	133	134	133.8
39	132	130	118	136	129.0
40	133	138	145	132	137.0

Sample no.	DATA				Mean
41	139	123	126	137	131.3
42	140	132	124	129	131.3
43	137	135	130	112	128.5
44	137	125	139	125	131.5
45	130	119	132	131	128.0
46	133	145	129	134	135.3
47	134	124	131	129	129.5
48	143	127	128	131	132.3
49	132	132	122	131	129.3
50	134	143	130	132	134.8

SAMPLING EXPERIMENT

DATASET NUMBER D 5   NAME _____

Sample no.	DATA				Mean
1	129	135	129	133	131.5
2	131	140	122	139	133.0
3	126	141	144	125	134.0
4	138	132	134	124	132.0
5	126	128	125	127	126.5
6	134	125	139	126	131.0
7	133	131	123	139	131.5
8	128	132	134	138	133.0
9	138	132	135	129	133.5
10	135	135	124	143	134.3
11	132	136	132	131	132.8
12	135	138	133	127	133.3
13	130	122	134	130	129.0
14	133	129	136	142	135.0
15	129	137	138	126	132.5
16	142	131	132	130	133.8
17	126	124	138	132	130.0
18	121	138	136	145	135.0
19	138	128	142	122	132.5
20	136	129	132	142	134.8
21	132	133	138	120	130.8
22	135	131	130	138	133.5
23	131	128	125	133	129.3
24	129	134	144	124	132.8
25	128	129	128	132	129.3
26	127	128	117	135	126.8

Sample no.	DATA				Mean
27	142	132	127	130	132.8
28	134	139	131	134	134.5
29	131	136	126	130	130.8
30	134	131	128	133	131.5
31	129	133	135	139	134.0
32	126	135	125	129	128.8
33	132	144	137	132	136.3
34	136	130	134	126	131.5
35	130	108	128	120	121.5
36	126	127	136	134	130.8
37	124	132	131	130	129.3
38	136	137	126	143	135.5
39	130	127	127	130	128.5
40	132	127	143	135	134.3
41	133	134	135	139	135.3
42	134	134	127	143	134.5
43	128	128	124	145	131.3
44	136	129	129	134	132.0
45	127	126	133	128	128.5
46	123	123	129	133	127.0
47	135	135	140	134	136.0
48	131	132	123	126	128.0
49	141	129	132	125	131.8
50	135	131	130	134	132.5

Appendix C

National and international standards relating to quality control

Much of the area of application of statistical methods to industry is covered by some useful national and international standards. The following list gives the reference numbers of those related to material in this volume. References are given to International (ISO), American (ANSI), British (BS), German (DIN) and Japanese (JIS) standards. In addition there are Draft International Standards (DIS) and Draft Proposals (DP). They are listed under the ISO reference, where applicable, with the following symbols relating to whether or not they are identical to the ISO standard:

$$\equiv \quad \text{completely identical}$$
$$= \quad \text{technically equivalent}$$
$$\neq \quad \text{related but not equivalent}$$

1. GENERAL TERMINOLOGY AND SYMBOLS

ISO 3534: 1977 *Statistics – Vocabulary and symbols*
 $\equiv$ BS 5532: Part 1: 1978 *Statistical terminology. Part 1. Glossary of terms relating to probability and general terms relating to statistics*
 $\neq$ JIS Z 8101–1981: *Glossary and terms used in quality control*
ISO/DP 3534–1 *Statistics – Vocabulary and symbols – Part 1: Probability and general statistical terms*
ISO/DIS 3534–2 *Statistics – Vocabulary and symbols – Part 2: Statistical quality control*
ISO 3534–3: 1985 *Statistics – Vocabulary and symbols – Part 3: Design of experiments*
 $\equiv$ BS 5532: Part 3: 1986 *Statistical terminology. Part 3. Glossary of terms relating to the design of experiments*

ISO 8402: 1986 *Quality – Vocabulary*
≡ BS 4778: Part 1: 1987 *Quality vocabulary. Part 1. International terms*
≡ DIN 55 350 Teil 11 (5/87) *Begriffe der Qualitätssicherung und Statistik; Grundbegriffe der Qualitätssicherung*
ANSI/ASQC A2–1987 *Terms, symbols and definitions for acceptance sampling*
ANSI/ASQC A3–1987 *Quality systems terminology*

2. ACQUISITION AND INTERPRETATION OF STATISTICAL DATA

ISO 377: 1985 *Wrought steel – Selection and preparation of sample and test pieces*
≠ BS 1837: 1970 *Methods for the sampling of iron, steel, permanent magnet alloys and ferro-alloys*
ISO 1988: 1975 *Hard coal – Sampling*
= BS 1017: Part 1: 1977 *Methods for sampling of coal and coke. Part 1. Sampling of coal*
ISO 2309: 1980 *Coke – Sampling*
≠ BS 1017: Part 2: 1960 (1988) *Methods for sampling of coal and coke. Part 2. Sampling of coke*
ISO 2602: 1980 *Statistical interpretation of test results – Estimation of the mean – Confidence interval*
≡ BS 2846: Part 2: 1981 *Statistical interpretation of data. Part 2. Estimation of the mean: confidence interval*
≠ JIS Z 9051–1963: *Interval estimation of the population mean (standard deviation unknown)*
ISO 2854: 1976 *Statistical interpretation of data – Techniques of estimation and tests relating to means and variances*
≡ BS 2846: Part 4: 1976 *Statistical interpretation of data. Part 4. Techniques of estimation and tests relating to means and variances*
= DIN 55 303 Teil 2 (5/84) *Statistiche Auswertung von Daten; Testverfahren und Vertrauensbereiche für Erwartungswerte und Varianzen*
≠ JIS Z 9042–1962: *Significance test of the difference between the population mean and a given value (standard deviation known, one-sided)*
≠ JIS Z 9043–1962: *Significance test of the difference between the population mean and a given value (standard deviation known, two-sided)*
≠ JIS Z 9044–1962: *Significance test of the difference between the population mean and a given value (standard deviation unknown,*

one-sided)

≠ JIS Z 9045–1962: *Significance test of the difference between the population mean and a given value (standard deviation unknown, two-sided)*

≠ JIS Z 9046–1965: *Significance test of the difference between two population means (standard deviation known, one-sided)*

≠ JIS Z 9047–1979: *Significance test of the difference between two population means (standard deviation known, two-sided)*

≠ JIS Z 9048–1979: *Significance test of the difference between two population means (standard deviation unknown, one-sided)*

≠ JIS Z 9049–1965: *Significance test of the difference between two population means (standard deviation unknown, two-sided)*

≠ JIS Z 9052–1963: *Interval estimation of the difference between two population means (standard deviation known)*

≠ JIS Z 9053–1963: *Interval estimation of the difference between two population means (standard deviation unknown)*

≠ JIS Z 9054–1966: *Significance test of equality of the population variance and a given value (one-sided)*

≠ JIS Z 9055–1966: *Significance test of equality of the population variance and a given value (two-sided)*

≠ JIS Z 9056–1979: *Significance test of equality of two population variances (one-sided)*

≠ JIS Z 9057–1966: *Significance test of equality of two population variances (two-sided)*

≠ JIS Z 9058–1966: *Interval estimation of the population variance*

≠ JIS Z 9059–1966: *Interval estimation of the population variance ratio*

ISO 3165: 1976 *Sampling of chemical products for industrial use – Safety in sampling*

≠ BS 5309: Part 1: 1976 *Methods for sampling chemical products. Part 1. Introduction and general principles*

ISO 3207: 1975 *Statistical interpretation of data – Determination of a statistical tolerance interval*

≡ BS 2846: Part 3: 1975 *Statistical interpretation of data. Part 3. Determination of a statistical tolerance interval*

≡ DIN 55 303 Teil 5 (2/87) *Statistiche Auswertung von Daten; Bestimmung eines statistichen Anteilsbereichs*

ISO 3301–1975 *Statistical interpretation of data – Comparison of two means in the case of paired observations*

≡ BS 2846: Part 6: 1976 *Statistical interpretation of data. Part 6. Comparison of two means in the case of paired observations*

ISO 3494–1976 *Statistical interpretation of data – Power of tests relating to means and variances*

≡ BS 2846: Part 5: 1977 *Statistical interpretation of data. Part 5. Power of tests relating to means and variances*

≡ DIN 55 303 Teil 2 (5/84) *Statistiche Auswertung von Daten; Testverfahren und Vertranensbereich für Erwartungswerte und Varianzen*

ISO 4259: 1979 *Petroleum products – Determination and application of precision data in relation to methods of test*

≡ BS 4306: 1981 (1988) *Method for determination and application of precision data in relation to methods of test for petroleum products*

ISO/DIS 5479 *Normality tests*

= BS 2846: Part 7: 1984 *Statistical interpretation of data. Part 7. Tests for departure from normality*

= DIN ISO 5479 *Test auf Normalverteilung*

ISO 5725: 1986 *Precision of test methods – Determination of repeatability and reproducibility for a standard test method by inter-laboratory tests*

≡ BS 5497: Part 1: 1987 *Precision of test methods. Part 1. Guide for the determination of repeatability and reproducibility for a standard test method by inter-laboratory tests*

= DIN ISO 5725 *Präzision von Meßverfahren; Ermittlung der Wiederhol – und Vergleichpräzision von festgelegten Meßverfahren durch Ringversuche*

≠ JIS Z 8402–1974: *General rules for permissible tolerance of chemical analysis and physical test*

ISO/DIS 7585 *Statistical interpretation of data – Comparison of a proportion with a given value*

ISO/DP 7868 *Estimation of a proportion*

ISO/DP 7874 *Applications of statistical methods in standardization and specifications (Guide)*

ISO/DP 7912 *Comparison of two proportions*

ISO 8213: 1986 *Chemical products for industrial use – Sampling techniques – Solid chemical products in the form of particles varying from powders to coarse lumps*

≠ BS 5309: Part 4: 1976 *Methods for sampling chemical products. Part 4. Sampling of solids*

ISO/DIS 8595 *Interpretation of statistical data – Estimation of a median*

ANSI/ASQC E2–1984 *Guide to inspection planning*

BS 2846: Part 1: 1975 *Statistical interpretation of data. Part 1. Routine analysis of quantitative data*

JIS Z 9041–1968: *Presentation and reduction of data*

BS 2987: 1958 *Notes on the application of statistics to paper testing*

BS 3518: Part 5: 1966 (1984) *Methods of fatigue testing. Part 5. Guide to the application of statistics*

BS 4237: 1967 *Report on the reproducibility of methods of chemical*

analysis used in the iron and steel industry
BS 5309: Part 2: 1976 *Methods for sampling chemical products. Part 2. Sampling of gases*
BS 5309: Part 3: 1976 *Methods for sampling chemical products. Part 3. Sampling of liquids*
BS 5324: 1976 *Guide to the application of statistics to rubber testing*
BS 6143: 1981 *Guide to the determination and use of quality related costs*
JIS Z 9031–1956: *Random sampling methods*
JIS Z 9050–1963: *Interval estimation of the population mean (standard deviation known)*

3. ACCEPTANCE SAMPLING

ISO/DP 2859 Part 0 *Sampling procedures for inspection by attributes – Introduction to the ISO 2859 attribute sampling system (Revision of ISO 2859 Addendum 1)*
 ≠ JIS Z 9001–1980: *General rules for sampling inspection procedure*
ISO 2859–1: 1989 *Sampling procedures for inspection by attributes – Part 1: Sampling plans indexed by acceptable quality level (AQL) for lot-by-lot inspection*
 ≠ ANSI/ASQC Z1.4–1981 *Sampling procedures and tables for inspection by attributes*
 = BS 6001: Part 1: 1972 *Sampling procedures and tables for inspection by attributes. Part 1. Specification for sampling plans indexed by acceptable quality level (AQL) for lot-by-lot inspection*
 ≠ JIS Z 9002–1956: *Single sampling inspection plans for desired operating characteristics by attributes*
 ≠ JIS Z 9015–1980: *Sampling inspection procedures and tables by attributes with severity adjustment (receiving inspection where a consumer can select suppliers)*
ISO 2859–2: 1985 *Sampling procedures for inspection by attributes – Part 2: Sampling plans indexed by limiting quality (LQ) for isolated lot inspection*
 = BS 6001: Part 2: 1984 *Sampling procedures for inspection by attributes. Part 2. Specification for sampling plans indexed by limiting quality (LQ) for isolated lot inspection*
 = DIN 40 080 Teil 2 *Annahmestichprobemprüfung anhand der Anzahl fehlerhafter Einheiten oder Fehler (Attributprüfung); Nach der rückzuweisenden Qualitätsgrenzlage (LQ) geordnete Stichprobenanweisungen für die Prüfung einzelner Lose*
ISO/DIS 2859–3.2: *Sampling procedures and charts for inspection by*

attributes – Skip lot sampling procedures
= ANSI S1–1987 *An attribute skip-lot sampling program*
= BS 6001: Part 3: 1986 *Sampling procedures for inspection by attributes. Part 3. Specification for skip-lot procedures*
ISO 3951–1989 *Sampling procedures and charts for inspection by variables for percent nonconforming*
≠ ANSI Z1.9–1980 *Sampling procedures and tables for inspection by variables for percent non-conforming*
≠ BS 6002: 1979 *Sampling procedures and charts for inspection by variables for percent defective*
≠ 00DIN ISO 3951 *Verfahren und Tabellen für Stichprobenprüfungen auf den Anteil fehlerhafter Einheiten in Prozent anhand quantitativer Merkmale (Variablenprüfung)*
≠ JIS Z 9003–1979: *Single sampling inspection plans having desired operating characteristics by variables (standard deviation known)*
≠ JIS Z 9004–1983: *Single sampling inspection plans having desired operating characteristics by variables (standard deviation unknown and single limit specified)*
ISO 5022–1979 *Shaped refractory products – Sampling and acceptance testing*
≡ BS 6065: 1981 *Methods for sampling and acceptance testing of shaped refractory products*
ISO/DIS 8422.2 *Sequential sampling plans for inspection by attributes (proportion of non-conforming items, and mean number of non-conformities per unit)*
≠ JIS Z 9009–1962: *Sequential sampling inspection plans having desired operating characteristics by attributes*
ISO/DIS 8423.2 *Sequential sampling plans for inspection by variables for percent non-conforming (known standard deviation)*
≠ JIS Z 9010–1979: *Sequential sampling inspection plans having desired operating characteristics by variables (standard deviation known)*
ISO/DP 8550 *Guide for selection of an acceptance sampling system, scheme or plan for inspection of discrete items in lots* (to be published as a Technical Report)
BS 2635: 1955 *Drafting specifications based on limiting the number of defectives permitted in small samples*
JIS Z 9006–1956: *Single sampling inspection plans with screening by attributes*
JIS Z 9008–1958: *Continuous sampling inspection plans for continuous production by attributes*
JIS Z 9011–1963: *Single sampling inspection plans by attributes with adjustment*

4. STATISTICAL PROCESS CONTROL

ISO/Draft TR 7871 *Introduction to cumulative sum charts*
ISO/DIS 7873 *Control charts for arithmetic average with warning limits*
ISO/DIS 7870 *Control charts – General guide and introduction*
ISO/DIS 7966 *Acceptance control charts*
ISO/DIS 8258 *Shewhart control charts*
   = JIS Z 9021–1954: *Control chart method*
   ≠ JIS Z 9022–1959: *Median control chart*
   ≠ JIS Z 9023–1963: *x control chart*
ANSI/ASQC A1–1987 *Definitions, symbols, formulas and tables for control charts*
ANSI/ASQC B1–1986 *Guide for quality control charts*
ANSI/ASQC B2–1986 *Control chart method for analyzing data*
ANSI/ASQC B3–1986 *Control chart method of controlling quality during production*
BS 600: 1935 *Application of statistical methods to industrial standardization and quality control*
BS 2564: 1955 *Control chart technique when manufacturing to a specification, with special reference to articles machined to dimensional tolerances*
BS 5700: 1984 *Guide to process control using quality control chart methods and CuSum techniques*
BS 5701: 1980 *Guide to number-defective charts for quality control*
BS 5703: Part 1: 1980 *Guide to data analysis and quality control using CuSum techniques. Part 1. Introduction to CuSum charting*
BS 5703: Part 2: 1980 *Guide to data analysis and quality control using CuSum techniques. Part 2. Decision rules and statistical tests for CuSum charts and tabulations*
BS 5703: Part 3: 1981 *Guide to data analysis and quality control using CuSum techniques. Part 3. CuSum methods for process/quality control by measurement*
BS 5703: Part 4: 1982 *Guide to data analysis and quality control using CuSum techniques. Part 4. CuSums for counted/attributes data*
JIS Z 8206–1982: *Graphical symbols for process chart*

5. QUALITY MANAGEMENT

ISO 9000: 1987 *Quality management and quality assurance standards – Guidelines for selection and use*
   ≡ ANSI/ASQC Q90–1987 *Quality management and quality assurance standards – Guidelines for selection and use*
   ≡ BS 5750: Part 0: Section 0.1: 1987 *Quality systems. Part 0. Principal*

concepts and applications. Section 0.1. Guide to selection and use
≡ DIN ISO 9000 (5/87) *Leitfaden zur Auswahl und Anwendung der Normen zu Qualitätsmanagement, Elementen eines Qualitätssicherungssystems und zu Qualitätssicherungs-Nachweisstufen*
ISO 9001: 1987 *Quality systems – Model for quality assurance in design/development, production, installation and servicing*
≡ ANSI/ASQC Q91–1987 *Quality systems – Model for quality assurance in design/development, production, installation and servicing*
≡ BS 5750: Part 1: 1987 *Quality systems. Part 1. Specification for design/development, production, installation and servicing*
≡ DIN ISO 9001 (5/87) *Qualitätssicherungssysteme; Qualitätssicherungs-Nachweisstufe für Entwicklung und Konstruktion, Produktion, Montage und Kundendienst*
ISO 9002: 1987 *Quality systems – Model for quality assurance in production and installation*
≡ ANSI/ASQC Q92–1987 *Quality systems – Model for quality assurance assurance in production and installation*
≡ BS 5750: Part 2: 1987 *Quality systems. Part 2. Specification for production and installation*
≡ DIN ISO 9002 (5/87) *Qualitätssicherungssysteme; Qualitätssicherungs-Nachweisstufe für Produktion und Montage*
ISO 9003: 1987 *Quality systems – Model for quality assurance in final inspection and test*
≡ ANSI/ASQC Q93–1987 *Quality systems – Model for quality assurance in final inspection and test*
≡ BS 5750: Part 3: 1987 *Quality systems. Part 3. Specification for final inspection and test*
≡ DIN ISO 9003 (5/87) *Qualitätssicherungssysteme; Qualitätssicherungs-Nachweisstufe für Endprufungen*
ISO 9004: 1987 *Quality management and quality system elements – Guidelines*
≡ ANSI/ASQC Q94–1987 *Quality management and quality system elements – Guidelines*
≡ BS 5750: Part 0: Section 0.2: 1987 *Quality systems. Part 0. Principal concepts and applications. Section 0.2. Guide to quality management and quality system elements*
≡ DIN ISO 9004 (5/87) *Qualitätsmanagement und Elemente eines Qualitätssicherungssystems; Leitfaden*
ANSI/ASQC C1–1985 *Specifications of general requirements for a quality program, REVISED EDITION*
ANSI/ASQC Q1–1986 *Generic guidelines for auditing of quality systems*
ANSI/ASQC Z1.15–1979 *Generic guidelines for quality systems*
BS 5750: Part 4: 1981 *Quality systems – Guide to the use of BS 5750:*

Part 1 'Specification for design, manufacture and installation'
BS 5750: Part 5: 1981 *Quality systems – Guide to the use of BS 5750: Part 2 'Specification for manufacture and installation'*
BS 5750: Part 6: 1981 *Quality systems – Guide to the use of BS 5750: Part 3 'Specification for final inspection and test'*

References

American Supplier Institute (1987) *Fifth Symposium on Taguchi Methods*, Dearborn, Michigan.

Anscombe, F. J. (1958) Rectifying inspection of a continuous output. *J. Amer. Statist. Ass.*, **53**, 702–19.

ASF Tables (1944) *Sampling Inspection Procedures; Quality Control*, Army Services Forces, Office of the Chief of Ordnance, Washington.

Bagshaw, M. L. and Johnson, N. L. (1975) The effect of serial correlation on the performance of CUSUM tests. II, *Technometrics*, **17**, 73–80.

Baillie, D. (1987) Multivariate Acceptance Sampling in *Frontiers in Statistical Quality Control*, **3**, Physica-Verlag, Heidelberg 83–115.

Baillie, D. H. (1988) The revision of ISO 3951 (1981). *J. Qual. Technology,* **20**, 21–49.

Baillie, D. (1989) Multivariate Acceptance Sampling: combined attributes and variables plans. To be published.

Banzhaf, R. A. and Bruger, R. M. (1970) MIL-STD-1235 (ORD) single and multi-level continuous sampling procedures and tables for inspection by attributes. *J. Qual. Tech.*, **2**, 41–53.

Barnard, G. A. (1959) Control charts and stochastic processes. *J. R. Statist. Soc.*, B, **21**, 239–71.

Beattie, D. W. (1962) A continuous acceptance sampling procedure based upon a cumulative sum chart for the number of defectives. *Applied Statistics*, **11**, 137–47.

Beattie, D. W. (1968) Patrol inspection. *Applied Statistics*, **17**, 1–16.

Becknell, D. (1987) Die cast 5.0L throttle body porosity study. *Fifth Symposium on Taguchi Methods*, American Supplier Institute, Dearborn, Michigan.

Bishop, A. B. (1957) A model for optimum control of stochastic sampled data systems. *Operations Research*, **5**, 546–50.

Bishop, A. B. (1960) Discrete random feedback models in industrial quality control. *The Ohio State University Engineering Experimental Station Bull.*, 183v, 29n, 5 September.

Bissell, A. F. (1969) Cusum techniques for quality control. *Applied Statistics*, **18**, 1–30.

Bissell, A. F. (1973) Process monitoring with variable element sizes. *Applied Statistics*, **22**, 226–38.

Bissell, A. F. (1979) A semi-parabolic mask for CuSum charts. *The Statistician*, **28**, 1–7.

Bowker, A. H. (1956) Continuous sampling plans, *Proc. Third Berkeley Symp. Math. Statist. & Prob.*, University of California Press, Berkeley and Los Angeles, pp. 75–85.

Bowker, A. H. and Good, H. P. (1952) *Sampling Inspection by Variables*, McGraw-Hill, New York.

Box, G. E. P. and Jenkins, G. M. (1962) Some statistical aspects of adaptive optimisation and control, *J. R. Statist. Soc.,* B, **24**, 297–343.

Box, G. E. P. and Jenkins, G. M. (1963) *Further Contributions to Adaptive Quality Control: Simultaneous Estimation of Dynamics: Non-zero Costs,* Technical Report No. 19, Dept. of Statistics, University of Wisconsin.

Box, G. E. P. and Jenkins, G. M. (1976) *Time Series Analysis: Forecasting and Control*, Holden-Day, San Francisco, C.A.

Bravo, P. C. (1980) Sampling inspection by variables with known variance. *Bull. App. Statistics,* **7**, 203–22.

Bravo, P. C. (1981) Correction to 'Sampling inspection by variables with known variance'. *Bull. App. Statistics,* **8**, 116–26.

Bravo, P. C. (1984) Sampling plans by variables with double specification limits. *Frontiers in Statistical Quality Control,* **2**, 160–74. Physica-Verlag, Würzburg.

Brook, D. and Evans, D. A. (1972) An approach to the probability distribution of cusum run length. *Biometrika,* **59**, 539–50.

BS 24, (1985) *BSI Handbook 24. Quality Control*, British Standards Institute, London.

Champ, C. W. and Woodall, W. H. (1987) Exact results for Shewhart control charts with supplementary runs rules. *Technometrics,* **29**, 393–401.

Chatfield, C. (1984) *Statistics for Technology*, Penguin Books, Harmondsworth, Middlesex.

Chiu, W. K. (1973) Comments on the economic design of $\bar{x}$-charts. *J. Amer. Statist. Ass.,* **68**, 919–21.

Chiu, W. K. and Wetherill, G. B. (1973) The economic design of continuous inspection procedures: a review paper. *Inst. Stat. Rev.,* **41**, 357–73.

Chiu, W. K. and Wetherill, G. B. (1975) Quality control practices. *Int. J. Prod. Res.,* **13**, 175–82.

Collani, E. von (1989) *The Economic Design of Control Charts*. B. G. Teubner, Stuttgart.

Crosby, P. (1985) *Quality is Free*, McGraw-Hill, New York.

Crowder, S. V. (1987) A simple method for studying run-length distributions of exponentially weighted moving average charts. *Technometrics,* **29**, 401–7.

Daffin, C., Duncombe, P., Hills, M. G., North, P. M. and Wetherill, G. B. (1986) A micro computer survey analysis package designed for the developing countries. *Pacific Statistical Congress,* 238–42. Elsevier Science Publishers, B.V.

Davies, O. L. and Goldsmith, P. (1972) *Statistical Methods in Research and Production* (4th edn.), Oliver and Boyd, Edinburgh.

De Bruyn, O. S. Van Dobben (1968) *Cumulative Sum Tests: Theory and Practice*, Griffin, London.

Deming, W. E. (1982) *Out of the Crisis: Quality, Production and Competitive Position*, Cambridge University Press, Cambridge.

Derman, C., Johns, M. V. (Jr) and Lieberman, G. J. (1959) Continuous sampling procedures without control. *Ann. Math. Statist.,* **30**, 1175–91.

Dodge, H. F. (1943) A sampling inspection plan for continuous production. *Ann. Math. Statist.,* **14**, 264–79.

Dodge, H. F. (1955) Chain sampling inspection plan. *Industrial Quality Control*, **11**, 10–13.

Dodge, H. F. (1956) Skip-lot sampling plan. *Industrial Quality Control*, **12**, 3–5.

Dodge, H. F. and Romig, H. G. (1929) A method of sampling inspection. *Bell Syst. Tech. J.*, **8**, 613–31.

Dodge, H. F. and Romig, H. G. (1959) *Sampling Inspection Tables; Single and Double Sampling* (2nd edn.), John Wiley, New York.

Dodge, H. F. and Torrey, M. N. (1951a) Additional continuous sampling inspection plans. *Industrial Quality Control*, **7**, 5–9.

Dodge, H. F. and Torrey, M. N. (1951b) *Continuous Sampling Inspection Plans*, Monograph 1834, Bell Telephone System Technical Publications.

Duncan, A. J. (1974) *Quality Control and Industrial Statistics*, Irwin, Homewood, Illinois.

Enkawa, T. (1980) *Quality*, **10**(4).

Ewan, W. D. and Kemp, K. W. (1960) Sampling inspection of continuous processes with no autocorrelation between successive results. *Biometrika*, **47**, 363–80.

Flesselles, J. (1985) Compliments pratiques pour la détermination des éléments d'un plan de contrôle par la méthode d'Enkawa. *Revue de Statistiques Appliquees*, **33**(4), 5–13.

Freeman, H. A., Friedman, H., Mosteller, F. and Wallis, W. A. (1948) *Sampling Inspection*, McGraw-Hill, New York.

Freund, R. A. (1957) Acceptance control charts. *Industrial Quality Control*, **14**(4), 13–23.

Girshick, M. A. and Rubin, H. (1952) A Bayes approach to a quality control model. *Ann. Math. Statist.*, **23**, 114–25.

Goel, A. L. and Wu, S. M. (1971) Determination of ARL and a contour nomogram for CuSum charts to control normal mean. *Technometrics*, **13**, 221–30.

Goldsmith, P. L. and Whitfield, H. (1961) Average run lengths in cumulative chart quality control schemes. *Technometrics*, **3**, 11–20.

Gorsky, J. (1987) Achieving reduced variation in 3.8L V6 camshaft lobe carbide. *Fifth Symposium on Taguchi Methods*, American Supplier Institute, Dearborn, Michigan.

Grant, E. L. and Leavenworth, R. S. (1972) *Statistical Quality Control* (4th edn.), McGraw-Hill, Tokyo.

Grubbs, F. E. (1946) The difference control chart with an example of its use. *Industrial Quality Control*, **2**, 22–25.

Hald, A. (1952) *Statistical Theory with Engineering Applications*, John Wiley, New York.

Hald, A. (1960) The compound hypergeometric distribution and a system of single sampling inspection plans based on prior distributions and costs. *Technometrics*, **2**, 275–340.

Hald, A. (1967) The determination of single sampling attribute plans with given producer's and consumer's risk. *Technometrics*, **9**, 401–15.

Hald, A. (1976) *Statistical Theory of Sampling Inspection*, Part 1, Institute of Mathematical Statistics, University of Copenhagen.

Hald, A. (1978) *Statistical Theory of Sampling Inspection*, Part 2, Institute of Mathematical Statistics, University of Copenhagen.

Hald, A. and Kousgaard (1967) *A Table for Solving the Equation B(n, p) = P for c = 0(1)100 and 15 values of P*, Institute of Mathematical Statistics, University of Copenhagen.

Hamaker, H. C. (1979) Acceptance sampling for per cent defective by variables and by attributes. *J. Qual. Tech.*, **11**, 139–48.

Healy, J. H. (1987) A note on multivariate CuSum procedures. *Technometrics*, **29**, 409–12.

Hill, I. D. (1956) Modified control limits. *Applied Statistics*, **5**, 12–19.

Hill, I. D. (1960) The economic incentive provided by inspection. *Applied Statistics*, **9**, 69–81.

Hill, I. D. (1962) Sampling inspection and defence specification DEF-131. *J. R. Statist. Soc.*, A, **125**, 31–87.

Hillier, F. S. (1961) *New Criteria for Selecting Continuous Sampling Plans*, Technical Report No. 30, Applied Mathematics and Statistics Laboratories, Stanford University.

Hillier, F. S. (1964) New criteria for selecting continuous sampling plans. *Technometrics*, **6**, 161–78.

Horsnell, G. (1954) The determination of single sample schemes for percentage defectives. *Applied Statistics*, **3**, 150–8.

Hunter, J. S. (1986) The exponentially weighted moving average. *J. Qual. Tech.*, **18**, 203–10.

Jackson, J. E. (1959) Quality control methods for several related variables. *Technometrics*, **1**, 359–77.

Jackson, J. E. (1980) Principal components and factor analysis: part I – principal components. *Journal of Quality Technology*, **12**, 201–13.

Jackson, J. E. and Morris, R. H. (1957) An application of multivariate quality control to photographic processing. *Journal of the American Statistical Association*, **52**, 186–99.

Jackson, J. E. and Mudhalkar, G. S. (1979) Control procedures for residuals associated with principal component analysis. *Technometrics*, **21**, 341–9.

Johnson, N. L. (1961) A simple theoretical approach to cumulative sum charts. *J. Amer. Stat. Assoc.*, **56**, 835–40.

Johnson, N. L. (1966) Cumulative sum charts and the Weibull distribution. *Technometrics*, **8**, 481–91.

Johnson, N. L. and Bagshaw, M. L. (1974) The effect of serial correlation on the performance of CUSUM tests. *Technometrics*, **16**, 103–12.

Kemp, K. W. (1958) Formulae for calculating the operating characteristics and the average sample number of some sequential tests. *J. R. Statist. Soc.*, **20**, 379–86.

Kemp, K. W. (1962) The use of cumulative sums for sampling inspection schemes. *Applied Statistics*, **11**, 16–31.

Kemp, K. W. (1971) Formal expressions which can be applied to CUSUM charts. *J. R. Statist. Soc.*, B, **33**, 331–60.

Kemp, K. W. (1981) The average run length of the cumulative sum chart when a V-mask is used. *J. R. Statist. Soc.*, B, **23**, 149–53.

Köllerström, J. K. and Wetherill, G. B. (1981) Sampling by variables with a normal–gamma prior. *Frontiers in Statistical Quality Control*, I, 133–47. Physica-Verlag, Würzburg.

Lai, T. L. (1974) Control charts based on weighted sums. *Ann. Statist.*, **2**, 134–47.

Lenz, H. J. and Rendtel, U. (1984) Performance evaluation of the MIL-STD-105D SKIP-LOT sampling plans and Bayesian single sampling plans. *Frontiers in Statistical Quality Control*, **2**, 92–106.

Lenz, H. J. and Wilrich, P. Th. (1978) Comparison of two sampling systems – MIL-STD-105D and skip lot. *Operat. Res. Verfahren*, **29**, 649–56.

Lieberman, G. J. (1953) A note on Dodge's continuous inspection plan. *Ann. Math. Statist.*, **24**, 480–4.

Lieberman, G. J. (1965) Statistical process control and the impact of automatic process control. *Technometrics*, 7, 283–92.

Lieberman, G. J. and Resnikoff, G. J. (1955) Sampling plans for inspection by variables. *J. Amer. Statist. Ass.*, 50, 457–516, 1333.

Lieberman, G. J. and Solomon, H. (1954) *Multi-level Continuous Sampling Plans*, Technical Report No. 17, Applied Mathematics and Statistics Laboratory, Stanford University.

Lieberman, G. J. and Solomon, H. (1955) Multi-level continuous sampling plans. *Ann. Math. Statist.*, 26, 686–704.

Montgomery, D. C. (1985) *Statistical Quality Control*, John Wiley, New York, pp. 12–19.

Mood, A. M. (1943) On the dependence of sampling inspection plans upon population distributions. *Ann. Math. Statist.*, 14, 415–25.

Murphy, B. J. (1987) Selecting out of control variables with the T^2 multivariate quality control procedure. *The Statistician*, 36, 571–83.

Owen, D. B. (1964) Control of percentages in both tails of the normal distribution. *Technometrics*, 6, 377–88.

Owen, D. B. (1967) Variables sampling plans based on the normal distribution. *Technometrics*, 9, 417–23.

Owen, D. B. (1969) Summary of recent work on variables acceptance sampling with emphasis on non-normality. *Technometrics*, 11, 631–7.

Page, E. S. (1954) Continuous inspection schemes. *Biometrika*, 41, 100–15.

Page, E. S. (1955) Control charts with warning lines, *Biometrika*, 42, 243–57.

Page, E. S. (1961) Cumulative sum charts, *Technometrics*, 3, 1–9.

Pandit, S. K. and Wu, S. (1983) *Time Series and System Analysis with Applications*, John Wiley, New York.

Peach, P. (1947) *Industrial Statistics and Quality Control* (2nd edn.), Edwards and Broughton, Raleigh, N.C.

Perry, R. L. (1973) Skip-lot sampling plans. *J. Qual. Tech.*, 5, 123–30.

Phillips, M. J. (1969) A survey of sampling procedures for continuous production. *J. R. Statist. Soc.*, A, 132, 100.

Prairie, R. R. and Zimmer, W. J. (1970) Continuous sampling plans based on cumulative sums. *Applied Statistics*, 19, 222–30.

Rai, G. (1971) Continuous acceptance sampling procedure based on cumulative sum chart for mean. *Trabajos de Estadistica, Investigacion Operativa*, 22, 213–19.

Read, D. R. and Beattie, D. W. (1961). The variable lot-size acceptance sampling plan for continuous production. *Applied Statistics*, 10, 147–56.

Roberts, S. W. (1958) Properties of central chart zone tests. *Bell System Technical Journal*, 37, 83–114.

Roberts, S. W. (1959) Control chart tests based on geometric moving averages. *Technometrics*, 1, 239–50.

Roberts, S. W. (1966) A comparison of some control chart procedures. *Technometrics*, 8, 411–30.

Rowlands, R. J. (1976) *Formulae for Performance Characteristics of CuSum Schemes when the Observations are Autocorrelated*, Ph.D. thesis, University of Wales (Cardiff).

Rowlands, R. J., Nix, A. B. J., Abdollahian, M. A. and Kemp, K. W. (1982). Snub nosed V-mask control schemes. *The Statistician*, 31, 133–42.

Rutherford, E. and Geiger, H. (1920) *Phil. Mag. Ser.*, series 6, 20, (Data also in Aitken, A. C. (1949), *Statistical Mathematics*, Oliver and Boyd, London.)

Savage, I. R. (1959) A production model and continuous sampling plan. *J.*

Amer. Statist. Ass., **54**, 231–47.

Schilling, E. G. (1982) *Acceptance Sampling in Quality Control*. Marcel Dekker, New York.

Shewhart, W. A. (1931) *Economic Control of Quality of Manufactured Product*, Reinhold Company, Princeton, N.J.

Stange, K. von (1961) Verzerrte und unverzerrte Schätzwerte bei messender Prufung. *Metrika*, **4**, 1–29.

Taguchi, G. (1986a) *Introduction to Quality Engineering*, Asian Productivity Organisation, Tokyo.

Taguchi, G. (1986b) *Introduction to Quality Engineering: Designing Quality into Products and Processes*, White Plains, N. Y. Kraus International Publications.

Taguchi, G. and Phadke, M. S. (1984) Quality engineering through design optimisation, in *Conference Record* (vol. 3), IEEE Globecom 1984 Conference, Atlanta, Georgia, New York, *Institute of Electrical and Electronics Engineers*, 1106–13.

Tauchi, G. and Wu, Y. (1985) *Introduction to Off-line Quality Control*, Central Quality Control Association, Nagaya, Japan.

Tukey, J. W. (1977) *Exploratory Data Analysis*, Addison-Wesley, Reading, Mass.

Tuprah, K. and Ncube, M. (1987) A comparison of dispersion control charts. *Sequential Analysis*, **6**, 155–64.

Uspensky, J. V. (1937) *Introduction to Mathematical Probability*, McGraw-Hill, New York.

Vasilopoulos, A. V. and Stamboulis, A. P. (1978) Modification of control charts limits in the presence of data correlation. *J. Qual. Tech.*, **10**(1), 20–9.

Wetherill, G. B. (1977) *Sampling Inspection and Quality Control*. Chapman and Hall, London.

Wetherill, G. B. (1982) *Elementary Statistical Methods* (3rd edn.), Chapman and Hall, London.

Wetherill, G. B. and Chiu, W. K. (1974) A simplified attribute sampling scheme, *Applied Statistics*, **23**, 143–8.

Wetherill, G. B. and Chiu, W. K. (1975) A review of acceptance sampling schemes with emphasis on the economic aspect. *Int. Stat. Rev.*, **43**, 191–209.

Wetherill, G. B. and Curram, J. B. (1984) Computer aided design in sampling inspection and quality control. *Frontiers in Statistical Quality Control*, **2**, 121–130. Physica-Verlag, Würzburg.

Wetherill, G. B. and Gerson, M. E. (1987) Computer aids to data quality control, *The Statistician*, **36**, 589–92.

Wetherill, G. B. and Glazebrook, K. D. (1986) *Sequential Methods in Statistics*, Chapman and Hall, London.

Wetherill, G. B. and Kollerström, J. K. (1979) Sampling inspection simplified. *J. R. Statist. Soc.*, A, **142**, 1–32.

Wetherill, G. B., Curram, J. B. and others (1985a) The design and evaluation of statistical software for microcomputers. *The Statistician*, **34**, 391–427.

Wetherill, G. B., Daffin, C. and Duncombe, P. (1985b) A user friendly survey analysis program. *Bull. Int. Statist. Inst.*, **51**, Book 3, 20.4.1–20.4.14.

Wetherill, G. B., Duncombe, P., Kenward, M., Kollerström, J., Paul, S. R. and Vowden, B. J. (1986) Regression analysis with applications. Chapman and Hall, London.

White, L. S. (1965) Markovian decision models for the evaluation of a large class of continuous sampling inspection plans. *Ann. Math. Statist.,* **36**, 1408–20.

Williams, M. K. (1988) ExpCheck – an intelligent diagnostic system in APL. *Vector*, **4**(3), 83–8.

Wilrich, P.-Th. (1970) Nomogramme zur Ermittlung von Stichprobenplanen fur messende Prüfung bei einer einseitig vorgeschriebenen Toleranzgrenze. Teil 2: Pläne bei unbekannter Varianz der Fertigung. *Qualitat und Zuverlassigkeit*, **15**, 181–7.

Wilrich, P.-Th. and Hennings, H. J. (1987) *Formeln und Tabellen der Angewandten Mathematischen Statistik,* Springer Verlag.

Woodall, W. H. and Ncube, M. M. (1983) Multivariate CuSum quality control procedures. *Technometrics*, **27**, 285–92.

Woodward, R. H. and Goldsmith, P. L. (1964) *Cumulative Sum Techniques*, I.C.I. Monograph No. 3, Oliver and Boyd, Edinburgh.

Index